W9-DGI-379

Social Policy and Economic Development
in the Nordic Countries

Social Policy in a Development Context

General Editors: **Thandika Mkandawire and Huck-Ju Kwon**, both at UNRISD

Social Policy in a Development Context is a new series which places social policy at the centre of research while maintaining the United Nations Research Institute for Social Development (UNRISD)'s unified approach to social development. The series provides a new and exciting contribution to the literature on economic development and social policy. In economic development, social policy has been recognized as an integral part of development, but the literature often falls short of elaborating social policy for a unified approach to economic and social development. In social policy, analysis has concentrated mainly on European and North American countries, and studies on developing countries often lack comparative rigour. The bridge between economic development and social policy will not only contribute to the academic research but also inform the policy debate at the international and national levels.

Titles include:

Olli Kangas and Joakim Palme *(editors)*
SOCIAL POLICY AND ECONOMIC DEVELOPMENT IN THE NORDIC COUNTRIES

Huck-Ju Kwon *(editor)*
THE DEVELOPMENTAL WELFARE STATE AND POLICY REFORMS IN EAST ASIA

Maureen Mackintosh and Meri Koivusalo *(editors)*
COMMERCIALIZATION OF HEALTH CARE
Global and Local Dynamics and Policy Responses

Thandika Mkandawire *(editor)*
SOCIAL POLICY IN A DEVELOPMENT CONTEXT

Social Policy in a Development Context
Series Standing Order ISBN 1–4039–4295–1 (hardback) 1–4039–4296–X (paperback)
(outside North America only)

You can receive future titles in this series as they are published by placing a standing order. Please contact your bookseller or, in case of difficulty, write to us at the address below with your name and address, the title of the series and the ISBN quoted above.

Customer Services Department, Macmillan Distribution Ltd, Houndmills, Basingstoke, Hampshire RG21 6XS, England

Social Policy and Economic Development in the Nordic Countries

Edited by

Olli Kangas

and

Joakim Palme

First published 2005 by
PALGRAVE MACMILLAN
Houndmills, Basingstoke, Hampshire RG21 6XS and
175 Fifth Avenue, New York, N.Y. 10010
Companies and representatives throughout the world

PALGRAVE MACMILLAN is the global academic imprint of the Palgrave Macmillan division of St. Martin's Press, LLC and of Palgrave Macmillan Ltd. Macmillan® is a registered trademark in the United States, United Kingdom and other countries. Palgrave is a registered trademark in the European Union and other countries.

ISBN13: 978-1-4039-4163-3
ISBN10: 1-4039-4163-7

This book is printed on paper suitable for recycling and made from fully managed and sustained forest sources.

A catalogue record for this book is available from the British Library.

Library of Congress Cataloging-in-Publication Data
Social policy and economic development in the Nordic countries / edited by
   Olli Kangas and Joakim Palme.
      p. cm.
   Includes bibliographical references and index.
   ISBN 1-4039-4163-7
   1. Scandinavia—Social policy. 2. Economic development—Social
aspects—Scandinavia. I. Kangas, Olli. II. Palme, Joakim.
   HV318.S594 2005
   361.6'1'0948—dc22   2004063619

10   9   8   7   6   5   4   3
14 13 12 11 10 09 08 07 06

Printed and bound in Great Britain by
Antony Rowe Ltd, Chippenham and Eastbourne

Contents

List of Tables

List of Figures

Notes on the Contributors

Anneli Anttonen is a professor of social policy at the University of Tampere, Finland. She researches on and has published widely in the areas of women and the welfare state, social care services and care in a comparative framework. Her most recent publication is *The Young, the Old and the State – Social Care Systems in Five Industrial Nations* (with John Baldock and Jorma Sipilä, 2003). She is a member of several international research groups and networks.

Eero Carroll is a postdoctoral research fellow at the Swedish Institute for Social Research, Stockholm University. His 1999 dissertation deals with the macrosocial concomitants of early social insurance enactments and of unemployment insurance extension among developed countries. He has contributed chapters in edited volumes on globalization and welfare, and a co-edited volume on welfare politics will be published by Aksant in 2005. Carroll has represented Sweden on the Management Committee of the EU COST A15 research network, and has served as consultant on social statistics collection for Eurostat and the Council of Europe.

Gøsta Esping-Andersen is Professor of Sociology at Universitat Pompeu Fabra, Barcelona. He has previously taught at Universita di Trento, the European University Institute and at Harvard University. He has also worked extensively for international organizations including the OECD, the World Bank, the UN, and the Portuguese and Belgian presidencies of the European Union. His research centres on themes related to social stratification, employment, social policy and welfare states. His most recent books include *Social Foundations of Postindustrial Economies* (1999), *Why Deregulate Labour Markets?* (with M. Regini, 2000) and *Why We Need a New Welfare State* (with D. Gallie, A. Hemerijck and J. Myles, 2003).

Tommy Ferrarini is Assistant Professor and Deputy Director at the Swedish Institute for Social Research, Stockholm University. His research is in the field of comparative welfare state development, in particular the causes and consequences of family policy institutions in post-war welfare democracies. He is currently involved in a research project that compares social policy institutions and their outcomes in East and West Europe.

Katja Forssén is Professor of Social Work at the University of Turku, Finland. Her research focuses on themes related to family policy, single parenthood, well-being of children and their families, child poverty and child protection. She is a member of an international research project on 'Welfare policy and employment in the context of family change' funded by the Nordic Council of Ministers (2001–5). She is currently directing a research project on 'Gender, family structure and social policy' funded by the Academy of Finland.

Johan Fritzell is Professor of Sociology at the Centre for Health Equity Studies, Stockholm University/Karolinska Institutet. He has conducted research for many years on the determinants and distribution of welfare in Sweden, most recently within the Swedish Welfare Commission 1999–2001. A major focus in Fritzell's work concerns comparative studies of poverty and income distribution. Recent publications include *Nordic Welfare States in the European Context* (co-editor, 2001). He currently directs two larger research programmes on 'Income, income distribution and health' and on 'Welfare States, welfare services and welfare outcomes' with support from Swedish research councils.

Pekka Himanen is the author of *The Hacker Ethic* (2001) and *The Information Society and the Welfare State: The Finnish Model* with Professor Manuel Castells (2002). Himanen has also acted as an adviser to the Finnish President and the Parliament, as well as to leading global organizations on information society issues. Himanen currently works at the Helsinki Institute for Information Technology, a joint research institute of the Helsinki University of Technology and the University of Helsinki.

Olli Kangas is currently Research Professor at the Danish National Institute for Social Research, Copenhagen. His main interests are the causes and consequences of social institutions and comparative methods. He is author of *The Politics of Social Rights* (1999). He has published numerous articles in refereed journals and edited volumes on the making of the welfare state, the institutional bases of social policy programmes and their consequences in terms of legitimacy and income distribution.

Jaakko Kiander is a Research Director at the Government Institute for Economic Research (VATT) in Helsinki, Finland. His main fields of expertise include macroeconomic policy and economic crises, labour economics and questions related to the determinants of economic growth such as integration and migration, technology policy, welfare state and social capital. He was the leader of a multidisciplinary research programme on the Finnish economic crisis of the 1990s. He is an adviser to the Bank of Finland supervisory committee and has been a member of many government committees. He has published numerous books and articles in academic journals.

Walter Korpi is Professor of Social Policy at the Swedish Institute for Social Research, Stockholm University, and works on comparative welfare state development, political sociology, political economy, class and gender. Books in English include *The Working Class in Welfare Capitalism* (1978) and *The Democratic Class Struggle* (1983). Recent articles include 'Faces of Inequality' (*Social Politics*, 2000), 'Contentious Institutions' (*Rationality and Society*, 2001), 'The Great Trough in Unemployment' (*Politics & Society*, 2002) and (with Joakim Palme) 'New Politics and Class Politics in the Context of Austerity and Globalization' (*American Political Science Review*, 2003).

Olle Lundberg is Professor of Health Equity Studies at the Centre for Health Equity Studies, Stockholm University/Karolinska Institutet, of which he is co-director. He has conducted research on living conditions with a special focus on health and health inequalities, in particular the mechanisms generating such inequalities. He has also studied the impact of childhood conditions on adult health, the links between income and health and living conditions among the old. Lundberg was a member of the Swedish Welfare Commission 1999–2001. Recent publications in journals such as *Social Science & Medicine* and the *Scandinavian Journal of Public Health* address the development of health inequalities in the Nordic countries and analyses of income, relative deprivation and health.

Joakim Palme is Director of the Institute for Futures Studies and Professor (Adjunct) at the Swedish Institute for Social Research, Stockholm University. His work focuses on comparative welfare state research, particularly on pensions. He has published (together with Walter Korpi) on the welfare state and redistribution and the new politics of the welfare state, and (with Olli Kangas) on the public–private mix in pension policy. He was chairman of the Swedish Welfare Commission 1999–2001. He has also written on the Nordic model in the context of the European Union.

Ola Sjöberg is Assistant Professor at the Swedish Institute for Social Research, Stockholm University. He researches and publishes mainly in the areas of comparative social policy, and his research interests include the financing of the welfare state and incentives and labour supply. His current research focuses on post-communist countries in Central and Eastern Europe.

Foreword

This book is part of the UNRISD series, *Social Policy in a Development Context*, which examines ways in which social policy can be instrumental to economic development while maintaining its intrinsic goal of social protection and equity.

Although the Nordic countries are among the 'late industrializers', their experience rarely features in development studies. This is partly due to the misconception that because their economic and social status places them among the most developed countries, their experience has little relevance to developing countries. It is also partly because of the 'Chinese Wall' that separates development studies and the study of welfare states. As a result, the literature on welfare regimes is rarely evoked in debates on democracy, equity or the development process – presumably on the grounds that its analytical tools are only relevant to developed countries. Although social policy in the Nordic region has been well scrutinized, the literature tends to emphasize the aspect of social protection, and pays less attention to the developmental aspect of the social policy.

And yet a historical look at the experiences of these countries suggests that they provide quintessential examples of 'democratic developmental states' and that the welfare regimes they created quite early on their developmental path provide important lessons with respect to the relationship of social policy and economic development. More specifically their experiences suggest that the successful tackling of poverty demands addressing issues of production, protection and redistribution simultaneously because social policy not only addresses fundamental goals of equity and human dignity, but also provides essential instruments for economic development and consolidation of a democratic order.

This volume is a unique attempt to put Nordic social policy in such a context. As the editors of the volume argue, 'a social policy is much more than just guaranteeing security against various social risks. Social policy creates and fortifies social bonds and may enhance the development of social capital. Social policy may also be used to accumulate real capital.' This book shows that the welfare state has played an important role in the economic development of the Nordic countries: not only in the past when these societies were poor, but also at present when they are among the richest in the world. It also challenges the contention that there is an unavoidable trade-off between equality and efficiency, and shows that social protection and economic development can go hand in hand. Of course, it is also instructive to shed a critical light on the welfare state in the Nordic countries and to examine with care the challenges that face the social protection system in the Nordic countries, such as ageing, family changes, 'revolutions' in information technology and globalization.

For all their similarities, the Nordic countries exhibit significant differences in their social policies and institutional arrangements, reflecting different historical trajectories traversed, different political and class configurations and different resource endowments. However, while learning from 'the Nordic experience' demands that one bear in mind its context specificity, there can be no doubt that the experience contains useful lessons for contemporary debates on democratization, development and inequality. It definitely contains rich material for serious comparative social development studies.

The papers in this volume were presented and discussed at a workshop in Stockholm, Sweden, in April 2003. UNRISD would like to take this opportunity to thank the Institute for Futures Studies for hosting this workshop.

UNRISD is grateful to the Swedish International Development Cooperation Agency (Sida) and the United Kingdom Department for International Development (DFID) for their financial support for the research on which this volume is based. As is the case with all UNRISD projects, work on the Social Policy in a Development Context project would not have been possible without the core funding provided by the governments of Denmark, Finland, Mexico, Norway, Sweden, Switzerland and the United Kingdom. Let me once again take this opportunity to express our gratitude.

THANDIKA MKANDAWIRE
Director, UNRISD

Acknowledgements

The Nordic model divides opinions. On one hand, there are those who think that the Nordic welfare state is the best of all possible worlds, a cornucopia that provides everyone with enough resources to fulfil various life projects. On the other hand, there are those with a more apocalyptic view, predicting a miserable end for the Nordic countries, as a result of the cardinal sin of interfering with the free play of market forces. Our opinion is that the extreme views expressed in both camps are often based on myth rather than reality: Heaven is being compared to Hell. Our hope is that the comparative studies included in this volume can contribute to policy discussions by contrasting different strategies, their advantages and problems, with empirical data. We view the 'Scandinavian way' as an alternative development path to learn from, through both trial and error. We argue that there are at least three aspects of the Nordic experience that deserve special attention. First, while democratization can bring pressures for expanded social policy, social policy can also contribute to democratization. Secondly, the clearest achievement of the Scandinavian welfare state has been poverty reduction and a high level of participation in society. The third aspect relates to the role played by the state in terms of economic development. The Scandinavian countries have experienced high levels of prosperity and rapid economic growth, 'despite' their high social spending and a high degree of state responsibility. This suggests that it may not only be possible to unify social protection with competitive and growth oriented economies but also that there are ways in which properly designed social policies can contribute to growth. However, the Nordic countries have also been obliged to adapt themselves to new challenges created by globalization and demographic change. These adaptation strategies – involving reform and redesign of policy as well as retrenchment – may offer some lessons. Exactly what lessons have been learned remain for the reader of this volume to judge.

This volume is one of the research outputs within the UNRISD project on 'Social Policy in a Development Context', which explores the ways in which social policy can be developmental while also pursuing intrinsic goals of social protection. We would like to thank Thandika Mkandawire, UNRISD Director, who launched the whole project and provided inspiration for this volume. Thank you for trusting us with the case, and for thinking that the Nordic experience is of genuine relevance in a development context. From the beginning to the end of this project, we have greatly benefited from Huck-ju Kwon's professionalism as a project director and for putting all the pieces in their right place. Josephine Grin-Yates has shown the same professionalism in organizing the whole venture. At various stages, we have been helped by Justin McDermott and Alexander Peyre – who, despite their names, are 'true' Scandinavians. Initially, we had thought-provoking discussions with the other teams at the Palais des Nations in Geneva. The book project would never have come to fruction without the scholarly efforts of our contributors. Our warmest collective thanks to you all!

Copenhagen and Stockholm

Olli Kangas
Joakim Palme

List of Abbreviations and Acronyms

AFDC	Aid for Families with Dependent Children (USA)
ALP	Active labour market policy
AMS	Labour Market Board (Finland, Sweden)
ATP	Earnings-related pension scheme (Sweden)
CHCA	Child care home allowance (Finland)
CPCA	Children's private care allowance (Finland)
ECHP	European Household Panel Survey
ECU	European Currency Unit
EDI	Equivalent disposable income
EEC	European Economic Community
EFTA	European Free Trade Association
EMS	European Monetary System
ERM	Exchange Rate Mechanism (EU)
Etla	The Research Institute of the Finnish Economy
EU	European Union
EVA	Finnish Business and Policy Forum
GDP	Gross domestic product
GSM	Global System of Mobile Communication
HDI	Human Development Index
IALS	International Adult Literacy Survey (Statistics Canada)
IDC	International Data Corporation
IKL	Isänmaallinen Kansanliike, successor party of the ultra-patriotic Lapua movement in Finland
IRC	Internet chatroom protocol
ISCED	International System Classification of Education
IT	Information technology
ITs	Information technologies
LIS	Luxembourg Income Study
LO	Confederation of Trade Unions (Norway)
LO	Trade union confederation (Sweden)
MNE	Multinational enterprise

MP	Member of Parliament
NGO	Non-governmental organization
NMT	Nordic mobile telecommunications network
NOSOSCO	Nordic Social Statistical Committee
NOU	Norges Offentlige Utredninger (Reports from the Government Commissions, Norway)
PISA	Program for International Student Assessment
PPP	Purchasing power parity
R&D	Research and development
SAJ	Finnish Confederation of Trade Unions
SAK	Finnish Confederation of Trade Unions
SCIP	Social Citizenship Indicators Project (Sweden)
SDP	Social Democratic Party (Finland)
SKDL	Communist popular front party (Finland)
SME	Small and medium-sized enterprise
SMP	Smallholders' party (Finland)
SNS	Centre for Business and Policy Studies (Sweden)
SOU	Sveriges Offentliga Utredningar (Reports from the Government Commissions, Sweden)
SSH	Encrypted Internet communication protocol
SSPTW	*Social Security Programmes Throughout the World*
STPC	Science and Technology Policy Council (Finland)
TAI	Technology Achievement Index (UN)
UK	United Kingdom
UN	United Nations
USA	United States
WEF	World Economic Forum

1
Social Policy and Economic Development in the Nordic Countries: An Introduction

Olli Kangas and Joakim Palme

'Constructive destruction'

The nineteenth and twentieth centuries witnessed major transformations of economic systems around the world. The first was the creation of capitalist markets in the Western hemisphere. The second was the transition from capitalism to socialism in several countries. The third was the transition in the reverse direction: from centrally planned command systems back to market-based economies. The new globalization of business attached to an explosive expansion of information technologies (ITs) and the rapid IT-based industrialization of the Asian economies may constitute a fourth great transformation that will change the economic order of the globe. During such great transformations, there are always winners and losers. In the wake of such changes, old forms of security vanish and new ones take shape. A crucial issue here is how destructive or constructive change actually becomes. In a Schumpeterian sense, we can speak about a 'constructive destruction' (Schumpeter 1950). This term refers to a situation where old, inefficient forms of social activities are destroyed and replaced by more efficient and better systems. An interesting question is how and to what extent different countries, or groups of countries, have managed to harness the destruction, in a socially justifiable way, and to create social and economic institutions that can effectively utilize the potentials and possibilities the new situation creates. How can the Nordic experience be interpreted in this perspective?

Nature and consequences of the 'Nordic model'

Different approaches to the question of social protection have been elaborated among countries with the most advanced industrial market economies. In this context, the Scandinavian or Nordic welfare state model is an established concept world-wide. Yet there appears to be something of a mystery about the nature and consequences of the model. Some scholars have gained their academic credentials by launching the idea of a model

1

and defining its characteristics, while others have claimed that such a model does not exist at all, that there only are country-specific development paths and outcomes and that instead of the Nordic model we should speak about the Danish, Finnish, Norwegian and Swedish models.

The views concerning the merits and drawbacks of the model also diverge widely among different observers. There are Candide-like opinions that the Nordic welfare state is the best of all possible thinkable worlds, guaranteeing high levels of well-being and decent life-chances to all regardless of circumstances. The most notable achievement in this field is poverty reduction: Nordic poverty rates are among the lowest in the world. For these analysts, the Nordic countries are a good example of how it is possible to unify equality, a 'big' welfare state and a high level of taxation with economic growth. However, critical voices describe the situation quite differently: by equalising incomes through lavish welfare benefits the welfare state creates work disincentives and kills individual initiative, which hampers economic growth. In the longer run, this 'passion for equality' is also detrimental for the poor.

Our opinion is that the extreme views expressed on both sides are often based on wishful thinking or prejudice, on myth rather than reality. This is a challenge for social science research. If we want to take social policy making as seriously a 'learning process', we need to base our evaluation of different social policy strategies on facts and systematic analysis, not on assumptions. Comparative studies can make a contribution by contrasting different solutions, their advantages and their problems. The purpose of this volume is to discuss these and other issues related to Nordic social policy and development from a historical and comparative perspective.

The aim here is not to dig too deeply into the debate about the 'true nature' of the Scandinavian welfare state, our approach is more pragmatic. We think that there are important commonalities as well as essential differences between the Nordic countries that all deserve to be described. Given the long common and tightly interwoven history of these countries, any other state of affairs would perhaps be surprising. Without denying national variations and differences between the countries, for practical reasons and space considerations we emphasize here commonalities more than country-specific characteristics. This is also a question of perspective: The wider perspective, the more homogeneous the Nordic[1] hemisphere appears to be, while a closer focus would generate a more heterogeneous picture.

In a developmental perspective (Mkandawire 2001), we argue that there are at least three important things to be learned from the Nordic model. First, while democratization can bring pressures for expanded social policy, social policy can also contribute to democratization. In this respect, the Nordic countries, with their universal and all-encompassing social policies, may serve as good examples. Indeed, the link between social policy and democratization has historically been very close in Scandinavia. Secondly, the clearest achievement of the Scandinavian welfare state has been in poverty reduction programmes and there are also lessons to be learned from performance here. The third aspect relates to the role ascribed to the state. Some neo-liberal thinkers suggest that the state should retreat from social provision and leave a more active role to non-governmental organizations (NGOs); only in that way can countries safeguard economic growth. However, the Scandinavian countries display a high level of prosperity and rapid economic growth despite their high social spending. In this respect, the Nordic countries thus demonstrate that is possible to unify social protection with competitive and growth oriented economies.

Yet the relationship between the welfare state and efficiency is poorly theorized and little studied, both theoretically and empirically. Several factors have contributed to thus. One is that intentions have been confused with actual outcomes. Another is that the architects behind the systems may have feared a critical examination of the outcomes (Sørensen 1998). There has also been an unfortunate starting point in some of the neo-classical analyses that all forms of taxation must mean efficiency loss, and instead of comparing different kinds of intervention the actual interventions are contrasted with a no-intervention situation: being Hell is compared to blessings of Heaven. A more realistic approach would be to examine different kinds of interventions by utilising comparative research more extensively.

The model's historical legacy

In order to be able to understand the present situation, it would appear useful to identify the basic elements of the model's historical legacy and ask four key questions:

- What are the basic elements of the model?
- What have been the driving forces behind its development?
- What have been its achievements?
- What have been the negative unintended consequences?

This may then help us to address two more questions:

- What are the problems and dilemmas facing the model?
- Can we identify any solutions to these dilemmas?

We would argue that the historical lesson here is that reforms of social policy programmes are responses to changing economic and social structures as well as to political mobilization. The fact that structural changes have been important for social policy reform implies neither that values have been unimportant for shaping the institutions, nor that decisions have come about without political action. Once established, institutions create interests, but also become bearers of values and expectations, and thus create their own *path dependency*; the essence of these institutions can either enhance or inhibit reforms.

Themes of the volume

This volume includes a number of special studies organized around four different themes, which have been given the following broad headings:

- The history of the model
- The consequences of policy design
- Economic and social policy
- The information society and challenges to social policy.

The history of the model

Chapter 2, by Kangas and Palme, 'Coming Late – Catching Up: The Formation of a 'Nordic Model', provides both a historical account of the the the Nordic experience and a conceptual framework for the entire book. Most of the issues that are taken up in Chapter 2 are analysed and discussed in more detail in the chapters that follow. The first outlines the broad historical commonalities in the social, economic and political structures of the Nordic nations, while also recognising the evident differences. The emergence of modern social policy legislation is also traced back in history. Four sections on different policy areas or programmes follow. The emergence and formation of old-age pension are followed during the course of the twentieth century. A section on sickness insurance (i.e sickness cash benefits) follows. There is a section on the particularities of unemployment insurance before the covereage and adequacy of various benefits among the Nordic countries are compared to those in the other advanced industrial nations. Coverage is clearly higher than in other countries, adequacy is high but not outstanding. The focus is then moved to what, in broad terms, can be labelled 'family support'. The social services sector, including education, is described and the cash benefits analysed. There is a clear Nordic exceptionalism when it comes to the social services. Four sections analyse various aspects of poverty and inequality from a social policy perspective, the reduction of poverty and inequality turns out to be substantial among the Nordic countries. The effects of different policy designs are also discussed in a section on labour supply. Here, the effects appear to go in different directions: labour force participation is high among the Nordic countries whereas the number of hours worked per employee is modest. Social trust is analysed in a social perspective in the next section. The chapter concludes with a section on the economic crisis of the 1990s, which struck Finland and Sweden particularly hard. Here, both policy changes and the consequences of welfare cuts are given attention, as well as the strategic choices made in the two countries regarding social policy design.

The focus in Eero Carroll's Chapter 3, 'Voluntary State-Subsidized Social Insurance in the Advanced Industrialized World since the 1890s: The Nordic Experience in Comparative Perspective' is on the institutional emergence and 'mortality' of voluntary social insurance in the highly industrialized

North. According to Carroll, one major site of welfare cooperation between states and social movements in the industrialized North has been voluntary state-subsidized social insurance institutions, particularly for the sick and for the unemployed. When they emerged, in the latter decades of the nineteenth century and extending into the 1930s, many such programmes were no less untried than what contemporary state – NGO cooperation ventures have been in facilitating Southern social development. Carroll argues that the question of whether this Northern experience can also inform development strategy discussions in the South is linked to the larger questions of whether socioeconomic development paths are multiple, and of whether Southern countries can usefully follow or learn from Northern precedents.

According to Carroll, the voluntarist model is interesting in how the state uses NGOs to develop institutions which the state lacks capacity or will to develop itself. In current development debates, state disengagement from social provision is advocated to cut costs and enable states to con-centrate on 'core activities'. Given possible countervailing disadvantages, Carroll emphasizes the diversity of policy considerations about 'third-sector' provision that should be borne in mind from European historical experience when considering such policies elsewhere today.

When discussing the costs and benefits of voluntarism, Carroll emphasizes that state-subsidized voluntarism may be motivated if certain conditions are met. State-subsidized sickness and unemployment insurance funds have historically constituted vital 'schools of democracy' in the Nordic countries, not least for working-class constituencies traditionally under-represented in voluntary organizations. Especially if embedded in a broader network of corporatist institutions, voluntary subsidized insurance institutions may constitute sites where 'bridging social capital' can be generated. Participation of union officials in administering state-sanctioned social welfare may bind civil society and the state more closely together – in ways that facilitate not only union membership but also social development, and the greater overlap of special and general interests.

However, Carroll warns that such benefits by no means automatically fol-low from voluntarism. Policy makers should particularly be warned against the idea that voluntarism can constitute an easy 'stepping stone' to com-pulsory insurance later, as well as against exaggerated visions of budgetary savings. Differences in costs may end up being minimal if state subsidies keep expanding in order to reach broader inclusion.

Carroll's general conclusion is that the complicated interplay of public, civil and private organizations runs throughout the social landscapes of both the global North and the global South. Criticism against 'one-size-fits-all' recommendations to developing countries, and of the unconditionally voluntarism-friendly Third Way variety, may be the only 'best practice'. If combined at all, state and voluntary provision should aim for *complement-arity*, with clear jurisdictions and uniting the best of both methods.

The consequences of policy design

The starting point in Anneli Anttonen's Chapter 4, 'Empowering Social Policy: The Role of Social Care Services in Modern Welfare States', is that while anchored to its national and normative contexts, care is exposed to many pressures when societies are changing. According to Anttonen, this is not a matter of ideological change taking place in the economy and politics, change that generally arises from structural adaptations to economic competition. Some ideological shifts appear to be relatively isolated from changes in the economy and patterns of employment – for example, moral debates about family responsibilities. Others are more clearly rooted in changes in everyday life – such as the discrepancies between social policy assumptions and the growing participation of women in paid employment. Although the forces of change are, to some extent, pushing in the same direction, they have not yet produced much cross-national uniformity in care policies. Unlike social security systems, care arrangements remain distinctly national and local innovations are common.

However, care is changing as both an informal and a formal activity, and quite rapidly. Most importantly, care is leaving the intimate sphere of family and kinship: it is going public everywhere. One consequence of the change in the locus of care from the family to other sectors is that it becomes *monetized*: it has to be paid for and its costs are revealed. This form of 'going public' may happen independently of social policy decisions, simply because more households need or choose to buy care services. Another side of the coin is that governments may create a public policy of care so that care becomes a social good and social right of citizens. Some governments have been much more active in the process of care 'going public' than others. The Nordic democracies have been active in favouring women-friendly solutions in care and family policies; internationally generous social care provision has promoted gender equality in terms of women's labour market participation.

The Scandinavian experience demonstrates that social solidarity and individual autonomy can be enhanced through legislation and the idea of universal social citizenship may be realized. It has meant that marginalized and other oppressed groups, such as women, have become a part of the social policy contract. It has been extremely important for women to extend social rights to cover such things as the caring of young children and the elderly, sick and disabled members of society. In Scandinavia, women have been more successful then elsewhere in combining their dual role as mothers and workers, and social policy arrangements have been an integral part of gender equality policy.

Anttonen sums up by pinpointing the fact that women's changing role as mothers, carers and workers has brought into being a society in which care relations have to be reorganized and renegotiated. A public policy of care is thus becoming a more and more important part of welfare states. When we talk about 'caring', we are talking about shifting boundaries between private and public responsibilities: caring is also sharing in the sense that there are now more social actors producing care and care services.

The focus in Tommy Ferrarini's and Katja Forssén's Chapter 5, 'Family Policy and Cross-National Patterns of Poverty', shifts to the cash side of public support to families. Historically, children have been the most vulnerable group exposed to poverty. Anti-poverty measures directed towards children and their families have always been constrained by tensions between the interests of the state and the rights and responsibilities of the parent. Poverty in families with children may have severe consequences for the individuals living under such circumstances not only in the short run, but also in the longer perspective. The shortage of external resources is reflected either directly or indirectly in the well-being of the child, which in a longer run may have detrimental consequences for the child's future development. These statements form the general starting point for Ferrarini's and Forssén's chapter.

The authors distinguish three different family policy regimes according to two separate dimensions, depending on whether they support a *traditional* family (general family support), where the father is the main earner and the mother mainly is expected to see to care work, or whether they support a *dual-earner* family (dual-earner support). The third variant is the so-called 'market oriented' model. According to Ferrarini and Forssén the main motive behind family policy programmes in the Nordic countries has in recent decades been to support the dual-earner family, while Continental European countries have primarily maintained family policies in support of traditional family patterns, with a main male earner and a female home-maker. Family policies in the English-speaking countries are market oriented, and support for both the traditional and the dual-earner family has consequently been less developed, leaving larger room for means-tested benefits with a more direct ambition of alleviating poverty.

The comparisons presented indicate that support for the dual-earner family policy is most effective at reducing poverty among all families with children. Welfare states with the lowest universal and earnings-related benefits, as well as low utilization rates of public child care, and thus heavily reliant on means-tested benefits in the provision of economic resources to poor families, also have the highest poverty levels. Countries with the most generous earnings-related parental leave benefits and high utilization of public child care also have the lowest poverty levels among families with children. Thus the answer to the main question the authors pose – whether family policy is related to cross-national patterns of poverty for families with children – is unanimously 'yes'. The analyses carried out suggest a strong link between social policy institutions and distributive outcomes. In particular, dual-earner models of family policy, such as those developed in the Nordic welfare states, seem effective in reducing poverty. Such welfare states are probably particularly effective at reducing poverty because family policy programmes provide both adequate benefits to families with children, that are often earnings-related and universal, and because transfers and services also provide incentives for female labour force participation as well as for male participation in care work. Furthermore, according to Ferrarini and Forssén, welfare states with family policy models that largely support traditional family patterns generally have medium levels of poverty among families with children. Countries with market oriented family polices, largely reliant on targeted benefits and services to the poorest families, have the highest poverty levels, contrary to what proponents of selective measures would predict.

In Chapter 6, 'Education and Equal Life-Chances: Investing in Children', Gøsta Esping-Andersen examines two factors that underpin the study of educational systems. First, knowledge-intensive economies push up skills premiums and when the returns from education are rising the less skilled are in danger of falling behind in the earnings distribution. According to Esping-Andersen, youth with poor cognitive skills or inadequate schooling today will become tomorrow's marginalized workers, likely to face a life-time of low wages, poor-quality jobs and frequent spells of unemployment or assistance dependency. The second feature has to do with the relatively large share of low-qualified jobs that coexist with service economy growth. This would appear to negate the argument that low-skilled workers are at risk were it not for the strong likelihood that such jobs will become dead-end, low-paid career traps. Current policy fashion advocates activation, retraining, and life-long learning as a way to combat such entrapment, but these programmes are ineffective unless participants already have strong cognitive and motivational abilities. Mobility is a realistic possibility only for those who already possess skills from youth.

Esping-Andersen points out that the advanced economies face a rising skill problem as far as individuals' life-chances are concerned. Yet, from the point of view of the collective good, the problem is the same. The advanced economies must rely almost exclusively on their human capital to gain a competitive edge in the world economy. Our societies are ageing very rapidly and future working-age cohorts are bound to be very small. Sustaining the welfare of a large aged population necessitates a highly productive labour force. In the new economy, countries can no longer afford social inheritance. What can we do?

Esping-Andersen offers two answers and policy options. First, the design of *school systems* can make a difference. Few would doubt that early tracking or segmentation based on ethnicity, race or social class help reinforce stratification. The important conclusion, however, is that equal opportunities will not come about solely through education policy. Secondly, we must rethink the link between *education and social policies*. This is clear when we recognize the potentially very negative effects of economic hardship on educational attainment and subsequent life-chances. One lesson from the Nordic welfare states is that the eradication of child poverty can yield very positive results, not only in terms of alleviating material hardship in childhood but also because economic security is a vital precondition for later achievement. Thirdly, according to Esping-Andersen, 'money' is a necessary but not a sufficient precondition for good life-chances. The data he presents show that cognitive inequalities are substantially lower in Scandinavia, and the trend towards declining social inheritance coincides almost perfectly with the era of building up universal day care, indicating that that life-long learning must begin at age one.

Esping-Andersen concludes up by arguing that if our sole concern is to fulfil the 'caring vacuum', the USA has shown that fairly broad access *can* be achieved through the market system. If we aim to build part of our equal opportunities policy into child care provision, however, then clearly an American-style approach will fail and perhaps something can be learned from the Nordic experience.

Health is one of the most important elements in an individual's welfare, as all level-of-living surveys done in the Nordic countries indicate. In their Chapter 7, 'Fighting Inequalities in Health and Income: One Important Road to Welfare and Development', Johan Fritzell and Olle Lundberg introduce some basic elements in the Swedish/Nordic welfare survey tradition and discuss the Nordic approach to research on welfare and its relation to various forms of social and other policies. Their analysis focuses on income and health as important factors for welfare, development and inclusion. The Nordic countries are well known for their low poverty rates and modest income differentials. Internationally speaking, the overall performance in terms of general health objectives appears to be good among the Nordic countries: low infant mortality and long life expectancy are two examples. Inequalities in health also persist in Nordic countries, however Fritzell and Lundberg give data on health differences by social status in selected countries. They emphasize that the consequences of income inequality for health have been recognized in comparative research but that the mechanisms have been far from fully explored. One major task in their chapters is to fill this gap. Drawing on Swedish as well as comparative research, their study helps to improve our understanding of the links between health, inequality and growth, and how policies as well as inequalities can affect these relationships

Fritzell and Lundberg have four principal findings. First, welfare is a *multidimensional* concept and so welfare measurement should:

- Study the prevalence of inferior conditions rather than those where people are faring well economically
- Use descriptive rather than subjective indicators
- Study how welfare areas are inter-related.

They find that health and income are two key components of level of living. Secondly, comparative analyses have shown that the Nordic countries have small income differentials and low poverty rates compared with other rich nations. These outcomes are closely related to a relatively *universal social insurance system*, but also to *high employment rates*. Thirdly, *relative health inequalities* are not consistently lower in the Nordic countries in comparison with other European countries. However, this is partly, in the Swedish case at least, dependent on a very good health status among the upper social strata of the population. In the Finnish case, research evidence suggests that the relatively unfavourable statistics are mostly due to historical conditions and consequently seen only among the elderly. In infant and child mortality rates, all the Nordic countries perform extremely well. Finally, the association between income and health is *curvilinear*. In other words, for both individuals and for nations we find diminishing marginal health returns of income. This implies that reducing income inequalities can lead to improvements in population health status.

Fritzell and Lundberg emphasize that health cannot be 'redistributed' in the same manner as income. Structural forces leading to class differentials in health are not easily eradicated, and fully understanding these is of great interest from a purely scientific view point. It may be that from a public policy point of view, however, it is more of interest to focus on the health status of vulnerable groups when making a comparative evaluation. Seen in that perspective, the Nordic countries also perform comparatively well, which is likely to foster economic and social growth and development. Fritzell and Lundberg argue finally that what really matters is to improve living conditions and lessen inequalities in conditions. In other words, they suggest that it is the Nordic social policy model at large that is of the greatest importance in understanding the health status of the population.

Economic and social policy

The starting point in Walter Korpi's Chapter 8, 'Does the Welfare State Harm Economic Growth? Sweden as a Strategic Test Case', is a critical discussion of the previous analyses on the relationships between economic growth and social policy. Korpi's case study is Sweden, as displayed in economists' analyses. Neo-classical economics predicts that taxes and other political measures associated with welfare states generate distortions in the functioning of markets. Sweden, as perhaps the most developed welfare state, has constantly been used to illustrate this argument: because of 'Swedosclerosis' the Swedish economy is lagging behind other comparable economies. According to Korpi, the empirical work here reveals more efforts to find figures illustrating theoretically assumed outcomes than studies testing hypotheses concerning possible outcomes.

Korpi focuses on the often-overlooked problems of *reliability* in the empirical data used in analyses of comparative growth rates. Data reliability can generate problems especially in the middle-range countries where Sweden and the other Nordic areas are often clustered. Because of the clustering of countries, small and relatively unimportant differences among them affect rankings. Recognizing this problem, Korpi pinpoints the fact that measures of GDP levels adjusted to purchasing power parities (PPPs) are unreliable and should not be used in detailed country rankings and should be used only for broad groupings of countries. Sweden would then come in the same category as Australia, Belgium, Canada, Finland, France, Germany, Ireland, Italy, Japan, The Netherlands, and the UK. The conclusion is thus that Sweden is not doing as badly as argued in economists' analysis.

From a neo-classical theoretical perspective, strong predictions have been derived to the effect that with increasing taxation and welfare state expansion labour supply as well as growth rates will suffer. Korpi demonstrates that empirical studies on the sensitivity of labour supply to taxation have shown only rather limited negative effects, although somewhat more for women than for men. He demonstrates that in analyses of comparative growth rates, data are much more shaky, and that it has proved difficult to establish evidence for major negative growth effects, including for Sweden, where such negative effects would appear to be most likely to emerge. The efforts to prove major negative effects of welfare states on labour supply and growth have not so far been very successful.

Korpi demands more evidence-based policy recommendations. According to him, it is necessary to have empirical verification of the bases upon which policy advices are founded. From a policy-related perspective, what is needed is studies of the instances where hypotheses on negative effects of taxes and welfare programmes can be empirically analysed. Such studies should focus on the microlevel as well as on the macrolevel. Korpi's policy advice is that it is also necessary to analyse consequences of welfare states that can be seen as positive, and to attempt to consider how to balance potentially positive and negative aspects.

Walter Korpi's chapter covers a period up to the early 1990s. Chapter 9, by Jaakko Kiander, 'Growth and Employment in "Nordic Welfare States" in the 1990s: Crisis and Revival', takes a close look at the 1990s alone. Kiander's contribution indicates that after the deep recessions of the early 1990s, all Nordic countries experienced a strong recovery. On average, post-recession Nordic growth rates of output, employment and productivity are almost the same as in the USA in the same period, and much better than the EU average. Within the Nordic group, output growth has been fastest in Finland and Iceland, and employment growth about 2 per cent per annum in Finland, Iceland and Norway. The highest productivity growth has been achieved in Finland and Denmark. According to Kiander, the good economic record of the latter half of the 1990s may indicate, that the Nordic economies still are functioning well, notwithstanding the earlier crises.

Kiander asks what role of economic integration had in explaining the good performance of the Nordic countries, and he highlights two answers. First there are several commonalities in the Nordic economies: they are all subject to the single market regulations of the European Union, for example. Nordic countries have also been ahead of European deregulation by being the first to liberalize telecoms and electricity markets under deliberate state policies. Secondly, a central part of the Nordic integration processes in the 1980s and 1990s involved changing monetary regimes. In the 1980s, all the Nordic countries fixed exchange rate targets, attempting imitate the Exchange Rate Mechanism (ERM) of the European Monetary System (EMS), although they were formally outside of it. After the currency crises of 1992 the paths of the Nordic countries started to diverge. Finland's goal was to join EMU. Denmark decided for political and clearly non-economic reasons to stay formally outside the monetary union but still have a fixed exchange rate *vis-à-vis* the euro. Sweden, Norway and Iceland remained in a floating exchange rate regime with explicit inflation targets. In spite of their different choices, all the Nordic countries adopted a policy of low inflation and central bank independence. The adjustment process to a new regime of stable prices was initially painful for them all, although the new regime has proven to function well in the long run.

Kiander concludes that the Nordic welfare model survived the test of the 1990s. The model faced a real crisis when public deficits and unemployment rose to record levels in the mid-1990s due to world-wide recession. However, instead of being locked into an 'unemployment trap' the Nordic countries recovered quickly after 1995 and enjoyed similar and sometimes even better growth rates of output, productivity and employment than the US economy. Between 1995 and 2000, all the Nordic countries successfully reduced open unemployment significantly and turned public finances from deficit to surplus, while maintaining their welfare states. The adjustment was made by raising taxes and restricting the growth of public expenditures, but not by changing the basic structure of the national welfare model. The Nordic countries can still thus be regarded as advanced welfare states with high public employment, universal benefit systems, extensive publicly provided welfare services, high taxes, low poverty and corporatist labour market structures.

However, Kiander also highlights some possible problems. In the future, extensive welfare systems, although they seem at present to be functioning well, are likely to face further challenges from integration, globalization and demographic change. Further integration of European economies may increase pressure for tax competition, which could threaten the financial basis of the welfare state. The Nordic countries have already responded to tax competition by lowering corporate tax rates and taxes on capital income. These changes have been compensated by other tax increases and labour incomes and private consumption are now heavily taxed. It is not clear how sustainable such a regime of high taxes will be in the future if mobility of goods and employees increases. If further pressure to lower taxation emerges, the financing of the increasing public pension and health care expenditures of an ageing population may be difficult – possibly more difficult for the Nordic countries than for other European countries, because the initial level of taxation is so high and there is less scope to increase labour supply because of already high labour force participation rates. Some leeway for the Nordic governments may, however, be provided by their exceptionally good fiscal positions.

Ola Sjöberg's Chapter 10 is entitled, 'Financing "Big-Tax" Welfare States: Sweden during Crisis and Recovery'. Sustainability of taxation is, of course, a critical question since most countries are facing a number of important challenges to the financing of their social protection systems. Changing demographic structures mean that a larger portion of the population will have to be supported by a shrinking one. Many predict that the globalization and internationalization of the world economy will also put important constraints on the financing of social protection, in terms of both what overall level of taxation is feasible as well as the rate at which different tax bases can be levied. Sweden can in this context be considered as something of a crucial 'test case' concerning the financial viability of large welfare states. Social expenditures and the total tax burden in Sweden are among the highest in the world, and in the 1990s Sweden experienced a severe economic recession which put heavy pressure on the public finances.

With this as a background, Sjöberg describes the financing of the Swedish welfare state from a historical and comparative perspective. The first part is devoted to a description and analysis of how social security programmes have been financed in Sweden against the background of developments in the OECD area. The focus then shifts to the financing of local government activities in the welfare arena. Given the importance of taxes on wages and income from work for the financing of almost all levels of the Swedish welfare state, Sjöberg concludes with a discussion and analysis of taxation and labour supply.

Sjöberg draws three main conclusions from his analysis. First, Sweden (like most other industrialized countries) is, and will in the foreseeable future continue to be, highly dependent on *taxation on labour* for financing the welfare state. The question of how to put as many people as possible to work is thus of vital importance. It is of crucial importance to recognize the complex relationship between the financing of the welfare state and other areas of welfare provision. Secondly, the way in which social protection is financed is not only, and perhaps not even primarily, a question of *economics*. Sjöberg demonstrates that the question of how to divide the costs of social protection in society can have important, and sometimes decisive, importance for how social policy reform is viewed by the public and for the legitimacy of social policy institutions. Thirdly, the way in which social security programmes are financed is to an important extent dependent upon which *institutional social policy model* is being applied. The financing structures of today may constitute an important foundation for the possibilities of future reform.

The 'information society' and challenges to social policy

The central issue in Pekka Himanen's Chapter 11, 'The "Nordic Model" of the "Information Society": The Finnish Case', is about the political choices available in the 'information age'. He addresses the following question:

- Does the rise of the information age necessarily increase social inequality and exclusion, as seems to be the dominant trend in the world?

In many political circles, it is believed that the answer is 'yes'. Many countries have thus chosen the route of competing in the global world by cutting back the welfare state. However, Himanen emphasizes that if we look at empirical data on which countries have succeeded as 'information societies', the picture is much more complicated. The Nordic welfare states have for many years topped the International Data Corporation (IDC) Information Society Index, which reflects the adoption of new information technology (IT) – such as computers, internet and telecoms – in society. According to the UN Technology Achievement Index (TAI), Finland is the world leader, followed by the USA and Sweden. It thus makes sense to talk about 'a Nordic model of the information society'. To shed light on the model, combining a dynamic 'information economy' with the welfare state as its foundation, Himanen analyses Finland in depth, and thus gives a concrete content to the idea.

Himanen traces two factors that have contributed to Finnish success. First the key element is the interaction between *business and the state*, between the 'information society' and the welfare state. Although the Finnish model is market-driven, there has been a conscious government policy to push the Finnish business towards the 'information economy', e.g. a Science and Technology Policy Council was formed in 1986. Secondly, Himanen shows that the Finnish government has deliberately invested in research and development (R&D). By 2000, the national R&D investment exceeded 3 per cent of GDP and is currently close to 4 per cent, the highest in the world (with Sweden) and almost double the average in other advanced economies. Thirdly, Himanen refers to the fact that Finland's public education system provides highly skilled people to drive innovatation in IT 'cluster'. It has also helped to create a special culture of innovation – the *open-source culture* – that has been the basis of key technological innovations. The Finnish welfare state has supported this innovation culture; the free and public education system, in which university students receive a small student salary, allows students to explore new ideas and applications, as they do not have an immediate pressure to graduate to earn a living.

Himanen points out that up to now the Finnish model has continued to work well, even during the late 1990s downturn of the IT field and the world economy. Relative to its competitors, both the Finnish economy and the leading technology companies, such as Nokia, managed recession better. However, Himanen warns of several problems that the Finnish model may come to suffer. First, the level of *start-up entrepreneurialism* is relatively low: entrepreneurialism could be an important way of expanding techno-logical innovativeness to completely new areas and thus broadening the basis for future growth. Second, *openness to foreign talent* is relatively weak. Third, global competition for talented and high-skill workers may increase pressures towards higher income inequalities; the central issue is how to bal-ance equality issues with a courageous policy to create more work and make employment more profitable to both companies and the workforce. Finally, the *structures of the welfare state* have not been 'upgraded' to the 'information age'. While the Finnish 'information economy' has reformed its work and management culture and used IT innovatively to increase productivity, the public services sector has reacted much more slowly. As the population ages, the pressure on the costs of the welfare state will become stronger and there will need to be productivity growth to avoid the cutting of services. One solution to these problems Himanen offers is the so-called 'E-welfare state', that would exploit the innovative potential of the well-educated workers in the public sector, linking up with ideas from the private sector and the workforce. Ultimately, the future of the Nordic model of a 'virtuous cycle' between the 'information society' and the welfare state will depend on each country's ability, and courage, to reform its welfare state into an 'E-welfare state'.

The current challenges to social policy in the Nordic countries are dis-cussed by Olli Kangas and Joakim Palme in Chapter 12, 'Does the Most Brilliant Future of the "Nordic Model" have to be in the Past?' This final chapter is intended to be future oriented in three different ways. First, it describes the pension reforms that have taken place in the Nordic region, examining primarily the Finnish and Swedish cases. The changes have long-term consequences for the sustainability and scope of public intervention in the pension area. Secondly, it reviews the 'universality' of the Nordic welfare states, paying special attention to the areas where both principles and prac-tices appear to be threatened by erosion. Thirdly, it tries to take a 'holistic approach' to social policy developments, starting from the observation that the old Keynesian legacy has disappeared and that we must find new macro–micro linkages in both design and evaluation of policies. The chapter tries to outline some basic principles that are congruent with a developmental perspective on social policy.

The basic argument is that the sustainability of the Nordic model of social policy hinges on the number of taxpayers that can be mobilized. In order to be successful, governments need to take a combined, or 'holistic' approach, and consider both micro motives and macro considerations. Incentive struc-tures need to be improved: investment in human capital and social services are critical for both labour supply and productivity improvements. However, unless such measures are combined with successful macroeconomic policies they are unlikely to achieve anything close to their full potential.

Note

1   In principle, there are five Nordic countries: Denmark, Finland, Iceland, Norway, and Sweden. Iceland is omitted here, mainly because of lack of availability of data. In a strict sense, the concept of 'Scandinavia' covers only Denmark, Norway and Sweden. Here we, however, use 'Nordic' and 'Scandinavia' as interchangeable concepts.

Bibliography

Mkandawire, T. (2001) 'Social Policy in a Development Context', United Nations Research Institute for Social Development. Social Policy and Development, Paper 7. Geneva: UNRISD.
Schumpeter, J. (1950) *Capitalism, Socialism and Democracy*. New York: Harper.
Sørensen, A. B. (1998) 'On Kings, Pietism and Rent-seeking in Scandinavian Welfare States'. *Acta Sociologica*, 41(4): 363–76.

2
Coming Late – Catching Up: The Formation of a 'Nordic Model'

Olli Kangas and Joakim Palme

Introduction

The purpose of this chapter is to provide a historical and comparative frame-work for the discussion of contemporary social policy developments in the Nordic countries. Present reforms and policy trends illustrate dilemmas for social policy that are common to many countries, and some of the reforms can be seen as alternative strategies to deal with the dilemmas. The relevance of the Scandinavian case for the discussion of different alternative social policy approaches in other parts of the world should be seen in relation to the fact that the Scandinavian model is seen as an 'ideal type'. Its merits, as well as its drawbacks, deserve to be taken seriously.

The structure of the chapter is as follows. We begin with a short historical review to give the reader a broad overview of the background of social policy making in the Nordic hemisphere, since the summary of how the central social insurance programmes were made may be of interest from a developmental point of view. A section enumerating the 'Nordic model's' achievements in terms of social policy coverage and generosity then follows. Poverty cycles – i.e. the incidence of poverty in different phases of life – are then evaluated. After a section on the relationship between the welfare state and economy we discuss the current challenges and reforms that are taking place to adapt the Nordic welfare state to its changing surroundings.

Historical background

Historically, Scandinavia has been a battlefield between two local 'super-powers', Denmark and Sweden which dominated the Northern hemisphere up to the early twentieth century. Norway was a Danish province more than four centuries until the Swedes formed a union with the Norwegians in 1814. The Swedes, who had for hundreds of years occupied territories around the Baltic Sea, began to lose their importance to the rising Germanic and Russian empires. By the end of the Napoleonic wars Sweden had lost all its Baltic provinces and by the Treaty of Tilsit in 1807 Finland was annexed to Russia in 1809. The union between Sweden and Norway was peacefully dissolved in 1905. When Finland gained independence from Russia in 1917 and Iceland from Denmark in 1944, the five Nordic countries took their present form (Alestalo and Kuhnle 1987).

Because of a common political history and administrative practices, the countries share similarities that played an important role when the first social policy programmes were planned and developed. One such aspect is the ability of the state to implement reforms, the focus of many welfare state analyses (see, e.g., Orloff and Skocpol 1984; Evans, Rueschmeyer and Skocpol 1985; Immergut 1992; Skocpol 1992). 'State capacity' is created by an interaction of several factors. First, the state itself must have a *structure* that facilitates reforms. In comparative studies, it has been shown that unitary states can more rapidly carry through reforms than federal states. In the latter case, relatively independent states can oppose federal-level decisions and prevent them from coming into force. The state must also have *bureaucratic ability and power* to plan and execute reforms (Heclo 1974; Orloff and Skocpol 1984; Katz 2001). Both the unitary state structure and a well-educated bureaucracy were at present in Scandinavia, but in rather a special way that combined central government actions with local-level agencies in the municipalities.

The founder of the Swedish kingdom, Gustaf Vasa (*b*.1496; *r*.1523–60), paid special attention to the administration of the country, keeping records of Swedish population mainly for taxation purposes and military conscription. But it took two hundred years until fully-fledged population censuses were conducted (in 1749 in Sweden and 1769 in Denmark). The access to individual citizens' income and assets created a basis for effective taxation which was a crucial precondition to the independency of the state *vis-à-vis* other societal actors and later for building up the welfare state.

Despite the tendency to centralize the administration, the local level played a crucial role in the provision of public services. Traditionally it was the local municipality, or parish, that was responsible for tax collection, delivering help to the poor and some other basic public goods. In order to cover the costs of these tasks, municipalities and parishes could collect and keep a certain part of tax revenues for their own disposal while the rest was sent to the central government. Within certain limits the municipalities could also decide on their own activities including welfare provision and municipal tax rates. Very early, the Scandinavian countries had thus established a functioning local-level democracy that was combined with and coordinated by the central government.

One important precondition to this was the power balance between the Crown and the aristocracy (Alestalo and Kuhnle 1987: 8). In Scandinavia, neither monarchical absolutism nor privileges of aristocracy reached such proportions as in Continental Europe. In such a balanced situation, both the royal family and nobility had to seek support, which improved the possibility that the voice of peasants would also be heard. This combination of a centralized state and local democratic decision-making had important ramifications for the subsequent development of all the Nordic societies.

In contrast to many other developing and poor countries, the state in Scandinavia came to be strong and powerful enough not to be harnessed merely as a vehicle of particular interests; the state was able to make its own plans and decisions to promote the collective or national good rather than merely promoting group-specific endeavours. This was an important precondition for the rapid industrialization of rural and poor societies (see also Vartiainen 1995).

The local character of decision making safeguarded the legitimacy of the public sector. The possibility of the grass-roots participating in municipal decision making created and fortified a general feeling of inclusion; it created a 'virtuous circle' between democracy and social policy. In Denmark, for example, municipalities that took care of everyday issues became the carriers of the first statutory pension scheme in 1891. The distance between the state/public sector and civil society came thus be close and blurred, and it is often hard to say where the civil society ended and the public sector began. One indication of this was that in Scandinavia the word 'state' was often used synonymously with 'society' (Allardt 1986) and the state was not perceived as such a hostile and alien force to the individual as in many other countries.

Nobility and landed aristocracy thus never played such an important role in Scandinavia as they did in feudal Central Europe – where arable land was mainly owned by the aristocracy, serfdom was more common and peasants at best only rented the plots of land they cultivated, whereas in the Nordic hemisphere they owned their fields. Nordic agriculture was individualized (Alestalo and Kuhnle 1987). This independent peasantry with rather strong formal rights constituted the nucleus of the Nordic democratic tradition: it had its say through municipal decision making and also had collective representation at the central government level in the meetings of four of the estates of the realm (peasantry, priests, bourgeoisie, and nobility). The independent peasantry could regard the state as an impartial and even benevolent agent and a counterbalancing force *vis-à-vis* the urban bourgeoisie. The same goes for social democracy; when Nordic social democrats chose to support parliamentary reformism, the state became a vehicle to promote class interests for the growing industrial working class (Esping-Andersen 1985: 141). The germ of grass-roots democracy or democracy from below was already planted in the prehistory or the Scandinavian welfare state.

When industrialization – where the state *de facto* was an important actor in building up railways and other basic infrastructure needed for the breakthrough of the new form of production – gave impetus to the emergence of an industrial working class, the peculiar Nordic tripolar class structure began to take shape (for a fuller description see, e.g., Castles 1979; Alestalo and Kuhnle 1987). On the one hand, there was the traditional class of capital owners and urban bourgeoisie and, at the other end of this continuum, there was the industrial working class. In that sense, the Nordic countries did not deviate from the rest of Europe. Yet since the independent peasantry formed their own distinct social class with political representation, the Nordic class structure, instead of being bipolar as in most other countries, came to be tripolar. This class structure was more or less directly mirrored in the political sphere. In addition to the left- and right-wing parties, relatively strong agrarian (later centre) parties were important political forces, which conditioned early Nordic social policy making. Their own political representation meant that the interests of the rural population could not be neglected when the first measures of social policy were planned. The Scandinavians therefore began to legislate *national* insurance covering the whole population, rather than *workers'* insurance limited only to the industrial working class, as in many Central European countries (Baldwin 1990; Kangas and Palme 1993). In the second place, the agrarian parties in the middle split the homogeneity of the non-socialist block and made it easier for social democrats to pursue their politics. As argued by Francis Castles (1979), the social democratic hegemony in Scandinavia is based not only on the strength of the left, but also on the weakness of the right.

The structural peculiarity of the Nordic countries in comparison to the rest of Europe becomes obvious if we depict the levels of socioeconomic development (measured as a sum of urbanization and industrialization) against the timing of the first social insurance laws, as is done in Figure 2.1 (cf. Alber 1981). The abbreviations in the figure refer to work-accident (WA), sickness (SI), pension (PI) and unemployment (UI) insurance. The vertical axis shows the degree of socioeconomic development and the year of legislation is displayed on the horizontal axis. The interpretation of the graph is straightforward. For example, in Norway the first social insurance form, work-accident (WA), was introduced in 1895 when the level of socioeconomic development was about 40 per cent and the last insurance (pensions, PI) were implemented in 1937 at the developmental level of about 50 per cent.

There are substantial differences between the countries and groups of countries in timing and the level of socioeconomic development. One extreme is the UK, where legislation of social insurance took place during a very short period of time and at a high level of modernization. The other extreme is Finland, where social policy was made in relatively agrarian surroundings and where the legislative process lasted a long time. The Finnish case is a good example of a country where social policy legislation lagged behind in terms of chronological time, but in terms of developmental time the reforms came 'too early' (see Flora and Alber 1981; Flora 1986). The same goes for the other Nordic countries as well. This pattern of structural and

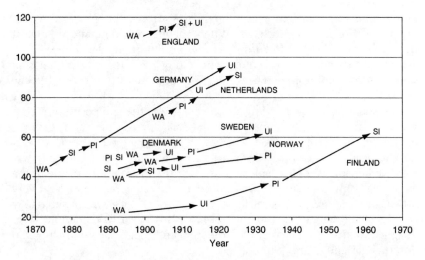

Figure 2.1 Level of socioeconomic development and introduction of first social insurance laws, Nordic countries and selected European countries, 1870–1970.
Note: 'Socioeconomic Development' = Industrialization and Labourization.

political surroundings had its ramifications for the kind of social policy that it was possible to implement.

Three aspects in this early development deserve to be emphasized. First, there is a striking similarity between the Nordic countries in poor law legislation and municipal administrative responsibilities (Kuhnle 1981: 136). In fact, in 1890 the Scandinavian countries spent more (about 1 per cent) of their GDP on social transfers, consisting mainly of poor help, than any other country at that time (Lindert 2004: 12–13). This poor-help tradition was one starting point when the early initiatives on social insurance were planned. Secondly, insurance schemes at various stages were based on wide, albeit varying, coalitions between political parties and/or social classes. Thirdly, state intervention in several fields was based on 'mobilization from below'. As will discussed later, both sickness cash benefits and unemployment insurance were first organized in the form of voluntary, independent insurance funds, often organized by trade unions and eventually subsidized by the state. There were some country-specific differences in this pattern. Denmark and Sweden, with a stronger urban and liberal tradition, relied more on voluntarism than Norway and the most agrarian country, Finland (Kuhnle 1981; Esping-Andersen and Korpi 1984 and 1987).

An advantage of this popular-movement model was that the state did not have to start with a major investment in a large administrative apparatus for paying the benefits. The legitimacy of the insurance was sustained by strict social control in what were fairly small insurance funds. The mobilization in various forms of social movements, such as trade unions and the temperance movement, was strong: this provided a base for organizing friendly societies. When these received financial support from the government, and thus became voluntary state-subsidized programmes, this became very important, along with the size of the subsidies, for expanding the coverage of the programmes (Kangas and Palme 1993).

A crucial aspect in expanding the coverage was the composition of class structure and the political representation of class-based interests. The implementation of the first pension schemes illustrates the point. In most Central European countries, the Bismarckian workers' insurance principle was applied: benefits were available according to the insurance principle to the employees only. Peasants, as well as agricultural labourers, would get very little if anything out of a contributory Bismarckian-type system since they got much of their pay in kind and not in cash. The early programmes were designed to meet the needs of both the rural and urban parts of the population (Kangas and Palme 1992).

Old-age pensions

Denmark was one of the first countries in the world to institute a legislated pension scheme (1891) only two years later than Bismarck had introduced his contributory pensions for the German wage earners (Palme 1990: 43). Despite the almost identical timing, the philosophy underpinning the Danish pension law was totally different from the German system. In Germany, pensions, and more generally all social insurance, were for the working-class 'aristocracy', whereas in Denmark the pension law tried to modify the existing poor-law practices and to remove the aged from poor relief by providing them with proper pensions. The emphasis was thus more on the lower end of the income ladder, on poor people, reflecting the key idea that the main goal of the pension reform was not to solve legitimacy problems of an authoritarian regime, as in Germany, but rather to help the poor elderly and also to solve municipal poor relief problems. The scheme instituted non-contributory (although means-tested) pensions financed through taxes, three-quarters coming from local sources and the rest from central government (Nørby Johansen 1986: 298). To facilitate administration, the scheme was run by local authorities (Salminen 1993: 169).

Sweden's first pension reform (1913) combined fully-funded contributory pensions with means-tested supplements (Elmér 1960). The intention was to provide both the urban and rural populations with economic security in old age and the scheme followed the Danish rather than the Bismarckian approach. As proposed by Esping-Andersen and Korpi (1987: 45) it was the first piece of social legislation that recognized full universalism by covering the whole population under one single scheme. In 1946, the contributory and funded system was dissolved and instead, tax-financed pay-as-you-go flat-rate pensions for every citizen over 65 years of age were introduced.

Norway introduced the first pension law in 1936 that also instituted universal coverage and universal financial responsibilities, but benefits were conditioned by means testing (Kuhnle 1986: 121). In fact, local initiatives figured in the first Norwegian pension scheme, which was a replicate of the municipal pension scheme implemented in 1923 in Oslo.

The Finnish development followed the Swedish way with couple of decades' delay and, corresponding the 1913 Swedish scheme Finland carried through in 1937 a fully-funded individual account-based scheme that covered all citizens. In that scheme, pensions for the first generation were to be means-tested.

The Second World War formed a turning point in social policy thinking, and in the mid-1950s the other Nordic countries followed the Swedish path trodden by the 1946 reform and changed their national pension schemes to guarantee universal flat-rate tax-financed pensions. The breakthrough of universalism, nascent in the first national pension laws, thus took place during the first decade after the war. In pensions, the Nordic countries began with the agrarian 'little but to everybody' principle.

When we study the post-war period, it is important to emphasize that the development of benefits, services and taxation interacted with changes in the labour market. Two important phases, or systemic shifts, can be identified in the pension area – and, in fact, they are characteristic for social policy at large. The abolition of means testing in the basic pensions system created the broadest possible political base for combating poverty among the elderly. Since all elderly persons received pensions and everybody of active age could look forward to getting statutory pension in their old age, it was in the interests of all to support such a system. This reform strategy was also well designed to meet the needs of countries which were becoming industrialized but still had large agrarian populations. Because benefit levels went up as pensions were introduced for all members of the community, there was a corresponding drop in public assistance payments to the elderly. Yet the levels of compensation the Nordic pensions offered in relation to an ordinary industrial worker's wage were still low (or, at best, modest) by international standards in 1960 (Palme 1990: 50–1).

The golden age of post-war economic growth meant that Scandinavian countries rapidly industrialized. This also meant a growing need to compensate the working population for loss of earned income in the case of incapacity to work because of age or other social risks. Along with the growth in the number of salaried staff and other employees in the service sector, the percentage of agricultural employees declined. Meanwhile something was taking shape which, in Britain, Richard Titmuss (1955) referred to as 'the two nations of welfare' – i.e. part of the population had to make do with quite small national pensions while other groups could rely on more generous, occupational benefits paid by the employer. This social division of welfare in society could, Titmuss argued, be counteracted only by means of universal earnings-related pensions. In Scandinavia, that debate became actual in the 1950s and 1960s.

The history and the success of endeavours to establish earnings-related pension schemes vary between the Nordic countries (for an excellent summary, see Salminen 1993). In Sweden, which was again the pioneer, the debate on and the making of the supplementary pension scheme (ATP) was highly politicized. The bourgeois parties backed by the Swedish Employers' Federation advocated either the universal flat-rate scheme proposed by the centre party or voluntary occupational pensions based on collective agreements proposed by the conservatives; social democrats in contrast insisted on a compulsory, legislated and state-run scheme that guaranteed similar benefits to all categories of employees (Olsson 1990). The basic idea was that social policy should not only guarantee against losses of income but that social policy may also unify and divide groups of people. This idea was a central element in Bismarck's social insurance programmes, with separate schemes with different benefits for different groups of employees. Where Bismarck tried to prevent the development of a common employee interest, the Swedish social democrats used the reverse strategy: by pooling the wage earners and the salaried employees in the same risk pool a common class identity – that was hoped to be social democratic – was to be created (Esping-Andersen 1985). In 1959, the Swedish Parliament, by a majority of one vote, passed the pension law according to social democratic principles and Sweden got its earnings-related pension programme, one of the most generous schemes in the world.

Finland was the next Nordic country to legislate on earnings-related pensions (1961). The political history of the Finnish scheme is totally different from that of the other countries. In Finland, the social democrats sought support for their social policy proposals from the conservatives, and trade unions had direct negotiations with the employer federation. The reason for this was the fact that the Agrarian Party, favouring universal flat-rate benefits, occupied such a strong position in parliament that it could have jeopardized the whole idea of earnings-related benefits (Niemelä 1988; Salminen 1993). For social democrats it was rather easy to accept a deal with the Employers' Federation promising earnings-related, employer-financed and completely legislated pensions that were decentralized and run by private insurance companies, not by state agencies as in the other Nordic countries. In comparison to the Swedish case, the Finnish scheme resulted from more consensual policy making and a much broader class-compromise. The Finnish scheme was less generous: the target level was 60 per cent of final income after forty years in employment, whereas the Swedes had a target level at least as high but with full pension already earned after thirty working years.

The Swedish ATP model figured in the Norwegian discussions on legislated earnings-related pensions. In the beginning, the social democrats were sceptical about the Swedish model but when they realized that it were a good weapon with which to attack the bourgeois bloc they adopted the idea. On the other hand, the non-socialist parties were reluctant to let the pension question to be politicized along party lines to the extent that had happened in Sweden. As a consequence, the Norwegian supplementary pension scheme was instituted rather consensually in 1966 (Kuhnle 1986: 123; Salminen 1993: 279–9). The basic structure of the scheme was similar to the Swedish model, but instead of thirty years in employment the claimant had to work for forty years to be entitled to a full pension.

In Denmark, the first initiatives for earnings-related supplementary schemes were taken in the early 1960s. The Social Democratic Cabinet made a Bill in 1964 on a supplementary pension scheme. In contrast to the other Nordic countries, the scheme was not to be earnings-related but a flat-rate system where the benefits were related to the number of years in employment not to the worker's wage. Since then, there have been several attempts to institute a proper earnings-related pension scheme, but all attempts have failed. In its pension system Denmark deviates from other Nordic countries, and in their typology of pension systems Korpi and Palme (1998) classify Finland, Norway and Sweden as the best representatives of the so-called 'encompassing welfare state model', offering universal basic security on flat-rate basis to all residents. On top of that basic security, homogeneous earnings-related benefits to all the employed are guaranteed; Denmark, due to the lack of an employment-related component, is a typical 'basic security' country. In Denmark, earnings-relatedness is obtained through labour market benefits that in the early twenty-first century cover nearly all the employees.

As stated above, social policy is much more than just guaranteeing security against various social risks. Social policy creates and fortifies social bonds and may enhance the development of social capital. Social policy may also be used to accumulate 'real' capital as well. Pension funds are a huge source of capital accumulation that can be used for different purposes. A closer inspection of the Finnish and Swedish cases illustrates the point. In Sweden, the state-controlled ATP funds were used to provide housing in urban areas expanding with migration from the countryside. The pension funds were used both to fortify and to mitigate the structural transformation from an agrarian into an industrial society. In Finland, the national pension funds were used in the 1950s to build up national basic infrastructure such as power stations and electrical networks, whereas the employment-related funds were mainly invested in national industry and to provide investment capital to industrialize society. The Nordic countries provide a good example on how it is possible to merge social policy goals with economic goals to build up a modern industrial market economy.

Sickness insurance

The early initiatives to seek help in the case of sickness involved various forms of support provided by kin and the neighbourhood. Emerging social legislation, first in the form of poor laws, later provided some relief. Various forms self-help organizations, such as guilds and other mutual arrangements, provided protection in the case of sickness, old age and death. Gradually, the state began to subsidize, and consequently supervise, these mutual and voluntary schemes (see Carroll, Chapter 3 in this volume). But as a rule, the benefit levels were meagre and the coverage rates of the early programmes limited. The nucleus of these mutual organizations were skilled, unionized workers, while unskilled labourers were excluded from the benefit societies. Applicants who were young, male and healthy were preferred to older workers and women because of their higher risk propensity. This accentuated the central problem in purely voluntary systems: the greater the need for protection, the more unlikely that help would be available.

In order to meet the needs of people who were bad risks, various forms of 'public' funds were established; nevertheless, in most countries, poor relief continued to be the most important form of social protection for ill workers. The numbers of sick, disabled and poor workers contributed nothing to the municipal budgets but strained local poor relief programmes. In other words, the public authorities were obliged to take responsibility for workers with 'bad risks', those who were excluded from the more selective workers' funds. Because of the local character and small size of membership, funds often became unable to carry the financial burden caused by long-term illness of an individual member, or by epidemics simultaneously hitting several members. Then the final responsibility fell on the public authorities. This increased pressures to carry through more fully-fledged insurance programmes and establish risk-pooling on wider national bases (Ritter 1986: 41–2,76). Wider risk-pooling also became necessary because of the very characteristics of local or strictly occupational-based funds that prevented the geographic and occupational mobility that was a precondition for a well-functioning market economy.

In addition to the primary function of guaranteeing protection in the case of illness, the early sickness funds had important latent functions as well, which came to affect the strategies chosen by the different political actors. Since the funds were often an organizational part of the activities of the emerging labour movement, the funds promoted the recruitment of new members for the trade unions. The sickness benefit system based on the activity of unions thus contributed to the formation of the working class and strengthened class solidarity among the workers (see, e.g., Ritter 1986: 71–82; Quadagno 1988: 53).

As noted above, the first Nordic social policy programmes were amalgamations of peasant liberalism and nascent social democratic ideas, and later of the emerging cross-class alliance between blue- and white collar-workers labelled 'socio-political development' (e.g. Esping-Andersen 1985; Esping-Andersen and Korpi 1987; Baldwin 1990; Olsson 1990). The emphasis and timing in this coalition-building differs to some extent. In Denmark, the liberal tradition was the strongest, social democracy was from the 1930s the dominant political force in Sweden and the same goes, perhaps, for Norway, whereas agrarian hegemony – more conservative than liberal – was up until the 1960s prevalent in Finland.

Following a stronger liberalistic stream, Denmark was far ahead of her Northern neighbours in the development of voluntary sickness funds; the state began to subsidize funds in 1892 and the financial basis of the funds were fortified further in 1907 (Hansen and Henriksen 1984: 85–6). As a consequence, the number of fund members rapidly increased. At the beginning of the 1890s, the Danish funds covered less than one-tenth of the total population but by 1930 the coverage was two-thirds of the total population or 90 per cent of the labour force (Kolstrup 1996: 263). In 1933, membership in sickness funds became obligatory; the 1971 National Health Security Act dissolved the funds and their activities were levied on the public authorities (Nørby-Johansen 1986: 298–9). The Danish experience demonstrates that in some instances it is possible to get extensive coverage rates even by voluntary measures, but that there must be some state involvement to solve collective action problems of moral hazard and adverse selection.

In Sweden, the first law to subsidy voluntary sickness funds was passed in 1891, but compared to Denmark subsidies were much smaller, which was mirrored in the slower membership development during the formative decades of the scheme. The Swedish sickness fund activities were like the Free Church or Temperance movements – also actively involved in the sickness fund activities – organized as a popular movement that had much wider backing than just the working class (see Lindqvist 1990; Olsson 1990; Johansson 2003).

In their hayday in the early 1950, the sickness funds covered about 60 per cent of the adult Swedish population. One of the most severe problems in Sweden was that those who were most in need never became members. Just as the most sinful did not enter Free Churches and the most notorious drinkers avoided the Temperance movement, the poorest and the most sick were not covered by sickness funds. Furthermore, the income loss compensation for the insiders was only very modest (at the beginning of the 1940s a vast majority of members had a compensation rate that covered less than 10 per cent of the income losses, Lindqvist 1990: 83). Like the Danes, the Swedes tried to make the fund-based insurance more efficient, and in 1955 a mandatory scheme where the existing funds were insurance carriers was implemented and universal coverage of all population categories was realized.

In Norway and Finland the voluntary sickness fund movement never gained the same importance as in Denmark and Sweden and consequently, the routes to compulsory and universal insurance were different (Kuhnle 1981). In Norway, the first sickness law of 1909 introduced obligatory insurance. Strangely enough, the poor and the rich were excluded form the coverage, nor were the self-employed included; voluntary solutions were available to those who were excluded from compulsory coverage (Seip 1994: 198). In a way, the Norwegians followed the German idea since the core of the insured came from the industrial working-class. The expansion of the scheme also followed the German model: new groups were gradually added to the insurance. In 1953, the scheme was made compulsory for all wage-earners and three years later for all citizens (Kuhnle 1986: 124).

Finland was the last European country to implement sickness insurance (1963). The struggle over insurance was between the two main political forces – i.e., the social democrats and the agrarian party. On the social democratic agenda, adequate income loss compensation was given priority and the strategy aimed at insurance for workers but not necessarily for other socioeconomic groups. On the agrarian agenda, universal coverage was combined with flat-rate daily allowances mirroring the interests of the agrarian sector (Kangas 1991: 150). Through judicious tactical coalitions, sometimes with the communist, sometimes with the right-wing parties, the agrarians managed to reject social democratic initiatives for workers' insurance unless the programme universally covered the total population. Had the social democrats been more powerful in Finland, the law on sickness benefits would have been carried through much earlier in all probability following the Norwegian pattern.

Unemployment insurance

Comparative studies on OECD countries have shown that unemployment security was the last social insurance form to be implemented (Alber 1981).[1] The reason for that is that the unemployment insurance, perhaps more than the other insurance forms, intervenes in the labour–capital relationship. By providing alternative means of livelihood to work unemployment benefits reduce employees' dependence on the market and weaken the employers' position. Moreover, moral hazard problems and inspection/screening of the claimants are bigger than in, say, pensions or work-accidents (Carroll 1999: 120).

The primary goal of social policy is to provide social protection. However, important secondary goals of latent functions are involved in the making of social policies. The issue of social policy's ability to enhance collective group identity was touched on earlier when discussing the latent functions of sickness benefits. The history of the Nordic unemployment insurance programmes offers perhaps the most illuminative story about the relationship between the administrative form of a social policy programme and the bases for collective action, showing how voluntary funds can be effective devices for class-mobilization and also showing the obvious limits of voluntary social policy programmes.

Initially, all the Nordic countries began with the so-called 'Ghent system': the scheme was based on voluntary membership in a state-subsidized and trade union-run insurance scheme. Norway was the first country to subsidize funds (1906) followed by Denmark (1907) and Finland (1917). This time, it was Sweden (1934) that lagged behind its neighbours (Carroll 1999: 127, and Chapter 3 in this volume). One of the most serious problems with voluntary funds is that they may become financially unstable if the risk against which they guarantee protection becomes widespread in society. This was what happened in the late 1920s and early 1930s. In Norway, the unions were unable to manage cost-cutting and some funds went bankrupt; the Labour Government decided to 'socialize' the risk of unemployment by introducing a compulsory and state-led system (Rothstein 1992: 45), whereas Denmark and Finland continued to rely on the voluntary principle. When the depression hit Sweden the country had not yet introduced any unemployment insurance at all, and it was too late to combat mass unemployment through creating insurance. Instead, the Swedish government began to establish subsidized jobs for the unemployed: the so-called 'active labour market policy' (ALP) had been invented.

Denmark, Finland and Sweden are the only Western countries that still have the 'Ghent system' in use. Interestingly enough, these three countries also display the highest union membership rates involving 80–90 per cent of employees, while the average for other countries is less than half of that (Rothstein 1992). The case of unemployment insurance clearly shows how social policy can create loyalties and social bonds, which in turn have important consequences for the distribution of power in society. The initial constructors of the system may have been unaware of the latent functions of the union-based unemployment scheme but the present-day policy-makers know rather more. The left-wing parties that have usually spoken for state-led and universal insurance schemes are in Denmark; Finland and Sweden more in favour of the present unemployment insurance system. Consequently, bourgeois parties, usually opposing centralized statutory systems and warmly supporting self-help organizations and 'third-sector' NGO solutions, vehemently desire to socialize the unemployment scheme.

Late starters – great leaps forward

The history of the coming of social insurance in the Nordic hemisphere tell the political side of the story. Another aspect is the level of benefits and the extension of coverage of social insurance guarantees. Figure 2.2 shows the compound indices[2] for coverage[3] and generosity expressed as an average

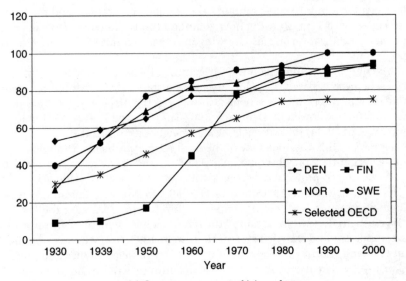

(a) Coverage: per cent of labour force

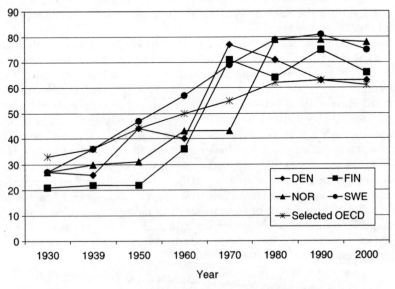

(b) Generosity: per cent of wage

Figure 2.2 Coverage and generosity of social insurance, Nordic countries and selected OECD countries, 1930–2000

replacement rate.[4] The coverage index varies between 0, indicating that nobody is insured under any scheme, and 100, indicating that the coverage is complete in all schemes. The range for generosity is 0–100, 0 pertaining to a situation where no benefits are available at all and 100 that benefits from all schemes fully correspond to the claimant's wage. In principle, it is possible to produce figures for eighteen industrialized OECD countries, but for the sake of simplicity we display data separately only for the four Nordic countries and merge the other fourteen countries together ('Other') and present averages only for the non-Nordic cases.

Figure 2.2 can be read from two points of view. Perhaps the first and most obvious way of seeing it is as a chronological and cross-sectional inspection. A reader interested in welfare state typologies will be able to see if the Nordic countries at different points in time belonged to the same welfare state regime. If we take the initial situation in 1930, and try to see if the countries display a similar pattern, our answer is negative. When it comes to the coverage of the scheme, Denmark and Sweden are more universal that the other countries, Norway hovers around the mean but catches up the two leading countries by 1950, while Finland lags far behind and reaches Nordic coverage rates only in the 1970s. Since then, the Nordic bloc has been rather homogeneous with high, near to universal, coverage rates. In that sense 'universalism' has been, and still is, the Nordic trademark.

The story concerning generosity is rather different. Initially the replacement rates in Scandinavia were lower than in the rest of the developed countries, and it was not until the mid-1970s that replacement rates in all the Nordic countries exceeded the general mean. By the turn of the millennium the Nordic 'cluster' is more homogeneous and distinct in terms of coverage than in terms of benefit generosity. If we drew a scatter-plot where countries were plotted on generosity and coverage, up to the mid-1950s the Nordic pattern would have been associated with wide coverage and low benefit levels. Later, when income-graduated components were added to basic security, the 'encompassing' Scandinavian welfare state as we know it nowadays would show the widest coverage and high, but not necessarily the highest, benefits levels (see Korpi and Palme 1998).

We could also read Figure 2.2 developmentally, and try to see if there were similar developmental patterns between countries. It may be that a group of countries follows a similar developmental path but because of differences in their socioeconomic development their timing is different. This may explain the deviance of Finland. As we know that the share of the agrarian labour force in Finland was the same in 1960 as it was in 1930 in Denmark and Sweden, one could compare the 1960 Finnish coverage and replacement rates with the 1930 situation in the other countries. That kind of comparison would reveal a nice fit; in all cases, coverage rates were about 40 per cent and replacement levels close to 35 per cent. In sum, the Nordic countries have followed a pretty similar pattern, but the timing has been different depending on nation-specific circumstances: the countries have been chronologically heterogeneous but developmentally homogeneous. When industrialization proceeded, chronological differences diminished.

Universal service delivery and mass education

An abundance of studies revolve around the question of possible convergence trends between different welfare states. In these studies, one central question has dealt with the distinctiveness of the Scandinavian model: whether it still exists or not. Concerning the income-maintenance programmes analysed above, one can argue that there still is a trait of Scandinavian distinctiveness that lies the universality of benefits, not necessarily in better income-loss compensation. Another feature that is typical of the Scandinavian welfare state model is the comprehensive social services. In that respect the Nordic countries can be labelled as 'service states', contrasted with the 'transfer states' of Continental Europe. In Figure 2.3 social spending is disaggregated into services and transfers expressed as a percentage of GDP. The division of social expenditures gives some support to this thesis: Sweden is in the lead in both social transfers and services, while Denmark and Norway display somewhat higher social service spending than other countries. Finland is closer to France and Germany than the Scandinavian countries.

Universality has also been one of the cornerstones of public service delivery in Scandinavia. In the very beginning the municipal poor-help and local

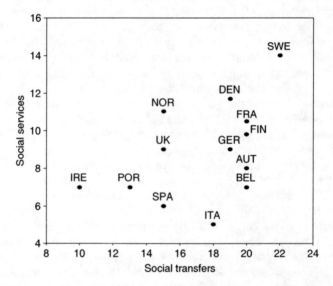

Figure 2.3   Social spending, services and transfers, Europe, 2000, per cent of GDP

poorhouse system paved the way. The local poorhouses were gradually transformed via 'communal' and 'old people's' houses to 'service centres'. The change in the name reflects the fact that today these institutions offer a vide variety of personal and social services, not only basic care. The hospital care that gradually began to take shape in Scandinavia after the 1850s (the first hospital laws were carried though 1860 in pioneering Norway and 1885 in late-comer Finland) established a system where municipalities, either alone or in collaboration with other municipalities, were responsible for organizing hospitals. The state supervised and subsidized these local activities in varying degrees. The system of 'decentralized centralization' continues today and universal health services that are either totally free or heavily subsidized by the state are organized on municipal or regional bases. Hospitals are predominantly public, although there is a slowly growing tendency towards private health care (Lehto, Moss and Rostgaard 1999). The Nordic health care system seems to have been fairly egalitarian and universal, in the sense that there is neither substantial geographic variation nor socioeconomic variation in the use of services. Use is linked to the need and health status of the claimant more than to access barriers dictated by traditional socioeconomic factors (see Fritzell and Lundberg, chapter 7 in this volume).

The same endeavour to establish universal access was present in the path the mass-education systems in Scandinavia and in building up the educational system the grass-roots level was harnessed to accomplish the task; as in the case of people's insurance, the very name of the educational system, *folkskola* (people's school), indicated the overarching idea that the whole population should have access to education. In Sweden, compulsory education was introduced in 1842, when parishes became responsible for organizing basic education, mainly run and financed at local bases under state supervision. In 1962, nine-year compulsory basic education was introduced. In principle, the story for the other Scandinavian countries is very similar although the timing of the reforms varies. In Denmark, compulsory education was introduced earlier than in Sweden but the transformation to homogeneous mass education took rather longer. In Finland, the *folkskola* began 1866 and in 1968 the comprehensive school system replaced the old 'parallel tracks schools'; all pupils became subject to ten years' basic education. The main goal of these reforms was to extend free education to every child under a certain age limit. One peculiarity deserves to be mentioned: in Finland and Sweden schools also provide all pupils with free lunches.

World-wide, the Nordic countries are big spenders in education (see Figure 2.4) but among the developed OECD countries Nordic spending in absolute terms is not strikingly high; despite this Nordic students have achieved high marks in various student achievement tests (see http://www.pisa.oecd.org/; Lindert 2004: 234–5). Moreover, student performance in Nordic countries is less than in most other countries related to the student's family background (e.g. Finland scored highest in the 2000

34

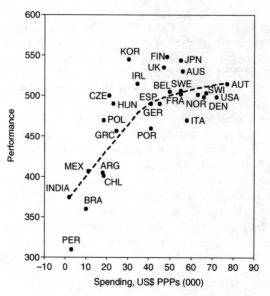

(a) Spending and educational performance, US$ PPPs, 000

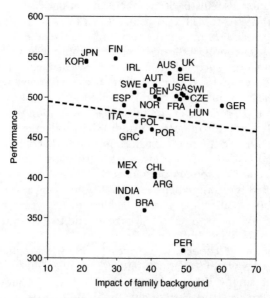

(b) Impact of family background and educational performance

Figure 2.4 Students' educational performance, educational spending and impact of family background on performance, 2000

Source: OECD PISA (Program for International Student Assessment) http://www.pisa.oecd.org/.

PISA literary skills study, and of high-score countries only Japan, Hong Kong and Korea did the student's family background have less impact than in Finland). Results presented by Esping-Andersen (Chapter 6 in this volume) point in the same direction and indicate that the educational reforms that have been carried through in Scandinavia have managed to diminish the inheritance of educational attainment and, consequently, social position attached to educational achievement. In this context, the emergence and consequences of the 'dual-earner model' becomes important, not least in relation to the design of family support.

Family support

Starting in the 1890s, European countries all went through demographic and social processes that had drastic repercussions on family life. The increased numbers of women involved in paid labour accentuated the problem of compensating income losses during pre- and post-natal maternal leave. The early sickness insurance laws included some (albeit rudimentary) maternity-leave arrangements. The increasing costs associated with bringing up children in industrial societies created fundamental problems, mirrored in heavily reduced birth rates (e.g. Wennemo 1994; Ferrarini 2003). Public family support grew from these processes of structural change but was also a result of political mobilization, creating country-specific variations in solving similar problems.

During the years 1900–30, the issue came on to the political agenda as a 'population question'. In the 1930s, concerns about demographic policy interacted with pre-existing motives in feminist mobilization and resulted in an approach that came to influence reforms. Perhaps the best example of this is given by Sweden. In 1934, Alva and Gunnar Myrdal published a book – *Kris i befolkningsfrågan* (The Crisis of the Population Question) – which was not only important for the way family support in Sweden was organized but was also influential in neighbouring countries. A host of different family policy reforms, emphasising the voluntary nature of parenthood, were recommended. The ambition was to *enable* women to combine economic activity with family life, and also to improve children's living conditions. However, despite its clear agenda-setting, the real expansion of universal family support did not take place until the post-war era.

The introduction of public family support was based on different motives and different forms (see, e.g., Wennemo 1994; Hiilamo 2002; Ferrarini 2003), but in principle two main strategies were applied. One was to give families more cash by paying benefits directly. The first child allowances were paid in France and in some other Continental European countries before the Second World War, whereas in Scandinavia they were implemented after the war (Hiilamo 2002). In Scandinavia, universal child benefits were first established in Norway (1946), followed two years later by Sweden and Finland.

Denmark started with tax allowances (1952), to be replaced by universal child allowances (1961). The Nordic peculiarity is that benefits are payable to the mother. The level of allowances in relation to the average wage level is high, but not necessarily the highest in Europe. Changes in the 1970s signified a breakthrough for the modern version of family support in terms of benefits in both cash and kind. Parental leave was paid out at the same level as sickness cash benefit, even if the duration was limited to start with. Today the benefit period is about a year and the average benefit levels range from 70 per cent of the wage in Denmark and Finland to 100 per cent in Norway (SSPTW 2003).

A second strategy is to enhance the earnings capacity of families by providing public subsidies to child care, thus making it possible for single parents to earn a market income or for two-parent families to have a second earner. The expansion of publicly subsidized day care made it possible for an increasing number of parents to combine work on the market with caring responsibilities for children (Palme 1999; Ferrarini 2003). However, in the Nordic political discourse on day care the goals were much more ambitious than simply providing 'parking places' for children while their parents were at work. Alva Myrdal succinctly expressed these ideas in her extensive writings on the topics in the 1930s and 1940s. Child care institutions should have important educational tasks: children coming from different backgrounds should have equal right to care which in the longer run would also even up unequal life possibilities caused by differences in family background.

The Nordic countries are a good example of how the 'male-breadwinner' model has been transformed into a 'dual-earner' model (Lewis 1992; Korpi 2000). It is evident that this has required significant policy changes. The fact that women, over the post-war period, have taken part in education to a higher and higher degree is one important factor behind their massive entrance on the labour market (Skrede 1999). Women simply acquired the necessary human skills and resources. The expansion of child care and care for the elderly are important, both as resources for women and men with care responsibilities, and as employment opportunities (see Anttonen, Chapter 4 in this volume).

These changes were facilitated by changes in the tax system. In the Nordic countries, taxes are imposed on individuals not on families, which provides better incentives for married women to enter paid employment. This stands in contrast to the traditional way of designing such systems in the countries of Continental Europe, even if there have also been important changes there more recently, and the female employment ratio has increased (Hemerijck 2002; OECD 2002: 72–3). However, the so-called 'gender employment gap' (the percentage point difference between employment rates for men and women) among persons aged twenty-five–fifty-four still displays high variation between countries (Figure 2.5). For men and women without children there is no gap at all in Finland and Sweden. At the other end of the

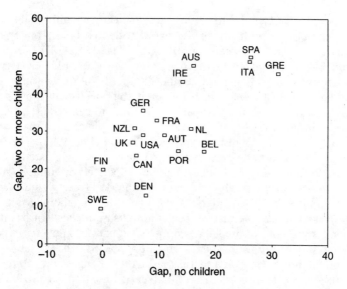

Figure 2.5 'Gender employment gap' (male–female employment, percentage points), persons aged twenty-five–fifty-four, selected OECD countries, 2000
Source: OECD (2002: 77).

horizontal axis are Greece, Spain and Italy, with gaps of around 30 per cent points. In the rest of the selected countries, the gap varies 10–20 points. The presence of children increases the gap everywhere but the Nordic countries still display the lowest disparities, indicating that in those countries it is easier to combine employment and parenthood. Even in Scandinavia, however, gaps still exist.

The Scandinavian welfare state model has certainly helped women to enter the labour market, and the income differentials between males and females appear to be smaller. However, the gender relations are perhaps not as equal as might seem on first glance. The other side of the coin is that the Nordic women predominantly work in the welfare sector, which leads to high degree of occupational segregation by gender in these countries (see, e.g., OECD 2002: 89–90; Mandel and Semeynov 2003). This occupational segregation has a double effect upon gender equality. First, women may be stacked in low-paid public sector occupations and their representation in the high-pay occupations may be lower than in countries with smaller public sectors. Recent studies have shown that low-paid women in Scandinavia are doing relatively well in comparison to men in lower-income brackets or if compared to a corresponding group of women in other countries, whereas women on the upper part of income ladder are doing better, say in the USA, in comparison both to men and Scandinavian high-salaried women.

However, in comparison to the Nordic dual-earner family policy model perhaps the biggest problems in the market oriented family policy model applied in the Anglo-American countries, most clearly the USA (Korpi 2000; Ferrarini 2003), are linked to the high prevalence of child poverty, most notably poverty in single-parent families (Korpi 2000). As shown by Ferrarini and Forssén in Chapter 5 in this volume, the poverty rate among single parents varies from less than 10 per cent in Finland close to 50 per cent in Canada and the USA. Here we have another example of dilemmas in social policy or paradoxes of redistribution (Korpi and Palme 1998). The Nordic dual-earner model is not especially targeted at poor or single-parent families, while Anglo-American social policy making deliberately attempts to support families in need and typically with benefits directed to single mothers; the Aid for Families with Dependent Children (AFDC) programme is perhaps the clearest example. The case of single mothers is an excellent example of the shortcomings of this model, not only to combat child poverty in general but also to support single mothers – who are supposed to be the target group of the programmes (Hobson and Takahashi 1996; Kangas and Palme 2000). Interestingly, it is the importance of market income that is contributing to the relatively good economic position of single mothers in the Nordic countries. With regard to both family support and pensions, comparative research indicates that expansion as well as design of policies has had substantial effects on poverty and inequality.

Poverty and inequality

The principal goal of the welfare state is often defined in terms of poverty reduction, but the Scandinavian countries have gone further and also included the ambition of reducing overall inequalities in society (Erikson 1993). In the Nordic social policy paradigm, perhaps more than in any other, the relative character of poverty is recognized: poverty is inability to participate in the way of life prevailing in the society where the individual lives (Townsend 1979; Gordon and Townsend 2000). Poverty equates to the lack of resources needed to participate in the normal way of life of the surrounding society. This 'lack of resources' comes close to the concept of 'functionings' or 'capabilities' as defined by Amartya Sen (1992, 1998). The lack of functionings in turn leads to 'poverty of agency'. This opens up the whole poverty discourse to deal with much wider issues than just of scarcity of money. Education, cultural and social capital, etc. will be involved in the bundle of capabilities needed for full participation in societal activities. This idea is expressed in the Nordic tradition of welfare studies (e.g. Johansson 1979; Allardt 1975; Erikson 1993), where the starting point has been those resources – or if you prefer, capabilities – that individuals have at their disposal. From this perspective, Bo Rothstein (1998: 218) convincingly argues against selectivism and the minimal welfare state: by providing the widest possible bundle of capabilities 'the universal welfare state does not prescribe to citizens which life projects are better than others'. In such a way the state enhances the real freedom and autonomy of its citizens.

Even if systems of social protection have other and wider goals than just fighting monetary poverty, it can still be argued, following Rawls' (1971) principles of justice, that the situation of the worst-off in society is a powerful indicator of how successful the entire system of social protection is. If the welfare state programmes prove to be most important for those who lack resources derived from the family or the market, the situation of children provides a special rationale for the welfare state. Children do not choose to be born and brought up by poor parents; it can therefore be argued that governments have a responsibility to ensure that children in their countries have equal rights to participate in education, health care, etc., and that they should be entitled to the necessary resources in terms of nutrition and housing so that they can take full advantage of these rights (see, e.g., Esping-Andersen's Chapter 6 in this volume). Old persons are also vulnerable because of their declining work capacity, and their situation is of particular relevance in a social policy context. Special attention to the position of these two vulnerable groups is thus warranted.

John Rawls' *A Theory of Social Justice* (1971) offers a heuristic starting point for such a study of poverty, and it also is the implicit underpinning idea connecting all contributions in this volume. There are three notions in Rawls's concept of justice that are relevant for our purposes in analysing the effect of social policy: (1) the original distribution of primary goods behind 'the veil of ignorance'; (2) the requirement that the institutions or positions that produce inequality are open to all; (3) the 'difference principle' that allows for inequalities under specific conditions. These notions have more or less been used deliberately in recent political discourse on the role and tasks of the welfare state.

According to the first proposition, a maximally just society would be one planned by *rational and mutually self-interested people ignorant of their own future status in that society*. The decisions about how and on what basis societal goods should be distributed are made in this planning situation 'behind the veil of ignorance', which would also conceal what personal qualities each would possess in the society to come. This would guarantee that no rational planner in the original position would propose or accept unreasonable differences in citizens' benefits, knowing that he might be the one who gets the last slice of the pie. Furthermore, since the planners do not know in what phase in the life cycle they would be placed, the probabilities of poverty would be pretty low and even during the life-cycle. However, if we also take generational issues into account we could think that since the planners do not know to what generation they would belong they would not, for example, plan for too excessive benefits for which that future generations had to pay.

Rawls' second condition of justice involves openness of the *positions and institutions* that create inequality. Whatever differences rational decision makers behind a 'veil of ignorance' would allow they would also be likely to incorporate mechanisms which would enable individuals to improve an initially disadvantaged position. Difference-producing institutions should be accessible to everyone: society would be a society of open opportunities. No one would be doomed to the same miserable position for life. In social policy terms, this means, for example, that educational attainment should not be conditioned on family background and there should be high degree of mobility away from poverty.

The third basic condition is the so-called 'difference principle', according to which *societal inequalities* are allowed provided that they also profit the disadvantaged. In principle, the starting point is that the division of primary goods in society, including income and wealth, should be equal unless there are reasons why the unequal distribution of those benefits will help the worse-off. Since there are severe incentive problems in strictly equal distribution, it is unreasonable to stop at absolute equality (Rawls 1996: 282–3). Therefore, income differences, for example, are acceptable on the condition that they cause people to work harder, and because of this hard work national wealth is increased more rapidly and the increase will also gradually diffuse to the worse-off. The same idea is expressed from another perspective in the 'trickle-down' theory. In countries where there are real incentives to work, economic growth will be stronger and, in the long run, the standard of living of the poor will be higher, than in countries where such incentives are weakened or totally destroyed by redistributive policies. It is therefore just to let income differences grow, and in fact this expansion is also the most effective way to help the poor (Schmidtz 1998: 6).

Poverty cycles

In his study on poverty in York, Rowntree (1901) observed that poverty was linked to age and family formation in a cyclical fashion. The first poverty cycle a person experienced was 'childhood', when his/her parents had many dependents to feed and when the earnings of one person were not enough to meet the needs of many. Poverty eased in the 'youth phase' when the young person left home and began to earn her/his own living. Economically, the situation became worse again when she/he got married and had children of her/his own. This stage of the early middle age years – the 'family phase' – continued until the children grew up, began to contribute to the family income and then, one by one, left home (see Figure 2.6). An economically easier 'empty nest' period began. This stage lasted until old age brought on a lower capacity for work. Because of inadequate pension systems in the early 1900s, old age meant a transition to persistent poverty.

During the post Second World War period, improved social policies in all countries had effects on poverty cycles; in many countries, the cycle

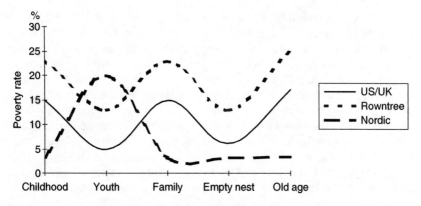

Figure 2.6 Rowntree's poverty cycle in York, 1899 and the 2000s cycle in Scandinavia, the UK and the USA

of poverty flattened out and the life-stages in many countries became no longer significantly different (Kangas and Palme 2000). Some systematic differences, however, remain between countries. The results on the situation of the elderly indicate first of all that their position has relatively speaking improved as pension systems have matured. The case of pensions speaks very strongly in favour of the 'social politics matter' thesis. The kinds of pension policies countries pursue make for differences in their poverty profiles. In the mid-1960s, for example, the incidence of poverty among the elderly was high (say about 20 per cent) in almost all countries. In 2004, there is a huge difference. In Scandinavia, old-age poverty is about 5 per cent whereas in the UK and USA the corresponding figure is over 20 per cent. High poverty rates among families with children also continue to be an Anglo-American problem (see Ferrarini and Forssén, chapter 5 in this volume), and only small improvement in this area has taken place over the years; there is a striking difference compared to the Nordic countries' child poverty levels below 5 per cent (see, e.g., http://www.lisproject/keyfigures/povertytable.htm).

When we compare poverty rates there are clear indications that social policy provisions are important for explaining both cross-national and over-time variations in poverty. The clearest impact is found in the pension area. In countries where the right to a basic pension is based on citizen-ship/residence, poverty among the elderly is virtually non-existent, at least on the kind of measurement that we have used here. When it comes to the 'family phase', there appears to be an important potential for redu-cing poverty by combining cash benefits with public child care services that increase the earnings capacity of both single parents and couples. This aspect is one of the special features of the Scandinavian model, which helps to combine family and work in such a way that both fertility and economic growth are supported.

The big challenge that the Nordic countries have to meet is the high level of 'youth' poverty, which is mostly explained by the status of students living on small study grants (available for every student) that are so small that the students are classified as 'poor'. The positive interpretation for the youth poverty 'peak' is that the phenomenon is temporary and when the students have got their degrees they will escape poverty. In that sense, the Rawlsian demand for openness is satisfied. However, there is an alternative explanation that is a bit less sunny for the Nordic model. Higher unemployment rates have also made it more difficult for young people to enter the labour market and compared to the Anglo-American situation entry may be harder in Scandinavia, which may lead to a 'vicious cycle' of persistent unemployment and poverty among youth (see Esping-Andersen's chapters 6 in this volume).

Poor, absolutely speaking

It can be argued, of course, that using national poverty rates that are derived from national income distributions and national poverty lines does a disservice to richer countries such as the USA. The income level at which a family is deemed 'poor' in these wealthy nations might correspond to the medium-if not high-income level in a less well-to-do country. In a global world, we should not only look at national and relative figures but also at the *absolute standards* of the poor in different countries. There is an additional reason for doing so. The general Rawlsian idea might be that the proportional differences displayed in poverty rates might be acceptable if they were connected to higher material standards displayed in the absolute income levels of the poor households. In other words, the 'difference principle' would allow higher proportional poverty rates for a country if the real income level of the poor in that country were higher than in other countries. To fulfil this criterion, income levels of the poor should be higher in countries with high poverty rates. However, this is not the case in practice. For example, the real income level (measured as US dollars using PPPs) of poor children (equivalent income below 50 per cent of the median) was 1.6 times higher in Norway (1.4 for Denmark and Sweden and 1.3 for Finland) than it was in the USA in the mid-1990s (Smeeding 2002). Of the thirteen advanced OECD countries included in the comparison, only the UK displayed lower absolute levels than the USA. The other side of the coin is, of course, that no other country can compete with the USA when it comes to the absolute income level of rich families with children.

On the basis of European Household Panel Survey (ECHP), where all EU countries are represented, it is possible to calculate correlations between long-term poverty rates (poor during 1995–8) and the absolute income levels of the long-term poor. The correlation in the EU sample is − 0.73, which also indicates that it is hard to defend high poverty levels by referring to higher absolute income of the poor (see also Kangas 2002; Kenworthy 2004). Relative poverty seems to be related to absolute deprivation.

It should be emphasized that inequality *per se* is not necessarily unjust or unfair (for a fuller discussion, see Saunders 1994: 81–3; Goodin *et al.* 1999). Much depends on the mechanisms that produce inequalities: some people work harder, educate themselves, ontake better use of their resources, etc. It is therefore justifiable that some people get more than others. Even large income differences are permissible if the institutions producing such differences are equally accessible to all. If income differences are based, say, on educational attainment, and education is available to everyone, wage differences may be seen as justified. Justice is thus a virtue of an open society.

One way to measure the 'openness' of a society is to investigate *income mobility*. This is particularly pertinent in comparisons between countries with equal and countries with unequal income distributions. If income mobility is higher in countries with higher inequality than in more equal countries, a high degree of temporary inequality could be forgiven. Correspondingly, if in countries with low level of poverty, poverty is a permanent phenomenon for the destitute, we are dealing with injustice.

In their longitudinal comparative three-country study, Goodin *et al.* (1999) found that countries that displayed the lowest cross-sectional poverty also displayed the lowest long-term poverty rates. Similar results can be read from the ECHP. Short-term poverty is closely connected with long-term poverty, as indicated in Figure 2.7 (Penttilä *et al.* 2003). The correlation between these variables is as high as 0.98, which indicates that those social policy measures that are effective to combat short-term poverty are also effective to reduce long-term destitution. Unfortunately, ECHP does not provide sufficient data for Sweden (not fully participating in ECHP) and Norway (not a member of the European Union), but the qualified guess is that those two would be placed into low-left-hand corner of Figure 2.7 and would join the Danish–Finnish block with low poverty levels and short spells of poverty.

Another possible way to evaluate the 'openness' of societies is to look at *generational income mobility* – i.e. the degree to which parents' levels of income determine children's incomes. A strong correlation would indicate that societal institutions are not particularly open and home background is a discriminating factor. The problem in examining generational income mobility is that long-term successive data on parents' and children's incomes are scarce, and there have been only a few studies on the subject. The essential finding in these studies has been that in all countries children's incomes are correlated with parents' incomes (Aaberge *et al.* 2000; Österbacka 2004). Childhood background everywhere has a deciding influence, so none of the countries studied is a completely 'open' society, though some are more so than others. The Nordic countries appear somewhat more 'open' than most other countries; the intergenerational correlation between parents and children varies in between 0.15 and 0.20, whereas in the USA the corresponding

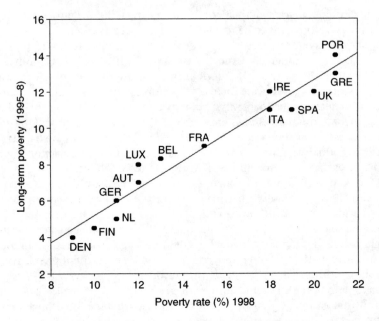

Figure 2.7 Short-term poverty[a] and long-term poverty[b] (*poor in three years in 1995–98*), European Union, 1998

Notes: [a] per cent; poverty line = 60 per cent of the median.
  [b] Poor in three years 1995–8.

figure is 0.40–0.60 (depending on the measurement and data sets used; see Österbacka 2004). Student achievement tests indicate the same thing (see also Esping-Andersen, chapter 6 in this volume).

The third way of looking at the 'openness' of societies is to inspect *class mobility*. Basically the story told by comparative studies of class mobility in industrial societies is the same as the story told by income mobility. In all societies, there is a more or less persistent pattern of unequal class mobility, and the pattern did not really alter throughout the twentieth century (Erikson and Goldthorpe 1992; Marshall 1997). Fluidity rates appear to be somewhat higher in Sweden, for example, than in the other European societies, and fluidity rates in Australia and the USA are no higher compared to the European ones (Erikson 1990; Erikson and Goldthorpe 1992: 336–7, 373; for Sweden, see also Jonsson 1993).

Economic growth and the position of the poor

During the period of Keynesian economic policy making after the Second World War, redistribution through social policy measures was regarded as an important factor in enhancing stable economic growth. In particular, improving the lot of those in the lowest income brackets was regarded as an efficient means of ensuring smooth economic growth. It was assumed that the stable consumption capacity of the poor had a countervailing effect upon economic downturns, and thus that equality not only helped the poor but also had a beneficial impact on economic activity as a whole. Especially in the Nordic countries, much of the legitimacy of welfare state institutions and equalization of income through taxation, free social services and social transfers was based on this assumption. In the 1950s and 1960s the most prominent economists and social planners (e.g. Myrdal 1960; Kuusi 1966) emphasized the positive link between equality and growth.

Much has changed since then. The prevailing political discourse, instead of emphasizing social rights, equality and redistribution, now puts more stress on social duties, diversity and the need to accumulate wealth. The conceptualization of the relationship between social policy and economic growth has essentially changed: equality and redistribution are now often seen as severe obstacles to economic growth, especially in Europe, where the high level of social protection is regarded as one important reason why the European economic and employment performance lags behind its American counterpart. The problem is regarded as being most severe in the Nordic countries, where heavy taxes and lavish welfare provision is argued to erad-icate all incentives to work (for a summary of the discussion, see Korpi, Chapter 8 in this volume; Esping-Andersen 1994). The economic crisis in Finland and Sweden in the early 1990s was seen as indisputable evidence of this thesis. Therefore, instead of pleas for equality, there are vociferous political calls for income inequality in order to increase incentives to work and thereby enhance economic growth. It is argued that this is also the only way to improve the lot of the poor: when the economy is boom-ing the worst-off sections in society will also get their share of the rising economic tide.

However, the situation is not necessarily as the theory predicts. Empirical findings suggest the opposite, and it is very hard empirically to justify social inequalities by referring to their beneficial effects on economic growth and the position of the poor (see, e.g., Goodin *et al.* 1999; Kangas 2002; Hein-rich 2003; Kenworthy 2004). Other factors than inequality seem to explain successful economic performance. The theory performs no better when it comes to the position of the poor: the absolute level of economic well-being of the poor is not higher in countries with higher income inequalities and poverty rates, neither is their position improving more rapidly than in coun-tries with smaller inequalities. Here again, the reverse seems to be the truth, and in this respect the 'trickle-down' theory is definitely refuted. The finding that the Nordic countries, with their equal income distribution, have a high absolute income level of the poor contradicts the theory.

The story about economic growth and the position of the poor is slightly trickier. In the short run, the association between the two variables is shown to be insignificant and indicates that if the comparison deals with rich countries and over a relatively short period of time other factors as economic growth are important. However, it is also true that over a short period economic changes may have an impact upon the position of the poor. This is clearly proved by the Finnish and Swedish experiences in the early 1990s. In both these countries, GDP *per capita* fell in three consecutive years and consequently the income of the poor clearly dropped. In these instances, the 'trickle-down' theory emphasizing the priority and importance of economic growth is definitely supported. For sure, the rising economic tide does not lift all income groups equally, and it is here that distributional issues enter the picture. There are huge national variations in the 'lifting' capacity of the rising tide and that capacity depends on the set-up of national social policy programmes. In the Western hemisphere, the incidence of poverty is thus more associated with political factors than with economic prosperity, and for this reason there is misery and want among plenty.

In addition to the classical social goals discussed above, there are of course a number of other criteria for evaluating how efficient a system of social protection is. These are important because they are related to the underlying issue of *combining efficiency and equality*. It should, of course, not be denied that the design and reform of systems of social protection sometimes involve real goal-conflicts: the goal of reducing inequalities might come into conflict with efficiency considerations, for example. But judgements about how these two kinds of goals are balanced depend on values and our vision of a good society (see, e.g., Goodin *et al.* 1999). This means that there are always alternative solutions and we, following our values, can choose more or less equality/efficiency. Arguments implying that there are no choices are in this context false: notwithstanding that social policies often can enable people to make choices that they would otherwise not have been able to make, individual choice is always, in some sense, circumscribed by state intervention in the form of taxation and social protection. This suggests that state intervention should focus on dealing with social issues that are relevant for all of us, and that it is always important to promote individual choice, even in areas that have become subject to state intervention.

The welfare state and work

The critique of the welfare state as such is a fundamental challenge for those who believe that there are rational grounds for defending the system of social protection. Different kinds of criticisms have been advanced, based on various observations and assumptions. One important criticism is that the welfare state does not deliver what it aims to deliver – that it does not, for instance, reduce poverty and inequality successfully. This critique deserves to be taken seriously. We also need to examine the bases for these claims, empirical and otherwise. Many critics of the welfare state do not actually deny its achievements (e.g. Lindbeck 1997). Their critique has focused on *unintended* and *indirect* effects. These have to do with the creation of disincentives to work, partly via the high levels of taxation and inefficiencies inherent in all kinds of taxes, partly as 'pull' effects where generous benefit programmes are considered to have discouraged people from taking an active part in the labour market. A major issue is whether 'excessive' welfare state spending has directly or indirectly created – or at least contributed substantially to – the present crisis of the European economies.

During the decades following the Second World War, the Nordic economies combined several objectives traditionally regarded as incompatible. High economic growth was combined with far-reaching economic equalization and full employment. The oil crises of the 1970s were followed by a slower growth rate, but this was a feature common to all the most affluent industrialized countries, including those with quite different welfare models and a completely different, less equal distribution, of economic resources (e.g. Switzerland and the USA). Nor does empirical research in this field serve to show that major welfare state commitments in themselves have a negative impact on growth. A comprehensive welfare state appears to be compatible with growth (cf. Dowrick 1996, Atkinson 1998; see also Korpi, Chapter 8 in this volume) and the Finnish and Swedish economic crises of the 1990s appear to be a result of macroeconomic policy failures rather than over-commitments in the social policy field. One reason that the economy overheated and then suddenly slowed down was the uncontrolled and mismanaged deregulation of credit markets. Basically the story is the same in all countries. The Ministry of Finance advised governments to deregulate the credit market, and the sooner the better. The rapid liberalization led to unbroked credit expansion and when the credit bubble burst, the banking sector came close to bankruptcy and had to rely on public subsidies (for a closer description of the crisis, see Kiander, Chapter 9 in this volume).

Criticism of 'big' welfare states of the Scandinavian kind has focused on the incentive problems associated with high levels of taxation, and the lack of control over the growth of public expenditure (see Sjöberg, Chapter 10 in this volume). As far as actual labour market behaviour is concerned, however, it is hard to find any pronounced negative deviations in the Nordic patterns of economic activity in comparison with those prevailing in other kinds of welfare state in the Western world. On the contrary, Sweden, Denmark and Norway have some of the world's highest employment participation rates, while the Finnish figures correspond to the OECD median, this is largely due to the high participation among women (Korpi 2000).

The relationships between the levels of social rights (or 'decommodification' to use Esping-Andersen's, 1990, vocabulary), is depicted in Figure 2.8 (the Social Rights Index is a mean for coverage and replacement rates in sickness, pension, unemployment and work-accident insurance programmes). As can be seen on the basis of the labour force participation rate, it is

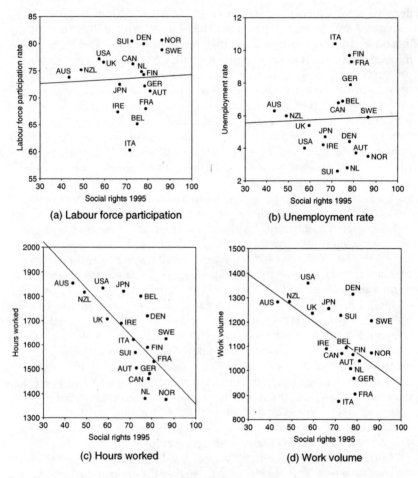

Figure 2.8   Social rights and labour force indicators, selected OECD countries, 2000
Note: [a] Work volume Employment rate x hours worked/100.

hard to verify the disincentive theory. The overall cross-sectional association between the level of social rights and unemployment is also negligible. However, there is some indirect evidence for the disincentive hypothesis. Most countries that have low social rights' scores display low levels of unemployment but the opposite does not hold, and not all countries with low unemployment display low social rights (Norway, for example, has managed to combine high social rights with low level of unemployment, and comparatively speaking the same also goes for Denmark and Sweden).

The story is a different when it comes to the hours actually worked per person employed. Here the correlation is strongly negative: the better the social rights the fewer hours people work. In fact, there is nothing surprising in that: the negative relationship can be anticipated since the level of social rights is strongly associated with many other 'decommodifying' measures such as part-time work compensated/supplemented by benefits rights to paid vacation, etc. In addition, the actual hours worked per employee do not tell everything about the work volume conducted in a country. In some countries working hours may be long, but if the employment rate is low then the overall work volume may be low. The degree of social rights is plotted against work volume. The overall correlation here is clearly negative but the correlation is weaker than in the case of hours worked. There are no cases with low social rights and low work volume but there are cases (Denmark as the best example) where high social rights are combined with high work volume. When we take into consideration the forced restriction on the number of hours worked imposed by legislation on paid vacation, the differences among countries are substantially modified. As shown by Andersen and Molander (2003), the differences between, for example, Sweden and the USA disappear when we compare work volume after having taken differences in paid vacation into account. The central question is whether we work to live or live to work.

Administrative form and social trust

With regard to the social justice and economic criteria discussed above, there are two issues to be noted concerning universal welfare states of the Scandinavian type. The administrative cost-efficiency of universal programmes is a clear advantage. Another strength of universal earnings-related systems is that they reduce 'transaction costs' on the labour market: individuals, firms and unions do not have to spend time negotiating about the provision of basic insurance and services such as health care. Mobility and flexibility in the labour market is also promoted because the universal character of the system means that workers do not lose their earned rights when they move from one job to another – the 'portability' of social insurance is high. This was one important reason why the Nordic countries tried to change from voluntary and enterprise-based occupational schemes to legislated pensions. In the present situation where the European Union forms a common labour market, strongly instituted and 'portable' social rights will grow in importance. An additional advantage in earnings-related benefits is that incentives to work are part of their essence: the more you work, the higher your social insurance compensation will be. One aspect, largely neglected in the public debate, is the fact that in universal homogeneous systems it is in principle easier to control the incentive structure and cost expansion than in more fragmented systems. The expansion of health costs is a telling example: since the 1970s expenditures on health have skyrocketed in decentralized or insurance-based schemes, whereas cost increases in public health-service based systems have been more modest (see, e.g., OECD 2004).

One of the most important roles of social institutions is to promote stability and predictability in society. Social policy had such functions from the first, as is evident in the measures that were taken by authoritarian regimes in Europe in the late 1880s (see, e.g., Flora and Alber 1981). North (1990) has found that stable economic institutions such as property rights are important for growth. Among the most advanced industrial nations, growth rates were higher in the post-war years in countries with the most stable institutions for interest mediation. Social policy is not only a distributional issue: who gets what and how much. The institutional set-ups of social policy programmes unify and divide both people and social groups. Social protection has thus contributed to the interest mediation and the stability of society.

Recent social and political science discourse largely revolves around the concept of *social capital*. Social capital deals with trust, social bonds and loyalty (Putnam 1993, 2000; Hardin 1995; Cook 2001; Rothstein 2003). In the opening paragraphs of his *Bowling Alone*, Robert Putnam (2000: 22) makes a distinction between *bridging* (or inclusive) and *bonding* (or exclusive) social capital (cf. Granovetter's, 1973, 'weak' and 'strong' ties). The 'bridging' form of social capital generates broader identities and brings larger sections of society together by unifying them by weak ties, whereas 'bonding' social capital pertains to specific, group-based solidarity. The 'bonding' form of social capital generates strong ties; however, because of its intra-group solidarity, it may create strong out-group antagonism. There is a thus danger that 'exclusive' social capital may turnout to be antisocial and detrimental for society as a whole.

Throughout its history social policy has had both 'bridging' and 'bonding' functions. In some countries such as the Nordic area the emphasis has more or less deliberately and consciously been on the 'bridging' side: the basic principle in Scandinavian social policy schemes has been universalism expressed in people's insurance or people's education, as described above. When it comes to the legitimacy of social policy, the universal schemes are extremely popular (e.g. Svallfors 1989; Ervasti and Kangas 1994). Some comparative studies have shown that the general level of trust, or social capital, is extremely high in the Nordic countries (e.g. van Oorschot 2003).

In many other countries – especially in Continental Europe and Asia/Africa – the welfare schemes have been based on membership in a certain occupational group or category of people. These schemes have relied on 'bonding' social capital and have consequently created strong intra-group interests, as discussed above in the case of voluntary sickness and unemployment insurance funds (see also Ritter 1986: 71–82; Rothstein 1992, 1998). In some cases – notably in the Anglo-Saxon world – means-testing has conditioned eligibility. The formation of social bonds has been more diffuse and because of the 'fuzziness' of the client groups no interest formation has taken place among clients. As a rule, the overall legitimacy of means-tested schemes is low (see e.g. Korpi 1980; Kangas 1995): means testing neither creates 'bridging' nor 'bonding' social capital.

These questions are crucial when considering the problem of collective action. In his classic books *The Logic of Collective Action* and *The Rise and Decline of Nations* Mancur Olson (1965, 1982; see also Pierson 1994) Olson says that small-scale interest organizations have a specific or concentrated interest to defend. They are small enough to feel strong social bonds – or if you prefer, the amount of 'bonding' social capital is large. Therefore they are ready to act immediately when needed. In bigger groups, the bonds are based on 'bridging' social capital and members of these groups do not necessarily have that much in common. They lack specific interest and intra-group solidarity strong enough to bring members to the barricades (cf. Pierson 1994). Universal norms, and consequently universal institutions, suffer from vagueness and free-riding problem (Hardin 1995). This may explain why it has been easier to reform universal and homogeneous schemes, such as national pensions in Scandinavia or employment-related pensions in Finland and Sweden. In homogeneous schemes both improvements and cuts are supposed to be distributed evenly across clienteles; occupational schemes generating more 'binding' solidarity are harder to attack. Ironically enough, the trust that universal social institutions create facilitates cutting those very institutions, as became evident during the crisis of the 1990s.

The crisis of the 1990s

Systems of social protection have always been intrinsically connected with the employment question. When Beveridge (1942) in the 1940s designed the reform of the British system of social protection, he did this on the precondition that what he called the 'social services' could be organized under full employment. Many countries in Europe have experienced twenty years of mass unemployment when systems of social protection have been severely challenged, but have not fallen apart. In some countries it has even proved possible to run a budget surplus despite persistently high levels of unemployment. However, this is not to argue that such systems work in terms of protecting all categories, but rather to indicate that they have survived under conditions that they were not designed for, nor were expected to cope with.

The 1990s treated the Nordic countries very differently. Finland and Sweden experienced the most severe macroeconomic crisis since the 1930s; Norway mostly avoided the crisis, while Denmark suffered a lot immediately after the oil crisis of the 1970s but her economic development was thereafter fairly stable. In Norway, real GDP *per capita* in 1989–99 increased by 2.9 per cent compared to the OECD average of 1.6 per cent. In 1993 the unemployment rate reached a peak of 6 per cent but because of the strong economy open unemployment had decreased below 4 per cent by 1998 (OECD 2000: 48; OECD 2002: 303). The decades that were hard for the rest of Europe were a success for the Norwegian 'oil-sheiks' who could introduce a number of improvements in social security – lengthening the duration in maternity/paternity benefits from 35 to 52 weeks for example, as was done in Denmark in 2002. No major downward adjustments in income loss compensations had to be made in Norway and the country was able to maintain its high replacement rates – 100 per cent in sickness and maternity and about 70 per cent in unemployment and pensions (Eirtheim and Kuhnle 2000; NOSOSCO 2002). Denmark was regarded in the 1970s and early 1980s as the Nordic 'sick man': unemployment rates were high, welfare benefits lavish and the public sector suffered from chronic deficits (see Goul-Andersen 2000). However, the measures taken in the 1980s helped the country to muddle through the most severe financial problems and when the recession of the 1990 was in its deepest, the Danish welfare state was in a good shape (even if benefits were not as generous as those in Norway) to meet the challenges (in 1993, economic growth was zero and the unemployment rate 10 per cent, which was halved by the turn of the millennium, OECD 2002: 303). These two cases are success stories, demonstrating that it is possible to combine a high level of social protection, high employment and stable economic growth.

The story of Finland and Sweden is very different. In 1991–3, GDP growth was negative, employment declined and open unemployment in Sweden rose from 1.7 in 1990 to 8.4 in 1994. In Finland, the corresponding figures were 3.2 and 16.7 per cent. The employment crisis had a catastrophic impact on public finances, as the downturn in employment led to a massive increase in public expenditures, as well as to drastically eroded revenues. In Finland, a mediocre level of social security spending in the European context (25 per cent of GDP) increased by 10 per cent points. The budgets in both countries went from surpluses to deficits of 10 per cent of GDP and public debt increased rapidly. The bleak economic prospects increased crisis awareness both among political parties and the population at large and fortified the political consensus to accept welfare cuts that were regarded as necessary to put the economy on its feet again. Virtually all social programmes were subject to change: In Sweden, sickness, maternity and unemployment benefits were cut from 90 to 80 and then from 80 to 75 per cent. In Finland, sickness benefits were reduced from 80 to 70 and unemployment benefits from 70 to 60. In both countries waiting periods were prolonged and the eligibility criteria for benefit purposes tightened (see, e.g., Timonen 2003).

In both countries the governments applied a 'planing' strategy: they tried to preserve the basic structure of the welfare state but 'plane' a bit off to balance the budgets. More stringent qualification requirements were introduced for a number of benefits. As a result of the lower level of employment, the degree of coverage in earnings-related insurance schemes fell and in some schemes (e.g. in sickness and pensions) cuts in legislated schemes were compensated by expansion of various occupational arrangements (i.e. there was a tendency to shift public responsibilities to the private sphere). In the case of social assistance, stiffer requirements were introduced and benefit levels declined as a result of both legislative change and of the way regulations were applied at the municipal level. In the welfare service sector, different – and even divergent – developments were observed in different areas, although some general patterns emerged. There was an overall increase in decentralization. Another general trend was an increase in user financing. Higher fees were introduced for both child care and old-age care and were income-related to a greater extent than before. Patients' financing of medical care increased significantly as a result of higher patients' fees and larger personal contributions to medicines and dental care. Denmark is now the only country that has no fees for medical services. The privatization of both financing and management remained a marginal phenomenon, while publicly financed services produced by private actors increased substantially in all welfare service sectors – child care, education, medical care, old-age care, care of substance abusers and child and youth welfare services. Market oriented administrative practices also became more widespread in that part of the welfare service sector which remained under public control. Taken as a whole, the 1990s were a period of greater decentralization, user financing and market orientation. The tendency was clearest in Sweden and Finland but neither Norway nor Denmark were free of such pressures.

Public finances in the Scandinavian countries now are in a better shape than in many other EU countries, and their economic performance has been much stronger than the OECD average, e.g., in the late 1990s Finland was second after Ireland in GDP growth rates (see, e.g., OECD 2000). Moreover, all the Nordic countries perform extremely well in the world competitiveness rankings.

These facts can be interpreted in different ways. For critics of the Nordic welfare state, this is evidence that they were right: more cuts and the countries will do even better. Defenders of the model say that the cuts were marginal, and cannot explain the recovery. Thus there is nothing fundamentally wrong with the model.

The model can be criticized also for the fact that many of the cuts hit the worst-off in society (Kangas and Ritakallio 2003; Palme *et al.* 2002) and many critical voices have argued that the welfare state failed badly in its task of protecting the vulnerable. However, the 1990 crisis also showed that the universal and advanced welfare states were able to absorb macroeconomic shocks and stabilize living conditions when needed (Kuhnle 2000: 392). Despite skyrocketing unemployment and rising factor income differences,

differences and poverty in disposable incomes did not change that dramatic-ally. One can only imagine what would have happened in a meaner welfare state if unemployment had risen from 4 to 18 per cent and GDP fallen by one-fifth. Against that background the Finnish and Swedish – or, if you prefer, the Scandinavian – record was fairly reasonable and the model passed the survival test of a deep recession.

Notes

1 The result is true for the rest of the developed countries, as well. Among 172 coun-tries the median year of the introduction of the first law was 1939 for work-accident, 1952 for pensions, 1957 for sickness, 1978 for family and 1981 for unemployment insurance. In the case of unemployment insurance, there are more right-hand cen-sored cases (i.e. countries that have not introduced the scheme of unemployment insurance). These cases are coded as if they had introduced the scheme in 2003. Data are from various issues of *Social Security Programs Throughout the World* (SSPTW 2003).
2 Data is derived from a comparative welfare state research project, the Social Cit-izenship Indicators Project (SCIP), led by Walter Korpi and Joakim Palme. The SCIP is housed at the Swedish Institute for Social Research, University of Stockholm. The SCIP database contains a broad array of data on coverage, qualifying conditions, financing and replacement rates for five major social insurance programmes in eighteen OECD countries at five-year intervals between 1930 and 1995 (see Korpi and Palme 1998).
3 Pensions: insured/population of 15–64 years of age, other three insurance forms as a percentage of labour force; the coverage index is average for the four coverage rates.
4 Replacement for pensions is single minimum pension and a work-merit pension for a worker who has worked for forty years; other insurance forms: net benefit/net wage, per cent.

Bibliography

Books and articles

Aaberge, R., Björklund, A., Jäntti, M., Pedersen, P., Smith, N. and Wennemo, T. (2000) 'Unemployment Shocks and Income Distribution: How did the Nordic Countries Fare During their Crises?' *Scandinavian Journal of Economics*, 102(1). 77–99.
Alber, J. (1981) *Vom Armenhaus zum Wohlfahrtsstaat: Analysen zur Entwicklung der Sozialversicherung in Europa*. Frankfurt: Campus. (From Poor-house to Welfare State: Analyses of Social Insurance Development in Europe)
Alestalo, M. and Kuhnle, S. (1987) 'The Scandinavian Route: Economic, Social, and Political Developments in Denmark, Finland, Norway and Sweden'. In R. Erikson, E.J. Hansen, S. Ringen and H. Uusitalo, (eds.), *The Scandinavian Model: Welfare States and Welfare Research*. New York: M.E. Sharpe: 3–38.
Allardt, E. (1975) *Att ha, att älska att vara. Om välfärd i Norden*. Lund: Argos. (Having, Loving, Being, Welfare in the Nordic Countries.)

Allardt, E. (1986) 'The Civic Conception of the Welfare State in Scandinavia'. In R. Rose and R. Shriatori (eds.), *The Welfare State. East and West*. New York: Oxford University Press: 107–25.

Andersen, T. and Molander, P. (2003) 'Policy Options for Reforming the Welfare State'. In T. Andersen and P. Molander (eds.) *Alternatives for Welfare Policy: Coping with Internationalization and Demographic Change*. Cambridge: Cambridge University Press: 350–75.

Atkinson, A. (1998) *Excusion, Employment and Opportunity*. London: London School of Economics, CASE.

Baldwin, P. (1990) *Politics of Social Solidarity*. Cambridge: Cambridge University Press.

Beveridge, W. (1942) *Full Employment in Free Society*. New York: Norton.

Carroll, E. (1999) *Emergence and Structuring of Social Insurance Institutions: Comparative Studies on Social Policy and Employment Insurance*. Stockholm: Stockholm University.

Castles, F. (1979) *The Social Democratic Image of Society*. London: Routledge & Kegan Paul.

Cook, K. (ed.) (2001) *Trust in Society*. New York: Russell Sage.

Dowrick, S. (1996) 'Swedish Economic Performance and Swedish Economic Debate: A View from Outside'. *Economic Journal*, 106 (439): 1772–9.

Eirtheim, P. and Kuhnle, S. (2000) 'Nordic Welfare States in the 1990s: Institutional Stability, Signs of Divergence'. In S. Kuhnle (ed.), *Survival of the European Welfare State, Routledge/ECPR Studies in European Political Science*. New York: Routledge: 39–57.

Elmér, Å. (1960) *Folkpensioneringen i Sverige*. Lund: CWK Gleerup.

Erikson, R. (1990) *Vinnare och förlorade i välfärdsutvecklingen*. Stockholm : Swedish Institute för social Research. (Winners and Loosers in Welfare Development).

Erikson, R. (1993) *Descriptions of Inequality: The Swedish Approach to Welfare Research*. Stockholm : Swedish Institute for Social Research.

Erikson, R. and Goldthorpe, J.H. (1992) *The Constant Flux: A Study of Class Mobility in Industrial societies*. Oxford: Clarendon Press.

Ervasti, H. and Kangas, O. (1994) *Class Bases of Universal Social Policy: Pension Policy Attitudes in Finland*. Turku: University of Turku.

Esping-Andersen, G. (1985) *Politics against Markets. The Social Democratic Road to Power*. Princeton: Princeton University Press.

Esping-Andersen, G. (1990) *The Three Worlds of Welfare Capitalism*. Cambridge: Polity Press.

Esping-Andersen, G. (1994) 'Welfare State and Economy'. In N.J.Smelsenr and R. Svedberg (eds.), *The Handbook of Economic Sociology*. Princeton: Russell Sage Foundation.

Esping-Andersen, G. and Korpi, W. (1984) 'Social Policy as Class Politics in Post-War Capitalism.' In J.H. Goldthorpe (ed.), *Crisis and Order in Contemporary Capitalism*. Oxford: Clarendon Press.

Esping-Andersen, G. and Korpi, W. (1987) From Poor Relief to Institutional Welfare State: the Development of Scandinavian Social Policy'. In R. Erikson, E.J. Hansen, S. Ringen and H. Uusitalo (eds.), *The Scandinavian Model: Welfare States and Welfare Research*. New York: M.E. Sharpe 39–74.

Evans, P., Rueschmeyer, D. and Skocpol, T. (1985) *Bringing the State back in*. Cambridge: Cambridge University Press.

Ferrarini, T. (2003) 'Parental Leave Institutions in Eighteen Post War Welfare States'. Swedish Institute for Social Research, Doctoral Dissertation Series 58. Stockholm: Swedish Institute for Social Research.

Flora, P. (1986) *Growth to Limits: The Western European Welfare States since World War II*. Berlin: De Gruyter.

Flora, P. and Alber, J. (1981) 'Modernization, Democratization, and the Development of Welfare States in Western Europe'. In P. Flora and A. Heidenheimer (eds.), *The Development of Welfare States in Europe and America*. New Brunswick and London: Transaction Books: 37–80.

Goodin, R.E., Headey, B., Muffels, R. and Dirven, H.-J. (1999) *The Real Worlds of Welfare Capitalism*. Cambridge: Cambridge University Press.

Gordon, D. and Townsend, P. (eds.) (2000) *Breadline Europe: The Measurement of Poverty*. London: Policy Press.

Goul-Andersen, J. (2000) 'Welfare Crisis and Beyond: Danish Welfare Policies in the 1980 and 1990s'. In S. Kuhnle (ed.), *Survival of the European Welfare State*. London and New York: Routledge: 69–87.

Granovetter, M. (1973) 'The Strength of Weak Ties'. *American Journal of Sociology*, 78: 1360–80.

Hansen, S.A. and Henriksen, I. (1984) *Dansk social historie 1914–39: Sociale brydninger*. Copenhagen: Nordisk Forlag. (Danish Social History 1914–39: Social Breaktroughs.)

Hardin, R. (1995) *One for All: The Logic of Group Conflict*. Princeton: Princeton University Press.

Heclo, H. (1974) *Modern Social Politics in Britain and Sweden*. New Haven: Yale University Press.

Heinrich, G. (2003) 'More is Not Necessarily Better: An Empirical Analysis of the Ineqality – Growth Tradeoff Using the Luxembourg Income Study'. Luxembourg Income Study, Working Papers, 344. Luxembourg: LIS.

Hemerijck, A. (2002) 'The Self-Transformation of the European Social Model(s)'. In G. Esping-Andersen (ed.), *Why We Need a New Welfare State*. Oxford: Oxford University Press: 173–213.

Hiilamo, H. (2002) *Rise and Fall of Nordic Family Policy? Historical Development and Change during the 1990s in Sweden and Finland*. Helsinki: Stakes.

Hobson, B. and Takahashi, M. (1996) 'The Parent–Worker Model: Lone Mothers in Sweden'. In J. Lewis (ed.), *Lone Mothers in European Welfare Regimes: Shifting Policy Logics*. London and Philadelphia: Jessica Kingsley: 121–39.

Immergut, E. (1992) *The Political Construction of Interests: National Health Insurance Politics in Switzerland, France and Sweden, 1930–1970*. New York: Cambridge University Press.

Johansson, P. (2003) *Fast i det Förflutna: Institutioner och Intressen i Svensk Sjukförsäkringspolitik 1891–1931*, Lund: Arkiv. (Stuck in the Past: Institutions and Interests in Swedish Sickness Insurance Politics 1891–1931.)

Johansson, S. (1979) *Mot en teori för social rapportering* (*Towards a Theory of Social Reporting*). Stockholm: Swedish Institute for Social Research.

Jonsson, J. (1993) *Ursprung och utbildning: social snedrekrytering till högre studier*. Stockholm: Allmännaförlaget. (Social origin and Education: Social Selection to Higher Education.)

Kangas, O. (1991) *The Politics of Social Rights: Studies on the Dimensions of Sickness Insurance in OECD Countries*. Stockholm: Swedish Institute for Social Research.

Kangas, O. (1995) 'Attitudes on Means-Tested Social Benefits in Finland'. *Acta Sociologica*, 38: 299–310.

Kangas, O. (2002) 'Economic Growth, Inequality and the Economic Position of the Poor in OECD Countries'. *International Journal of Health Services*, 32(2): 213–27.

Kangas, O. and Palme, J. (1992) 'Public–Private Mix in Old Age Pensions'. In J.-E. Kolberg, (ed.), *The Study of Welfare State Regimes*. New York: M.E. Sharpe: 199–237.

Kangas, O. and Palme, J. (1993) 'Eroding Statism – Challenges to the Scandinavian Models'. In R. Erikson, E.J. Hansen, S. Ringen and H. Uusitalo (eds.), *Welfare Trends in the Scandinavian Countries*. New York: M.E. Sharpe: 3–24.

Kangas, O. and Palme, J. (2000) 'Does Social Policy Matter? Poverty Cycles in OECD Countries'. *International Journal of Health Services*, 30 (2): 335–52.

Kangas, O. and Ritakallio, V.-M. (2003) *Eri metodit, eri trendit: köyhyys Suomessa 1990-luvulla*. Turku: Turun yliopisto. (Different Methods, Different Trends: Poverty in Finland in the 1990s.)

Katz, M. (2001) *The Prize of Citizenship: Redefining the American Welfare State*. New York: Metropolitan Books.

Kenworthy, L. (2004) 'Welfare States: Real Income and Poverty'. Luxembourg Income Study, Working Papers 370. Luxembourg: LIS.

Kolstrup, Søren (1996) *Velfærdsstatens rødder: Fra kommunesocialisme til folkepension*. Viborg: SFAH. (The Roots of the Welfare State. From Communal Socialism to 'People's Pensions'.)

Korpi, W. (1980) 'Social Policy and Distributional Conflict in the Capitalist Democracies'. *West European Politics*, 3: 294–316.

Korpi, W. (2000) 'Faces of Inequality: Gender, Class and Patterns of Inequalities in Different Types of Welfare States'. *Social Politics*, 7(2): 127–91.

Korpi, W. and Palme, J. (1998) 'The Paradox of Redistribution and Strategies of Equality: Welfare State Institutions, Inequality and Poverty in the Western Countries'. *American Sociological Review*, 63: 661–87.

Kuhnle, S. (1981) 'The Growth of Social Insurance Programs in Scandinavia: Outside Influences and Internal Forces'. In P. Flora and A.J. Heidenheimer (eds.), *The Development of Welfare States in Europe and America*. New Brunswick and London: Transaction Books: 125–50.

Kuhnle, S. (1986) 'Norway'. In P. Flora (ed.), *Growth to Limits: The Western European Welfare States since World War II*. Berlin: Walter de Gruyter: 117–96.

Kuhnle, S. (ed.) (2000) *Survival of the European Welfare State, Routledge/ECPR Studies in European Political Science*. New York: Routledge.

Kuusi, P. (1966) *Social Policy for the Sixties: A Plan for Finland*. Helsinki: Social Policy Association.

Lehto, J., Moss, N. and Rostgaard, T. (1999). 'Universal Public Social Care and Health Services?' In M. Kautto, M. Heikkilä, B. Hvinden, S. Marklund and N. Ploug (eds.), *Nordic Social Policy: Changing Welfare States*. London: Routledge: 104–32.

Lewis, J. (1992) 'Gender and the Development of Welfare Regimes'. *Journal of European Social Policy*, 2(3): 159–73.

Lindbeck, A. (1997) 'The Swedish Experiment'. *Journal of Economic Literature*, 35: 1273–319.

Lindert, P. (2004) *Growing Public: Social Spending and Economic Growth Since the Eighteenth Century*. Cambridge: Cambridge University Press.

Lindqvist, R. (1990) *Från folkrörelse till välfärdsbyråkrati: Det svenska sjukförsäkringssystemets utveckling 1900–1990*. Lund: Arkiv. (From Social Movement to Welfare Bureaucracy: The Swedish Sickness Insurance Development 1900–1990.)

Mandel, H. and Semeynov, M. (2003) 'Welfare, Family Policies and Gender Earnings Inequality: A Cross-National Comparative Analysis': Luxembourg Income Study, Working Papers, 364. Luxembourg: LIS.

Marshall, G. (1997) *Repositioning Class: Socal inequality in Industrial Societies*. London: Sage.

Myrdal, G. (1960) *Beyond the Welfare State*. London: University Paperback.

Myrdal, A. and Myrdal, G. (1934) *Kris i befolkningsfrågan* (*Crisis in the Population Question*). Stockholm: Bonniers.

Niemelä, Heikki (1988) *Kokonaiseläkejärjestelmän muotoutuminen Suomessa* (*The Formation of the Pension System Totality in Finland*). Helsinki: KELA.

Nørby-Johansen, L. (1986) 'Denmark'. in P. Flora (ed.), *Growth to Limits: The Western European Welfare States since World War II*. Berlin: Walter de Gruyter: 293–381.

North, D.C. (1990) *Institutions, Institutional Change and Economic Performance*. Cambridge: Cambridge University Press.

NOSOSCO Nordic Social Statistical Committee, (2002) *Social Protection in the Nordic Countries 2000*. Copenhagen: NOSOSCO.

OECD (2000) *Historical Statistics 1970–1999*. Paris: OECD.

OECD (2002) *Employment Outlook 2002*. Paris: OECD.

OECD (2004) *Towards High-Performing Health Systems*. Paris: OECD.

Olson, Mancur (1965) *The Logic of Collective Action: Public Goods and the Theory of Groups*. Cambridge, Mass.: Harvard University Press.

Olson, Mancur (1982) *The Rise and Decline of Nations*. New Haven: Yale University Press.

Olsson, S.E. (1990) *Social Policy and Welfare State in Sweden*. Lund: Arkiv.

van Oorschot, W. (2003) 'Changing Welfare States, Changing Social Commitments': A Key-Note Speech given at the EuroConference, 'European Societies or European Society'. Helsinki, 20–24 September.

Orloff, A.S. and Skocpol, T. (1984) 'Why not Equal Protection?: Explaining the Politics of Public Spending in Britain, 1900–1911, and the United States, 1880s–1920. *American Sociological Review*, 49: 726–50.

Österbacka, E. (2004) *It Runs in the Family: Empirical Analyses of Family Background and Economic*. Åbo: Åbo Akademi University Press.

Palme, J. (1990) *Pension Rights in Welfare Capitalism: The Development of Old-Age Pensions in 18 OECD Countries 1930 to 1985*. Stockholm: Stockholm University.

Palme, J. (1999) *The Nordic Model of Social Protection and the Modernization of Social Protection in Europe*. Copenhagen: Nordic Council of Ministers.

Palme, J., Bergmark, Å., Bäckman, O., Estrada, F., Fritzell, J., Lundberg, O., Sjöberg, O., Sommestad L. and Szebehely, M. (2002) *Welfare in Sweden: The Balance Sheet for the 1990s*. Stockholm: Fritzes.

Penttilä, I. Kangas, O. Nordberg L. and Ritakallio, V-M. (2003) *Suomalainen köyhyys 1990-luvun lopulla – väliaikaista vai pysyvää?* (*Finnish Poverty in the 1990s: Temporary or Permanent*). Helsinki: Ministry of Social Affairs.

Pierson, P. (1994) *Dismantling the Welfare State? Reagan, Thatcher, and Politics of Retrenchment*. Cambridge: Cambridge University Press.

Putnam, R. (1993) *Making Democracy Work*. Princeton: Princeton University Press.

Putnam, R. (2000) *Bowling Alone: The Collapse and Revival of American Community*. New York: Simon & Schuster.

Quadagno, J. (1988) *The Transformation of Old Age Security: Class and Politics in the American Welfare State*. Chicago: University of Chicago Press.

Rawls, J. (1971) *A Theory of Social Justice*. Cambridge, Mass.: Harvard University Press.

Rawls, J. (1996) *Political Liberalism*. New York: Columbia University Press.

Ritter, G. (1982) *Social Welfare in Germany and Britain*. Leamington Spa and New York: Berg Publishers.

Rothstein, B. (1992) 'Labour-Market Institutions and Working-Class Strength. In S. Steinmo, K. Thelen and F. Longstreth (eds.), *Structuring Politics: Historical Insitutionalism in Comparative Analysis*. Cambridge: Cambridge University Press: 33–56.

Rothstein, B. (1998) *Just Institutions Matter: The Moral and Political Logic of the Universal Welfare State.* Cambridge: Cambridge University Press.

Rothstein B. (2003) 'Social Capital, Economic Growth and Quality of Government'. *New Political Economy*, 8(1): 49–71.

Salminen, K. (1993) *Pension Schemes in the Making: A Comparative Study of the Scandinavian Countries.* Helsinki: The Central Pension Security Institute.

Rowntree, S. (1901) *Poverty: The Study of Town Life.* London: Macmillan.

Saunders, P. (1994) *Welfare and Inequality: National and International Perspectives on the Australian Welfare State.* Cambridge: Cambridge University Press.

Schmidtz, D. (1998) *Social Welfare and Individual Responsibility.* Cambridge: Cambridge University Press.

Seip, A-L. (1994) *Veiene till velferdsstaten: Norsk sosialpolitikk 1920–75* Oslo: Gyldendal. (The Roads to the Welfare State: Norwegian Social Policy 1920–75.)

Sen, A. (1992) *Inequality Re-Examined.* Oxford: Oxford University Press.

Sen, A. (1998) *Development as Freedom.* New York: Random House.

Skocpol, T. (1992) *Protecting Soldiers and Mothers: The Political Origins of Social Policy in the United States.* Cambridge, Mass: Harvard University Press.

Skrede, K. (1999) 'Shaping Gender Equality – The Role of the State: Norwegian Experiences, Present Policies and Future Challenges'. In *Comparing Social Welfare Systems in Nordic Europe and France.* Paris: MIRE: 169–200.

Smeeding, T.M. (2002) *No Child Left Behind?* Luxembourg Income Study Working Papers, 319. Luxembourg: LIS.

SSPTW (2003), *Social Security Programs Throughout the World.* Washington, DC: US Department of Health and Welfare.

Svallfors, S. (1989) *Vem älskar välfärdsstaten?: Attityder, organiserade intressen och svensk välfärdspolitik.* Lund: Arkiv (Who Loves the Welfare State? Attitudes organized interests and Swedish Welfare Policy.)

Timonen, V. (2003) *Restructuring the Welfare State: Globalization and Social Policy Reform in Finland and Sweden.* Northampton, VT: Edward Elgar.

Titmuss, R.M. (1955) 'Pension System and Population Change'. *Political Quarterly*, 26: 152–66.

Townsend, P. (1979) *Poverty in the United Kingdom: A Survey of Household Resources and Standard of Living.* Harmondsworth: Penguin.

Vartiainen, J. (1995) 'The State and Structural Change: What can be Learnt from the Successful Late Industrializers?'. In H.-J. Chang and R. Rowthorn (eds.), The *Role of the State in Economic Change.* Oxford: Clarendon Press: 137–69.

Wennemo, I. (1994) *Sharing the Costs of Children. Studies on the Development of Family Support in OECD Countries.* Stockholm: Swedish Institute for Social Research.

Websites

http://www.lisproject/keyfigures/povertytable.htm.
http://www.pisa.oecd.org/.

3
Voluntary State-Subsidized Social Insurance in the Advanced Industrialized World since the 1890s: The Nordic Experience in Comparative Perspective

Eero Carroll

Introduction

The historic tension between voluntarism and statism remains politicized in today's welfare debates. Voluntarism without state intervention, in accordance with Alexis de Tocqueville's idea of 'the slow and quiet action of society upon itself,'[1] has become compromised. States increasingly engage with social movements, and vice versa, financially, regulatorily and interorganizationally. This sharpens the question of what organizations and citizens gain or lose by this inter-articulation of 'sectors' in what is (utterly ahistorically) called the 'new mixed economy of welfare'.

The focus of this chapter is on the institutional emergence and (to some extent) also the mortality of voluntary social insurance in the highly industrialized North. The first section focuses on relations between states and social movements in development debate and the 'social capital' concept – ending with some overarching questions. Historical narrative analyses follow on programme development in the Swedish, Norwegian, Finnish and Danish cases, exemplifying problems of administration, inclusion and legitimacy. A comparative data section follows on the extent of social insurance for the sick and the unemployed since 1930 in selected OECD countries.[2] A broader policy discussion section concludes the chapter.

Background: social movements, states and social policy voluntarism

State involvement in social movements has a long history in both the global North and the South. One major site of welfare cooperation between states and social movements in the industrialized North has been constituted by voluntary state-subsidized social insurance institutions, particularly for the sick and the unemployed. Voluntary state-subsidized social insurance is one of at least five overarching 'models of social policy' (see, e.g., Korpi and Palme 1998). The voluntarist model is interesting for how the state uses social movements to develop institutions which the state lacks the capacity or will to develop itself. In current development debate, state disengagement from social provision is advocated so as to cut costs and enable states to concentrate on 'core' activities. Given possible countervailing disadvantages, I emphasize the diversity of policy considerations on 'third-sector' provision from European historical experience that should be kept in mind when considering such policies today.

The long-term viability of voluntary state-subsidized social insurance has also been limited in the advanced industrialized countries. Initial enthusiasm for such programmes ran high: workers' organizations, trade unions and locally or regionally based associations throughout the industrializing North created funds or benefit organizations to offer cash benefits to their members (not least upon sickness or unemployment) in exchange for membership contributions. When public subsidies and recognition began to be granted to such organizations, their membership often increased further and their development contributed to the institutionalization of welfare states themselves – politicians of many stripes, from Socialist to Catholic to liberal, often saw state recognition of voluntary social protection as a central response to the so-called 'workers' question' (see, e.g., Carroll and Johansson 2000). Yet, as will be seen below, few countries retained such programmes for the sick or unemployed into the new millennium – for various reasons, voluntary social insurance for the risks of work accidents, old age and parenthood was never extensively institutionalized, or accorded long-term state recognition and legislated subsidies when it did emerge.

To the extent that it has been tried and retained in the industrialized North, a voluntary state-subsidized social insurance programme entails recognition of one or more voluntary organizations, based on membership, as designated insurance carriers for protection against members' wage loss in certain situations of social risk. However, such programmes entail a wider set of consequences, and tie in to several development concerns. One set of theoretical concerns raised in both Northern and Southern debate on social policy deals with the role of institutions and networks in consolidating bonds of reciprocal trust among members of society, often referred to as 'social capital' (see, e.g., Coleman 1990). A number of contextual factors may influence levels of trust in welfare institutions; here we may mention the level of social conflict, the strength of intermediate organizations such as political parties and trade unions, cultural norms of reciprocity, or prior levels of trust in people and/or institutions. Prior levels of institutionalized trust are sometimes referred to as existing 'stocks' of social capital, viewed as less malleable or 'constructible' by policy means. Robert Putnam's (1993) now classic account of the societal preconditions of good governance in the Italian regions emphasizes the role of already existing social capital in explaining why good governance succeeds (for a discussion, see Evans 1996: 1124; Fox 1996).

However, other treatments of 'social capital' place much more emphasis on politics and state intervention as ways of designing institutional contexts generating trust. The consolidation of social capital through policy, in instances ranging from construction of local irrigation design institutions in Taiwan to health care popularization in Northeast Brazil, may ensure that 'networks of trust and collaboration ... are created [that] span the public/private boundary and bind state and civil society together' (Evans 1996: 1122).

Strong states and strong societies may thus not be at odds, as implied in some accounts of 'social capital' development placing stronger faith in voluntary organizations' efficiency, but indeed can go hand in hand. This seems to have been the case in Sweden, where the voluntary sector is no smaller than in countries with 'smaller' states and where state – social movement relations in the welfare domain are closely cooperative, with a pro-state orientation on voluntary organizations' part to welfare services nationalization (Lundström and Svedberg 2003; Rothstein and Stolle 2003). Including voluntarist components in social provision may increase trust by bringing the welfare state 'closer' to its beneficiaries, through organizational members' direct participation in decisions on their welfare. In African context, beneficiary participation is argued potentially to lower the cost of social policy interventions and 'ensur[e] that they more closely reflect the preferences of the population they are designed to serve' (Hoddinott 2002: 146).

Closely linked to the issue of social capital's political 'malleability' is one of legitimacy: of whether increasing state intervention in or funding of the 'third sector' compromises the legitimacy of one, or both, sets of actors. Whereas one set of views is fairly optimistic on this score, emphasizing the 'synergies' of states' and social actors' co-involvement in producing welfare services (Evans 1996; Ostrom 1996), another set of views is more pessimistic, particularly in its views on international agencies' funding of NGOs. Proponents of these views hold that states and international donors may bureaucratize or coopt formerly more 'lateral' and membership-oriented civil organizations. Further, if voluntary movements depend more on official funding, this may compromise performance in key areas of provision. This may mean that both national decision makers and organizational leaderships become less accountable, to voters and to organizational members, respectively, and that voluntary organizations lose legitimacy as uncompromising defenders of their members' interests (Edwards and Hulme 1996).

Parallel considerations of legitimacy, funding and institutionalized trust also run through the history of Nordic voluntarism, regarding the potential strengths and pitfalls of national state financing of voluntary organizations. I shall therefore address a number of subsidiary questions. Historical narratives on voluntary state social insurance development in the Nordic cases will consider what initial and later divisions of administrative responsibility for programmes were debated between state elites and voluntary organizations (and as organized nationally), as well as what agreement and disagreement existed on definitions of the risks to be insured, the constituencies to be taken into account, the subsidy and recognition conditions to be followed and choices of institutional models for the programmes enacted. Such matters can be viewed in terms of nationally organized political debates on issues of administration, legitimacy and inclusion. More overall comparisons with quantitative data address how voluntary state-subsidized social insurance coverage developed, and what institutionally governed logic can be seen in the confluence of other aspects of programme scope and generosity, such as in programme financing and in benefit rates, duration and contribution requirements. A final discussion will consider the more global issue of what the balance is between policy benefits of 'third-sector' social provision (participation of the insured, strengthened civil society and social capital) and its possible costs, such as reducing the reach of parliamentary democracy, fostering of separate interests, increasing administrative costs and institutional fragmentation.

The Nordic history of subsidized social risk since 1891

How did administrative, legitimacy and inclusion concerns, as well as national organization/politics, interact in voluntary insurance development? Norwegian, Finnish and Swedish unemployment insurance, as well as Danish and Swedish (and partly also compulsory Norwegian) sickness insurance, are here examined to examine these questions more closely.

Starting with the Norwegian case, late industrialization and mass emigration (as in Sweden) somewhat predisposed elites to political solutions for the 'social question' of integrating the emergent industrial working class. Institutional designs nonetheless differed. For the sick, compulsory insurance was the first Norwegian law of choice. The Norwegian unemployment insurance law of 1906 sought to resolve the conflict between legislators' belief that public provision was necessary with misgivings that the state might not be able administratively to undertake it. This task was delegated to existing trade unions, however weak they still were. By 1904, there were sixteen privately organized unemployment funds in Norway with more than 10,000 members, all union-administered (Bjørnson and Haavet 1994: 83). The funds could include or exclude anyone the union chose, and serve whatever purposes fitted the organization's goals:

> the funds were a means of the union members' wage struggle. This was clearly indicated by the [funds'] statutes, which said that workers who had quit work when employers cut wages, or who had quit because they demanded better pay, had the right to assistance from the unemployment

fund. They were counted as 'involuntary unemployed', with all the rights which followed therefrom. (Bjørnson and Haavet 1994: 83).

Policy experts such as Oscar Jaeger, the social liberal economist chairing the 1904 State Commission investigating unemployment insurance, partly disregarded the fact that public subsidies to union funds might be controversial. He felt that issues of oversight were more important: unions were viewed as better and more legitimate supervisors of unemployed fund members' willingness to work, which public support otherwise might compromise: 'Jaeger was of the opinion that union organizations had better possibilities to exercise control over their members than any public authority, for example to verify that only the involuntarily unemployed would be paid benefits' (Bjørnson and Haavet 1994: 86; cf. Olson 1965).

The eventuality that union and state officials might have very different definitions of who counted as 'involuntarily unemployed', and thus was entitled to support, was also disregarded. Public funding would subsidize the wage struggle as long as unions and insurance funds were not administratively separated, and strikers regarded as entitled to support – and politicians and unionists disagreed vehemently over the justice in such demands, as they did over whether the non-unionized should be allowed to join the funds. In administrative practice, decades after public support had been implemented, union funds 'could have a broader definition of the concept 'involuntary unemployment' than what was provided for by law. The authorities' control, and the tug-of-war about who would be defined as involuntarily unemployed, however occurred in the same instant as the funds sought subsidies for the expenses they had taken on' (Bjørnson and Haavet 1994: 91).

The unions were also dissatisfied with the low subsidies – at one-quarter of the funds' costs when the first law was passed (Kuhnle 1978: 25). The rate was not increased to half of the funds' costs until after the First World War. The government in office in 1918 was willing to do this since it was feared that European demobilization would lead to mass unemployment; it was also dissatisfied with how slowly fund membership had grown (Bjørnson and Haavet 1994: 94). Yet as subsidies increased, so did the protests from both government officials and right-wing parliamentarians to the effect that public funds were effectively being misused to support the unions' wage struggle – despite the fact that, formally, 'the [original] law had been modelled so that the trade unions' opportunities to use the unemployment fund in a wage dispute were strongly restricted' (Bjørnson 2001: 203). The unions' opportunities to use their control of the funds as a power resource, even though legally restricted, thus nevertheless continued to arouse political controversy, as elsewhere where voluntarism was retained.

By the 1920s, as the funds proved unable to substantially increase (or even retain) membership in the wake of increased unemployment, debate on voluntarism's justification intensified – and the Depression made things worse. Norwegian unions had not mandated fund membership even of their own members, and no more than a quarter of the full members of the Confederation of Trade Unions (LO) belonged to the funds as late as 1935 – arguably, 'these voluntary organizations had failed ... pav[ing] the way for a state-financed system' (Bjørnson 2001: 208). The Labour Party government under Johan Nygaardsvold, taking his cue from sceptics of voluntarism within the unions, abolished the voluntary legislation and enacted a new compulsory law in 1938.

This account of the developments by which voluntary sector failure led to compulsory statism in Norwegian unemployment policy is also endorsed in theoretical and historical accounts (Kuhnle 1978). Compulsory social insurance programmes tended to emerge either when the very broadest pre-existing voluntarist movements gave a platform for their easy enactment or when a weak pre-existing movement proved entirely unable to meet the demands of running the system. Voluntary unemployment insurance failure in Norway by 1938 seems to fit the latter category well – although not only the quantity, but also the quality, of administrative capacity seemed to matter for the outcome, on the part of both the state and voluntary movements.

Voluntarism's failure was not preordained: to those involved, it seemed like a good idea at the time. As a solution to the 'agrarian question' in Norwegian society, voluntarism also had political reasons in its favour. The Agrarian Party opposed the original legislation precisely because it excluded agricultural workers (Kuhnle 1986: 121), and their continued resistance was obviated by a financing design wherein 'rural communities and farmers did not have to contribute' (Bjørnson 2001: 203). Though the Norwegian compulsory sickness programme of 1909 is an interesting contrasting case, agrarian politics also made the Swedish voluntary sickness insurance law of 1891 a motivated design choice.

The Swedish sickness insurance law of 1891 provided existing funds with only a limited administrative costs subsidy and legal recognition if they registered with the state. This entailed relatively less political conflict and more continuity with a stronger voluntarist movement providing sickness benefits than did the somewhat later Norwegian proposal for a compulsory state law (first made in 1897) directed only to the industrial working class. The Norwegian law entailed a sharp break with liberalism and its voluntarist emphasis, and as such 'was more in accordance with the German models than with the Danish and Swedish ones' (Kuhnle 1978: 27). Yet precisely by making issues of inclusion and entitlement that otherwise would have been resolved within voluntary funds into political questions, the legal proposal of 1897 also raised greater political conflict: 'representatives from the countryside opposed the proposal and succeeded in postponing the enactment until 1909' (Johansson 2003: 264). Once finally enacted, the law also lessened opposition by similar means as for the voluntarist unemployment

insurance law: the insured 'were supposed to pay six-tenths themselves ...
the rural population was less prone to disease than the industrial workers
and consequently paid less' (Bjørnson 2001: 203).

Despite attendant higher conflict, Norwegian politicians were readier to
push through corporatistic compulsory legislation of sickness insurance
because of the greater perceived weakness of the voluntarist alternative.
The Norwegian sickness insurance funds, also within the industrial working
class, were not seen as sufficiently developed to serve as national programme
carriers even with subsidy – decision makers preferred to build up their
own municipal sickness administration institutions, in a way which Swedish
policy makers considering measures in the same insurance domain did not.
Voluntarism was a more attractive alternative in the Swedish case, as long as
the farmers were not expected to contribute much to the urban population's
greater risks (see Lundberg and Åmark 2001).

The voluntary sickness insurance programme in Sweden certainly changed
after inception, with reforms in both 1910 and 1931 strengthening the state's
demands on organizational routines of the funds, as well as raising subsidies
to include also benefits and not only administrative costs. However, proposals for compulsory insurance which began to be made were actively opposed
by the voluntary funds – not least by the so-called National Sickness Insurance Funds' Central Organization, one of two competing national organizations of sickness funds in Sweden. The national funds, with membership
drawn from several municipalities, were against a new localist administration which would leave the competing locally based funds' membership
bases more intact. Breaking away in 1916 from the Sickness Insurance Funds'
Federation, founded in 1907, the National Sickness Insurance Funds' Central
Organization constituted itself in opposition to the former organization's
readiness to support compulsory insurance (Johansson 2003: 48). And both
national and local funds objected to the likely exclusion of the middle-class
members they had from the envisioned compulsory systems (Johansson
2003: 268–9, cf. Chapters 5–6).

This institutionally and organizationally centered account distinguishes
different reasons for the long-term continuity of voluntary sickness insurance in Sweden (not abolished until 1955) than do more traditional social
policy and economic – historical accounts, emphasizing the statist component in the Swedish welfare state's development, as well as the economic
reasons for delays in enacting it for the sick (Olson 1986; Edebalk 2000).
The weight of institutional precedence is underestimated here – this sets up
special interests to be respected, making dismantlement or integration more
difficult in later stages of policy making.

Another case of long-term persistence in voluntarism further illustrates
this: that of Danish sickness insurance development since 1892. Early
and strong commitment to social policy voluntarism characterized the
Danish welfare state in several respects, reflecting the long-term dominance

of Manchester liberalism and liberal political elites in the Danish social order. Economic growth, party system modernization and trade union strength were furthest-advanced and earliest in Denmark (among the Nordic countries), as was the 'depth' of voluntarist organizing itself (Kuhnle 1978: 15, 20). Voluntary unemployment insurance, enacted in 1907, took off earlier and reached higher levels of coverage than almost anywhere else under similar conditions, remaining in force today. Yet we should avoid too rosy a view of how the Danish voluntary sickness insurance system worked – institutional continuity's own force once again constituted an obstacle for expansion or reform, especially when voluntarism was initially combined with the rather different logic of targeting.[3]

This double logic was evident in the first proposals of the state Inquiry Commission on sickness insurance convened by the Minister of the Interior, which presented its report in 1887. While proposing extensive state subsidies to the benefit societies, covering both free health care and cash sickness benefits, the Commission also expressed the will to target expenditure upon the most needy, 'those without means' *('de ubemidlede')*. If a benefit society was to register with the state, and thereby obtain public subsidy, state authorities desired to influence who was to be a member, or at least to partake in benefits to be subsidized with state means.

The Commission saw that these categorizations opposed the idea of a free movement of benefit societies which could develop in accordance with own goals. According to the Commission's own studies, some 20 per cent of all members in the benefit societies of Copenhagen fell outside of the Commission's (largely occupational!) definition of 'those without means' (Betænkning 1887: 28–9). The enacted law also illustrates how the Danish state wished to target its subsidies to the most needy, whereas the voluntary benefit society movement had developed without regard to the fact that only those most lacking in means would be regarded as fully entitled members.

The 1892 Law, despite its contradictions, contributed to the sickness benefit societies' subsequent growth, and the societies founded a national federation soon after the turn of the century. Yet, as in Sweden, national organization brought new interests into play, which had to be respected and which exacerbated conflicts of institutional logic. The Danish national organization of sickness funds demanded changes, not least that those with means should be allowed to remain members and receive subsidized benefits if their economic situation became worse.

Governments responded by appointing new commissions, and by making proposals in the spirit of these demands. Yet new legislation in 1915 still enshrined the principle that the worst off had privileged access, also stipulating that the Minister of the Interior issue a declaration on entitled categories of members every fifth year to benefit societies and municipal council executives *(kommunalstyrelserna)*. This led to proliferating regulations, continued discontent by fund organizers attempting to enlarge categories of subsidized members and decades of further battles between state and membership organizations on whose definitions of entitlement should prevail. Occupational and class-related entitlement limits were abolished in 1927, with definitive income and assets tests adopted instead. Targeting was retained until the reform of 1933, in principle establishing universalist coverage with voluntarist carriers. Other contradictions ensued, since 'the principle of universal compulsory social insurance was only cosmetic. Thus, people could choose between active and passive membership in funds[, yet p]assive membership entailed payment of a ridiculously low fee and in no way guaranteed protection' (Nørby-Johansen 1986: 299–300). The 1960 Law was also 'semi-compulsory' (Kangas 1991: 64) – the sickness funds were not definitively dissolved and their tasks transferred to state authorities until 1971 (Nørby-Johansen 1986: 303).

Long-lived welfare co-provision by states and voluntary organizations may also go through fairly divisive debates as to which actors take the leading roles and how programme constituencies are defined. This occurred for programmes retained today: the Finnish voluntary unemployment insurance enacted in 1917 as well as the Swedish programme enacted since 1934.

The Finnish programme was characterized by low legitimacy from the very start – basic political conflicts about the legitimacy of trade unionism, and indeed on the future of Finnish democracy, carried over into conflicts on social insurance. The voluntary programme's enactor, a non-socialist parliamentary majority, passed the law in November 1917 just prior to independence (declared on 6 December) from now-revolutionary Russia. In the five-month civil war starting in January 1918, with Russian garrisons intervening on the 'Red' government's side and German expeditionary forces on the 'White' government's side, the Reds were defeated. In the aftermath, working class mobilization went into a wintry hiatus. Union membership fell rapidly (not to recover more stably until mass unemployment had been weathered by the late 1930s), with the organizations' very existence threatened (see Alapuro 1988).

Parliamentary debates in the 1920s and 1930s indicated that other problems, similar to those raised in Norway, remained partially unresolved in the early Finnish system, in their turn exacerbated by the low level of trust and regulation obtaining in labour relations. State funding was fairly modest. The Government's Legal Proposition 31 from 1926, in its third paragraph (§20), differentiated subsidy rates by family status of recipients, at three-fifths of all compensation paid to those with at least one child under sixteen and two-fifths of compensation paid to all others (Finnish Parliament VP 1926 VM no. 31, III, n.d., p. 9). Leftist MPs argued throughout the 1920s and 1930s that subsidies were too low, and also rejected rightist MPs' suggestions that the state's neutrality in labour market conflicts was threatened since the funds' own rules, as modified, had come to specify that the locked-out or strikers not be supported. Rightist and centrist MPs, on the other hand, continued to question whether the unions could be trusted, and repeatedly brought up (to a degree realistic) fears of communist subversion.

Revolutionary ambitions were thus continually ascribed to, and/or subscribed to by, the unions. Mutual suspicion and conflict was exacerbated by agitation from the extreme right – organized in the extra-parliamentary Lapua movement, most active in the so-called 'yeomens' march' on Helsinki in the summer of 1930 and the armed (albeit small-scale and bloodlessly subjugated) Mäntsälä uprising in February 1932. State repression was also directed at unions – the first Finnish Confederation of Trade Unions (SAJ), founded in 1907, was outlawed in 1930 after its takeover by communists (themselves banned as a party by extraordinary legislation in the same year, in force until 1944). Also the social democratically-run successor confederation (SAK), formed in 1930, saw activists blacklisted by employers, and union leaders were recurringly jailed on trumped-up charges of state treason – employers were also uncompromising, with strikebreakers recruited via a national organization (*Vientirauha*, or Export Peace).

The unions and their funds were severely weakened, and at first did not have much to put up against repression by the right-centre and agrarian elites ruling the post-civil war country. Coverage in the 1930s was very low, on the order of 1 per cent of all employees, in itself with feedback effects on legitimacy. Subsidies to the funds were apparently also complemented by external assistance, used for the larger social struggle. In fact, Social Democratic Party (SDP) leader K. A. Fagerholm admitted as much in debate with the Lapua movement successor party IKL's (Finnish Patriotic People's Movement) representative Somersalo in 1933, while hinting at external support to the latter's camp:

> As far as the issue is concerned of where the present unemployment funds have gotten the means with which they have paid out more support than what they have gotten in through members' contributions and state subsidies, this is a question which I honestly have no interest of illuminating more closely. Rep. Arne Somersalo looks very victorious as I say this, but this is after all for about the same reasons that Rep. Arne Somersalo does not wish to more closely illuminate from where the Lapua movement got funding for the Mäntsälä uprising, and for one and the other of the doings which these gentlemen have to their account. (Finnish Parliament VPP PI 1933, n.d., p. 634)

Clandestine and semi-legal manoeuvring, coinciding with restrictions on the rights of unions to organize, were even such that Finnish democracy could almost be said to be verging on semi-authoritarianism by the 1930s. Unemployment funds were restricted in their activity. Continually debated, paragraph 1 of the Unemployment Funds Law of 1934 (125/34) stipulated that funds could not operate in conjunction with any labour organization even if they were administratively separate – a limitation claimed to have contributed to the suspension of eight of the ten unemployment funds still then formally constituted (Finnish Parliament VPP II, 16 December 1936, p. 1298).

It appears that voluntarist social provision cannot be expected to work when more basic civil rights, such as those to organize, are not firmly institutionalized or are recurringly threatened. When democracy is threatened in the state, it inescapably becomes so also in the world of voluntary organizations. Work on the history of civil-societal organizing in Mexico indicates that voluntary organization from below may also succeed under repression by local governmental elites (Fox 1996), but it is evident that solving broader issues of democracy and inclusion can be crucial before civil-societal organizing can take place.

Starting in the 1940s, voluntary unemployment insurance could be increasingly appreciated as an incentive to union membership by many union administrators in the SAK, and the social democrats generally defended it (though party factions did in 1954 also put forward a motion in favour of a national insurance programme administered centrally by the labour market partners). The only major reform in the system before the mid-1980s, resulting in a complementary means-tested state unemployment assistance law in 1960 (included with the benefit improvements legislated through Statute 328), was enough to address the otherwise staunchly universalist Agrarian Party's major objection to the system, that it did not sufficiently protect farmers. This new programme brought the Agrarians round to supporting continued voluntarism – to the consternation of the (partly rurally based) communist popular front party SKDL, who had hoped to abolish the voluntary system entirely (see Finnish Parliament VPP PI, 29 February 1960, pp. 608–20). The SKDL and the populist smallholders' party SMP continually raised (into the 1980s) parliamentary motions to enact compulsory insurance, as did the Conservative Coalition Party – the SDP was to retain its commitment to voluntarism.

The system thus was continually contested, even as social democratic and communist unionists resolved some differences and united in a strengthened SAK. By 1985, another reform strengthened second-tier benefits offered to fund non-members. Its income test was removed and a third-tier system introduced in 1994, as re-emergent mass unemployment passed 20 per cent of the labour force. Despite recurring proposals for a compulsory system from government experts, membership trumped citizenship – although coverage had expanded to more than 80 per cent of employees with increasing unionization before second-tier benefits became comprehensive in 1994.

Finnish unemployment insurance developments were an afterthought in the welfare state's development for reasons parallel to those in Sweden: compensation was less of a priority in the Nordic countries (excepting Denmark, particularly after 1973) than employment policies. Thus, throughout the period 1945–80 (with shortlived exceptions, mainly in the late 1970s),

Finnish labour market policy expenditure was much more strongly oriented to public works than to unemployment compensation (Alestalo and Uusitalo 1986: 214). Sweden's expenditures initially favoured compensation in the mid-1950s, though there was at that time hardly any unemployment to spend money on. By the mid-1960s, public works and relocation benefits had expanded radically, bypassing compensation in both absolute levels and proportionally – retraining expanded from the mid-1970s (Olson 1986: 22). Voluntary unemployment benefits may work best not only when implementation responsibilities, labour peace and union concertation issues are resolved, but also when they are embedded within full employment policies. The Swedish case provides significant confirmation of this reasoning and I shall conclude by giving a brief account of the Swedish voluntary insurance programme's institutionalization.

Precisely because of historical delay, the Swedish programme may have avoided being caught in the crossfire of more basic labour market conflicts, as in the Norwegian and Finnish systems. These latter countries' systems assigned greater responsibility for supervising the unemployed, and their market availability, to the labour union funds, engendering suspicion as to whether these roles were discharged, and at what level of competition with municipal employment exchanges and Social Affairs ministries using different definitions of unemployment and availability. In Sweden, by contrast, 'public employment exchanges were set up starting in 1902 ... in which half the representatives ... were taken from the labour movement and half from local employers' organizations' (Rothstein 2001: 213). Such extensions of corporatist interest representation into state or government institutions enabled conflict resolution through other channels than parliament, and cleared the institutional ground for fund subsidies in 1934 by obviating some of the suspicions on their purposes as voiced elsewhere.

The law's legitimacy was still questioned by unionists, since public works programmes of the same period did not embody a similar corporatist consensus. In order to qualify for state assistance and public works before 1934, workers could still be required to strikebreak and were not paid a market wage – an order which the ascendant Social Democratic government of 1932 was sworn to change (Rothstein 1989). The social democrats agreed with the Agrarian Party in 1933 on the financing of market-wage public works, in what political punsters dubbed the 'cow-lition' agreement. Special concessions for agriculture were used to buy out the farmers' representatives, otherwise in favour of 'public works [being] emergency projects, as such [to] be paid for at emergency (i.e. lower) rates' (Samuelsson 1968: 238; Rothstein 1989).

As described by Lundberg and Åmark (2001: 161), initial unionist objections resembled those raised in Norway and Finland: 'Many trade unions thought that the [state's] economic contribution was too small to compensate for the price they had to pay. For example, they feared that they would have to let strikebreakers become members of the unemployment funds.' Registration of funds for support in the 1930s was slow – it was only in 1941, when rules changed to meet union demands, that registration took off. Political indeterminacy also played a role. The Social Democratic Minister of Social Affairs, Gustav Möller, favoured compulsory insurance; disunity continued until Möller resigned in 1951, over failures of the timely implementation of this principle in sickness insurance, and disagreements with unions on whether social benefits should be earnings-related or flat-rate.

A further precondition for unemployment insurance becoming a power resource for the unions was arguably the dissolution of the State Unemployment Commission in favour of the corporatist and unionist-dominated Labour Market Board (AMS), founded by 1946 (Rothstein 1989). Union control over 'passive' labour market policy was then extended under centralized forms to 'active' channels of labour market training and education. In Denmark, this problem was 'solved' by the relative unimportance of active policies and more complete union control of job placement (through the funds). Only a systemic 1967 reform realized 'a transfer of employment services from the unemployment funds to a state system of employment agencies' (Nørby-Johansen 1986: 359), signed up to by unions in exchange for radical increases in subsidies and benefits.

In Sweden, corporatist negotiation was also not enough to keep voluntarism or unionization expanding. State financing had to expand before coverage took off (Carroll 1997), with steady coverage increases coinciding fairly closely with almost continuously increased state subsidies to the funds. Yet subsidies still left other groups unaccounted for – an exclusively state-financed (though modest) alternative assistance benefit was thus enacted in 1974, and its assets test removed by 1984, so as to give non-members protection. Formally full coverage had resulted among employees by that time, albeit soon delimited when 16–19-year-olds were excluded from assistance benefit in 1986. Mass unemployment in the 1990s (now largely overcome) called voluntarism into question, and amplified Conservative Party and Liberal People's Party demands for a compulsory system (voiced since the early post-war period). Yet the overall framework of voluntary insurance remained: here, 'trade union power was more important to the labour movement than the principle of universalism' (Lundberg and Åmark 2001: 162).

Contextualizing the Nordic experience: statistics on programme development

How do the overall developments of social insurance generosity and inclusivity look also among the advanced industrialized countries as a whole? Principal data for such comparisons are derived from the Social Citizenship Indicators Project (SCIP).[4] Figures 3.1 and 3.2 depict formal coverage developments for unemployment insurance among employees and

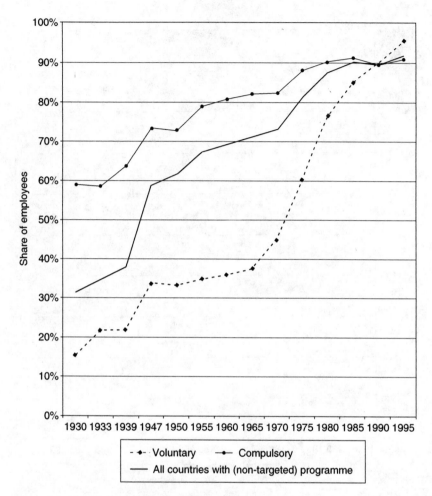

Figure 3.1 Unemployment insurance coverage among employees under voluntary, compulsory, and all (non-targeted) legislation for 18 OECD countries, 1930–1995

sickness insurance in the labour force. Both include average development for all countries with (non-targeted) insurance programmes, but also for the country sub-samples with either voluntary or some variant of compulsory insurance for either risk.[5] Coverage thus assessed is indeterminate when benefits are targeted, since no unconditional entitlements then exist. Tables 3.1 and 3.2 document changes in the number of countries in each sub-sample – crucial to interpreting mean figures.

Measuring coverage in terms of formal entitlement to benefits can be seen as problematic, insofar as this disregards differences in actual recipient levels

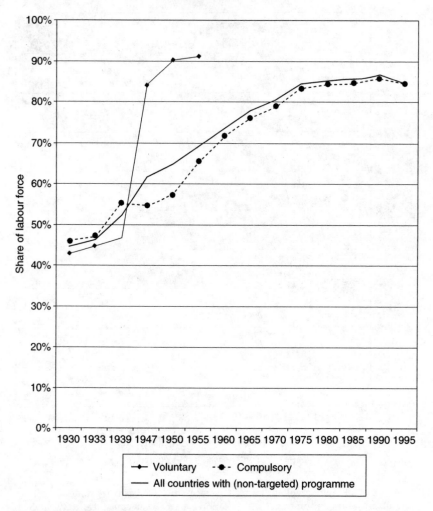

Figure 3.2 Sickness insurance coverage in labour force under voluntary, compulsory, and all (non-targeted) legislation for 18 OECD countries, 1930–1995

(harder or impossible to assess) as well as in the actual implementation of formal laws. Differences in formal entitlements nevertheless say something important about how inclusive programmes are designed to be, and obviate the insurmountable problems currently posed by the gathering of comparable figures on what shares of programme target groups actually receive benefits. Formal coverage indicators also more strictly reflect the level of inclusionary ambitions among legislators, rather than (for example) the overall state of the economy or of the labour market.

Table 3.1 Voluntary and compulsory unemployment insurance programmes in force, selected OECD countries, 1930–95

Year	1930–3	1939	1947	1950	1955–65	1970–5	1980–95
Voluntary	7	8	4	4	4	4	3
Compulsory	4	5	7	10	11	12	13
Total	**11**	**13**	**11**	**14**	**15**	**16**	**16**

Note:
The four countries which had some form of compulsory unemployment insurance legislation in force (at least formally) already in 1930–3 are Germany, Ireland, Italy, and the UK. The seven countries with voluntary systems at that time are Belgium, Denmark, Finland, France, the Netherlands, Norway and Switzerland. By 1939, Sweden has entered the voluntary family, and the United States has entered the compulsory family (both through first laws ever passed). By 1947, Canada has entered the compulsory family and Norway has switched to it, as has Belgium – the German system had, however, practically ceased to exist, and is not coded as being in force in this year (though coverage as a share of the labour force is set to equal that of 1939 in later codings). Also by 1947, France and the Netherlands have gone over to a third kind of system (not counted here), targeted benefits, which temporarily takes them out of this sample of cases and decreases the total amount of systems in force. By 1950, Austria (going over from a pre-war targeted system), Germany (with a revised compulsory law) and Japan (with a new law) have also (re-)entered the compulsory family. By 1955 and 1970 respectively, the Netherlands and France also do so, with Switzerland switching families from the voluntary side by 1980.

Table 3.2 Voluntary and compulsory sickness insurance programmes in force in SCIP 'census years', selected OECD countries, 1930–95

Year	1930–9	1947	1950	1955	1960	1965–70	1975–95
Voluntary	5	3	3	2	1	1	1
Compulsory	8	10	10	11	12	13	14
Total	**13**	**13**	**13**	**13**	**13**	**14**	**15**

Note:
The eight countries with compulsory sickness insurance law in force already in 1930–39 are Austria, France, Germany, Ireland, Japan, Netherlands, Norway, and the UK. The five countries with voluntary systems at that time are Belgium, Denmark, Italy, Sweden, and Switzerland. Belgium and Italy have switched over to the compulsory family by 1947 – Sweden has followed this path by 1955 and Denmark (as coded here) has done the same by 1960. Finland has entered the compulsory family with a delayed first law by 1965, and Canada has done the same by 1975. As in the case of unemployment insurance, Australia and New Zealand have never had anything else than a targeted system, and are never counted here – the United States has not yet legislatively adopted any kind of national sickness insurance (although state-level so-called temporary disability programmes do exist today for some sectors of the work force in California, Hawaii and Rhode Island).

The story of voluntary state-subsidized social insurance provision in the advanced industrialized countries is one of increasing coverage beyond core fund 'membership groups' of the administering organizations. Though administering sickness insurance funds were sometimes regionally based, the organization behind a voluntary fund (even more so for the unemployed) was typically a labour union. As argued particularly for unemployment insurance in Sweden and Denmark (Pedersen 1981; Rothstein 1989; Toft 1995; Carroll 1999), union-controlled voluntary insurance worked as an incentive (albeit indirect) to join the unions. The development of voluntary insurance coverage was intimately connected with increases in the power of Scandinavian trade unions.

Coverage increased under voluntary programmes remaining in force by the 1990s even to levels (if not greatly) above those prevailing under formally compulsory programmes. This success story's other side, however, is one of decreasing institutional prevalence of voluntarism. In force in almost half the sampled countries by the end of the 1930s, voluntary unemployment insurance programmes existed by 1995 only in Sweden, Denmark and Finland. Norway abandoned voluntarism in 1938, before the Second World War and German occupation. The same wartime circumstances contributed to similar programmes' demise in France, the Netherlands and Belgium, as the free labour movements went underground or were crushed in the 1940s. The Finnish programme's development long remained abortive – in the context of 1930s prohibitions on union and fund organization, as well as infighting among social democrats and communists for control of the unions. This infighting declined only in the late 1960s, when socialist and communist wings of the blue-collar Trade Union Confederation (SAK) concluded a power-sharing agreement. Only in one other country, Switzerland, did voluntary unemployment insurance remain in force more continuously (until 1977) – coverage stagnated at about 30 per cent of the labour force, not least since state subsidies remained very low.

Coverage of unemployment insurance was conspicuously higher in countries enacting compulsory programmes. Winston Churchill's wartime call (in 1943) for extending British compulsory insurance led to abolition of 'horizontal' restrictions on industries covered, previously excluding many groups. For other kinds of compulsory insurance on the corporatistic model (Korpi 2001), such as the 1927 Law enacted in Weimar Germany, Bismarckian traditions remained influential in that restrictions were also 'vertical'. Workers were insured separately by occupational group, and those either above a definitive income ceiling or without firm occupational attachment were excluded (Carroll 1999). It was not until the 1980s that coverage levels under the compulsory programmes, regardless of character, were rivalled (by 1995, exceeded) by those under remaining voluntary programmes. And by then, voluntary institutions had changed so much that structured differences between programme types were no longer what they had been.

For sickness insurance, compulsory laws were more often first laws, some of them (as in Canada and in Finland) conspicuously delayed in enactment into the 1960s and 1970s. Sweden's and Denmark's laws, enacted in 1891 and 1892, respectively, remained in force for decades, despite accumulating steps towards a logic of compulsory organization in practice. Belgium's modest and Italy's languishing system, the latter with roots as far back as the Berti Law granting legal recognition to sickness funds in 1886, also fell victim to wartime fascism. Italy went over to a compulsory system under authoritarian auspices in 1943 (Kangas 1991: 64). Unlike the cases of the Low Countries, and regardless of the localist subsidiarity element in Social Catholicism, return to voluntarism was never seriously countenanced in the post-war social insurance settlements of the Italian republic.

By 1960 and into the present, voluntary sickness insurance development among the advanced industrialized countries is a story of Swiss exceptionalism. The Swiss system reached universal coverage by the 1970s, demonstrating that voluntarism need not exclude broad constituencies from social provision. However, figures may overestimate inclusion because coverage for three different kinds of benefits, some for hospitalization only, cannot be mutually distinguished in Swiss administrative records (Kangas 1991: 70). Since the figures are thus difficult to interpret, they have been left out of the descriptive series for voluntary systems in Figure 3.2 starting in the year when the Swiss voluntary regime is the only one remaining.

Coverage has thus on average increased everywhere since the 1930s, for both the sick and the unemployed. Compulsory systems' citizenship focus long distinguished their reach in comparison to that of the narrower membership focus of voluntary programmes. However, intermediate-level institutional variables, such as those of funding, duration, generosity and contributory requirements, also vary within categories of countries with the same institutional tradition. We thus need more specific information as to what extent choices of institutional form for programmes appear to go together with a broader range of programme characteristics besides those of coverage.

Replacement rates of benefits are thus focused on below-average net post-tax benefits paid in four typical situations of income loss for households headed by an industrial worker are here assessed as a share of the industrial worker's wage. Also included here is the percentage share of total programme financing derived from individuals' insurance contributions (as distinct from employers' or the state's contributions). Inclusionary ambitions can also be seen as reflected, albeit more indirectly than by coverage, in the average legal maximum benefit duration (here measured in weeks), as well as qualifying conditions, here measured as the number of weeks for which an industrial worker must have worked in covered employment in order to receive benefits.

Table 3.3 depicts these programme characteristics within unemployment insurance, in 1939 and in 1995, respectively, while Table 3.4 depicts sickness insurance scheme characteristics in the same years. Institutional traditions of voluntarism, compulsory statism and targeting may interact with certain central tendencies towards characteristic levels of coverage,

Table 3.3 Institutional aspects of unemployment insurance, selected OECD countries, 1939 and 1995 (median averages for sub-groups of countries by institutional design)

(a) 1939

Countries	Insurance desgn	Coverage (%)	Net repl. rate (%)	Financing share individs insrd	Duration (weeks)	Qualif. condtn (weeks)
GER, IRL, ITA, UK, USA	Compulsory	61.0	41.0	37.0	17.0	30
BEL, DAN, FIN, FRA, NDR, NOR, SWE, SUI	Voluntary	18.5	28.5	60.0	12.0	28
AUT, NZL	Targeted	n/a	35.0	16.5	Unlimited[a]	10.0
(All, median average)		**39.0**	**34.0**	**49.0**	**15.0**	**26.0**

(b) 1995

Countries	Insurance desgn	Coverage (%)	Net repl. rate (%)	Financing share individs insrd	Duration (weeks)	Qualif. condtn (weeks)
AUT, BEL, CAN, FRA, GER, IRL, ITA, JPN, NDR, NOR, SUI, UK, USA	Compulsory	99.3	58.0	32.2	52.0	26.0
DAN, FIN, SWE	Voluntary	98.4	62.0	17.0	100	26.0
AUS, NZL	Targeted	n/a	35.5	0.0	Unlimited	0.0
(All, median average)		**97.9**	**57.5**	**28.9**	**62.5**	**26.0**

Notes:
In 1939, Australia, Canada and Japan did not yet have any unemployment insurance law in force, and thus have no systems comparable with those of the other fifteen countries included here.
[a] The Austrian programme's twenty-week duration is not possible to meaningfully average with the unlimited duration characterizing the more typical New Zealand programme. Elements of means-testing in the otherwise voluntary programme of Denmark had been removed by 1933.
n/a = Data not applicable

Table 3.4 Institutional aspects of sickness insurance, selected OECD countries, 1939 and 1995 (median averages for sub-groups of countries by institutional design)

(a) 1939

Countries	Insurance desgn	Coverage (%)	Net repl. rate (%)	Financing share individs insrd	Duration (weeks)	Qualif. condtn (weeks)
AUT, FRA, GER, IRL, JPN, NDR, UK, USA	Compulsory	55.0	35.5	47.5	26.0	0.0
BEL, DAN, ITA, SWE, SUI	Voluntary	46.0	24.5	69.5	26.0	9.5
NZL	Targeted	n/a	32.0	0.0	26.0	0.0
(All, median average)		**50.0**	**34.0**	**50.0**	**26.0**	**0.0**

(b) 1995

Countries	Insurance desgn	Coverage (%)	Net repl. rate (%)	Financing share individs insrd	Duration (weeks)	Qualif. condtn (weeks)
AUT, BEL, CAN, DAN, FIN, FRA, GER, IRL, ITA, JPN, NDR, NOR, SWE, UK	Compulsory	85.0	75.5	37.1	52.0	1.5
SUI	Voluntary	n.c.[a]	81.0	50.0	103.0	13.0
AUS, NZL	Targeted	n/a	37.5	0.0	Unlimited	0.0
(All, median average)		**85.0**	**74.0**	**34.7**	**52.0**	**0.0**

Note:

In 1939, Australia, Canada, Finland and the United States did not have any sickness insurance law in force, and thus have no systems comparable with those of the other fourteen countries included here.

[a] Swiss coverage has been estimated at 100% of employees for 1990 and 84% in 1995 – this may reflect administrative changes rather than actual exclusions, and is viewed as non-codeable for purposes of representative comparison.

n/a = not applicable

generosity, duration and programme contribution requirements. Institutional precedents are seen by many researchers as having independent impacts on continued social policy development (see, e.g., Pierson 1994) – voluntarist institutions can thus be expected to go together with lower coverage overall, though more so (as indicated above) in the 1930s than in the 1990s. This institutionalist reasoning may be further confirmed by assessing the share of programme financing derived from individual contributions (either earmarked taxes or membership fees to funds), with high levels of financing individualism (Esping-Andersen 1985) presumed both to characterize voluntarist programmes overall and to go together with lower coverage.

Data on the scope and generosity of insurance provision in Table 3.3 and 3.4 is grouped with respect to whether voluntarism, compulsory state programmes or targeted programmes are in force, to see whether voluntarism is associated not only with lower overall levels of coverage, but also with higher levels of financing individualism, shorter legal benefit durations and higher contribution requirements. Here, high 'financing individualism' could also be expected to be relevant for lowering coverage under voluntarism.

An examination of Table 3.3a indicates that voluntary insurance design and lower coverage were strongly associated within unemployment insurance in 1939. For those countries when voluntarism was in force in 1939, average unemployment insurance coverage was at just under 20 per cent or so of all employees, compared to about triple that share for all those countries where some variant of compulsory insurance programme was in force. Financing individualism also was higher under voluntarism: the share of programme financing derived from individual insurance contributions under voluntarism amounted to more than half of programme income, while amounting (on median average) to only a third of programme incomes under compulsory regimes. Besides being restricted in coverage, as Table 3.3a indicates, voluntary programmes were also below average in terms of benefit generosity and duration. Voluntary programmes did not, however, require (on median average) longer contribution periods than did compulsory programmes, or programmes overall. Targeted unemployment benefits were actually somewhat more generous, also in duration, than those within voluntary programmes, and were closer to (if not yet entirely of) non-contributory design.

By 1995, the voluntary regimes remaining in force are much more collectively financed and have (partly in consequence) become much more inclusive, on average almost as much as compulsory programmes. They are also more somewhat more generous (and are paid out for longer) than benefits in either compulsory programmes as a group or in all programmes overall, with benefit rates now being much higher than those retained under targeted regimes. However, targeted regimes remain the most liberal in now being entirely non-contributory and in providing benefits for as long as need and unemployment continue. Overall, in unemployment insurance design, voluntary institutions limiting universalism also appear to have been accepted by leftist parties in Scandinavia, since these provide excludable benefits for unions running the funds. Within this framework, by increasing state financing, coverage can be increased in the long term – but at the price of exclusion of those who choose not to become members in union-related funds.

For sickness insurance (see Tables 3.4a and 3.4b), coverage appears to be less strongly related to institutional choices between compulsory and voluntary insurance as such. Coverage levels are somewhat lower for countries with voluntary programmes in the 1930s than they are for countries with compulsory programmes, and median coverage levels for compulsory regimes are above the median average overall (while the opposite is true for countries with voluntary regimes). Benefit rate generosity is lower, contribution requirements more strict and financing individualism also higher under voluntarism in the 1930s. However, coverage differences between countries within the voluntarist and compulsory camps are not strong (and, as mentioned, are no longer reliably calculable by the 1990s), and 1930s benefit durations were uniformly low regardless of institutional regime.

By 1995, sickness insurance financing has been collectivized everywhere almost regardless of institutional regime, though the Swiss programme is still more 'individualist' in providing only for social security contributions (half from the insured) rather than for any state contributions. Since voluntary sickness insurance programmes were much fewer from the start, and disappeared more rapidly, variation is restricted on the institutional variable, also weakening conclusions on 'financing individualism'. Reliance on contributions has here more often been the same as relying on obligatory employees' social security contributions, channelled through the tax system and harder not to pay, rather than on membership contributions keeping people out of autonomous funds in the absence of higher state subsidies. Contribution requirements in terms of weeks of prior work are also much less typical for sickness insurance programmes than for unemployment benefits overall. Benefit durations are now, however, longer in the sole voluntary regime in Switzerland than on the overall average, and contribution requirements in terms of weeks of prior work are also still enforced. Formally unlimited duration with non-contributory financing is now (as in unemployment) exclusively the rule in targeted regimes. Benefits are, again, now least generous under targeting.

Taken together, these results indicate that institutional design has some relevance for financing, coverage, generosity, duration and requirements for programme affiliation in social policy, albeit in different ways over time and by the programmes in question. In particular, it appears that political parties may have been able to make much less consistent use of voluntarism to create politically useful 'excludable benefits' among the sick than among the unemployed. The policy recommendations which narratives, numbers and history may bequeath to latterday decision makers are now discussed.

Discussion: voluntary insurance problems and potentials of state-subsidized programmes

Comparisons of statist programme emergence and voluntarist programme mortality under war- and Depression-related duress entails increased institutional and temporal reach in understanding welfare state developments. In sickness insurance, voluntary state-subsidized legislation has been abolished almost everywhere, while surviving to our day for the unemployed in Sweden, Finland and Denmark. The reason for this seems to be that trade unions in these countries, supported by leftist parties, ended up seeing the unemployment insurance system as a source of strength (and thus as a potential power resource) rather than as a liability, which is what the underdeveloped Norwegian voluntary system ended up being seen as by their sister organizations. Sickness insurance, less exclusively linked to unionism from the start, was partly less valuable as an excludable power resource, but was also more linked to national cross-class constituencies, politics and organizing logic – and thus a stronger candidate for long-term nationalization. Interesting axes of further comparison occur between programmes in these countries and consolidating social programmes in developing countries, themselves often at 'new beginnings' with respect to informal civil-societal alternatives.

In practice, targeting and voluntarism have not been entirely mutually exclusive. They are certainly not so in current development policy debate, where voluntary organizations' involvement as programme practicioners has been motivated by actors such as the World Bank on the grounds that community organizations can be more efficient at targeting social provision than can states or donor organizations. Though involving communities in targeting can make for gains in increasing benefits channelled to the poor based on locally available information, potential drawbacks exist. Being delegated as 'targeters' may give administrators incentives to rent-seek. Programmes may also be captured by (not necessarily pro-poor) local elites and targeting may be modified in unforeseen strategic ways to ensure preferential funding; targeted programmes may also experience declines in political support (Conning and Kevane 2002). As the historical facts of the Danish experiment with 'targeted voluntary' sickness insurance from 1892 to the 1930s also demonstrate, the logic of targeting and of voluntarism are in practice very hard to combine with any justice to the autonomy and social composition of voluntary organizations. This should give pause to organizations advocating a combination of the same measures to promote social development in the developing countries today.

What about the costs and benefits of voluntarism itself? Although guardedly, this chapter's author would emphasize that the advantages of voluntarism should not be under-estimated, and that this may favour enacting voluntary state-subsidized programmes if certain conditions are met. State-subsidized sickness and unemployment insurance funds have historically constituted vital 'schools of democracy' in the Nordic countries, not least for working-class constituencies traditionally under-represented in voluntary organizations. Especially if embedded in a broader network of corporatist institutions, voluntary subsidized insurance institutions may constitute sites where 'bridging social capital' (Rothstein and Stolle 2003) can be generated. Participation of union officials in administering state-sanctioned social welfare may bind civil society and the state more closely together – in ways facilitating not only union membership but also social development and the greater overlap of special and general interests. Although coverage was initially limited by voluntarism, it has increased considerably by the 1990s in those countries where it has been retained, with contributory logic also being less strict and benefit rates higher. Political controversies over divisions of responsibility for schemes and definitions of risks to be insured, although by no means ended, have also abated somewhat, indicating that continued voluntarism need not be synonymous with low benefits and coverage nor with narrow interest-group politics.

However, such benefits by no means automatically follow from voluntarism. Policy makers should be particularly warned against the idea that voluntarism constitutes an easy 'stepping stone' to compulsory insurance later, as well against exaggerated visions of budgetary savings. Differences in costs may be minimal if state subsidies are to expand in ways seemingly needed to reach broader inclusion. Four overall conditions to be met are summarized here, which policy makers should keep in mind when considering implementation of voluntary state-subsidized social insurance.

First, *administrative capacity* on the part of both states and voluntary organizations may crucially impact also voluntarist programme success, and should be carefully assessed before implementation. It cannot necessarily be assumed that voluntary organizations will be more 'efficient' at programme implementation than states if membership depth, administrative resources, records and staffing are lacking. Non-synergy of administrative capacities may be exacerbated if there is no common conception of the purpose to which that capacity should be committed.

Secondly, *national organizations of insurance funds* may be strengthened by state subsidies, either directly or indirectly. Such national organizations of funds may come to constitute special interests which need to be negotiated with in the continued course of the programme's governance. Voluntary organizations may thus have views of their own on how issues of administration and inclusion should be solved, and disagreements in this respect with state elites may undermine the programme's legitimacy.

Disagreements in themselves need not be problematic, since interest-group politics are ineluctably part of political life, but the eventuality of voluntarism's leading to such politics being strengthened may constitute an obstacle to later change which decision makers may need to make political allowances for. While probably necessary to attain economies of scope in provision, national organizations of funds complicate negotiations over the future of any system. As evident particularly in the history of Swedish and Danish sickness insurance, such organizations tend to take on a political life of their own. If they are to be genuinely autonomous from direct state control (which may be desirable, and certainly is a part of the strict definition of the NGO, a category of organizations substantially overlapping with that of voluntary organizations writ large), their representatives may also argue for maintaining an existing order of subsidy even when subsequent parliamentary majorities would wish to see a new one. For better or worse, special-interest politics may broaden at the expense of parliamentary deliberation.

Thirdly, voluntarism will (exceptions notwithstanding) tend to entail inherent *institutional limits* to coverage (albeit not necessarily to benefit generosity), as well as strengthening possibly onerous contributory financing, in ways which economic under-development may exacerbate – and also invite political criticism which needs to be addressed. As the statistical results above indicate, unemployment insurance coverage can be severely limited by voluntarism, although sickness insurance development does not support a similar conclusion. Agrarian employment makes for further limitations, and fund have had problems maintaining membership in the absence of state subsidies when economic crises struck. Leftist parties may also see a voluntarist order as legitimate in tough times, as long as unions running it can be strengthened by the responsibility. Agrarian interests may also do so if they are not expected to subsidize other groups' unemployment or sickness risks. Such arrangements might, however, lead to further conflict about whether the voluntarist order sufficiently takes into account agrarian and/or employer interests, and thus intensify conflicts over legitimacy. Compulsory programmes are no legitimacy panaceas for disagreements about inclusion either, especially if these programmes are (through 'horizontal' or 'vertical' restrictions) in practice also more compulsory for some groups than for others.

Fourthly, it should be remembered that issues of *administration and inclusion* only partly overlap with broader issues of democracy and representation, while still being intimately linked to them – the absence of, or limits to, democracy are difficult to compensate by increasing either voluntarism or inclusion. The benefit–cost balance of voluntarism thus may depend partly on a prior level of institutionalization of democracy, which means that democratization is an important precondition for successful voluntarism rather than the other way around. As Finnish history in the 1920s and

1930s in particular indicates, an institutional order for nominal participation in welfare administration from below cannot generate democracy if the state is not doing enough from above. In labour policy, responsibility for employment exchanges has historically been a task for which voluntary organizations appear to be poorly suited, at least while running systems of 'excludable benefits' in ways permitting public oversight. This should probably give pause to those hoping to give voluntary organizations extensive responsibilities for implementing public policy functions beyond the provision of members' benefits.

A complicated interplay of public, civil and private organizations runs throughout the social landscapes of both the global North and the global South. Criticism against 'one-size-fits-all' recommendations to developing countries, particularly of the unconditionally voluntarism-friendly Third Way variety, may be the only 'best practice'. If combined at all, state and voluntary provision may need to aim for complementarity with clear jurisdictions, uniting the 'best' of both (unobstructed free organization and fairly extensive subsidies from the entire social comity).

Notes

1 Quoted from *De la Démocratie en Amérique* [1835–40], 1, in 'Tocqueville, Alexis de', *The Concise Oxford Dictionary of Quotations,* ed. Elizabeth Knowles. Oxford: Oxford University Press, 2001, available at http://www.oxfordreference.com/views/ENTRY.html?subview=Main&entry=t91.002397.

2 The sample includes Australia, Austria, Belgium, Canada, Denmark, Finland, France, (West) Germany, Ireland, Italy, Japan, the Netherlands, New Zealand, Norway, Sweden, Switzerland, and the UK, as well as the USA (sometimes represented in codings by a 'typical industrial state,' most often Michigan). Comparability problems entail exclusion of states with post-war non- or semi-democratic regimes such as Spain, Portugal, Greece, Turkey, Mexico, as well as the 'reforming socialist economies' of Eastern Europe. Countries with populations of under 1 million (for example, Iceland and Luxembourg) are excluded since they are much less autonomous as states from the international environment.

3 The account draws heavily on Carroll and Johansson (2000), where source documentation is more extensive.

4 This database includes information about coverage, benefit levels, qualifying conditions and financing of four social insurance programmes (old-age pensions, work accident insurance, sickness and unemployment insurance) for eighteen OECD countries in 'census years' since 1930, every fifth year starting in 1950. Coverage, the major factor focused on, is assessed as the percentage share of the labour force or of all employees who are formally entitled to benefits in situations of income loss – provided or subsidized by the state, or (alternatively) simply extensively regulated by the state.

5 Information is lacking on whether the German sickness insurance programme, formally remaining in force in 1947, included provisions for means-testing, as well as whether the Italian voluntary system of 1930–9 tried to do so. It has been assumed that no means test was used, and coverage levels under these systems were thus in the German case simply was assumed to be the same as in 1939).

Bibliography

Alapuro, R. (1988) *State and Revolution in Finland*. Berkeley: University of California Press.

Alestalo, M. and Uusitalo, H. (1986) 'Finland'. In P. Flora (ed.), *Growth to Limits: The Western European Welfare States since World War II*. Berlin: Walter de Gruyter: 197–292.

Betænkning (1887) *Øvervejelse av spørsmaalene om Sygekassernes Ordning og om Arbejdernes Sikring mod Følgerne af Ulykkestilæflde under Arbejdet*. Copenhagen. (Considerations on the Issues of the Organisation of Sickness Insurance Funds and of the Insurance of Workers with regard to the Consequences of Work Accidents.)

Bjørnson, Ø. (2001) 'The Social Democrats and the Norwegian Welfare State: Some Perspectives'. *Scandinavian Journal of History*, 26(3): 197–223.

Bjørnson, Ø. and Haavet, I.E. (1994) 'Arbeidsledighetsforsikringen: Et tidlig norsk eksperiment'. (Unemployment Insurance: An Early Norwegian Experiment.) In Bjørnson and I.E. Haavet, *Langsomt ble Landet et Velferdssamfunn: Trygdens Historie 1894–1994*. (*Slowly the Country Became a Welfare Society: The History of Social Insurance, 1894–1994*.) Oslo: Ad Notam Gyldendal: 81–103.

Carroll, E. (1997) 'Samspelet mellan 'aktiv' och 'passiv' arbetsmarknadspolitik'. (The Interplay Between 'Active' and 'Passive' Labour Market Policy.) In S. Ackum-Agell and J. Hassler (eds.), *Tretton inlägg om arbetslöshe*. (*Thirteen contributions on unemployment*.) Stockholm: LO: 73–92.

Carroll, E. (1999) *Emergence and Structuring of Social Insurance Institutions*. SOFI Dissertation Series, 38. Edsbruk: Akademitryck.

Carroll, E. and Johansson, P. (2000) 'Mutual Benefit Societies, Institutional Design, and the Emergence of Public Sickness Insurance Programs: A Comparative Analysis of Six European Nations'. Paper presented at the Foundation for International Social Security Studies Meetings, Sigtuna, June.

Coleman, J. (1990) *Foundations of Social Theory*. Cambridge, Mass.: Belknap Press of Harvard University Press.

Conning, J. and Kevane, M. (2002) 'Community-Based Targeting Mechanisms for Social Safety Nets: A Critical Review'. *World Development*, 30(3): 375–94.

Edebalk, P. (2000) 'Emergence of a Welfare State: Social Insurance in Sweden in the 1910s'. *Journal of Social Policy*, 29(4): 537–51.

Edwards M. and Hulme, D. (1996) 'Too Close for Comfort? The Impact of Official Aid on Nongovernmental Organizations'. *World Development*, 24(6): 961–73.

Esping-Andersen, G. (1985) 'Power and Distributional Regimes'. *Politics and Society*, 14(2): 223–56.

Evans, P. (1996) 'Government Action, Social Capital and Development: Reviewing the Evidence on Synergy'. *World Development*, 24(6): 1119–32.

Finnish Parliament (various years) *Official Protocols of Parliamentary Sessions and of Government Bills* (VPP-series, Valtiopäivien Pöytäkirjat, and VM-series, Valtionministeriö). Helsinki: Eduskunta.

Fox, J. (1996) 'How Does Civil Society Thicken? The Political Construction of Social Capital in Rural Mexico'. *World Development*, 24(6): 1089–1103.

Hoddinott, J. (2002) 'Participation and Poverty Reduction: An Analytical Framework and Overview of the Issues'. *Journal of African Economies*, 11(1): 146–68.

Johansson, P. (2003) *Fast i det Förflutna: Institutioner och Intressen i Svensk Sjukförsäkringspolitik 1891–1931*. (Stuck in the Past: Institutions and Interests in Swedish Sickness Insurance Policy, 1891–1931.) Lund: Arkiv.

Kangas, O. (1991) *The Politics of Social Rights: Studies on the Dimensions of Sickness Insurance in OECD Countries*. SOFI Dissertation Series, 19. Edsbruk: Akademitryck.

Knowles, E. (ed.) (2002) *The Oxford Dictionary of Modern Quotations*. Oxford: Oxford University Press, available at http://www.oxfordreference.com/views/.

Korpi, W. (2001) 'Contentious Institutions: An Augmented Rational-Actor Analysis of the Origins and Path Dependency of Welfare State Institutions in Western Countries', *Rationality and Society*, 13(2): 235–83.

Korpi, W. and Palme, J. (1998) 'The Paradox of Redistribution and the Strategy of Equality: Welfare State Institutions, Inequality and Poverty in Western Countries'. *American Sociological Review*, 63(5): 661–87.

Kuhnle, S. (1978) 'The Beginnings of the Nordic Welfare States: Similarities and Differences'. *Acta Sociologica*, 21, Supplement: 9–36.

Kuhnle, S. (1986) 'Norway'. In P. Flora (ed.), *Growth to Limits: The Western European Welfare States since World War II*. Berlin: Walter de Gruyter: 117–96.

Lundberg, U. and Åmark, K. (2001) 'Social Rights and Social Security: The Swedish Welfare State, 1900–2000'. *Scandinavian Journal of History*, 26(3): 157–76.

Lundström, T. and Svedberg, L. (2003) 'The Voluntary Sector in a Social Democratic Welfare State: The Case of Sweden'. *Journal of Social Policy*, 32(2): 217–38.

Nørby-Johansen, L. (1986) 'Denmark'. In P. Flora (ed.), *Growth to Limits: The Western European Welfare States since World War II*. Berlin: Walter de Gruyter: 293–381.

Olson, M. (1965) *The Logic of Collective Action: Public Goods and the Theory of Groups*. Cambridge, Mass.: Harvard University Press.

Olson, S. (1986) 'Sweden'. In P. Flora (ed.), *Growth to Limits: The Western European Welfare States since World War II*. Berlin: Walter de Gruyter: 1–116.

Ostrom, E. (1996) 'Crossing the Great Divide: Coproduction, Synergy and Development'. *World Development*, 24(6): 1073–87.

Pedersen, P. (1981) *Økonomiske Effekter av Arbejdsløshedsforsikring. (Economic Effects of Unemployment Insurance.)* Copenhagen: Tekniske Førlag.

Pierson, P. (1994). *Dismantling the Welfare State? Reagan, Thatcher and the Politics of Retrenchment*. Cambridge: Cambridge University Press.

Putnam, R. (1993) *Making Democracy Work: Civic Traditions in Modern Italy*. Princeton: Princeton University Press.

Rothstein, B. (1989) 'Marxism, Institutional Analysis, and Working Class Power: The Swedish Case'. *Politics and Society*, 18(3): 317–45.

Rothstein, B. (2001) 'Social Capital in the Social Democratic Welfare State'. *Politics and Society*, 29(2): 207–41.

Rothstein, B. and Stolle, D. (2003) 'Introduction: Social Capital in Scandinavia'. *Scandinavian Political Studies*, 26(1): 1–26.

Samuelsson, K. (1968) *From Great Power to Welfare State: 300 Years of Swedish Social Development*. London: George Allen & Unwin.

Toft, C. (1995) 'State Action, Trade Unions and Voluntary Unemployment Insurance in Great Britain, Germany and Scandinavia, 1900–34'. *European Economic Review*, 39(3–4):565–74.

4

Empowering Social Policy: The Role of Social Care Services in Modern Welfare States

Anneli Anttonen

Care 'going public?'

Care is a growing concern in welfare states and an ever-more frequent object of social policy reforms. Every post-industrial society is having to confront anew how to support families and individuals and organize the care of those who need regular help, particularly small children and those adults whose disabilities are linked to age or illness. Long-established forms of informal care are being rapidly undermined by economic and social change. Families are in particular no more self-evident care providers in the way they used to be. Social networks based on kinship have fragmented and even become transnational (Vuorela 2002). It is becoming more and more common for older people to live alone. The spread of female employment outside the home, above all, has changed the division of labour between the sexes. Unpaid work done by women at home and in the local community can no longer be treated as a resource to be drawn on freely.

The expression of 'reproduction going public' was coined by Helga Maria Hernes (1987) in the mid-1980s. By the slogan she implied that the division of reproductive work between the family and the rest of society had radically changed during the twentieth century. In feminist scholarship on social policy, reproduction had become one of the key concepts in the 1970s; feminist theorists made explicit that women's unpaid work was decisive in reproducing whole societies. In this chapter, I will use the concept of 'care' instead of 'social or human reproduction'. Care is one important element in social reproduction through which societies not only reproduce themselves but also set up standards and norms for reproductive activities such as child and elder care. Many of these standards and norms are gendered, as feminist research also has shown

In some countries, care has 'gone public' only to a very limited amount, while in others the state and/or other formal institutions such as welfare organizations have assumed a wide responsibility for caring activities. Yet, there is no doubt that in all societies there is a need to expand services linked to care. There are a number of reasons for this development:

- *Changes in the labour market*: Capitalism needs cheap labour – i.e. women in the labour market; employers no longer have any particular reason to pay 'family wages' to men; the mobility of labour is *estranging* the generations from each other. All these factors have now become more marked in a global labour market.
- *Changes in demography*: Children are fewer than before and the care of children does not tie women to the home for decades; old people are numerous and the services they require cannot be organized without society's interventions – especially when old people have fewer and fewer children and divorce is dissolving inter-generational obligations.
- *Changes in democracy*: Women participate more actively in politics and they push issues that are important for women, such as family and care policy.
- *Changes in consumption*: The value of domestic work is declining; capitalism creates intensively new needs, the satisfaction of which requires increased income that again means that dual-earner households become more and more common.
- *Changes in values and norms*: The stress on individualism is pushing 'familism' aside; the growth of gender equality and female paid employment is reducing informal care resources. All these changes mean that familial and inter-generational obligations in the field of care are weakening.

The changes listed above have affected primarily the 'Western' family institution. As care has been 'going public', family-based care arrangements have had to give way to other kind of arrangements. This does not mean that families no longer constitute the foundation on which the Western way of life is built. Social reproduction must to a critical extent take place in the home (or in informal settings), for neither the state nor any other formal institutions have the resources to take care of large numbers of children and elderly around the clock. The fact that family-based care arrangements have given ground means rather that social reproduction and care are no longer left solely in the hands of families. Supporting care requires services produced outside the home and, for at least part of the population, financial assistance.

However, acceptance has only very slowly arisen for the idea that responsibility for the care of children and elderly or infirm parents can belong to someone other than family members, and in particular female family members. State or public service provision and family care are sometimes seen as alternatives, even as opponents. It is often thought that when alternatives are available, families will withdraw, and services will then replace family obligations. Thus, as Daatland (2001: 18) has noted, public service provision is often seen to represent a moral risk for society.

Care is a social policy issue that raises moral and political passions. Public opinion tends to swing back and forth between two extreme positions, one stressing the responsibility of individuals and families for their own welfare and the other expecting the wider society to take responsibility for at least some aspects of care (Midre 1995: 115–35). In Scandinavian societies, public opinion has given strong support to the latter view ever since the idea of a universal welfare state became gradually institutionalized. The idea of universal service provision was brought into public political discourse by Swedish social democrats at the beginning of the twentieth century and it was closely connected to the promotion of gender equality and social solidarity (Myrdal and Myrdal 1935). 'Universalism' means that services such as education, health care and social care are designed for all people instead of those in greatest need and that citizens can use them without any stigma. Universalism also includes the idea of free-of-charge services or services strongly subsidized by central or local governments.

Care arrangements are an integral part of the wider order and structure of a society. The norms and assumptions that govern care policy are products of gendered, political, cultural and religious norms (Pfau-Effinger 1998). This again explains why the extent to which the family is responsible for the care of its members varies considerably from one country to another and why the provision of care services varies so much even within Western Europe (Anttonen, Baldock and Sipilä 2003). At one extreme, there are countries such as many Asian countries, where families right down to the present day have had wide responsibility for care; at the other extreme there are countries such as the Scandinavian countries, where the public authorities have assumed a very broad responsibility for the welfare of small children as well as for adult people in need of care and social support.

In this chapter, my aim is to describe and evaluate the processes by which care is 'going public'. In this evaluation, I will pay a special attention to the field of public policy of care. To make a distinction between *public policy of care* and *informal care*, that is the care provided at home, a theoretical term of 'social' care proves very useful. Through the concepts of 'social care' and 'social care services', I will underline the role of the state and local governments as well as other formal service providers. When estimating such a policy area as care is, however, one cannot take into account all care needs and all care situations. I will restrict my review to social care and social care services linked to the care of young children (child care) and to the care of elderly persons (elder care). Although my focus is on formal care providers, it is of great importance to look at changing boundaries between the private and public responsibilities. Indeed, care as a concept comprises care giving work done both in informal and in formal settings (Daly and Lewis 2000).

When estimating the processes by which care is 'going public', it is important first to describe the complexity of care provision. This will be done in the following section. After that, I will briefly look at the history of social care service provision. The phenomenon of 'social care' is then located in a comparative framework, better to understand national patterns and national differences in the public policy of social care. My fourth and final task is to describe more precisely the Scandinavian 'social care' model. All themes are discussed in such a way that both gendered assumptions and outcomes are taken into consideration. My overall aim is to make explicit that social care of young children and older people is closely linked to social policies. Without mapping the territory of care arrangements, we cannot properly understand the ways in which modern welfare states are operating, nor the demands social policies are confronting in trying to meet increasing care needs while the population is 'greying' and more and more women are taking part in paid labour.

In some countries, the process of care 'going public' has already reached its limits. In many of the Western welfare states demands for retrenchment have grown more insistent and welfare state cutbacks have taken place (Pierson 2001). In countries where care has 'gone public' to the greatest degree, such as in Finland and Sweden, for instance, governments have carried out reforms that have shrunk the scope of public service provision and limited citizens' access to some social care services by tightening eligibility rules or/and by raising the service fees that used earlier to be nominal ones (Anttonen 2001; Palme *et al.* 2002; Hort 2003). All this means that forerunners and late-comers in the public policy of care are facing the same problem: how to produce care in a situation where neither family-based care nor state-led social care service provision can be the only solution.

It is evident that innovations in the field of care will more and more often represent new welfare mixes, where there are no clear borderlines between private and public responsibilities. This is true even in the Scandinavian societies that from the late 1950s and 1960s strongly relied on public service provision in their social care policies. Policy recommendations and reforms based on new mixed modes of care are, however, difficult both to construct and to govern. It also seems to be almost impossible to break the umbilical cord between care and women as the main providers of care both at home and in paid labour.

Mapping the territory: different modes of social care provision

My first task is to clarify the complexity of care provision. I will begin by defining what 'social care' is about, and what it is not about. 'Social care' can be identified as something other than professional health care. According to Knijn and Kremer (1997: 328–30) 'care includes the provision of daily social, psychological, emotional and physical attention to people' who need care: the need to be cared for can be temporal or constant. Knijn and Kremer go on to argue that '[C]are can be provided by paid or unpaid work, on the basis of an agreement or voluntarily, and it can be given professionally or on the basis of moral obligation'. Daly and Lewis (1998: 6–7) suggest a similar approach, but seek definitions that will allow the concept of care to serve as an analytical tool for understanding the welfare state. For them, care is a multi-dimensional concept with three aspects meriting particular emphasis. The first is care as *labour*. Highlighting the labour aspect emphasizes 'care' as a verb and the 'carers' as actors. The second dimension of the concept sets care within normative framework of *obligations* and *responsibilities*. Care is not like other work or labour because it is often initiated and provided under conditions of social and/or familial responsibility. In their third dimension they see care as an *activity with costs*, both financial and emotional, which extends across private/public boundaries.

International comparisons (e.g. Anttonen and Sipilä 1996; Rostgaard and Fridberg 1998; Daly 2001; Anttonen, Baldock and Sipilä 2003) have shown that there are surprisingly large national differences in the scale, scope and targeting of formal social care services as well as in the operational practices used and the justifications adopted. One and the same function may be arranged through services provided by government, by private businesses, by voluntary organizations and associations or by various combinations of these public and private sources. Social care is particularly likely to exhibit this variety of form and source, as Table 4.1 shows. For example, carers and care recipients in some welfare systems may be offered cash benefits or tax concessions instead of services. Alternatively, a whole system may rely largely on social care being provided by relatives, family members, friends and neighbours, supported and encouraged by state policy to different degrees and in various ways.

Simplifying matters somewhat, we can start from the fact that care is produced in homes, in different kinds of welfare associations (charities, mutual aid societies), in public organizations and in markets. In households and homes social care is usually the responsibility of *female* family members. The rationales that drive it are complex: tradition, religion, reciprocity and love. Where families fail in terms of these codes of responsibility, or seek support from other sources such as local government, shame and stigma may follow. Family-based informal caring has, however, gone through major changes. There are societies whose social care policy is based on family-first priorities and societies where the role of the family has been thoroughly renegotiated. Even in Scandinavian welfare societies the renegotiated care pattern is primarily based on female labour inputs. The process of care 'going public' does not mean that women are freed from care work once and for all, but rather that the division of paid and unpaid care work in these societies has changed. Although care work is increasingly done in the formal care sector, there still are women who take care of young children and elderly persons.

Often social care is the 'duty' of religious or other value-based communities. Members provide care for each other but there are also welfare associations providing care to 'strangers'. Giving help brings moral and psychic

Table 4.1 Production modes of social care

Modes of provision	Resource allocation	Care provider	User	Care worker
Informal caring	Reciprocity, love, responsibility	Immediate community, household, family	Member of immediate community	(Female) family member, unpaid friend
Voluntary and charity work, volunteering	Collection, work contribution, mutual responsibility	Charity associations and suchlike	Person approved for help	Unpaid volunteer
Welfare organizations, NGOs	Collection, membership fees, public subsidies	Non-profit or for-profit welfare organizations	Consumer, customer	Paid or semi-paid (professional or semi-professional) worker
Commercial service producers	Service charges, public subsidies	Company, for-profit welfare organizations	Consumer, customer	Professional or semi-professional paid worker
Public authorities (state and local governments)	Taxation, income transfers, service fees	Local governments and suchlike, sub-contractors	Citizen (resident), customer, consumer	Professional or semi-professional paid worker

Source: Sipilä, Anttonen and Baldock (2003: 13), with some further developments by Anttonen for this chapter.

reward and even commercially or politically useful publicity to individuals and organizations. It raises the status of the people who act as helpers and helps to sustain forms of social order and cohesion. Local voluntary organizations may or may not be supported by the wider community through state subsidies or joint work with public agencies. The motives for care work might, however, be the same: moral and psychic reward. In the field of charities and welfare organizations female care takers are over-represented.

In market-based provision, social care is a commodity exchanged for money or for other goods. Commodity exchange is based on contracts and it can take place between strangers. Prudent people may prepare for their future needs by accumulating savings or taking out care insurance, and inequalities of income are likely to be reflected in the quantity and quality of care. Market-based provision of care has in some countries created new job opportunities for women in particular; unfortunately market-driven social care provision has most often meant an increase in low-paid jobs.

Finally, social care is frequently a statutory duty of local authorities. Such provision often has historical roots in public poor relief. More universal and modern forms of social care help integrate the local community and legitimate local government and politics. Local government may receive support from the central state, usually finance to run social care services. The growth of public social care services has meant a gradual 'feminization' of welfare states, and a majority of those working in education, health and social services are women.

Last but not least, we should also pay attention to care work that does not easily appear in statistics or other official documents. A considerable (and an increasing) amount of care work is being done by low-paid workers, often migrant women, in private households (see Anderson 2000). Hochschild (2000) introduced the term global care chain to categorize the phenomenon related to the globalization of care. In the first instance, there are those time-poor and money-rich people who need someone to take care of their children or adult relatives when they are working. Secondly, there are a lot of women in poor countries who badly need money (being money-poor) to keep their family and raise their children. These women move to rich countries to work – documented or undocumented – as domestic servants or nannies. I do not evaluate the role and growing importance of this part of care work in this chapter.

Most care is produced by complex and changing combinations of these sources and motives. From individuals' point of view the most important thing is that there are care resources available and to be used when in need, and that access to these care resources does not mean a loss of personal and financial autonomy. In modern societies, the 'care deficit' represents a new social risk for citizens and societies. There have always been people who have not had any family or kin to turn on when in need of care or livelihood, or people who have had no financial resources to pay for care. In a modern society and welfare state, one should have a right to be cared for in need of help and attendance: care should be an inseparable part of our well-being and personal welfare.

Social care services in historical context: mean, lean and local

Social care services have grown mainly out of the poor relief tradition and may still carry some features of the poor law, such as means- and income-testing. Local administrations were originally responsible for poor relief measures; accommodation had to be arranged for those people who were supported neither by kin nor by industrial patrons. Residential institutions proved to be an important means of dealing with such individuals; they were created essentially to allow relatively small numbers of 'carers' to manage relatively large numbers of needy, as well as to gather together categories of people for study and treatment according to whatever were the prevailing views of the time and place. Institutional care for deviants also tended to come under the jurisdiction of local administration and it was often centred in the same institutions as the care of vulnerable persons (Anttonen, Baldock and Sipilä 2003).

Locally administered poor relief systems underwent a differentiation process beginning in the nineteenth century, with different categories of poor being created. Children, criminals and handicapped persons were sent to separate institutions. Eventually only old people were left in the poor house and this was later developed into the old-age home-type of institution. The timetable for this differentiation, however, varied considerably from one country to another as shown in a number of social histories of poor relief and social services.

If locally administered poor relief forms one root of modern 'social care', then another is a charitable poor relief. In the first half of the nineteenth century care of the poor and vulnerable people interested numerous organizations. Charities and later other kinds of welfare associations as well as mutual aid societies, which in many cases were more or less explicitly women's organizations, took the initiative in arranging care for the most vulnerable members of society. Often their work was motivated by religious commitment, but educational, feminist and moral ideals were also involved. Through these associations, women were creating new public spaces and professional methods of providing help and care.

The work of charities and welfare organizations in all its diversity constituted a foundation for the differentiation process of poor relief practices. Many of these organizations specialized in working with some target group, such as children, prostitutes or poor single mothers. The differentiation process was accelerated by the growth of the social sciences. Scientific conceptions of social problems served as a new basis on which professional knowledge could be developed and implemented through charity work. Care of older people did not, however, turn easily into a professionally and scientifically led field of action. When comparing social care with other elements of social policy, the development of social care services has been slow in all industrial societies.

I would argue that it has rarely been possible to turn care into large-scale social policy issues in the same way as has been done with, for example, monetary income transfers and industrial health and safety. It has been easier to mobilize trade unions and labour parties behind demands relating to social insurance, and later other political groupings gave their support to the such developments. Social insurance is based nearly everywhere on laws, and functions as a system on the national level. Users of social care services are individually assessed, entitlements to social care are needs-tested and means-tests are often used. It is typical of social care services that they have remained services produced in local settings with no clear national regulations. This is especially the case for care services for older and disabled persons. The only exception here is pre-school system for young children.

There are several reasons for the slowness of social care service development. Perhaps one reason is that social care depends on human work and takes place in a personal relationship (Knijn and Kremer 1997). With the elderly there is a special problem because of the enormous variation in care needs. One individual needs the cleaning of her home, another needs medical help and assistance with shopping. It is therefore no cause for wonder that there is no country in the world where older people have unlimited access to social care services. The extensive socialization of care is also hindered by expense, costs being fundamentally related to the fact that it is labour-intensive work. Looking after young children and dependent older people are expensive activities that have become relatively more expensive over time, because they are areas where technical efficiency and economies of scale are very difficult to achieve.

Another reason for the slowness of social services' development lies in cultural norms and expectations. The restriction of social care to poor relief was a self-evident part of nineteenth-century social policy, which was based on the family model upheld by the male-breadwinner/worker ideology. In Pateman's interpretation (1989: 187) the male-breadwinner/female housewife model was first established in nineteenth-century Britain. A 'worker' became a man who had an economically dependent wife to take care of his daily needs and to look after his home and children, and eventually also his and her parents. By the end of the nineteenth century there was a powerful familistic undercurrent flowing through social policy, although social insurance, which had developed separately from poor relief, actually strengthened individualism and a breaking away from the patriarchal family and factory system on the one hand, and from the extended family on the other hand.

Social policy founded on the male-breadwinner ideology nevertheless allowed certain tasks to slip out of the compass of the family. In the course of its expansion health care began to take some of the responsibility for care of the elderly, since no clear boundary could be drawn between health care and social care: it has always been possible to designate old people needing care as sick. As a central institution in society, education also performs a care task during the time children are at school. In many countries pre-school has come to form an almost all-day day-care institution. The care load of families has also been crucially lightened by old-age pensions and the associated benefits by which elderly and disabled citizens may buy the social care services and support that they need.

Although the history of social care services can be described as being slow, mean and local, there are some distinctive aspects of social care development in different societies. Three main dimensions of change are revealed in the histories of modern industrial societies:

- A long-term historical dimension in which an increasing proportion of the care functions of a society are removed from the entirely private domestic economy of the household towards a greater overlap with the *formal economy of the market, the voluntary and charitable sector and the state.* The slogan of care 'going public' describes best this process.
- A dimension along which publicly funded or provided care services move from being entitlements that are available to families, or to individuals because of their role or status within the family, to becoming *services* that are available simply on the basis of individual citizenship. This process is related to the *individualization of social care.*
- A dimension along which publicly funded or provided care services move from being selective, usually in terms of income, or contingent upon some form of behaviour, often labour market participation, to their being genuinely *universal* in availability and take-up. This is the process of *universalization.*

These dimensions of change and development can be combined to generate a three-dimensional understanding of the evolution of social care, shown in Figure 4.1 (Anttonen, Sipilä and Baldock 2003: 173).

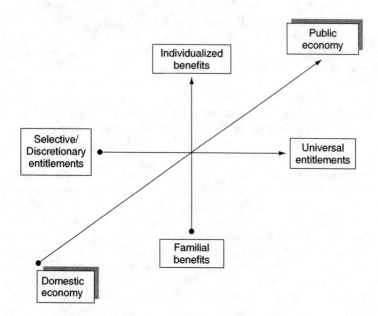

Figure 4.1 Dimensions of change in social care

In principle, Figure 4.1 creates eight segments or categories into which care provision might be placed. At one extreme are the discretionary, charitable handouts more typical of nineteenth-century philanthropy and intended to encourage families to attend to their needs in ways more acceptable to the donor; at the other is public, professional help provided to individuals in proportion to their need and entirely independently of their household or family circumstances. However, because countries' social care systems are highly segmented and differentiated, no nation's care arrangements can be placed at one single conjuncture of these three intersecting dimensions of change. Different aspects of a nation's care arrangements tend to be positioned at different points.

Some social care services are highly valued and are readily turned to when there is need; others are seen almost entirely negatively and are used only when no other sources of help is available. This difference may be characterized as the difference between services of first and last resort. Public services are not always those of last resort, although in many countries public social services even today carry the label of stigma and shame. An important distinction appears to be whether they are simply modern versions of previously selective, poor law-based provision rather than formerly 'middle-class' market-based services made public and universal.

When selective social services begin to reach the whole population, their nature changes. The function of modern social service is not to help people at the bottom of society with their individual troubles but to fulfil a *positive function towards respected members of the society*. The task of social welfare is thus constructed in a positive way to make it a service. However, it may not be possible to turn all that is included in social welfare into a service for all citizens; some social services such as social work have a controlling function in a society. Against this background day care for children seems to be by its nature a very special type of social care service; governments and the interest groups that represent them usually have a strong national interest in the upbringing of children, who are going to become the workforce and are an investment in the future (Esping-Andersen 2002; Mahon 2002).

Today, most European societies want to promote the labour market participation of mothers with small children, so the outputs of social care are very valuable. In the case of children, they have to do with the very reproduction of society itself. In the case of older people, the material benefit to the wider society is harder to discern. Although social care services have largely remained local and their development has been characterized by reluctance and slowness, some of the services have achieved a legitimate and stable position in the entirety of the welfare state. Yet in times of major social and political change, care arrangements can be among the first aspects of welfare provision to be questioned and 'reformed'. It is often argued that the status of social care services is related to their close association with the history of local social welfare institutions (e.g., Higgins 1981; Stjernø 1995). It really seems to be more difficult to develop a social service society than a social insurance society (Anttonen 1997).

Social services expenses in a comparative framework: differences among OECD countries

Current patterns of globalization in politics, economics and culture and the growing movements of people across borders have raised the significance of comparative social research, a field that has a long history in social policy analysis. Earlier comparative welfare state research was largely a matter of explaining differences in development between welfare states by seeking correlations between overall welfare expenditure and structural and political variables. The aim was to advance a 'grand theory' of welfare state development. More recent comparative research has, according to Clasen (1999), also begun to investigate 'the causes of policy changes within social policy components or programmes, such as health care, pensions or social care arrangements' (Clasen 1999: 2–3). Although there is a growing interest in comparative social policy knowledge, comparative studies on social care arrangements are rare. There are several reasons for this situation.

Anttonen and Sipilä (1996) have noticed that there is still no agreement in the comparative debate on welfare states on what count as social (care) services. This has to do with concepts and naming. The same service comes under different fields of administration in different countries, and the distinguishing line between health care and social care services as well as between educational and social services is not always clear. Secondly, statistical principles vary in the absence of any far-reaching standardization for social care services. A third problem arises from the fact that in some countries access is seen as a social right while in some others it is followed by shame and stigma. It is nonetheless of great importance to compare national social care models, and try to find answers to the questions of why there are such wide country differences in providing social (care) services. Table 4.2 can provide a crude understanding of differences in financing social services in OECD countries.

All countries and all kinds of welfare states use more money on income transfers than on social services, however, some countries do allocate a considerable amount of public funding to social services. Table 4.2 shows the distribution of social service expenses in twenty-six OECD countries. The differences are remarkable, with relatively high figures in the Nordic countries (Denmark, Sweden, Norway, Finland, Iceland), and some Continental European countries (France, the Netherlands, Germany) in the next tier. The lowest figures can be found in New Zealand, Turkey, Belgium, Korea, Mexico and the USA. Low investment in social services are obviously found in countries whose social expenses are generally low and also in those countries where

Table 4.2 Social services[a] expenses, selected OECD countries, 1998, per cent of GDP

Country	Social services as % of GDP	Country	Social services as % of GDP
Australia	1.2	Luxembourg	0.9
Austria	2.0	Mexico	0.3
Belgium	0.3	Netherlands	1.7
Denmark	5.2	New Zealand	0.1
Finland	3.0	Norway	4.7
France	1.9	Portugal	0.6
Germany	1.5	Slovak Republic	0.5
Greece	1.0	Spain	0.4
Iceland	3.2	Sweden	5.4
Ireland	0.5	Switzerland	0.8
Italy	0.5	Turkey	0.2
Japan	0.6	UK	1.3
Korea	0.3	USA	0.3

Note:
[a] Social services: aggregate public expenditure on services for the elderly and disabled people and family services as a percentage of GDP.

Source: OECD (2002).

social care is considered a private matter for families and individuals. The only exception among the low investors is Belgium, a country known for its well-developed public child care. Presumably Belgian child care costs are counted in the category of 'education' instead of 'social services'. Because of the unestablished status of social services, however, it is possible that expenses may not always be counted in a consistent way in international statistics.

Dong-Ho (2001) has compared public expenditure on income transfers and social services in fifteen OECD countries in 1994. Table 4.3 is based on his data and shows how the proportions of transfers and services differ in the countries compared. In Norway, for instance, the funds used for transfers are three times larger than those used on services, but in Belgium almost all the public welfare expenditure is invested in transfers. There are high proportions of income transfers in several Northern and Continental European countries and low proportions in the countries well known for their smaller welfare expenses. Social service expenses, however, are high only in four Northern European countries but generally low, even in the otherwize high-expense welfare states of Continental Europe. Once again we seem to see the classic difference between the 'Scandinavian' and 'Central European' welfare models. Iceland is a special case, with rather low income transfer expenses but high social services expenses.

Table 4.3 Public expenditure on income transfers and social services, selected OECD countries, 1994, per cent of GDP

Countries	Income transfers[a]	Social services[b]
Australia	8.3	1.0
Austria	20.1	0.9
Belgium	19.3	0.2
Finland	22.3	3.1
France	18.4	1.1
Germany	17.9	1.4
Iceland	9.4	2.9
Ireland	11.6	0.6
Italy	17.0	0.3
Japan	7.2	0.4
Netherlands	19.8	0.9
Norway	15.7	5.0
Sweden	19.4	5.2
UK	13.6	1.2
USA	8.8	0.3

Notes:
[a] Income transfers: aggregate public expenditure on old-age cash benefits, disability cash benefits, sickness benefits, family cash benefits, unemployment and low-income benefits as per cent of GDP, 1994.
[b] Social services: aggregate public expenditure on services for the elderly and disabled people and family services as per cent of GDP, 1994.
Source: OECD (2002).

One of the major conclusions Dong-Ho (2001) makes is that the countries favouring social services above income transfers have high local tax rates, whereas the countries with high income transfers but low social services expenses seem to have weaker power of leftist parties and favour nonprofit organizations in their service provision. In those countries where both income transfers and social service expenses are low, the population seems to be 'younger' (the share of people over 65 years of age is low), and often two of the following features are dominant: a weakness of left-wing parties, a strong non-profit sector and/or a constitution which makes it possible to block social legislation. However, once again the reader should be cautious about making too far-reaching interpretations based on the OECD database, there is a significant lack of reliable data when trying to 'cluster' national social service models.

This is why I will now look more closely at differences between social care models in five post-industrial societies only – those of Finland, Germany, Japan, the UK and the USA. These countries are on the one hand sufficiently similar, in terms of economic and social development and their exposure to the forces of globalization, and on the other hand clearly distinct from each other in their social care arrangements, representing different social care regimes (Anttonen and Sipilä 1996).

Five different social care patterns

The five countries examined represent different kinds of 'welfare mixes' in the social care policy field (Table 4.4). Finland represents a state-driven social care model: public authorities have assumed a large responsibility of producing and financing social services in the field of child and elder care. Germany is a country where the role of welfare organization in providing social services has been traditionally distinctive compared to many other countries. It is however important to remind ourselves that state financial support to these organizations has been remarkable. Germany was also the first nation to develop a national long-term care insurance system in the 1990s. The national social care pattern in Japan reflects the contradictions inherent in modernization: state policy has stressed the family's responsibility for care, and public care services have been seen as stigmatizing and marginal. The role of women and families is, however, changing rapidly, and new initiatives have been made by the state to meet the new situation and to increase social care services provision.

The USA shows a market-driven pattern of social care heavily supported by voluntary and *denominational* provision. The state plays a minor role even in terms of financing. There are no new initiatives being made by government to change the prevailing situation; people rely on combinations of family and for-profit care arrangements. In the UK, the social care pattern resembles that of Japan: families are in charge of arranging care for their members; state interventions have taken place selectively only where

Table 4.4 Key figures for the care environment, Finland, Germany, Japan, the UK and the USA, mid-1990s

Country	GDP in (PPP[a])	Fertility rate[b]	Elderly living alone[c]	Poverty rate[d]	Women in Parliament[e]
Finland	High (22.7)	Average (1.7)	High (38)	Low (5)	High (36)
Germany	High (23.8)	Low (1.3)	High (41)	Average (9)	High (31)
Japan	High (24.6)	Low (1.3)	Low (12)	Average (8)	Low (7)
UK	High (22.3)	Average (1.7)	High (38)	High (15)	Average (18)
USA	Very high (33.8)	High (2.1)	Average (30)	High (17)	Average (14)

Notes:
[a] GDP/capita (PPP), USD000, 1990.
[b] Total fertility rate, live births per woman, 2000. *Source:* www.Tilastokeskus.fi.
[c] Elderly people living alone (%), mid-1990s.
[d] Poverty line (50% of the median equivalent income), mid-1990s.
[e] Lower house in last election (%) (2001).

private provision has failed. Neither state nor private-for-profit provision is explicitly supported by public policy. During the early 2000s the 'New Labour' administration put in place a comprehensive child care policy, the first post-war government to do so.

I will now present some figures relevant to understanding and explaining the care environments in our five societies. The national products of the five countries are of a surprisingly similar size, and so it is difficult to use them as a basis from which to draw conclusions. There are considerable differences in birth rate; in Japan and Germany, there has been an extensive debate about how the low birth rate may be caused by deficiencies in family policy and also in the day care of small children. The explanations for the birth rate are controversial, but a more detailed analysis and a more precize measurement of family policy benefits supports the supposition that the birth rate is not a phenomenon that exists in isolation from the choices that people make. Family policy, and especially support for the employment of mothers, matters (see Ekert 1986; Gauthier 1996; Esping-Andersen 1996, 1999: 47–72). But of course family policy is not the only influential factor: the USA offers a good example of a high birth rate without a strong public family and care policy.

The share of elderly people living together with their families is highest in Japan, while the proportion of old people living alone is highest in Europe. It is probable that this phenomenon is also connected with socio-political choices: pensions and housing benefits make it easier to live alone and the same could also be said about the use of social services. The small difference between the European countries and the USA might perhaps have arisen because low-income Americans cannot afford to use home care services, and that diminishes their wish to live alone.

In Finland, the proportion of women MPs is markedly higher than in the other four countries. This difference naturally reflects how successfully women have been able to raise care issues at the national level in politics and how they have achieved results at that level. It is in Finland that care has been most widely taken under public control and where the public sector's role as a provider of care services is most extensive. The participation of women in politics and the comprehensiveness of public care services are intimately related.

Table 4.5 presents the main features of national social care patterns in our five countries. A description in tabular form is, of course, crude, in this case particularly because it does not distinguish the extent to which the family and other informal networks provide care compared with formal providers.

European state financial support in care policy is thus at a substantially higher level than in Japan and the USA. 'Familialism' has traditionally been strongest in Japan and the USA but, especially in the latter, the position of the family has changed as women have moved into paid employment on a large scale.

Table 4.5 National patterns of social care,[a] Finland, Germany, Japan, the UK and the USA, mid-1990s

Country	Regulative idea of social care policy	Main providers of social care apart from families	State support for social care arrangements	Relative emphasis in social policy[b]
Finland	State-driven social care policy	Local authorities	High	Trans 22 Serv 11
Germany	Subsidiarity and insurance policy	Welfare organizations, local authorities	Average	Trans 16 Serv 11
Japan	Extensive family responsibility	Local authorities, welfare organizations	Low	Trans 7 Serv 6
UK	Family responsibility	Local authorities, market	Low	Trans 15 Serv 8
USA	Market-driven social care policy	Market, welfare organizations	Low	Trans 9 Serv 7

Notes:
[a] Note that health services are included.
[b] The relative emphasis of social care expenditure as a per cent of GDP. Trans = Transfers as a per cent of GDP; Serv = Services as a per cent of GDP.
Source: OECD (1999: 41–7).

The question of the amount of income transfers and services and their inter-relationships is interesting when comparing the social policy systems of different countries. In Finland and Germany, income transfers and services are abundant, while in Japan and the USA both are relatively meagre. It is, however, necessary, to add that the figures for the USA are not directly comparable because instead of income transfers and subsidized services there are plentiful tax concessions to support the capacity to purchase social services. In the evaluation of both dimensions, the UK lies in the middle.

What it comes to the main question of the chapters, it is easy to argue that care is increasingly 'going public' in each of the five countries in the sense that its production is leaving the informal, domestic world of the household and family and is increasingly being managed and produced outside the home in more public ways by welfare organizations, market and state sectors. Three key trends can be identified in the process of care 'going public':

(1) The extension of state responsibility
(2) The extension of civil society responsibility
(3) The monetization of care.

These three development trends may take place concurrently or one of them may dominate.

I shall look at the extension of state responsibility in the following section when the 'Scandinavian' social care model is placed under scrutiny. The market-driven US model of social care gives us a good example with which to evaluate the process of the monetization of care. After that I shall take a brief look at the role of civil society-based provision.

The US market-driven model of social care has meant that care has become commercialized. However, in a market-reliant society different social groups have to rely on different solutions. As Heffernan (2003: 151–2) points out:

> Those from poor and low-income families are eligible for a limited number of publicly provided and subsidized places [in day care]. Children from middle- and upper-income households benefit from partial tax write-offs to purchase care from for-profit providers. Children from all income classes receive care in centres operated by churches and other non-profit centres. Children from all classes go to national chains of 'Jack and Jill Houses'.

The monetization of care represents one possible solution through which familial burden of care is relieved especially in a situation, where women with small children move into paid employment and work long hours, as they do in the USA. However, as Heffernan reminds us, the outcomes of the process of monetization are far from equality measures. When a crucial part of the familial care burden is moved into low-paid care workers and child minders in private households, new kinds of class and race divisions are brought into being. We should ask if monetization of care is a proper solution to care deficiency. In a global world, the monetization of care means that mainly migrant women work in low-paid care professions to extend the earning capacities of better-off white families. The same trends can now be identified in Central and Southern Europe, where more and more care work is done by documented and undocumented migrant care workers (Anderson 2000; Williams 2003). These low-paid care and domestic workers are nearly always migrant women.

To some extent, the monetization of care is thus also an European phenomenon. The UK represents a country where public care services became an important means of reducing the inequality between classes and building up a universal social citizenship; at an early stage, since the mid-1980s, however, many people in the UK have begun to relate more and more cautiously to publicly provided care services and instead to turn to private solutions. Finland is the country where state participation has not been regarded as problematic, even if developments that began at the beginning of the 1990s created several cracks in the practice of a state-led social care policy based on the ideal of universal service provision (Anttonen 2001).

Extended civil society responsibility is not a new phenomenon. Indeed, in nearly all countries charities and welfare organizations took the initiative to build up institutions to care and support vulnerable members of society. They also were active in creating new professional ways to care for different categories of needy persons. In some countries, even today, welfare organizations or the third sector plays the most important role in providing social care services; Germany is a good example of a country whose service provision is largely in the hands of third-sector actors. It is, however, important to stress that nation-wide welfare organizations in Germany are financially supported by the government.

Evers and Sachße (2003: 75) argue that social care services have only gradually gained a more universal and professional status, especially when contrasted with health care and education. The third-sector dominance is not the key explanation for the marginality of social care services. In Germany, the principle of subsidiarity has meant that the family comes first when it is a question of care obligations. The German example also makes clear that welfare organizations may play a crucial role in service provision even in situations where the state has assumed a large responsibility of financing and controlling service production. Universalization and individualization of social care services does not thus necessarily undermine the role of welfare organizations. Germany is the first country in the world that introduced long-term care insurance to meet the increasing care needs of older people.

As to the question of the alternatives which different societies have for replacing family care, it would seem that neither voluntary work nor a genuine market will suffice as a substitute for the family. Although social care represents in Rose's (1989) terms an area where there is a high substitutability between the monetary and the household sectors, the market will scarcely be able to provide a sufficient volume of care services for all citizens without public support. In societies which hold equality and justice as their ideals only the state or a form of social insurance subject to public control will be able to build a viable system for financing care. The services themselves can be produced by many kinds of providers: families, welfare associations (non-profit and for-profit), companies and local governments. The 'welfare mix' in the field of social care does not mean that care-related services and benefits are distributed unequally among citizens, what is important is that citizens have a right to and access to care service when in need, and that services are not too expensive for citizens to use.

The Scandinavian social care regime: the principle of universal service provision

The Nordic democracies differ from most post-industrial welfare societies in the extent to which informal caring has been transformed from a private matter for families to a public matter for the state. The comparative literature on the welfare states shows that in the Scandinavian welfare societies there is an extensive public provision of social care services for adult citizens who need regular help in their daily life. The Nordic societies are also generous in their support for families with small children.

In the field of social care services there are many important similarities between Finland, Sweden, Norway and Denmark. Sipilä *et al.* (1997: 39–40) have argued that in all the Nordic countries (with the exception of Iceland) social care services are widely available for both children and adult persons who need help. Secondly, the service system at large responds most specifically to the interests of women. Thirdly, the middle and upper classes are among the users of public social services. Finally, the municipalities are responsible for service provision. I feel that it is therefore justified to talk about a 'Scandinavian social care regime' (see also Anttonen and Sipilä 1996).

Whereas other countries with high social expenditures concentrate more on income transfers, the Scandinavian welfare states allocate relatively large resources to public consumption. Regarding their special emphasis on social care, they have been characterized as 'social services' or 'social care' states. When describing the Scandinavian social care regime reference is often made to the principle of *universalism* as opposed to selectivism and particularism (Anttonen 2002).

According to Therborn (1995: 97), *universal* rights 'entitle all citizens or residents to social services and income security, specified mainly by [only] their position in the human life-cycle'. In contrast, *particularist* rights are specific to occupational and other special social groups that are understood to be more needy or more deserving than others. In all definitions, an indispensable characteristic of universal social policy programmes is that they not are intended only for the poor. Usually the interpretation given to the concept is much wider: universalist social policies cover all social groups in a society.

One of the most famous formulations of the concept comes from Esping-Andersen (1990: 28) who states that within universalistic programmes of a social democratic welfare regime 'all benefit, all are dependent, and all will presumably feel obliged to pay'. This highlights the peculiar quality of universalistic social policies. Once they have been adopted, they become highly popular and reversing them turns often to be politically infeasible or, at least, problematic. However, this does not imply that creating universal policies will be uncomplicated. On the contrary, it requires a consensus between the political main players that is usually attainable only through significant mutual compromises. A willingness to make such concessions is a rare phenomenon in political life.

But what exactly does 'universalism' mean in social care? The concept is used conventionally but often sloppily, without specifying its different meanings and interpretations. Here, developing further a definition given originally by Sainsbury (1988), I suggest that within the provision of social care services universalism can refer to a number of different dimensions:

- There is a *public system* providing social care services.
- Services are available to *all citizens*, irrespective their economic status, gender or ethnic background: all citizens have access to same service system.
- The *middle and upper classes* are among the users of public social (care) services.
- The service system at large responds to the *interests of women* (gender equality).
- The system offers *uniform services* all over the country (regional equality).
- Services are produced by *professional care workers*.
- Citizens have *rights* to some social care services.
- Services are delivered *free of charge*, or they are heavily subsidized by local or central governments.
- The *municipalities* are responsible for service provision and the financing of services.

Universalist solutions in the field of social care have been prominent in Scandinavian social care policies. Social democrats saw at the beginning of the twentieth century that social services were needed to promote gender equality. The agrarian sector's demand for regional equality also favoured solutions that covered all citizens in the same terms. A third strong source of support for developing universal social services was the women's movement. One aim of the Scandinavian welfare state regime was that social care services should be available equally for all citizens; this guaranteed women's right to paid labour and helped women to reconcile home and work. Moreover, the politics of universalism were supported by the extensive public sector and its interest organizations. Many feminist scholars (Hernes 1987; Siim 1993; Anttonen 2002) have pointed out that universalism has brought into being a woman-friendly welfare society, where women's needs as mothers and workers are widely acknowledged through the public policy of social care services. National as well as comparative studies show that the Northern European democracies have the most advanced welfare systems for safeguarding women's social rights.

To understand the distinctive nature of the Scandinavian social care regime it is important to remind ourselves that municipalities are much more than administrative regions (Kröger 1996). Although the state sets the framework through its legislative power, municipalities have the main responsibility in running social services such as education, health care and social care. In these tasks they are subsidized by a central government grant, but the government does not control local activities in detail. It is also important to note that municipalities are democratic and self-governing institutions in the sense that their representatives are elected in municipal elections and they have the right to levy taxes.

Tax financing is in fact one of the cornerstones of the Scandinavian social care regime. Among Scandinavians it has been common to think that taxes are the best method of funding so that a certain benefit can be systematically made available either to all people or to those who according to certain criteria are judged to be in need. Taxes also allow the common good to be taken into account. All countries with extensive and universal service provision in fact rely mainly on tax revenues in funding.

Overall, universalism has served as an important goal for social policies in the Scandinavian countries and shaped the idea of 'universal social citizenship'. However, it is important to stress that even in Scandinavia universalism is not complete. It is more like an ideal type or never-attached goal, and in practice, the Nordic welfare state – with universalism as its trademark – does not fulfil all its universalistic premises. For instance, the supply of services available for the frail elderly, whether institutional or home help services, does not always meet the current demand. Likewise, the idea of equal services for poor and rich people does not always work in practice; there has always existed private service production alongside municipal services. Another kind of problem comes from the policy of service fees: they are staggered according to income and they can in some cases be so high that it makes more sense for service users to turn to the 'grey markets' or to subsidized services produced by voluntary organizations than to public authorities.

In Finland, universalist principles in the field of social care encountered further problems during the economic recession of the early 1990s. One of the main victims of cost containment was the state subsidy to local government, which hit the municipal social services hard. Services for the elderly became one of the main victims, and the economic recession, together with the growth of a liberal ideology, led to a profound restructuring of social care policy. The initial tendency was to reduce the costs of institutional care and now there seems to be a tendency to increase selectivism and self-payment, especially in the field of elder care services. The principle of universalism has become weaker in the field of social care services for older people, while in the field of child care service it has become stronger (Anttonen 2001).

However, the Scandinavian case also shows us that national and local governments are able to create social care systems with a wide range of services. The essential point today is that the state's financial support is not directed only to the professional provision of social services in the municipalities; alongside them, financial support for those taking care of their family members, both children and the elderly, has expanded since the 1980s. There is a new debate on 'cash or services?', illustrating new kind of 'welfare mixes' in the field of social care. Payments for care that are paid either to the person in need of care or to the carer have become more common since the 1980s in many European societies (Daly 2001). In many cases, for instance, it is less expensive for the government to pay a cash benefit than to provide institutional or home help services for older people. In the following section I shall highlight the idea of payments for care, using Finnish child care policy as an example.

Money or services? the Finnish child care policy in transition

Finnish child care policy is a good example of universal social service provision. In Finland, the first calls for public day care were made at the beginning of the twentieth century. Yet, it took more than fifty years for the first national law on day care to come into force in 1973. As late as in the 1950s, the number of municipal kindergartens and crèches was very limited; however, the pattern of women's labour market participation began to change rapidly, and so did the pattern of women's political participation. In the 1940s 70 per cent of women left work on the birth of their first child, while in the 1960s more than half of women returned to work during a period of twelve months after the first child was born (Rissanen 2000: 40). At least as important was the fact that in the 1960s the proportion of women in the Finnish Parliament rose from 15 to 22 per cent. These factors combined to set day care reform into motion: children's day care became one of the most-debated social policy issues in the 1960s and early 1970s.

Following a series of inevitable political disputes and compromises, the first National Day Care Act (1973) came into force. Local authorities were charged with the responsibility of supporting, first, the building of day care centres and, second, supervised day care in families. The latter option was recorded in the law partly because the advocates of the so-called 'mother's wage' remained in the minority: the alternative suggested was that all mothers with children under school age would be paid a flat-rate allowance so that they could themselves decide who they wanted to look after their child (Anttonen 1999).

Debates around a mother's wage in Finland have been closely associated with the policy of municipal child day care. Two contradictory policy lines have been put forward: the agrarian centre party promoted the idea of a 'mother's wage', while the political left supported building up a nationwide system of child day care centres. The pleas of the Centre Party to support families directly through flat-rate allowances were left unanswered in the 1970s. After the introduction of the National Day Care Act, the municipal day care system expanded very rapidly. In 1965 there were nearly 29,000 publicly funded day care places in Finland. After the 1973 reform the number of places rapidly increased, so that in 1980 the corresponding figure was around 130,000 places, and in 1998 around 220,000 place. Generous public support for municipal childcare left very little room for private provision.

In the mid-1980s, the child care legislation was revised quite radically. There was still a chronic shortage of day care places and municipalities were unable to meet the increasing demand. Moreover, the debate on alternative ways to provide child care had been going on since the 1973 Law was enacted. The Centre Party persisted in advocating cash benefits to families which could not make any use of day care services.

The child care reform implemented in 1985 represented a historic compromize between the two competing policies. By accepting a proposal for a revised Day Care Act, the Centre Party won the backing it needed to get a system of child home care allowances (CHCA) adopted. The new legislation consisted of two major parts. The new Day Care Act required local governments not only to organize day care services according to demand, but also established day care as a legal right of parents (or guardians) of child under three. This right became fully effective in 1990 and in 1996 was extended to cover all children under school age.

The second part of the reform was equally radical. In 1985, the Finnish Parliament passed a law which stipulated that as an alternative to a municipal day care place, the parents of children under age three were to be given the option of claiming a CHCA, either to look after their child themselves or to pay for private care (Sipilä and Korpinen 1998: 263). At the same time, the situation of parents who opted to stay at home was facilitated by an amendment to the Contracts of Employment Act which gave parents of children under three the right to take child care leave with full job security.

Almost as soon as it was introduced, the CHCA became immensely popular, although the new law was to be implemented gradually and did not cover all children under age three until 1990. In 1987 the number of children of families choosing the allowance out paced the number of children in the same age group in municipal day care. At the end of 1997, 45 per cent of children under three were in care arrangements subsidized by the benefit and the majority (more than 90 per cent) were looked after at home by a mother or father.

In 1997, the CHCA was accompanied by a new benefit, that of a children's private care allowance (CPCA) to be used by those families which preferred to purchase private day care services. The CPCA is paid to families with children under school age; with its introduction nearly all forms of care arrangements for small children are now covered by public support.

To sum up, the Finnish child care policy represents 'Nordic universalism' in service provision. There is a public system of providing child day care services. Services are available to all families irrespective of their economic status. Moreover, the system offers uniform services all over the country and access is guaranteed by social rights. Alongside uniform service provision there is a tendency to develop child care centres based on Montessori and other 'alternative' ideologies. Finally, a clear majority of parents use municipal child care services, even if private service provision is also now supported by government.

The idea of 'universalism' has changed during the decades. If it first meant that all families should have access to same kind of services across the country, the day care reform carried out in the mid 1980s brought the politics of choice into being. Parents can now decide if they want to use child care services or take care of their children themselves at home. According to Mahon (2002) this kind of turn in the Finnish child care policy represents neo-familialism rather than parental choice, because it is mainly unskilled women who decide to stay at home with the CHCA, even if nearly all women do extend the period of parental leave to stay longer at home with their babies. In a country where women have a long tradition of working full-time, extended parental leave is much valued among parents, and especially among women. Against this background, the Finnish child care policy represents a new 'welfare mix' in social care in which services and cash benefits are combined to reinforce pluralism in universalism.

High social care service provision: a sign of gender equality or a work society for all?

While anchored to its national and normative contexts, care is exposed to many pressures when societies are changing. This is not just a matter of ideological changes taking place in the economy and politics, changes that generally arise from structural adaptations to economic competition. Some ideological shifts at least appear to be relatively isolated from material changes in the economy and patterns of employment – for example, the never-ending moral debates about family responsibilities. Others are more clearly rooted in changes in everyday life, such as the discrepancies between social policy assumptions and the growing participation of women in paid employment. Although the forces of change are, to some extent, pushing in the same direction, they have not yet produced much cross-national uniformity in care policies. Unlike social security systems, care arrangements remain distinctly national and local innovations, such as the Finnish system of child home care allowances, are common.

I have shown in this chapter that social care is a field of informal and formal activities that are changing, and quite rapidly so. Most importantly, care is leaving the intimate sphere of family and kinship: it is 'going public' everywhere. One consequence of the change in the locus of care from family to other sectors is that it has become monetized; it has to be paid for and its costs are revealed. This form of 'going public' may happen quite independently of social policy simply because more households need or choose to buy, or it may be a consequence of greater state participation. Another side of the coin is that governments are able to create a public policy of care in such a way that care becomes a social good and social right of citizens. Some governments have been much more active than others in the process of care 'going public'. The Nordic democracies in particular have actively favoured women-friendly solutions in care and family policies. Internationally generous social care provision has promoted gender equality in terms of women's labour market participation. Of course there are also other equality indicators such as women's share in parliaments and women's educational level in a society. However, here I shall look only at women's labour market participation, using the same five countries as before.

Many feminist theorists (e.g. Lewis 1992; Pfau-Effinger 1998) have paid attention on the transformation of the male-breadwinner/female-housewife model. The reorganized male-breadwinner model has taken different forms in different societies. In countries where the dual-breadwinner model persists there are more social care services available for citizens than in countries where the main breadwinner is primarily still a male worker (Lewis 1992).

Table 4.6 summarizes the current patterns of women's participation in the labour markets of Finland, Germany, Japan, the UK and the USA. Overall, the levels of female involvement in paid work are quite similar. What mainly varies are the proportion and degree of part-time participation. One might expect part-time work to be more often selected by women in those countries where social care services are less available or flexible; Table 4.6 supports the argument except in the US case. The high level of full-time work by women is the USA is sustained both by a greater use of market-based child care and by the availability of state-funded social care for older people. In both cases, the availability of cheap, female and often migrant labour, plays a significant role.

In Finland, women most often work full-time. Yet this is no 'Scandinavian' phenomenon because in the other Nordic countries part-time work is much more common. The UK and Japan have highest shares in women's part-time work among the five nations. In the UK, there are now new policies to help women with small children to move into the labour market (Baldock 2003). In Japan, too, there are significant pressures to move towards a dual-earner

Table 4.6 Women's labour market participation, Finland, Germany, Japan, the UK and the USA, 1999

Women aged 15–64	Finland (%)	Germany (%)	Japan (%)	UK (%)	USA (%)
In paid work	71.3	62.8	63.8	67.5	71.5
Part-time[a]	13.5	33.1	39.7	40.6	19.0
Migrant workers	1.5	9.1	1.0	3.7	11.7

Note:
[a] Fewer than 30 hours per week.

Source: OECD (2001).

society and this means that social care services will have to be extended in the future. In Japan above all, the lack of congruence between policy assumptions, care services and the proportions of women in paid work has triggered falling levels of marriage and fertility among younger women, now a matter of great concern in public debate about the future of the Japanese economy (Takahashi 2003). In countries where the public social care service provision is high, fertility rates have also remained on a relatively higher level than in countries that invest little on public social care – with the USA as an exception.

What is required is a greater understanding of how the politics of social care produces diverse responses to the need to reconcile the actual pattern of women's (and men's) labour market roles and caring functions within a society. As global economic competition forces all nations to treat all adults as individual workers, *striking this balance in a sustainable way* becomes more critical for national economic and political success. Care arrangements have growing political significance; they impinge particularly on the lives of women, the disabled and poor people. In all societies, rich people can buy services and the help they need at the market price. However, many people even in rich countries are not able to pay for services without any financial support if they are produced at a market price. Social care services available for all citizens free of charge or subsidized by local or central government is a sign of a just society and equality between sexes and classes. Yet we know that in all affluent countries, care systems are undergoing reassessment and reorganization; economic globalization and the continuing crisis in the public sector are generating mounting pressures to find more competitive but politically acceptable care solutions.

According to Hernes (1987: 41) the Scandinavian experience gives us significant evidence that social solidarity and individual autonomy can be legislated through the idea of universal social citizenship. Marginalized and other oppressed groups such as women have become a part of the social policy contract at a time when it is important for women to extend social rights to cover such things as caring for young children and the elderly, sick and disabled members of society. Scholars such as Lewis (1992) and Pfau-Effinger (1998) have shown that in Scandinavian societies women really have succeeded in combining their dual role as mothers and workers and that, social policy arrangements have become an integral part of gender equality policy.

Women's changing role as mothers, carers and workers has brought into being a society in which care relations have to be reorganized and renegotiated. Public policy on care is becoming a more and more important part of the welfare state. When we talk about 'caring', we are talking about the shifting boundaries between private and public responsibilities. Caring is also 'sharing' in the sense that there are now more social actors producing care and care services even though care remains a predominantly female activity.

Bibliography

Anderson, B. (2000) *Doing the Dirty Work? The Global Politics of Domestic Labour.* London and New York: Zed Books.

Anttonen, A. (1997) 'The Welfare State and Social Citizenship'. In K. Kauppinen and T. Gordon (eds.), *Unresolved Dilemmas: Women, Work and the Family in the United States, Europe and the former Soviet Union.* Aldershot: Ashgate: 9–32.

Anttonen, A. (1999) *Lasten kotihoidon tuki suomalaisessa perhepolitiikassa.* Sosiaali-ja terveysturvan tutkimuksia, 52. Helsinki: Kela (Child home care allowance in Finnish Family policy: studies on social and health politics, 52.).

Anttonen, A. (2001) 'The Politics of Social Care in Finland: Child and Elder care in Transition'. in M. Daly (ed.), *Care Work: The Quest for Security.* Geneva: International Labour Office: 143–58.

Anttonen, A. (2002) 'Universalism and Social Policy: A Nordic – Feminist Revaluation'. *Nora – Nordic Journal of Women's Studies,* 10(2): 71–80.

Anttonen, A., Baldock, J. and Sipilä, J. (eds.), *The Young, the Old and the State: Social Care Systems in Five Industrial Societies.* Cheltenham: Edward Elgar.

Anttonen, A. and Sipilä, J. (1996) 'European Social Care Services: Is it Possible to Identify Models?'. *Journal of European Social Policy,* 6(2): 87–100.

Anttonen, A., Sipilä, J. and Baldock, J. (2003) 'Patterns of Social Care in Five Industrial Societies: Explaining Diversity'. In A. Anttonen, J. Baldock and J. Sipilä (eds.), *The Young, the Old and the State: Social Care Systems in Five Industrial Societies.* Cheltenham: Edward Elgar: 167–97.

Baldock, J. (2003) 'Social Care in the United Kingdom: A Pattern of Discretionary Social Administration'. in A. Anttonen, J. Baldock and J. Sipilä, J. (eds.), *The Young, the Old and the State: Social Care Systems in Five Industrial Societies.* Cheltenham: Edward Elgar: 109–42.

Clasen, J. (1999) 'Introduction'. In J. Clasen (ed.), *Comparative Social Policy: Concepts, Theories and Methods.* Oxford: Blackwell: 1–12.

Daatland, S.O. (2001) 'Ageing, Families and Welfare Systems: Comparative Perspectives'. *Zeitschrift für Gerontologie und Geriatrie,* 34(1): 16–20.

Daly, M. (2001) 'Care policies in Western Europe'. in M. Daly (ed.), *Care Work: The Quest for Security.* Geneva: International Labour Office: 33–55.

Daly, M. and Lewis, J. (2000) 'The Concept of Social Care and the Analysis of Contemporary Welfare States'. *British Journal of Sociology,* 51(2): 281–98.

Daly, M. and Lewis, J. (1998) 'Introduction: Conceptualising Social Care in the Context of Welfare State Restructuring'. in J. Lewis (ed.), *Gender, Social Care and Welfare State Restructuring in Europe.* Ashgate: Aldershot: 1–24.

Dong-Ho, J. (2001) *A Comparative Analysis on Redistribution Strategies among Welfare States in Income Transfers and Social Services.* Master's thesis, Department of Social Welfare, Chonbuk National University.

Ekert, O. (1986) 'Effets et limites des aides financières aux familles: une expérience et un modèle'. *Population,* 41(2): 327–48.

Esping-Andersen, G. (1990) *The Three Worlds of Welfare Capitalism.* Cambridge: Polity Press.

Esping-Andersen, G. (1996) 'Welfare States without Work: The Impasse of Labour Shedding and Familialism in Continental European Social Policy'. In G. Esping-Andersen (ed.), *Welfare States in Transition: National Adaptations in Global Economies.* New York and London: Sage 66–87.

Esping-Andersen, G. (1999) *Social Foundations of Postindustrial Economies.* Oxford: Oxford University Press.

Esping-Andersen, G. (2002) 'A Child-Centred Social Investment Strategy'. In G. Esping-Andersen with D. Gallie, A. Hemerijck and J. Myles, *Why We Need a New Welfare State*. Oxford: Oxford University Press 26–67.

Evers, A. and Sachße, C. (2003) 'Social Care Services for Children and Older People in Germany: Distinct and Separate Histories'. In A. Anttonen, J. Baldock and J. Sipilä (eds.), *The Young, the Old and the State: Social Care Systems in Five Industrial Societies*. Cheltenham: Edward Elgar: 55–80.

Gauthier, A.H. (1996) 'The Measured and Unmeasured Effects of Welfare Benefits on Families: Implications for Europe's Demographic Trends'. In D. Coleman (ed.), *Europe's Population in the 1990s*. Oxford: Oxford University Press: 297–331.

Heffernan, J. (2003) 'Care for Children and Older People in the United States: Laggard or Merely Different?'. In A. Anttonen, J. Baldock and J. Sipilä (eds.), *The Young, the Old and the State: Social Care Systems in Five Industrial Societies*. Cheltenham: Edward Elgar: 143–66.

Hernes, H.M. (1987) *Welfare States and Woman Power: Essays in State Feminism*: Oslo: Norwegian University Press.

Higgins, J. (1981) *States of Welfare: Comparative Analysis in Social Policy*. Oxford: Blackwell.

Hochschild, A.R. (2000) 'The Nanny Chain'. *The American Prospect*, 11(4): 32–6.

Hort, S.E. O. (2003) 'Back on Track – To the Future? The Making and Remaking of the Swedish Welfare State in the 1990s'. In N. Gilbert and R. A. Voorhis, (eds.), *Changing Patterns of Social Protection*. International Social Security Series, 9. New Brunswick and London: Transaction: 239–76.

Knijn, T. and Kremer, M. (1997) 'Gender and the Caring Dimension of Welfare States: Toward Inclusive Citizenship'. *Social Politics*, 4(3): 328–61.

Kröger, T. (1996) 'Policy-Makers in Social Services in Finland: The Municipality and The state'. *Scandinavian Journal of Social Welfare*, 5(2): 62–8.

Lewis, J. (1992) 'Gender and the Development of Welfare Regimes'. *Journal of European Social Policy*, 2(3): 159–73.

Mahon, R. (2002) 'Child Care: Toward What Kind of 'Social Europe?'. *Social Politics*, 9(2): 343–79.

Midre, G. (1995) *Bot, Bedring eller Brød? Om Bedømming of Behandling av Sosial Nød fra Reformasjonen til Velferdsstaten*. Oslo: Universitetsforlaget. (Cure, Improvement or Bread? On Judgements of Treatment of social Distress from the Reformation to the Welfare State.).

Myrdal, G. and Myrdal, A. (1935) *Kris i Befolkningsfrågan*, 3rd edition. Stockholm: Albert Bonniers Förlag: (Crisis in the Population Question.)

OECD (1999) *A Caring World. The New Social Policy Agenda*. Paris: OECD.

OECD (2001) *Labour Force Statistics 1979–1999*. Paris: OECD.

OECD (2002) *Online Social Expenditure Database 1980–1998*. Paris: OECD.

Palme, J., Bergmark, Å., Bäckman, O., Estrada, F., Fritzell, J., Lundberg, O., Sjöberg, O. and Szebehely, M. (2002) 'Welfare Trends in Sweden: Balancing the Books for the 1990s'. *Journal of European Social Policy*, 12(4): 329–46.

Pateman, C. (1989) *The Disorder of Women*. Stanford: Stanford University Press.

Pfau-Effinger, B. (1998) 'Gender Cultures and the Gender Arrangements. A Theoretical Framework for Cross National Gender Research'. *Innovation*, 11(2): 147–66.

Pierson, P. (2001) 'Introduction: Investigating the Welfare State at Century's End'. In P. Pierson (ed.), *The New Politics of the Welfare State*. Oxford: Oxford University Press: 1–14.

Rissanen, T. (2000) *Naisten ansiotyömallin muotoutuminen. Työnteon, toimeentulon ja lasten hoidon järjestäminen Suomessa 1920–1980 – luvuilla*. Master's dissertation.

Tampere: University of Tampere, Department of Social Policy and Social Work. (The formation of women's employment model. The organization of work, income and child care in Finland in the 1970-1990s.)

Rose, R. (1989) *Ordinary People in Public Policy: A Behavioural Analysis*. London: Sage.

Rostgaard, T. and Fridberg, T. (1998) *Caring for Children and Older People: A Comparison of European Policies and Practices*. Copenhagen: The Danish National Institute of Social Research.

Sainsbury, D. (1988) 'The Scandinavian Model and Women's Interests: The Issues of Universalism and Corporatism'. *Scandinavian Political Studies*, 11(4): 337–46.

Siim, B. (1993) 'The Gendered Scandinavian Welfare States: The Interplay between Women's Roles as Mothers, Workers and Citizens in Denmark'. in J. Lewis (ed.), *Women and Social Policies in Europe: Work, Family and the State*. Aldershot: Edward Elgar: 25–48.

Sipilä, J., Andersson, M., Hammarqvist, S.-E., Nordlander, L., Rauhala, P.-L., Thomsen, K. and Warming Nielsen, H. (1997) 'A Multitude of Universal, Public Services: How and Why did Four Scandinavian Countries get their Social Service Model?'. In J. Sipilä (ed.), *Social Care Services: the Key to the Scandinavian Welfare Model*. Aldershot: Avebury: 27–50.

Sipilä, J., Anttonen, A. and Baldock, J. (2003) 'The Importance of Social Care'. In A. Anttonen, J. Baldock. and J. Sipilä (eds.), *The Young, the Old and the State: Social Care Systems in Five Industrial Societies*. Cheltenham: Edward Elgar: 1–23.

Sipilä, J. and Korpinen, J. (1998) 'Cash versus Child Care Services in Finland'. *Social Policy and Administration*, 32(3): 263–77.

Stjernø, S. (1995) *Mellom kirke og capital*. Oslo: Universitetsforlaget. (Between Church and Capital.)

Takahashi, M. (2003) 'Care of Children and Older People in Japan: Modernizing the traditional'. In A. Anttonen, J. Baldock and J. Sipilä (eds.), *The Young, the Old and the State: Social Care Systems in Five Industrial Societies*. Cheltenham, Edward Elgar: 81–108.

Therborn, G. (1995) *European Modernity and Beyond: The Trajectory of European Societies 1945–2000*. London and New Delhi: Sage.

Vuorela, U. (2002) 'Transnational Families: Imagined and Real Communities'. In D. Bryceson and U. Vuorela (eds.), *The Transnational Family: New European Frontiers and Global Networks*. New York: Berg: 63–82.

Williams, F. (2003) *Rethinking Care in Social Policy*. Paper presented at the Conference of the Finnish Social Policy Association (Finland), Meetings, Joensuu, 24–25 October.

5

Family Policy and Cross-National Patterns of Poverty

Tommy Ferrarini and Katja Forssén

Poverty risks

Since the 1980s child poverty has become a new political issue in many countries. Anti-poverty measures directed towards children and their families have been constrained by tensions between the interests of the state and the rights and responsibilities of the parents. However, there exists wide consensus on the fact that child poverty should be lowered to the minimum level possible. Poverty in families with children may have severe consequences for the individuals living under such circumstances, not only in the short run but also in longer perspective. The shortage of external resources is reflected either directly or indirectly in the well-being of the child (Daniel and Ivatts 1998). For example, the shortage of material resources directly affects everyday life of the family and it has a negative effect on the health of family members, home environment, atmosphere of the family, stability of the family and parenthood (Conger *et al.* 1992; Zill *et al.* 1995; Jack and Jordan 1999; Duncan and Brooks-Gunn 2000). Socioeconomic status has an impact on children's well-being at multiple levels. The impact of low economic resources is moderated by children's own characteristics, functionality of the family, external support systems, etc. (Bradley and Corwyn 2002). Families can experience poverty in many different subjective ways; however, there is a strong connection between experience of poverty and overall well-being (Duncan and Brooks-Gunn 2000).

Living in poverty deprives all family members of potential choices and may restrict present opportunities to pursue their objectives. But low socioeconomic status also has consequences for the future life chances of the children growing up in poor economic positions (see Fergusson, Horwood and Lawton 1990). It has been argued that the risk of poverty and social exclusion of an adult in large part originates in early childhood, when crucial cognitive resources are acquired (see Esping-Andersen, chapter 6 in this volume). A lack of such resources, among other things, increases the risk of a precarious labour market position, which in turn is closely related to experienced poverty risks (see Haveman and Wolfe 1995). Economic means do not, of course, constitute the only type of resource that impacts upon the well-being of an individual; however, it is unarguably a central factor in this respect (Johansson 1973; Sen 1992).

A way to mitigate poverty risks among families with children is through the provision of social transfers, services and active labour force measures. Such social policy measures may of course have been developed with other main objectives than to alleviate poverty. In the Nordic countries, a main motive behind family policy programmes in recent decades has been to support the dual-earner family, while the Continental European countries have primarily maintained family policies in support of traditional family patterns with a main male earner and a female home maker. Family policies in English-speaking countries are mainly market oriented, and support for both the traditional and the dual-earner family has consequently been less developed, demanding larger reliance on means-tested benefits with a more explicit ambition to alleviate poverty.

Substantial cross-national differences in poverty and income inequalities among families with children are well documented in the highly industrialized countries (see Ritakallio 1994; 2002; Rainwater and Smeeding 1995; Hobson and Takahashi 1997; Bradbury and Jäntti 2001; Micklewright and Stewart 2001; Rainwater, Smeeding and Coder 2001; Sainsbury and Morissens 2002; Smeeding 2002). The cross-national patterns of poverty are also often found to be related to institutional differences in legislated family policy programmes in these welfare states (see Forssén 1998; Solera 1998, Kangas and Palme 2000; Ferrarini 2003). If these arguments are to be taken seriously, a closer examination of the relationship between family policy and poverty among families with children is needed, since such welfare state institutions may structure the present as well as the future poverty risks of children. The purpose of this chapter is to analyse how different family policy strategies link up with patterns of poverty among families with children in the Western welfare democracies.

This chapter combines institutional data on family policy institutions with micro-level data on income distributions to study the macro-relationship between policy and welfare outcomes. Our task is to analyse potential effects of family policy on child poverty. Special interest is devoted to connections of family structure, employment patterns of mothers and poverty dynamics. The institutional data on family policy transfers is from the Social Citizenship Indicator Programme (SCIP), which is being constructed at the Swedish Institute for Social Research, Stockholm University. These data, among other things, include information on the generosity of parental leave benefits and child benefits. The micro-income data is mainly from the Luxembourg Income Study (LIS), which comprises national income data sets that have been made comparable concerning income and demographic concepts. Beside the four Nordic countries (Denmark, Finland, Norway and

Sweden) twelve other Western welfare states are analysed with LIS data, namely Australia, Austria, Belgium, Canada, France, Germany, Ireland, Italy, the Netherlands, Switzerland, the UK and the USA. The main focus of this chapter is on the time period from the mid-1990s to the end of the 1990s.

Models of family policy

When comparing countries with different social policy regimes, a typology is valuable. In his institutional family policy typology, Walter Korpi (2000) arranges characteristics of family policy institutions into two separate dimensions, depending on whether they support a traditional family (general family support), where the father is the main earner and the mother is expected mainly to see to care work, or whether they support a dual-earner family (dual-earner support). These types of support are expected to structure the agency of parents in different ways. Three different existing family policy strategies has been discerned by Korpi in Western welfare democracies Figure 5.1 shows how these models are constituted along the two underlying analytical dimensions.

As is shown in Figure 5.1, the Nordic countries (Denmark, Finland, Norway and Sweden) have implemented dual-earner models of family policy, characterized not only by policies oriented towards extending mothers' capabilities to combine labour market careers with children, but where fathers also are provided with incentives to engage in care work. Continental European countries, and Ireland, cluster in a general family support model, oriented towards preserving traditional family patterns, while English-speaking countries, and Switzerland, have market oriented models of family policy with less developed support on both dimensions.[1]

Figure 5.1 Dimensions and models of family policy, selected welfare states
Sources: Based on Korpi (2000) and Ferrarini (2003).

As pointed out by Ferrarini (2003), a fourth ideal-typical model of family policy could potentially come into existence. As shown by the top right hand-side box in Figure 5.1, this is a model in which policies for both the dual-earner family and the traditional family are highly developed. Because of partly opposing motives and dimensions of simultaneously supporting both the dual-earner family and more traditional gender roles, such a model may be labelled 'contradictory'. No country has clearly developed the latter family policy model, even if developments of policy systems in some countries have been in this direction. Recent reforms of paternity insurance in France and Belgium, for example, has brought these countries closer to the dual-earner model of family policy, while developments in several Nordic countries in the 1990s were in the direction of strengthening traditional gender roles through the introduction of flat-rate child care leave benefits.

Institutional structure of family policy programmes

Programmes of family policy

Substantial cross-national differences in family policy programmes are well documented among welfare democracies regarding both cash transfers, such as child allowances (Wennemo 1994; Montanari 2000) and parental leave benefits (Moss and Deven 1999; Ferrarini 2003), as well as concerning social services such as public child care (Kamerman and Kahn 1994; Gornick, Myers and Ross 1996; Korpi 2000). Important family policy measures that structure well-being of children and parents alike are child benefits paid in cash or via the tax system, parental leave benefits and access to publicly subsidized child care and active labour market policy. The following sections aim to describe the institutional development and structure of important family policy programmes in the mid-1990s in sixteen Western welfare democracies. Finally an index of family policy measures is constructed.

Child benefits

Universal child benefits were typically introduced in the Western welfare democracies in the decade after the Second World War. Frequently, such cash benefit systems are complemented by different types of tax benefits targeted at families with children (Wennemo 1994; Montanari 2000). Child benefit transfers, distributed in cash as well as via the tax system, are generally paid from the time of birth of the child and throughout primary-school age. This section uses data on net family policy benefits from the SCIP database to describe the generosity of child benefits for eighteen welfare democracies.[2] Figure 5.2 shows the average net generosity of total child benefits, expressed as a percentage of an average production worker's net wage, in countries with different models of family policy between 1950 and 1995.[3] Child benefits in the countries with general family support have been relatively stable

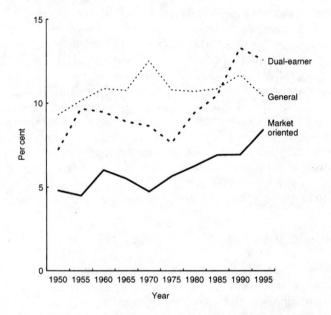

Figure 5.2 Average levels of child benefits, selected countries[a] with different models of family policy, 1950–95, per cent of average production worker's net wage
Note: 'Dual-earner' is an average of Denmark, Finland, Norway and Sweden; 'General' is an average of Austria, Belgium, France, Germany, Ireland, Italy and the Netherlands; and 'Market' is an average of Australia, Canada, Switzerland, the UK and the USA.

above 10 per cent of an average production worker's wage and was until the 1990s on average higher than in the other welfare states. The trend of rapidly increasing child benefits from the mid-1970s until the 1990s in countries with dual-earner models of family policy was broken in the early 1990s, when several of them were hit by a deep economic recession, but by the end of the period these countries still had the most generous child benefits. Countries with market oriented models on average had lower child benefits than countries with other family policy models, but here an unbroken increasing trend can be discerned from the mid-1970s.

Large cross-national differences do, however, exist between particular countries. Child benefit generosity, by type of benefit, is displayed in Figure 5.3 for each of the sixteen countries in the mid-1990s. Belgium and Finland have the highest net child benefits, corresponding to over 15 per cent of an average production worker's wage. The generosity of child benefits in Australia and Ireland are relatively low, around 5 per cent of an average production worker's wage, while the USA has the lowest generosity of such benefits of all countries, around 1 per cent. All other countries have child benefit generosities ranging between 8 and 13 per cent.

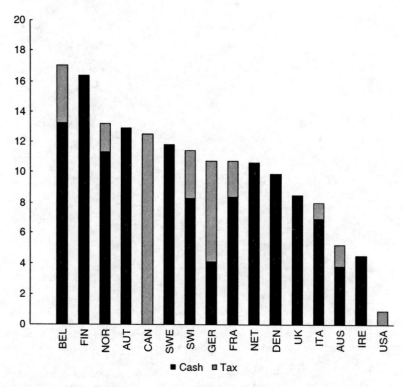

Figure 5.3 Net child benefit generosity, selected welfare states, by type of benefit, 1995, per cent of an average production worker's net wage

Most welfare states primarily rely on universal cash benefits, but a majority of countries also utilize the tax system for distribution of resources to families with children. In this respect important between-'cluster' differences also exist. Dual-earner model countries to a larger extent rely on cash benefits alone, with only Norway also providing a smaller share of child benefits via the tax system. Of the market oriented countries, the UK lacks tax child benefits while Canada and the USA rely solely on such benefits. The countries with general family policy models present a more mixed bag in this respect, with Austria, Ireland and the Netherlands relying exclusively on cash benefits while the other general family policy models also provide tax benefits, Germany notably providing larger shares of tax than cash child benefits.

Paid parental leave

If the trend in child benefit generosity on average is moderately increasing in our sixteen countries throughout the post-war period, paid parental leave shows a more dramatically escalating trend, in particular in dual-earner

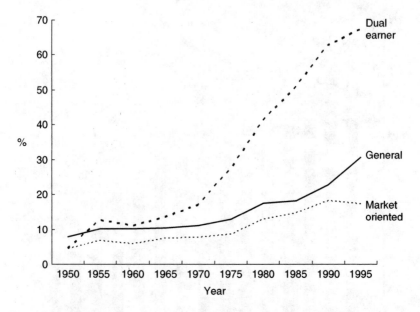

Figure 5.4   Average generosity of parental leave benefits first year after confinement in countries with different models of family policy, for a two-earner family, four Nordic and twelve other Western countries [a], 1950–95, per cent of an average production worker's net wage

Note: a 'Dual-earner' is an average of Denmark, Finland, Norway and Sweden; 'General' is an average of Austria, Belgium, France, Germany, Ireland, Italy and the Netherlands; and 'Market' is an average of Australia, Canada, Switzerland, the UK and the USA.

welfare states. Figure 5.4 shows the average net generosity of parental leave benefits after taxes for the countries with different family policy models between 1950 and 1995 for a two-earner household where one earner remains home with the infant during the first year after birth. Net benefit generosity is expressed in per cent of an average production worker's net wage. In the 1950s, net paid leave amounted to slightly above 5 per cent of such a wage in the welfare states which currently have different types of family policy models. In 1995, average benefit generosity has shown substantial increases in all family policy models, but cross-'cluster' differences have increased even more dramatically, with the average benefit generosity by the mid-1990s being over 60 per cent in dual-earner countries, around 30 per cent in countries with general family policy and around 20 per cent in welfare states with market oriented policies. The large differences stem primarily from the introduction and expansion of dual-earner model in the Nordic countries, including the introduction of earnings-related benefits to both parents and the extension of earnings-related parental insurance

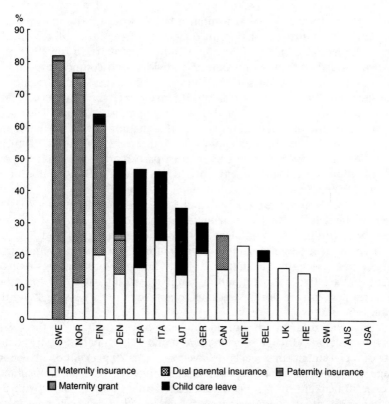

Figure 5.5 Net generosity of parental leave, first year after confinement, by type of benefit, two-earner family, selected countries, 1995, per cent of an average production worker's net wage, ranked by total benefit generosity

duration, but also from extensions of maternity insurance duration and the introduction of flat-rate child care leave benefits (see Ferrarini 2003).

Parental leave generosity in 1995 is displayed by type of benefit for each of our sixteen countries in Figure 5.5. Five types of benefits are separated: earnings-related social insurance benefits paid to the mother (maternity insurance), to both parents (dual parental insurance), or to the father in the form of 'daddy days' to be utilized simultaneously with maternity insurance (paternity insurance), lump-sum payments made in relation to childbirth (maternity grants) and flat-rate benefits (childcare leave) paid in continuation of earnings-related parental insurance benefits.

Three countries with dual-earner models, Finland, Norway and Sweden, have the most generous parental benefits, with Finland replacing nearly two-thirds of an average net wage, and Norway and Sweden having corresponding levels of around 80 per cent. These three countries have extended the duration of dual parental insurance benefits during the past decades. Sweden was the first country to introduce such benefits in 1974, with the two other Nordic countries following within a few years. In the 1990s first Norway and then Sweden introduced individualized components in dual parental insurance benefits in the form of 'daddy quotas' that cannot be transferred to the mother. Canada and Denmark have also introduced a dual parental insurance benefit, but this is less generous in terms of earnings replacement and duration. Important motives behind the introduction and extension of dual parental insurance programmes in the Nordic countries have been to support female labour force participation and facilitate the combination of paid and unpaid work in the family, with the ambition of promoting gender equality (Carlsen 1998; Ferrarini 2003).

The most common type of parental leave programme in the Western welfare states is earnings-related maternity insurance; only Australia and the USA, without any non-means-tested paid leave rights, and Sweden, with an all-dual parental insurance programme, lack maternity insurance programmes. Maternity insurance typically has generous earnings replacement, but relatively short duration compared to dual parental insurance programmes – on average ten weeks as compared to twenty-six weeks for the latter type of program.

Several countries also introduced child care leave benefits from the 1980s. Such benefits in principle provide leave rights to both parents, but the low rate of replacement (the weekly net average rate is 20 per cent of an average wage while the corresponding figure for earnings-related parental insurance is over 70 per cent) in practice create disincentives for the parent with the higher earnings, in most instances the father, to utilize such paid leave. The institutional structure of child care leave has led several researchers to categorize this type of benefit as supportive of traditional family patterns (Schiersmann 1991; Leira 1998; Bussemaker and Van Kersbergen 1999).

Paternity insurance benefits and maternity grants in general make minor contributions to the overall benefit generosity of paid parental leave. Lump-sum maternity grants have become less important in the paid parental leave package among our sixteen welfare democracies throughout the post-war era. Paternity insurance, on the other hand, has been introduced in an increasing number of countries, but has relatively short duration, ranging between three days and three weeks (Ferrarini 2003).

Public child care take-up

A central feature of the dual-earner model developed in the Nordic countries is the access to publicly subsidized child care for the youngest children that facilitates the labour market participation of women (and men). Welfare states with general family policy models have relatively well-developed services for older pre-school children, while countries with market oriented models have the least developed pre-school children services. Public services

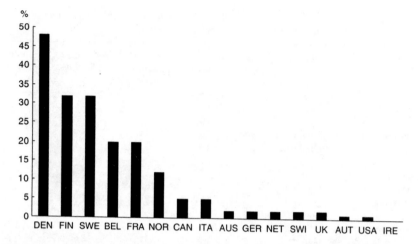

Figure 5.6 Percentage of children under three in public child care, selected countries, early to mid-1990s

Source: Korpi (2000).

are generally a less researched area than public transfers and longer time series on coverage and use of public child care are not available for all the countries included here. In Figure 5.6 the utilization of public child care for the youngest children in the early 1990s is shown.

Denmark has the highest proportion of the youngest children in public child care, by almost 50 per cent, followed by two other dual-earner model countries, Finland and Sweden, where a third of the youngest children are in public child care. The high public child care take-up in Denmark probably reflects the less generous parental leave benefits than the other Nordic countries, in terms both of duration and benefit level. In Belgium and France, every fifth child used public child care in the early 1990s. Norway clearly has the lowest utilization of public child care of the dual-earner countries, at 12 per cent, which is still, however above the average. In Canada and Italy, these figures are around 5 per cent, while all other countries have 2 or fewer than 2 per cent of children in public child care. It should perhaps be emphasized that this indicator may reflect a number of different factors, such as access, quality and costs of child care, length of paid parental leave and the existence of alternative services.

An index of family policy

To capture the central features of family policy relevant for poverty outcomes a family policy index is valuable. In Table 5.1 such an index is construc-ted from the family policy components presented above, together with the

Table 5.1 Model of family policy, family policy indicators and family policy index, early to mid-1990s, ranked by family policy index

	Family policy model	Child benefit	Paid parental leave	Under 3s in public child care	Family policy index
Sweden	Dual earner	12	81	32	42
Finland	Dual earner	16	64	32	37
Denmark	Dual earner	10	49	48	36
Norway	Dual earner	13	76	12	34
France	General	11	47	20	26
Belgium	General	17	22	20	20
Italy	General	8	46	5	20
Austria	General	13	32	1	15
Canada	Market oriented	13	26	5	15
Germany	General	11	30	2	14
Netherlands	General	11	23	2	12
UK	Market oriented	9	16	2	9
Ireland	General	5	15	0	7
Switzerland	Market oriented	11	9	2	7
Australia	Market oriented	5	0	2	2
USA	Market oriented	1	0	1	1

Sources: OECD and SCIP.

model of family policy. Countries are ranked by the family policy index which is the sum of the three indicators divided by three.

Not surprisingly, the four Nordic countries with dual-earner models of family policy have the highest scores on the index, while the countries with market oriented models have the lowest scores and welfare states with general family policy models take a middle position. There are two main exceptions to this pattern: Canada, which scores higher than expected, and Ireland, which scores somewhat lower. Before using the index in comparison with poverty levels in these welfare states, the following section presents patterns of poverty in the mid-to late 1990s.

Trends in child poverty

Child poverty rates

It is sometimes said that the outcomes of family policies reveal how children are valued in different countries. An extreme indicator of dysfunctionality of family policy is, of course, poverty. While the reduction of poverty among the elderly has been one of the great success stories of the post-war welfare state, many countries have seen a re-emergence of child poverty since the 1980s (Bradbury, Jenkins and Micklewright 2001; Forssén 1998; Kangas and Palme 2000; Ritakallio 2002). As mentioned earlier, child poverty varies widely across the industrialized countries. Explanations for the pattern of child poverty have usually focused on three factors: labour market participation patterns, family structure and the structure of welfare state institutions. These three factors are connected. For example, generous family support benefits together with universal child care provision increases women's possibility to participate in the labour force (Forssén and Hakovirta 1999; 2002; Gornick and Meyers 2003).

In this section of the chapter we present an overview of the development of child poverty in our sixteen countries using LIS data. The structure of this part of the study is as follows. First, the overall average trends of child poverty in sixteen countries with different family policy models from 1985 to 2000 are presented. After that, we proceed to investigate the child poverty rates in comparison to total population poverty rates in different countries in 1985 and 2000. Has any major shift occurred in this respect? Is childhood poverty still related to an increased risk of poverty? According to earlier studies, particular risk factors behind child poverty are single parenthood and labour market participation patterns, where adult members of the family are not in paid labour. We present how these factors have affected the poverty rates of families with children in different countries. Finally we examine the link between the family policy index and child poverty.

In all the following analyses, a relative low income poverty limit of 50 per cent of the median income in the population is applied, the indicator of poverty most often used in comparative studies. We also conduct sensitivity analyses by using different income poverty thresholds. Equivalence scales are also used to adjust family incomes to reflect the needs of families with different size and composition. The equivalence scale applied here is the so-called 'square root scale', which assumes relatively high economies of scale in a family. The use of an equivalence scale which assumes smaller economies of scale may change the poverty levels in individual countries, but does not alter the conclusions about cross-national relationships between family policy and child poverty.

Previous studies have shown that there exist remarkable variation in child poverty rates in countries at broadly similar levels of economic development. Figure 5.7 shows the average child poverty trends with different models of family policy from 1985 to 2000. Dual-earner model countries keep having the lowest child poverty rate. In these countries, child poverty rate has remained under 5 per cent during the whole fifteen-year period. In general family policy countries child poverty increased from 1985 to 1995 and the trend then declined slightly, but child poverty still remains at a much higher level than in dual-earner model countries. Child poverty seems also to be a serious problem in market oriented countries, although the trend has fallen slightly since 1995.

These slightly declining child poverty trends can be explained by the fact that in the late 1990s some governments committed themselves to reducing child

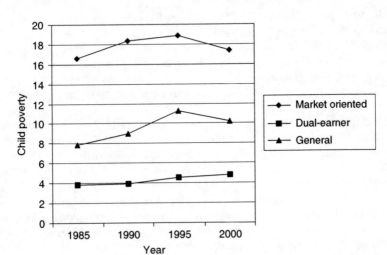

Figure 5.7 Average levels of child poverty, selected countries[a], with different models of family policy, 1985–2000

[a] See Figure 5.2.

Source: LIS data.

poverty. In 1999, for example, Tony Blair in the UK stated a mission to halve child poverty by 2010. The British government unveiled a package of measures aiming to fulfil this promize and child poverty statistics fall slightly after the new measures. The same kind of commitment to fight poverty was also made in Ireland and Belgium. In 2000, the European Union Council decided that member states should implement two-year action plans for combating poverty. In the first National Action Plans on Social Inclusion, each government assessed their level of poverty and described the policies they had implemented in order to deal with the problem (Vleminckx and Smeeding 2001). Once again, poverty has become a political issue in many countries.

Figure 5.8 demonstrates children's poverty rates in relation to the poverty rates for the total population of sixteen countries in 1985 and 2000. In 1985, child poverty was higher than the total poverty rate in all the market oriented countries and in Italy. Fifteen years later, the picture has remained about the same but Switzerland and Austria have joined the market oriented countries with higher child poverty rates. This finding is partly due to the fact that, regardless of welfare state model, all countries have developed social security schemes which lower adults' poverty risk but have no corresponding uniform principle regarding family policies. Of our sixteen countries, Finland, Sweden and Norway stand out as a group with a low incidence of poverty: both total and child poverty rates are below 7 per cent.

Figure 5.9 shows in more detail the differences in child poverty between individual countries: the differences between family policy regimes in child

131

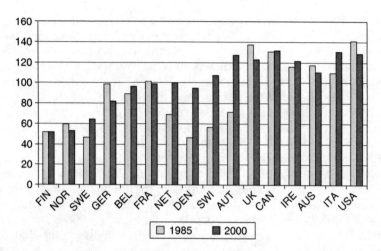

Figure 5.8 Children's poverty rate, in relation to the poverty rate of the total population, 1985 and 2000, per cent
Source: LIS data.

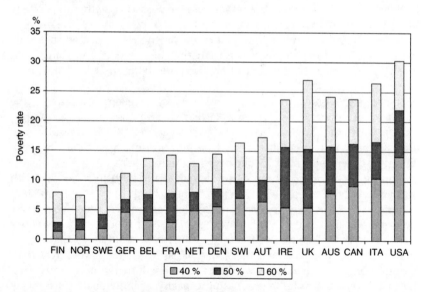

Figure 5.9 Poverty rates for children, by 40, 50 and 60 per cent of the median income, the most recent year[a]

Note: [a] Observation years: AUS = 1994; AUT = 1997; BEL = 1997; CAN = 2000; DEN = 1997; FIN = 2000; FRA = 1994; GER = 2000; IRE = 1996; ITA = 2000; NET = 1999; NOR = 2000; SWE = 2000; SWI = 1992; UK = 1999; USA = 2000.

Source: LIS data.

poverty and general poverty parallel each other: the dual-earner model countries (except Denmark) have low poverty rates, then come the general family
policy countries, and last the market oriented countries, where poverty is
fairly common. Figure 5.9 also shows child poverty rates by different levels of
median income. Figure 5.9 shows first the share of children living in extreme
poverty (40 per cent of the median) and then the share of children living
just above the traditionally used poverty line (50 per cent of the median).
This kind of analysis also works as a sensitivity test for the traditionally used
poverty line. In Finland, Norway and Sweden extreme poverty (40 per cent
of the median) is rare or almost non-existent. On the other hand, there exist
a relatively large number of children in low-income families (60 per cent
of the median) in these countries. Opposed to the situation of dual-earner
model countries are the market oriented countries together with Italy. In
these countries, more than every fourth child lives in poor or low-income
households. The USA represents the extreme end of poverty; there, almost
every third child is either poor or has a low income. However, it is notable
that in the UK and in Ireland the share of children living in extreme poverty
is at the same level as in most countries representing the general family
policy model.

Most of the countries maintain their relative position whether the poverty
threshold in 40 per cent, 50 per cent or 60 per cent of the median
income. Among the market oriented countries the UK's position measured
by 60 per cent threshold is worse than that of Australia and Canada. In
the UK, more than 25 per cent of children are living in at least near-poor
circumstances.

It has been argued that child poverty is an excellent indicator of the
'fairness' of different societies in a Rawlsian distributive sense (see Kangas
2000), with child poverty being one way to address Rawls' idea of a 'veil
of ignorance' in real empirical life. Children do not chose their own situation, and being born in a country with high child poverty can on this
reasoning be perceived as more unjust than being born in a country with
low poverty levels. Some would perhaps object here that it is not sufficient
to compare relative poverty levels for single years and that relative poverty
does not reveal the whole truth about actual standards of living when countries are compared. When comparing countries, it could be so that a poor
person in one welfare state actually has access to economic resources than
a non-poor person in another welfare state. We will therefore here first analyse poverty when holding purchasing capacity of individuals constant by
the use of so called Purchasing Power Parities (PPPs), which take costs of
a standardized bundle of goods and services as departure point to enable
comparison between countries; poverty is therefore measured here in a more
'absolute' sense.

In recent years, a different approach to the analysis of the 'family policy
package' have been evaluated (see Bradshaw and Finch 2002). For example,

Timothy Smeeding (2002) has examined differences in the standard of living among children at various points in the income distribution. In his analyses, he included the value of non-cash benefits for health care and education as well as money, and determined the value of public sector benefits compared to taxes paid for social transfers by this group. On this fuller-income basis, it is possible to assess the efforts of policy to provide access to basic goods and services, education and health care across a range of nations. Smeeding used the OECD estimates of PPP exchange rates to translate household incomes in each country into 1997 US dollars, adjust for family size and then compare income distribution for families with children relative to US median disposable income per equivalent adult. Smeeding also used PPP exchange rates to measure public health and education spending in 1997 US dollars (Smeeding 2002).

Figure 5.10 shows that the low-income children in most countries (except the UK) are better off in real income terms than low-income children in the USA when only cash income is considered. Swiss, Norwegian, Danish, and Swedish children are 37–57 per cents better off, while other European

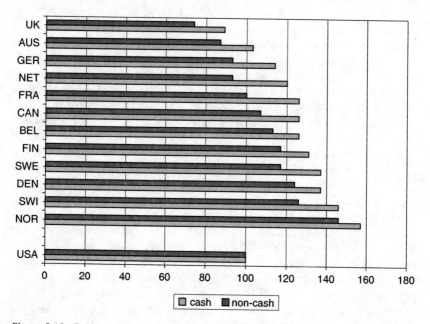

Figure 5.10 Real incomes of the low-income child: ^acash and non-cash, as per cent of US low-child income

Note: ^a Child in household at the 50th percentile (median) of the US equivalent income distribution for households with children, all other currencies converted to 1997 US dollars using PPPs.

Source: Smeeding (2002).

low-income children (Belgium, France and the Netherlands) are at least 20 per cent better off. Once non-cash benefits are added, the differences between US and other rich nations' low-income children become narrower. Now British, Australian, German and Dutch children are worse off, mainly because of their relatively low spending on education and health benefits. Smeeding concludes his study by writing that 'race, ethnicity, and single parenthood play roles in explaining these differences, but low parental wages and lack of social income support are the two most important factors that explain these results' (Smeeding 2002).

Along with concerns about the depth and severity of child poverty, the length of time children spend in poverty is important. The harmfulness of child poverty is connected to the length of time a person remains in poverty, since short-term poverty does not necessarily affect a child's well-being. Many studies have shown that parents try to protect their children in the situation where they are unable to make ends meet. In these situation, children are put first and the primary target of expenditure cuts are items related to the needs of parents. In long-lasting poverty, this 'shelter' mechanism does not necessarily work any longer.

Cross-national comparisons of children's movements into and out of poverty are rare because of lack of suitable data. Bradbury, Jenkins and Micklewright (2001) have studied children's exit rates from and entry rates to poverty in seven sample countries. Their results underline that the longitudinal perspective of child poverty adds a great deal to one's view of childhood deprivation. According to their results, around 60 per cent of low-income children in most countries in one year were still there the following year, 9 per cent of US children were in the poorest fifth in every year of a five-year period and around 6–8 per cent of children were in the same situation in Britain and Germany. There was notably higher rates of entry to poverty as well as lower rates of exit from poverty for children in single-parent households (Bradbury, Jenkins and Micklewright 2001).

Jonathan Bradshaw has analysed long-lasting poverty among children in the European Union by using the first four waves of the ECHP. 'Long-term poverty' was defined as being in poverty (50 per cent of the median) in each of the first four sweeps (1993–96) of the ECHP. Bradshaw's results deepened the picture of child poverty although the ranking between countries remains the same. Long-term poverty is very rare in Denmark (0.1 per cent) and rare in France (1.7 per cent) and the Netherlands (2.2 per cent) but it is higher in the UK (4.3 per cent), Ireland (4.3 per cent), Belgium (6 per cent) and the southern EU countries (Bradshaw 2002).

These studies prove that the risk of long-lasting poverty is highest in some market oriented countries and general family policy countries. This 'chronic poverty' increases the risk of social deprivation and exclusion. Nevertheless, although the focus on chronic poverty is essential, and there is a great need for more detailed studies on this area, transitory spells of poverty during childhood can also be damaging.

Family structure and child poverty

An increase in the proportion of single parents has been common in all industrialized countries since the 1980s. This increase has altered the picture of poverty. The central role of family structure in explaining poverty is self-evident: in single-parent families there is at the maximum one earner in the household which naturally affects the income level. Studies focused on single-parent families have noticed that single parents' higher risk of poverty can be explained by the fact that single parents are usually women and the income level (wages and also income transfers) of women is lower than that of men. Single parents also do not benefit from all aspects of economies of scale, especially those connected to housing (Forssén 1998.) The expenses of child rearing are also easier to bear if there are two adults sharing them instead of one. Motherhood itself lowers the incomes of women, because in some countries women leave the labour force or work part-time when they have young children. These care-related reductions in employment have far-reaching consequences for mothers' incomes. For example, in the USA the total lost earnings (the so called 'mommy tax') over the working life of a college-educated woman can easily be 1 million US dollars (Crittenden 2001; Gornick and Meyers 2003).

Figure 5.11a and 5.11b show the average levels of poverty for single-parent and two-parent families under different models of family policy from 1985 to 2000. Poverty rates for single-parent families are in all countries much higher than poverty rates for two-parent families. The highest poverty rates for single-parent households are found in market oriented countries. For example, in the USA, poverty rates for single-parent families increased markedly from the beginning of the 1980s, being 63 per cent in 1985. After that, the poverty rate started to decline but still almost half of the children in single-parent families lived in poverty. In Australia, the picture of single-parent poverty in the 1980s was similar to that of the USA but it started to decline much more rapidly.

Although poverty rates for single-parent families have always been at lower levels in the Nordic countries than elsewhere, the trend is also increasing in these countries. Especially in Finland, the single-parent families' economic situation weakened during the 1990s. The poverty rate of Finnish single parents was 4.7 per cent in the mid-1990s and 8.1 per cent at the end. One explanation for this is found in changes in the labour market, the share of single parent families outside the labour market having increased to 2000.

Figure 5.11b shows that two-parent families in all countries are better off than single-parent families. However, there are remarkable differences between different family policy models. Poverty rates for two-parent families have been stable and low in dual-earner family policy model countries.

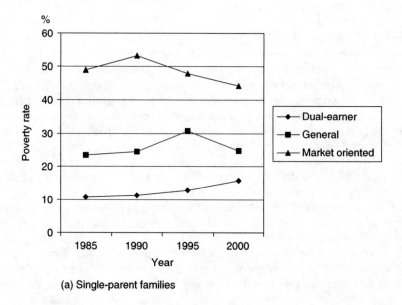

(a) Single-parent families

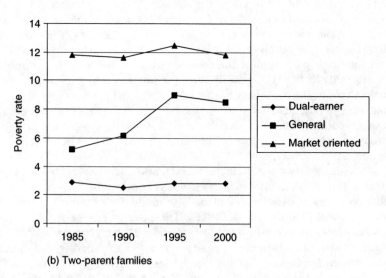

(b) Two-parent families

Figure 5.11 Average levels of poverty, in countries with different models of family policy, 1985–2000

Source: LIS data.

In general family policy countries, the poverty rate for two-parent families increased markedly from 1985 to 1995. This might indicate that traditional male-breadwinner model no longer guarantees an adequate income level. Increasing poverty rates of two-parent families outside the Nordic countries demonstrate the failure of family policy schemes to help families to reconcile employment and care.

In order to get a whole picture of the existence of child poverty the connection between the poverty rate and family structure has to be viewed together with the existence of different family types. In Figure 5.12 we present the share of children living in single-parent households in different countries.

Across our sixteen countries, the proportion of children living in single-parent families varies widely. The share of children living in single-parent families is the highest in the UK and in the USA. In the Nordic countries this share is clearly higher than in general family policy countries. From the children's point of view, the most problematic situation is in market oriented countries, where the share of children living in single-parent families is high and their poverty rate is also high. In some of these countries (Australia, Canada, UK, USA) the high rates of single parenthood and the lack of child benefits increases the risk of child poverty. If it were possible to include non-cash benefits (see Figure 5.10) such as child care and health care in

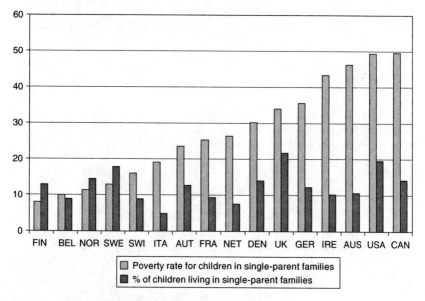

Figure 5.12 Poverty of single-parent families and share of children living in single-parent households, the most recent year[a]

Note: [a] See Figure 5.9.

Source: LIS data.

this analysis, the picture of child poverty in single-parent households would probably be even worse, especially in market oriented countries.

Employment and child poverty

As indicated earlier, the economic welfare of families with children is linked to the family structure, and especially to the employment of the parents. The rize in the labour market participation of women in general, and especially of mothers with young children, is a widely illustrated and internationally applicable social phenomenon. Although the participation of women in the labour market has increased everywhere, there are still significant differences between countries. The labour market behaviour of women in each country is a product of a complex mix of factors, including cultural beliefs and social norms. However, there is strong evidence that the family policy model has an effect on mothers' labour market behaviour.

Labour market conditions for mothers can be said to be governed by the country's real demand for female labour (Figure 5.13). The supply for part-time and flexible work arrangements has had an important effect on female labour force participation. On the other hand, in some countries labour market policies offer employers ways to avoid social security payments and job protection regulations by offering part-time work through temporary contracts. These jobs are often low-wage and low-skill jobs (Knudsen 1999; Gornick and Meyers 2003). Another factor that affects mothers' potential for participation in the labour force is the availability of child care services.

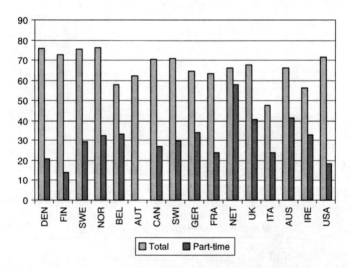

Figure 5.13   Female total labour force (fifteen–sixty-five years) and part-time employment as per cent of female employment, mid-1990s

Source: OECD (2002).

Although more and more women are in paid employment in all Western countries, marked differences still exist in both employment rates and the form of their employment. The highest female labour force participation rates are in the Nordic countries and the lowest in Italy, Ireland and Belgium. Part-time employment is the most common in Netherlands, Australia and the UK.

It has been considered self-evident that a single parent without employment income is in a weaker economic position than an employed single parent. Yet this is not so in all countries. In Figure 5.14a and 5.14b we present the poverty rates of single-parent and two-parent families, differentiated by numbers of earners.

The poverty rate for children living in workless families is much lower in some countries than in others. It is a consequence of variations in the level of the 'tax and benefit package' which exists in each country to support the incomes of families raising children. In all countries, a non-working single parent is at clear risk of poverty. The number of income earners in a two-parent family is also a significant poverty risk determinant. In all countries, the absence of employment income for both parents clearly increases the poverty risk. Moreover, if families have two earners, the poverty rate is very low in all countries. For two-parent families, employment also plays an important role, although there is diversity among countries as to how many earners are needed to prevent families from falling into poverty.

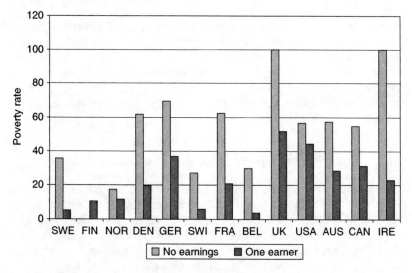

Figure 5.14 Poverty rates, by number of wage earners, the most recent year, per cent
a Single-parent families *b* Two-parent families
Source: LIS data.

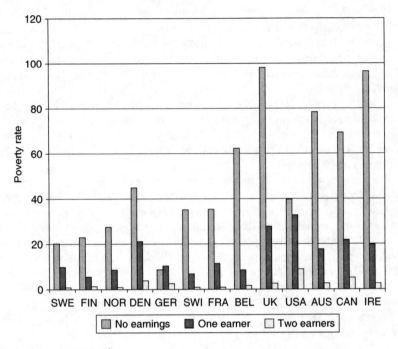

Figure 5.14   (continued)

Employment seems to be an effective shelter against poverty, especially for single-parent families. In many countries, there seems to be a need to resolve tensions arising from new economic and social arrangements in the family and the labour market in order to increase mothers' employment rates. For example, irregular or part-time working hours make new kind of demands on child care provision: child care arrangements should be flexible and affordable for low-income families.

Examining the family policy and poverty link

A first impression from the above discussion would suggest a negative relationship between family policy institutions and poverty in families with children. This seems particularly evident regarding the countries with the very lowest and the highest generosity of family policy, which take opposing positions regarding poverty levels. The relationship between the institutions of family policy and poverty will now be viewed more closely.

In Figure 5.15, an index of family policy is plotted against poverty levels for all households with dependent children. The correlation is strongly negative ($r = -0.76$), indicating that generous family policies considerably mitigate

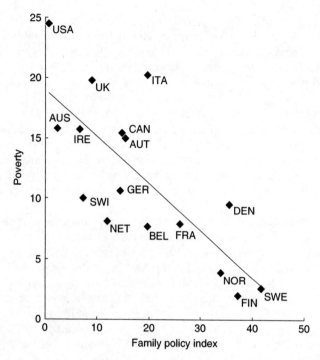

Figure 5.15 Index of family policy and poverty, households with dependent children, selected countries, the mid-1990s, poverty level: 50 per cent of median equivalized income

the risk for poverty in our sixteen welfare states. The Nordic countries, with dual-earner models of family policy, have high generosity in family policy and low poverty levels. Denmark has somewhat higher poverty levels than might be expected, which perhaps could be due to lower generosity in their family policy transfers than Finland, Norway and Sweden, as shown in Table 5.1. Countries with market oriented policies combine low generosity of family policy with relatively high poverty levels, suggesting that the greater reliance on means-tested benefits in these countries in general does not alleviate poverty more effectively than universal benefits.

One interpretation of the above exercise could be that increased family policy efforts seem effective at reducing poverty risks among families with children in general, particularly with a dual-earner model of family policy such as developed in the Nordic countries. But how robust are the results for the use of a different poverty threshold? The application of a poverty limit of 40 per cent of equivalized disposable income comes closer to what has been termed 'very low income' by Duncan *et al.* (1998) in their study of early childhood poverty and educational attainment. The 40 per cent level is also fairly close to the US official poverty line for recent years (Smeeding 1997). Utilizing a 40 per cent poverty line results in an overall decline in poverty levels as compared to the results in Figure 5.15. But the cross-national variation remains large, and the negative correlation between total paid parental leave and poverty is still negative, although somewhat weaker ($r = -0.64$). The generosity of paid leave thus also seems to be an important factor when explaining the cross-national variation among families with the poorest of the youngest individuals in these societies. Applying a 60 per cent level renders a correlation equal to that in Figure 5.15 ($r = -0.76$). LIS data for the years around 2000 exist only for a smaller number of these countries. However, a comparison between the family policy index for this point in time and child poverty does indicate a similar negative relationship between the two variables.

The analyses conducted in this section seem to indicate that support to the dual-earner family policy is most effective at reducing poverty among all families with children. The analyses do not seem to back up the idea put forward by proponents of selective redistributive strategies. Welfare states with the lowest universal and earnings-related benefits as well as with low utilization rates of public child care, and thus to the largest degree reliant on means-tested benefits in the provision of economic resources to poor families, also have the highest poverty levels. It is countries with the most generous earnings-related parental leave benefits and high utilization of public child care that also have the lowest poverty levels among families with children.

Conclusions

The results presented here show that child poverty is still a serious problem in Western welfare states. No matter how poverty has been measured, a large numbers of children live under poor circumstances in several of these countries. Poverty of families with children, however, also shows substantial cross-national variation. The results presented in this chapter indicate close relationships between the model of family policy implemented in a country, the generosity of family policy and the incidence of child poverty, with the risk of experiencing long-lasting poverty being highest in countries with least developed family policy systems and high child poverty.

If the purpose of this chapter is reformulated into the questions: 'Is family policy related to cross-national patterns of poverty for families with children?', or 'Does it matter in which developed society a child is born?', an answer to both would be 'yes'. In particular, dual-earner models of family policy, such as developed in the Nordic welfare states, seem effective in reducing poverty. Such welfare states are probably particularly effective at reducing poverty because family policy programmes provide both adequate benefits to families with children that often are earnings-related and universal, and transfers and services which provide incentives for female labour force participation as well as for male participation in care work. Welfare states with general family policy models that largely support traditional family patterns have medium-high levels of poverty among families with children. Countries with market oriented family policies, which to the largest extent rely on targeted benefits and services to the poorest families, have the highest poverty levels in this population group, contrary to what proponents of selectivist social policy measures would predict.

Living in poverty may not only deprive family members of opportunities to pursue their objectives but may also introduce substantial long-run life-course effects for individuals experiencing early childhood poverty. It has been argued that the risk of poverty and social exclusion of an adult in large part originates in early childhood, when crucial cognitive resources are acquired (Esping-Andersen, Chapter 6 in this volume). A lack of such resources, among other things, increases the risk of a precarious labour market position, which in turn is closely related to experience of poverty risks (for a review of previous research, see Haveman and Wolfe 1995). Duncan *et al.* (1998) show that economic living conditions during the first years of a child's life are strong determinants of school completion, in particular among children growing up in families with the lowest household incomes. The goal of abolishing child poverty can be achieved by supporting mothers' employment, which lowers poverty risks dramatically, and by an adequate 'family benefit package'. Mothers are often vulnerable in labour markets, this increases the importance of social services and an adequate basic income guarantee for families with children. In dual-earner model countries state-sponsored day care for children and extensive parental leave programmes facilitate the combination of employment and children. The poverty risks for families with young children may also have consequences for parents-to-be. Running the risk of becoming poor through childbirth constrains parents' choices to have children without suffering from potentially severe economic difficulties. Agency is thus affected not only for existing parents and children, but also for all potential parents.

The implications of family policy models and child poverty should perhaps also be viewed in the wider perspective of the changing age structures in Western countries, which probably pose one of the greatest challenges to policy makers in the history of the welfare state. The changing age structures of 'post-industrial' societies, with a growing proportion of elderly non-working individuals combined with decreasing fertility levels, create pressures on existing welfare states, since costs for elderly persons increase at the same time as tax revenues decline due to decreases in the economically active population. The 'ageing of societies' thus creates a demand for female labour force participation at the same time as children are needed to reproduce the existing population size.

The solution to several of these problems and challenges may be found in family policy intervention. Increased female labour force participation without provision of possibilities to reconcile paid and unpaid work is likely to decrease birth rates further, since large numbers of women (and perhaps also men) will opt for a career before having children, with those ending up childless becoming more numerous. Providing support to traditional gender roles could perhaps increase child births, but is likely to also decrease both female involvement in paid work and male involvement in care work. Improving parents' possibilities to reconcile paid and unpaid work, in particular through a family policy supportive of the dual-earner family, may thus not only improve family income and prevent poverty, but could at the same time also uphold child bearing at levels necessary for a stable social and economic social development in Western welfare states.

Notes

1   The institutional indicators used partly include aspects of paid leave, together with the scope of public services to families and other transfers paid in cash or via the tax system. The general family support dimension in the original typology is based on indicators reflecting tax benefits to dependent spouses and children, cash child benefits and child care facilities for older pre-school children. The dual-earner dimension of family support is based on the quality of public child care available to the youngest children (0–two years), the extent of social services provided to elderly persons and the generosity of earnings-related parental insurance benefits for mothers and the presence of a period of paid leave for fathers (Korpi 2000:145–6).
2   Besides our sixteen countries, SCIP also include Japan and New Zealand, for which no comparable micro-income data exists and therefore these two countries are not included in the following analyses.
3   The figures used here are based on a typical family with two adults and two children aged two and seven where one parent earns an average production worker's wage.

Bibliography

Bradbury, B. and Jäntti, M. (2001) 'Child Poverty Across Twenty-Five Countries'. In B. Bradbury, S.P. Jenkins and J. Micklewright (eds.), *The Dynamics of Child Poverty in Industrialized Countries*. Cambridge: Cambridge University Press.

Bradbury, B., Jenkins, S.P. and Micklewright, J. (2001) 'The Dynamics of Child Poverty in Seven Industrialized Nations'. In B. Bradbury, S.P. Jenkins and J. Micklewright (eds.), *The Dynamics of Child Poverty in Industrialized Countries*. Cambridge: Cambridge University Press.

Bradshaw, J. (2002) 'Comparisons of Child Poverty and Deprivation Internationally'. In J. Bradshaw (ed.), *The Well-Being of Children in the UK: Save the Children*. University of York: 17–26.

Bradshaw, J. and Finch, N. (2002) *A Comparison of Child Benefits' Packages in 22 Countries*. Department for Work and Pensions, Research report, 174.

Bradley, R. and Corwyn, R. (2002) 'Socioeconomic Status and Child Development'. *Annual Review of Psychology*, 53: 371–99.

Bussemaker, M. and van Kersbergen, V.K. (1999) 'Contemporary Social–Capitalist Welfare States and Gender Inequality.' In D. Sainsbury (ed.), *Gender and Welfare State Regimes*. Oxford: Oxford University Press: 15–46.

Carlsen, S. (1998) *Men on Parental Leave: How Men Use Parental Leave in the Nordic Countries*. Copenhagen: Nordic Council of Ministers.

Conger, R., Conger, K., Elder, G., Lorenz, F., Simons, R. and Whitbeck, L. (1992) 'A Family Process Model of Economic Hardship and Adjustment of Early Adolescent Boys'. *Child Development*, 63: 526–41.

Crittenden, A. (2001) *The Price of Motherhood*. New York: Metropolitan Books.

Daniel, P. and Ivatts, J. (1998) *Children and Social Policy*. London: Macmillan.

Duncan, G. and Brooks-Gunn, J. (2000) 'Family Poverty, Welfare Reform, and Child Development'. *Child Development*, 71: 188–96.

Duncan, G. J., Brooks-Gunn, J., Yeung, W.J. and Smith, J.R. (1998) 'How Much Does Childhood Poverty Affect the Life Chances of Children?'. *American Sociological Review*, 63: 406–23.

Fergusson, D., Horwood, L. and Lawton, J. (1990) 'Vulnerability to Childhood Problems and Family Social Background'. *Journal of Child Psychology and Psychiatry and Allied Disciplines*, 31: 1145–60.

Ferrarini, T. (2003) *Parental Leave Institutions in Eighteen Post-War Welfare States*. Stockholm: Swedish Institute for Social Research.

Forssén, K. (1998) *Children, Families and the Welfare State: Studies on the Outcomes of the Finnish Family Policy*. STAKES, Research Report, 92.

Forssén, K. and Hakovirta, M. (1999) 'Work Incentives in Single Parent Families'. In S. Ringen and P.R. de Jong (eds.), *Fighting Poverty: Children, Parents, The Elderly and Health*. Series of International Social Security, 6. Aldershot: Ashgate. 117–45.

Forssén, K. and Hakovirta, M. (2002) 'Family Policy, Work Incentives and the Employment of Mothers'. In R. Sigg and C. Behrendt (eds.), *Social Security in the Global Village*. International Social Security Series, 8. New Brunswick: Transaction: 297–312.

Gornick, J. and Myers, M. (2003) Families That Work: Policies for Reconciling Parenthood and Employment. New York: Russell Sage Foundation.

Gornick, J. Myers, M. and Ross, K. (1996) *Supporting the Employment of Mothers: Policy Variation Across Fourteen Welfare States*. Luxembourg Income Study Working Paper, 139.

Haveman, R. and Wolfe, B. (1995) 'The Determinants of Children's Attainments: A Review of Methods and Findings'. *Journal of Economic Literature*, 23: 1829–78.

Hobson, B. and Takahashi, M. (1997) 'The Parent–Worker Model: Lone Mothers in Sweden'. In J. Lewis (ed.), *Lone Mothers in European Welfare Regimes: Shifting Policy Logics*. London and Philadelphia: Jessica Kingsley: 121–39.

Jack, G. and Jordan, B. (1999) 'Social Capital and Child Welfare'. *Children and Society*, 13: 242–56.

Johansson, S. (1973) 'The Level of Living Survey: A Presentation'. *Acta Sociologica*, 3.

Kamerman, S.B. and Kahn, A.J. (1994) 'Family Policy and the Under-3s: Money, Services and Time in a Policy Package'. *International Social Security Review*, 47 (3–4): 31–43.

Kangas, O. (2000) 'Distributive Justice and Social Policy: Some Reflections on Rawls and Income Distribution'. *Social Policy and Administration*, 34 (5): 510–28.

Kangas, O. and Palme, J. (2000) Does Social Policy Matter? Poverty Cycles in OECD Countries. *International Journal of Health Services*, 30 (2): 335–52.

Knudsen, K. (1999) 'Married Womens' Labour Supply and Public Policies in an International Perspective'. Paper presented at the Population Association of America Annual Meeting, New York.

Korpi, W. (2000) 'Faces of Inequality: Gender, Class, and Patterns of Inequalities in Different Types of Welfare States'. *Social Politics*, 7 (2): 127–91.

Leira, A. (1998) 'Caring as a Social Right: Cash for Child Care and Daddy Leave'. *Social Politics*, 5 (3): 362–79.

Micklewright, J. and Stewart, K. (2001) *Is Child Welfare Conferging in the European Union?* Innocenti Occasional Papers, Economic and Social Policy Series, EPS 69.

Montanari, I. (2000) *Social Citizenship and Work in Welfare States: Comparative Studies on Convergence and on Gender*. Stockholm: Swedish Institute for Social Research.

Moss, P. and Deven, F. (1999) *Parental Leave: Progress or Pitfall? Research and Policy Issues in Europe*. Brussels: Vlaamse Gemeenschap.

Rainwater, L. and Smeeding, T. M. (1995) *Doing Poorly: The Real Income in American Children in a Comparative Perspective*. Luxembourg Income Study Working Paper, 127.

Rainwater, L., Smeeding, T. M. and Coder, J. (2001) 'Poverty across States, Nations, and Continents'. In K. Vleminckx and T. Smeeding (eds.), *Child Wellbeing, Child Poverty and Child Policy in Modern Nations: What do we Know?* Bristol: The Policy Press.

Ritakallio, V.-M. (1994) *Köyhyys Suomessa 1981–1990: Tutkimus tulonsiirtojen vaikutuksista* (Poverty in Finland 1981–1990: Study on effects of income transfers). Stakesin tutkimuksia (National Research and Development Centre for Welfare and Health, Studies), 39. Jyväskylä: Gummerus Kirjapaino Oy.

Ritakallio, V.-M. (2002) *New Recommendations for Compilation of Statistics will Change the Cross-National Picture of Poverty in Europe*. Paper presented at EU COST A15 Meeting, Urbino, 15 October.

Sainsbury, D. and Morissens, A. (2002) 'Poverty in Europe in the Mid-1990s: The Effectiveness of Means-Tested Benefits'. *Journal of European Social Policy*, 12 (4): 307–27.

Schiersmann, C. (1991) 'Recognizing the Value of Child Rearing'. In S. B. Kamerman and A. J. Kahn (eds), *Child Care Parental Leave and the Under 3s*. Westport, Conn.: Greenwood.

Sen, A. (1992) *Inequality Re-Examined*. Oxford: Oxford University Press.

Smeeding, T.M. (1997) 'Poverty in the Developed Countries: The Evidence from LIS'. *Poverty and Human Development*. United Nations Human Development Office, Human Development Papers: 195–240.

Smeeding, T.M. (2002) *No Child Left Behind?*. Luxembourg Income Study Working Paper, 319.

Solera, C. (1998) *Income Transfers and Support for Mothers, Employment: The Link to Family Poverty Risks. A Comparison between Italy, Sweden and the UK*. Luxembourg Income Study Working Paper Series, 192.

Vleminckx, K. and Smeeding, T. (2001) 'Ending Child Poverty in the Industrialized Nations'. In K. Vleminckx and T. Smeeding (eds.), *Child Wellbeing, Child Poverty and Child Policy in Modern Nations: What do we Know?* Bristol: The Policy Press.

Wennemo, I. (1994) *Sharing the Costs of Children: Studies on the Development of Family Support in the OECD Countries*. Swedish Institute for Social Research, 25.

Zill, N., Moore, K., Smith, E., Stief, T. and Coiro, M.J. (1995) 'The Life Circumstances and Development of Children in Welfare Families: A Profile Based on National Survey Data'. In P. Chase-Lansdale and J. Brooks-Gunn (eds.), *Escape from Poverty. What Makes a Difference for Children?* Melbourne: Cambridge University Press.

6

Education and Equal Life-Chances: Investing in Children

Gøsta Esping-Andersen

Skills, education and the new economy

Two core features of the new economy conspire to raise ever higher the human capital requisites for life-chances. First, and almost by definition, knowledge-intensive economies push up the skills premium. The returns to education are rising, and the less skilled are falling behind in the earnings distribution. Gone are the days when a semi-skilled 'standard production worker' could count on stable employment and good wages. The probability of unemployment – and especially long-term unemployment – doubles or even triples among workers with less than secondary-level education (OECD 2001). It is a pretty safe guess that youth with poor cognitive skills or inadequate schooling today will become tomorrow's precarious workers, likely to face a life-time of low wages, poor-quality jobs, and frequent spells of unemployment or assistance dependency. As pension systems move towards career-long earnings for benefit calculations, these same citizens can easily face poverty as they move into retirement.

The second feature, paradoxically, has to do with the relatively large share of low-qualified jobs that coexist with service economy growth. True, the emerging service economy is highly skill-intensive but, concomitantly, it also nourishes low-end 'MacJobs', in particular within personal (cleaners and waiters) and social (home helpers and nursing assistants) services. Population ageing will, additionally, spur the growth of labour-intensive and relatively low-skilled caring jobs. This would appear to negate the argument that low-skilled workers are at risk were it not for the strong likelihood that such jobs become dead-end, low-paid career traps. Current policy fashion advocates activation, retraining, and life-long learning as a way to combat entrapment, but it is well documented that remedial programmes are very ineffective unless participants come with strong cognitive and motivational abilities to begin with. Mobility is a realistic possibility only for those who already possess skills from youth.[1]

In brief, the advanced economies face a rising skill problem as far as individuals' life-chances are concerned. Yet, the same is the case from the point of view of the collective good. The advanced economies must rely almost exclusively on their human capital to gain a competitive edge in the world economy. Our societies are ageing very rapidly and future working-age cohorts are bound to be very small. Sustaining the welfare of a large aged population necessitates a homogeneously very productive workforce.

All in all, it is difficult to exaggerate the challenge we face in terms of *simultaneously* equalizing and raising the quality of our future human capital. A first question, however, is: What kind of human capital matters? There is a large body of research that points to the rising importance of 'unconventional' skills. Certainly, formal educational credentials remain as central as ever, but additional dimensions are gaining in importance, first and foremost cognitive abilities. The rising salience of relational skills, personality characteristics and social capital is also frequently noted.[2]

Cognititive abilities are, no doubt, the crux of the matter. It is cognitive skills which, in the first place, help determine a child's educational success. Moreover, intrinsic to knowledge-intensive production is the ability effectively to absorb and interpret information and then put it to productive use. The consensus view is that we must build our future on 'life-long learning' and continuous skill acquisition. The evidence shows that this is a practical reality only for those who already possess a strong cognitive base. What matters is the ability to *learn* in the first place and this ability is sown early in life, in great part *prior* to normal school age (Heckman and Lochner 2000).

Indeed, we must be very careful not to conflate formal education with cognitive abilities. In fact, the two are only modestly correlated (estimates from the IALS data show, for most countries, a simple correlation around 0.40).[3] This is also evident from standard earnings studies. In most earnings regressions, education explains only 20 or 25 per cent of the wage variation. Including a measure of cognitive abilities raises the variation explained by another 10 percentage points (Green and Riddell 2001; Esping-Andersen forthcoming). [4] In other words, formal education and cognitive skills represent two relatively distinct dimensions of human capital.[5]

Still, whether we are concerned with educational attainment or with cognitive development, in either case our focus needs to be directed at childhood – and, most importantly perhaps, early childhood. Traditionally, social policy for children has been preoccupied with the *material welfare* of child families. In the past, in fact, the prime concern had to do with the income problems that large families often experienced. Generally, family support was effectively divorced from educational policy, in large part because of one huge and – we now know – erroneous assumption, namely that educational expansion and democratization would resolve the problem of unequal opportunities. In other words, social policies were not conceived as part-and-parcel of the quest for equal opportunities.

The fundamental insight that guides this chapter is that a policy which seriously aims to both improve upon and also equalize human capital must re-integrate – quite radically – social and educational policy around a comprehensive 'package' aimed at investing in children's welfare and life-chances at once. As we shall see, the world can learn a lot from Scandinavian experience in this respect.

How people acquire human capital

International comparisons of cognitive skills and educational attainment yield a set of rather clear, broadly shared, but also surprising, conclusions. Beginning with education, we now have ample evidence in favour of the *constant flux* view. This implies that the impact of social origins and parental social status on children's educational achievement remains as strong today as it was in our fathers' and grandfathers' times. To be sure, there is 'mobility' in the sense that some youth attain more or less education than would be predicted from knowing their parents' education or occupational status. The sheer expansion of higher educational levels means, of course, that more youth will obtain schooling that is superior to that which their parents received. What is important to note is that there has been no noticable rise in *relative* mobility rates (that is, net of overall growth), notwithstanding a half-century of educational expansion and reform. The chances of mobility for working-class children, relative to middle or upper-class children, have not improved and accordingly the *flux* has been constant.[6]

Since innate intelligence is distributed normally across the population, it is clear that IQ cannot explain why children from less privileged social strata systematically perform more poorly than others, nor why children from privileged families systematically perform better. We find a very similar picture in studies of inter-generational income mobility (Solon 1999; Corak 2004). The children of low-income parents – gifted or not – have significantly fewer chances of high incomes and, vice versa, the children of the rich – dumb or not – are far less likely to experience downward income mobility. Economists routinely explain this in terms of Becker's human capital investment models: moneyed parents invest more in their children's education which, then, yields a positive dividend (Becker and Tomes 1986; Solon 1999). In this model, an increase in public spending on education should help reduce the impact of social origins and establish more equality of opportunity.

One problem that most explanations face is that more public spending on education does not result in more mobility. The *constant flux* seems to obtain equally across countries with very dissimilar levels of public investment in education and also seemingly independent of the design of a nation's educational system (Shavit and Blossfeld 1993). To be sure, as Erikson and Jonsson (1996) emphasize, some educational system designs do help reduce – or, alternatively, reinforce – the impact of social inheritance.

A powerful commitment to comprehensivity, as in the Swedish system, can be shown to equalize educational careers, while early tracking and selectivity (for example, through a dual private–public system) probably solidifies inheritance. Still, the prevailing conclusion is that educational systems by and large reproduce, rather than correct for, already existing inequalities among children. In other words, schools are inherently ill-suited to perform remedial and corrective functions if the children they receive already start out unequally in terms of their motivation to learn, their cognitive skills, or their cultural baggage.

Why opportunities remain unequal

Such insights have moved researchers to re-examine the mechanisms that explain educational achivement, mobility and opportunities. One important clue comes from a number of recent comparative studies which suggest that one case, namely Sweden, has indeed succeeded in diminishing social inheritance. There is clear evidence that the impact of social origins on Swedish youth's school achievement and also occupational mobility weakened in the last decades of the twentieth century (Erikson and Goldthorpe 1992; Shavit and Blossfeld 1993).

Considering Sweden's stature as world leader in egalitarian social policy, no wonder that most attention has focused on welfare state programmes. Among the key factors cited are Sweden's unusually generous family benefit 'package' and its successful fight against child poverty.[7] The absence of economic hardship in families should have a double salutary effect. It means that parents can better afford to keep their children in school; and less material insecurity implies greater resources and a longer time horizon so that parents are better positioned to plan ahead and to navigate their children through the school system. Naked trade-offs are less likely to arise.

The focus on family incomes is, of course, a variant of the 'investment model', but with a particular bent, namely the implicit idea that the core problem of unequal opportunities is concentrated at the bottom of society's income pyramid. Empirically, there is ample support for this view. We now have massive evidence that poverty, want and insecurity in childhood can have devastating effects on children's subsequent life-chances. American research suggests that poverty in childhood is associated with, on average, two years' fewer schooling and, later on, substantially lower wages. Especially alarming is the finding that children who grew up in poverty are far more likely to become, themselves, poor parents – thus reproducing the poverty syndrome from generation to generation (Duncan and Brooks-Gunn 1997; Mayer 1997; Duncan *et al.* 1998; Danziger and Waldvogel 2000). Similar, if perhaps less dramatic, findings come from European research (Machin 1998; Gregg and Machin 2001).[8] All this suggests that an attack on child poverty would be very effective in weakening the inter-generational transmission of underprivilege. In fact, this is very clear from evaluation research on the US Head Start programme, an early childhood intervention programme targeted at the truly disadvantaged (Heckman 1999). More indirectly, this conclusion also gains support from recent studies of inter-generational income mobility (Corak 2004). A major finding here is that mobility out of the bottom of the income distribution is, everywhere, exceptionally difficult.

One may interpret the problem in terms of the distance that needs to be travelled in order to escape from poverty and its associated evils. There are two factors of relevance here. (1) the more unequal the society, and the more extreme are the differentials, the longer must someone travel to experience effective mobility. (2) extreme poverty is likely to imply *cumulative* disadvantage and resourcelessness. Low income goes hand in hand with dissavings, sub-standard housing, residential concentration in impoverished and troubled neighbourhoods, lack of transportation and – very likely – social exclusion due to unemployment and assistance dependency. In short, the distance widens simply because families may lack all or many of the basic requisites for improving their conditions: cumulative disadvantage implies a strong likelihood of permanent entrapment. It is this which may explain why there is systematically far less income mobility and substantially more entrapment in countries such as the USA and Britain than in egalitarian societies such the Nordic countries (Bradbury, Jenkins and Micklewright 2001; Corak 2001 and 2004).

This said, one would expect that the Swedish success story should be matched by those other countries in which poverty in general, and child poverty in particular, is exceptionally low – the other Nordic countries *par excellence*. The shortcoming of existing mobility research is that it never includes the other Nordic countries in comparisons.[9] Tables 6.1 and 6.2 give substantial support to the hypothesis that Sweden's documented success in creating more equal opportunities is matched equally by Denmark and Norway. Table 6.1 presents a cohort comparison of the effect of fathers' education on child's probability of attaining secondary education. We compare here cohorts born in the 1940s with sequentially younger cohorts, the youngest being born in the 1970s.[10]

If the 'welfare state' hypothesis is correct, we would expect a clear and steady decline of the parental correlation as we move from older to younger cohorts. Indeed, this is what we see occurring in both Denmark and Norway – but not elsewhere. To illustrate, the probability of secondary schooling was more than twice as high among Danish children with a higher-educated father in the oldest cohort, dropping to almost parity (1.22) in the youngest. In contrast, the parental effect is basically constant in countries such as the USA, the UK and Germany.[11] Another way of illustrating the point is to note that the 'social inheritance' effect is pretty much the same for all countries in the oldest cohort; as we move across the younger cohorts, only the Nordic countries show any systematic declining trend. The same kind

Table 6.1 Impact of fathers' education on child's attainment of secondary education, logistic odds ratios, with controls for mother's education, gender, immigrant status and child's abilities[a, b]

	USA	UK	Denmark	Norway	Germany
Cohort born 1970–80	2.49***	1.66***	1.22*	1.40***	2.04***
Cohort born 1960–70	2.53***	1.83***	1.80***	1.37*	2.46***
Cohort born 1950–60	2.11**	1.52***	1.64***	1.46**	n.s.
Cohort born 1940–50	2.28***	1.76***	2.22***	2.43***	2.00***

Notes:
[a] Abilities are the scores obtained from IALS literacy tests, averaging the scores for document, prose and quantitative tests.
[b] Estimations based on IALS microdata from Statistics Canada, see n. 3.
Significance: * = 0.05; ** = 0.01; *** = 0.001
n.s. = non-significant

Data source: IALS.

Table 6.2 Impact of fathers' education on child's probability of attaining tertiary-level education, selected cohorts, 1935–75, logistic odds ratios, controlling for for mother's education, gender, immigrant status and child's abilities[a]

	USA	UK	Denmark	Norway	Germany
Cohort born 1965–75	1.96***	1.65***	1.33***	1.63***	2.01***
Cohort born 1955–65	1.63***	1.60***	1.42***	1.89***	2.08***
Cohort born 1945–55	1.89***	1.68***	1.82***	1.42***	2.35***
Cohort born 1935–45	1.58***	2.10***	1.67***	2.58***	2.23***

Note:
[a] See notes to Table 6.1.

Data source: IALS.

of analysis is replicated in Table 6.2, but this time we focus on tertiary-level education. Again, we discover exactly the same pattern: Denmark and Norway show, like earlier findings for Sweden, a systematic weakening of the influence of parental status on children's educational attainment while, in other countries, the *constant flux* continues to reign. The impact of social origins has actually risen in the USA.

An additional test that more directly speaks to the 'distance thesis' is to focus specifically on educational attainment among children who come from less privileged homes. Estimating a model similar to that used above, and again controlling for gender, cognitive skills and immigrant status, Table 6.3 shows the odds ratios of attaining secondary education among children whose fathers had *low* education – i.e. only primary school or less. We compare across the same youth cohorts as before. The results of this analysis

Table 6.3 Relative odds of attaining secondary education, children of low-educated fathers[a] selected cohorts, 1940–80

	USA	UK	Denmark	Norway	Germany
Cohort born 1970–80	0.115***	0.185***	0.449**	0.661	0.094***
Cohort born 1960–70	0.097***	0.153***	0.248***	0.447**	0.067***
Cohort born 1950–60	0.116***	0.359**	0.428***	0.445**	0.053***
Cohort born 1940–50	0.133***	0.162***	0.213***	0.205***	0.098***

Note:
[a] Defined as ISCED 0–2 (less than secondary level). For explanations and sources, see Table 6.1.
Data source: IALS.

clearly confirm our earlier conclusions – indeed, quite strongly so. We note, first, the impressive *relative* improvement in secondary attainment among children of low-educated parents in Denmark and Norway and, again, a basic constancy elsewhere. In the case of Denmark, for example, the chances of a Dane from low-education origins have more than doubled (in the oldest cohort, she was a fifth as likely to attain secondary education as children from more educated origins; in the youngest cohort, she is now only about half as likely). That is a substantial improvement when we compare not only with the constancy prevalent elsewhere, but also with the far lower probabilities reigning in the USA and Germany (here, the probability is only a tenth compared to children from more-educated origins), or in the UK (about a fifth). It is also important to remember that these differences cannot be attributed to countries' different immigration profiles.

The results so far must be interpreted with caution because they address only very indirectly the purported connection between income poverty and children's life-chances. We have no information on family income, and our 'inheritance variable' (parents' education) may just as well capture the cultural resources that parents transmit to their children.

As it turns out, there is an equally strong argument in favour of the import-ance of cultural factors. As developmental psychologists and pedagogical experts stress, the motivation to learn and the cognitive skills developed in children are key to their success in school and, indeed, throughout life (Duncan and Brooks-Gunn 1997; Mayer 1997; Waldvogel 2002; Warren Hauser and Sheridan 2002). In fact, the single most persuasive argument for why school systems – irrespective of design – generally replicate existing social inequalities is that children's learning skills are already implanted *prior* to their first encounter with school. Essentially, education systems simply reproduce – or, worse, widen – the cognitive inequalities that any cohort of children manifests. In other words, the key lies in early childhood, which is exactly when children's experience is most intensely shaped by the parental milieu.

If this is the case, we need to focus more directly on the process of *cognitive skill acquisition*. The OECD's PISA study provides us with a unique opportunity to identify far more precisely the mechanisms that link parental resources to children's attainment. The PISA study conducted detailed cognitive tests on fifteen–sixteen-year-olds in a large number of countries, and the data also provide information on both material and cultural resources in the parental home. Table 6.4 presents regression analyses for seven countries, estimating the relative impact of father's and mother's educational level, of their socioeconomic status and of the family's cultural milieu; it also controls for whether the mother is employed (part- or full-time) outside the home.[12] Note that I include controls for gender (girls normally perform better than boys in cognitive tests) and for immigrant status (foreign-born children usually perform poorer simply for language reasons). 'Immigrant children' are defined here in terms of being of foreign-born parents. We have no information on the duration of their residence in the country.

Many of the results confirm conventional wisdom. Girls systematically outperform boys, and immigrant children do more poorly than natives.[13] It is also evident that mothers' education matters more than fathers' – which is to be expected to the extent that mothers are likely to be far more intensely involved with the children when they are small. However, separate analyses (not shown) demonstrate that this is very gender-specific: mothers' education is systematically more decisive for girls, while fathers' matters more for boys. As will be examined much more thoroughly below, mothers' employment seems positive if they work part-time, and problematic only when they work full-time.

The key finding is that *both* material *and* cultural resources have a strong effect on cognitive performance, across the board. It is worth noting, however, that the impact of socioeconomic status is far lower in Denmark than elsewhere. This is fully consistent with our earlier results which show that the parental effect on children's schooling has declined sharply in Denmark. If both 'money' and 'culture' matter, it is nonetheless evident that the latter matters most. This emerges from a comparison of the standardized BETA coefficients (not shown) which indicates that the 'culture' variable is typically 2 1/2 times stronger than the socioeconomic status variable in determining cognitive performance.[14]

In other words, there exists a good case for the conventional welfare state explanation, namely that a reduction of child poverty and economic insecurity should help correct inequalities of opportunity. But the case for a 'cultural capital' explanation is, if anything, even stronger. If this is so, we need to widen our enquiry to what factors in the Nordic countries might account for their far more egalitarian opportunity structure.

A first important clue comes from a comparison of *cognitive inequalities* in the population. The national differences are substantial. If we simply examine the proportion of the adult population which falls in the bottom

Table 6.4 Family background characteristics and cognitive performance, fifteen-year-olds, late 1990s, OLS is regressions with unstandardized coefficients

	USA	UK	Germany	Netherlands	Denmark	Norway	Sweden
Constant	421.34***	444.86***	375.97***	465.29***	388.85***	406.06***	433.92***
Gender	18.68***	15.53***	25.57***	10.04***	20.24***	27.51***	27.51***
Immigrant	−15.98*	−14.01**	−40.92***	−30.87***	−25.48***	−35.25***	−35.66***
Father Education	3.57*	0.76	7.52***	0.58	8.19***	2.98*	−0.27
Mother educ: Secondary	13.79*	10.31	43.61***	27.24***	37.87***	30.83***	20.59*
Mother educ: Tertiary	13.88*	15.42*	50.01***	22.34***	52.72***	20.44**	17.07*
Socio-economic Level	1.10***	1.17***	0.90***	0.92***	0.50***	1.01***	1.06***
Cultural Capital	34.21***	40.65***	36.39***	35.82***	34.17***	38.73***	30.84***
Mother part-time	16.84**	12.92***	5.00	9.55**	8.24	4.76	5.05
Mother full-time	−8.91*	5.99**	−3.09	−10.66*	−0.77	2.91	7.41
R^2	0.182	0.200	0.247	0.230	0.199	0.170	0.170
N	2571	7458	3933	2169	3933	3470	3836

Notes:
We follow the same education coding procedure as before. Reference for mothers' education is less than secondary (ISCED 0-2). Reference for mothers' part-time/full-time employment is not employed. To make education systems more comparable, upper-secondary-level education includes, for the USA, also 'some college' (usually two years). For further details, see n. 12.
Significance levels: * = 0.05; ** = 0.01; *** = 0.001.

Data source: OECD PISA micro-data.

fifth of the IALS cognitive levels (a level defined as *de facto* dysfunctional), the Nordic countries hover around 6–8 per cent, compared to 24 and 28 per cent in the UK and the USA, respectively. Alternatively, if we compute a Gini coefficient for cognitive inequalities across the entire population, we find that inequalities in the USA are exactly twice as great as in Denmark (the most egalitarian of all IALS countries). What is especially telling is that these inequalities widen even further when we focus only on the youngest age groups: for the sixteen–twenty-four-year-olds, the Danish Gini is 2 points lower, and the American 8 points higher than for the population as a whole.

These noticeably lower cognitive inequalities, combined with far greater social mobility, suggest that there may be additional factors involved in the Nordic countries. Those factors must be related to the conditions of early childhood since this is when both material and cultural influences are most decisive. It is well known from many studies that emotional insecurity and familial malfunction can have serious consequences for children's development (Duncan and Brooks-Gunn 1997). Factors that are clearly decisive include parental unemployment, drug abuse, marital instability and divorce; lone motherhood is also highly associated with inferior child performance. Certainly, the Scandinavian countries stand out in terms of low unemployment risks. But we also note that Danish unemployment was quite high in the very same era in which we register a sustained decrease in social inheritance effects. Family instability and lone parenthood are also prevalent in the Nordic countries. Of course, a strong welfare state no doubt helps mitigate the potential welfare problems associated with unemployment, marital breakdown or lone motherhood.

Alternative stimulus structures

A far more tempting and persuasive explanation lies in what we might call children's 'stimulus structure'. If, as we know, the impact of parents' (and maybe especially mothers') educational level and cultural resources is so strong, one explanation for the Nordic phenomenon may simply lie in the far more homogeneous cultural and cognitive stimulus structure that ensues from practically universal attendance in pre-school child care of uniform high quality. If attendance becomes universal in such a system this should clearly equalize the kind of cognitive stimulus that children receive and should be of special benefit to children that come from disadvantaged or culturally weak homes. Any new cohort of children will arrive at the school gates far more homogeneous in terms of their cognitive preparation and their cultural baggage.

We know from research that high quality pre-school care can have very positive effects (Currie 2001; Waldvogel 2002). The fact that the decline in social inheritance in the Nordic countries coincides almost precisely with the period in which these countries moved towards a universal day care regime seems fully consistent with the argument that, (a) the stratification process begins very early, namely in the pre-school ages, and (b) high-quality pre-school care can equalize the cognitive abilities and educational chances of children *if* it is universal. The American Head Start programme has been shown to be quite effective for precisely the same reasons, because it provides middle-class-standard pedagogical stimulus to extremely disadvantaged children. Its shortcoming lies in its very narrow targeting, and one might expect that the USA would exhibit far less cognitive inequality (and social inheritance) were Head Start to expand its coverage, say, tenfold.

As many argue, the potential downside of the universal day care policy is that children's interaction with their parents diminishes drastically. Ermish and Francesconi (2004), for example, show that mothers' employment has negative effects on children's outcomes. The issue of mothers' employment is not only controversial but also hugely complex. We must, of course, first recognize that women's growing attachment to life-long employment is an inescapable fact in all advanced nations. This is unquestionably both positive and necessary for household and societal welfare. It is evident that mothers' employment is, by far, the single most effective bulwark against child poverty – in particular in an era in which single motherhood is rising and in which the earnings prospects of young males are deteriorating (Esping-Andersen *et al.* 2002). It is equally evident – indeed, officially recognized – that the long-term sustainability of the welfare state can be assured only if we manage to maximize female employment rates.

If, then, it is true that mothers' employment has problematic second-order effects for children's outcomes, a policy of encouraging a return to housewifery would not only be unrealistic but probably also counterproductive. The identification of an alternative policy is made difficult by the complexity of the issue. It is, first of all, well documented that the importance of parental closeness to their children is age-specific (Duncan and Brooks-Gunn 1997). The creation of emotional security, a clear precondition for later development, is especially important in the child's first year. Generous maternity and parental leave during the child's first year would thus be an obvious policy – is now pursued in the Nordic and many other EU countries.

Secondly, the possible harm that mothers' employment may do must no doubt depend on the kind of care alternative that the child is given. As Waldvogel (2002) shows, the quality of child care in the USA is extremely uneven, depending on the parents' ability to pay: low-income parents are thus likely to place their children in low-cost and low-quality care (probably parked in front of a neighbour's TV). The situation is pretty similar in the UK, and this may help explain why Ermish and Francesconi (using British data) find such negative effects.

Thirdly, any impact that mothers' employment may have depends very much on its precise nature. There is evidence that stressful, insecure, and unsatisfying work transplants itself negatively to the child (Duncan and

Brooks-Gunn 1997). A key issue has to do with employment intensity. For example, the problematic effects from Ermish and Francesconi's study are especially evident when mothers have full-time jobs. If we now return to the findings in Table 6.4, we note that there is considerable truth in this hypothesis. In most countries, full-time employment has negative effects, while part-time work seems to be neutral – or, indeed, *positive* – for children's cognitive development. The truly noticeable finding is that even full-time employment has no adverse effect whatsoever in the Nordic countries.[15] This provides strong, albeit circumstantial, evidence that a policy of generous parental leave, coupled to universal, high-quality day care, indeed more than compensates for any negative effects that may ensue from mothers' employment. To return, one final time, to the Ermish and Francesconi study, the negative employment effects they identify are in fact not solely due to mothers' but also to fathers' employment. If that is the case, it does not seem to matter which of the two parents is absent or present, as long as someone is. A policy of parental leave should thus be equally positive whether it is taken up by the mother or the father. In fact, one might speculate that boys' cognitive performance would benefit as a result in so far as they see the father as the prime role model.

Conclusions

Post-war welfare states put their faith in educational reform and expansion in their pursuit of strengthening human capital and equalizing opportunities. This, we now know, was a success in terms of broadening human capital, but a resounding failure in terms of attacking social inheritance. The challenge we face today is of a very different kind. On one side, our increasingly knowledge-intensive production system requires not only a more skilled population but one that is also biased towards 'new' kinds of skills. There is little doubt that we shall be moving towards a norm of continuous skill upgrading and life-long learning, and this implies that the labour force needs a solid cognitive base. On the other side, individual life-chances depend – and will increasingly so – on having adequate skills. The 'ante' in terms of the resources required is constantly rising. The low-skilled worker could, in the 'golden' post-war age, count on decent wages and job security. The low-skilled today are likely to face unemployment or low (and even falling) wages. One may, as a rule of thumb, predict that a youth who today fails to attain the equivalent of secondary-level education will, with substantial probability, inhabit tomorrow's poverty, unemployment and social assistance statistics.

The basic point is that equality and a nation's economic performance are intrinsically linked. If, as is the case in many OECD countries, 20 or 30 per cent of youth fail to obtain adequate education, our society in the decades to come may face a major problem of social exclusion or low wages, a new polarization that echoes the 'social question' of the distant past. This will, in turn, pose major problems for the economy, not simply because this population may burden our welfare finances, but also because the coming active population will be steadily shrinking in size. To compensate for our demographic imbalance, we will need to strengthen our reservoir of human capital to the utmost. A competitive knowledge-intensive economy must, above all, rely on the skills and abilities of its citizens; as emphasized by Thandika Mkandawire, our social policy (and also educational policy) must be 'developmental, democratic and inclusive'.

As is well established, citizens' life chances are powerfully over-determined by their social origins, and post-war welfare states have largely failed to improve upon this. School drop-out rates, educational attainment and also later earnings and job prospects are all associated with the kinds of resources that parents command. In other words, we arrive at the inescapable conclusion that, in the new economy, *we can no longer afford social inheritance*.

Once we fully realize that reforming schools and education systems will, alone, not equalize opportunities we find ourselves back at the drawing board. In other words, the advanced nations must design an alternative policy strategy. It is here that the Scandinavian countries' experience holds some relevance, mainly because these are the only cases so far known in which a genuine equalization of opportunities seems to have occurred. The question is: How? What are the real mechanisms that transmit, from one generation to the next, inherited privilege or disadvantage? And can these be modified through policy?

The analyses presented here suggest that it would be futile to think that there is one single 'smoking gun' and, hence, one simple remedy. First, but arguably least important, the design of *school systems* can make a difference. Few would doubt that early tracking or segmentation based on ethnicity, race or social class helps reinforce stratification. Under-funded education systems are likely to nurture the growth of private schools for the well-off, and this also hardens segmentation. Nevertheless, the important conclusion is that equal opportunities will not come about solely through education policy.

Secondly, it is quite evident that we must rethink the link between *education and social policies* – and, above all, pursue a far stronger integration between the two. This is clear when we recognize the potentially very negative effects of economic hardship on educational attainment and subsequent life-chances. Contemporary policy fashion sponsors 'work-friendly' and incentivating social benefits and turns its back on 'passive' income-support programmes. We hereby risk throwing the baby out with the bathwater because there is little doubt that adequate income guarantees to families with children is a *sine qua non* for any work-friendly approach to become realistic. One lesson that the Nordic welfare states teach us is that the eradication of child poverty yields very positive results indeed, not only in terms of alleviating material hardship in childhood but also because economic security is a vital precondition for later achievement (see also Ferrarini and Forssén, Chapter 5 in this volume).

Thirdly, education and social policy need also to be integrated along another dimension. 'Money' may be a necessary but it certainly is not a sufficient, precondition for good life chances. Perhaps the thorniest problem that any campaign for equal opportunities faces is that the *cultural capital* of parents exercises a major influence on children's cognitive development and school success. How can we possibly pass laws to augment parents' cultural resources? Most would answer that this would be naive thinking but, indirectly, the Scandinavian countries suggest an alternative route, namely that cognitive inequalities can be smoothed out if children, universally, attend high-quality pre-school institutions. The data show quite clearly that cognitive inequalities are substantially lower in Scandinavia and, tellingly, the trend towards declining social inheritance coincides almost precisely with the era of building up universal day care. Undoubtedly, we witness here an unintended consequence of a policy that was originally designed for a very different purpose, namely to help reconcile female employment with motherhood. Unintended or not, there is support for the argument that *if* child care is both universal and of high quality, the consequence is a potentially very powerful levelling in children's aptitudes prior to school age – and it is this early phase that is key for subsequent school performance. One way to put it is that life-long learning must begin at age one.

And we must not forget that history is already written as far as women's attachment to employment and careers is concerned. This implies, additionally, a potentially large caring and stimulus vacuum in the early ages of childhood. If our sole concern were the caring vacuum, the USA shows us that fairly broad access *can* be achieved through the market system. If we aim to build part of our equal opportunities policy into child care provision, then clearly an American-style approach will fail. Scandinavia's success in equalizing opportunities may, in part, have been the unanticipated consequence of an altogether different policy but nonetheless it teaches us that we can kill not only two, but three, birds with one stone: at once reconciling motherhood with careers, enhancing our human capital stock and attacking social inheritance. The returns that individuals will enjoy from a policy of investing in children will more than fully be shared by the entire society.

Notes

1 For a comparative overview of entrapment in low-end jobs, see Esping-Andersen (1993) and OECD (2001). For a comprehensive review of the effectiveness of remedial training, see Heckman (1999) and Heckman and Lochner (2000).
2 For a very comprehensive overview of empirical evidence, see Bowles, Gintis and Osborne (2001).

3 The IALS (International Adult Literacy Survey) data were collected by Statistics Canada in the late 1990s, covering a large number of countries. The data include intensive cognitive test information for the adult population aged sixteen–sixty-five. The IALS is one of the key micro-data sets to be used in this article.

4 Warren, Hauser and Sheridan (2002) distinguish the impact of formal education and cognitive skills on life-time occupational attainment . They show that educational credentials are primarily of importance for a person's early career moves and then gradually decline in salience. In contrast, cognitive abilities (as measured via test scores) retain a similar degree of importance throughout people's entire career.

5 They are separate only up to a point, of course, since cognitive skills, no doubt, play a causal role in determining school success.

6 In terms of cross-national comparisons of educational attainment and social inheritance, the most authoritative study is Shavit and Blossfeld (1993), but see also Erikson and Jonsson (1996). The concept of the 'constant flux' comes from the title of Erikson and Goldthorpe's (1992) mobility comparisons, a study which comes to virtually identical conclusions regarding occupational class mobility. A very interesting exception to the rule emerges in both Shavit and Blossfeld and in Erikson and Goldthrope, namely that Sweden (and possibly the Netherlands) do seem to have reduced social inheritance among younger cohorts.

7 For a comprehensive overview, see Erikson and Jonsson (1996), Esping-Andersen (2004) and Ferrarini and Forssén, Chapter 5 in this volume.

8 There is, similarly, abundant evidence that parental unemployment, alcoholism and marital instability have very adverse effects on child outcomes.

9 Neither Shavit and Blossfeld (1993) nor Erikson and Goldthorpe (1992), examined Denmark or Norway.

10 The analyses in Table 6.1 are based on the IALS micro-data (see n. 3). Fathers' education is measured according to international ISCED practice: ISCED 0–2 is less than secondary; ISCED 3 is secondary level. ISCED 4–5 is tertiary level.

11 Estimations for other countries (not shown here) confirm the uniqueness of the three Nordic countries as far as weakening social inheritance is concerned.

12 Socioeconomic status is an index value that weights the occupational status and income of the head of the household; cultural capital is a composite variable (derived from factor analysis) that captures (a) the number of books in the home, (b) the frequency of discussing cultural issues in the family and (c) a 'high culture' measure of frequenting the theatre, concerts and the like. The 'book' variable weighs most powerfully among the three. To avoid multi-collinearity problems, fathers' education is now measured in years, while mothers' is measured in ISCED levels.

13 Note that the immigrant 'penalty' is substantially larger in the non-English speaking countries, in Germany especially.

14 The relative dominance of 'culture' over 'money' is additionally confirmed when we also include another variable that captures family wealth (a measure of the size and amenities of the dwelling).

15 Any negative effect of full-time employment is very gender-specific. In those countries where it is highly negative, we typically find that it is concentrated in boys while, for girls, it is generally positive. This suggests that the girls react more to the mother in terms of role model.

Bibliography

Becker, G. and Tomes, N. (1986) 'Human Capital and the Rise and Fall of Families'. *Journal of Labour Economics*, 4: 1–39.

Bowles, S. Gintis, H. and Osborne, M. (2001) 'The Determinants of Earnings: A Behavioural Approach'. *Journal of Economic Literature*, 39: 1137–76.

Bradbury, B., Jenkins, S. and Micklewright, J. (2001) *The Dynamics of Child Poverty in Industrialized Countries*. Cambridge: Cambridge University Press.

Corak, M. (2001) *Are the Kids All Right? Intergenerational Mobility and Child Well-Being in Canada*. Working Paper, 171, Family and Labour Studies, Statistics Canada.

Corak, M. (ed.) (2004) *The Dynamics of Intergenerational Income Mobility*. Cambridge: Cambridge University Press.

Currie, J. (2001) 'Early Childhood Intervention Programs'. *Journal of Economic Perspectives*, 15: 213–38.

Danziger, S. and Waldvogel, J. (2000) *Securing the Future: Investing in Children from Birth to College*. New York: Russell Sage.

Duncan, G. and Brooks-Gunn, J. (1997) *Consequences of Growing up Poor*. New York: Russell Sage.

Duncan, G., Jean Yeung, W., Brooks-Gunn, J. and Smith, J. (1998) 'The Effects of Childhood Poverty on the Life Chances of Children'. *American Sociological Review*, 63: 406–23

Erikson, R. and Goldthorpe, J. (1992) *The Constant Flux*. Oxford: Clarendon Press.

Erikson, R. and Jonsson, J. (eds.) (1996) *Can Education be Equalized? The Swedish Case in Comparative Perspective*. Boulder, Col.: Westview Press.

Ermish, J. and Francesconi, M. 2004 'Intergenerational Mobility in Britain: New Evidence from the BHPS'. In M. Corak (ed.), *Generational Income Mobility in North America and Europe*. Cambridge: Cambridge University Press.

Esping-Andersen, G. (ed.) (1993) *Changing Classes*. London: Sage.

Esping-Andersen, G. (2004) 'Unequal opportunities and social inheritance.' In M. Corak (ed.) *Generational Income Mobility in North America and Europe*. Cambridge: Cambridge University Press.

Esping-Andersen, G. (forthcoming) 'Untying the Gordian knot of Social Inheritance'. *Research on Social Stratification and Mobility*.

Esping-Andersen, G., Gallie, D., Hemerijck, A. and Myles, J. (2002) *Why We Need a New Welfare State*. Oxford: Oxford University Press.

Green, D. and Riddell, W.C. (2001) 'Literacy, Numeracy and Labour Market Outcomes in Canada'. Ottowa: Statistics Canada.

Gregg, P. and Machin, S. (2001) 'Childhood Experiences, Educational Attainment and Adult Labour Market Performance'. In K. Vleminckx and T. Smeeding (eds.), *Child Well-Being, Child Poverty and Child Policy in Modern Nations*. Bristol: Policy Press: 129–50.

Heckman, J. (1999) 'Doing it Right: Job Training and Education'. *The Public Interest*, Spring: 86–106.

Heckman, J. and Lochner, L. (2000) 'Rethinking Education and Training Policy: Understanding the Sources of Skill Formation in a Modern Economy'. In S. Danziger and J. Waldvogel (eds.), *Securing the Future*. New York: Russell Sage: 47–86.

Machin, S. (1998) 'Childhood Disadvantage and Intergenerational Transmissions of Economic Status'. In A. Atkinson (ed.), *Exclusion, Employment and Opportunity*. London: London School of Economics (CASE).

Mayer, S. (1997) *What Money Can't Buy*. Cambridge, Mass.: Harvard University Press.

OECD (2001) *Education at a Glance*. Paris: OECD.

OECD (2002) *Knowledge and Skills for Life*. Paris: OECD.

Shavit, Y. and Blossfeld, H.P. (1993) *Persistent Inequality*. Boulder: Col.: Westview Press.

Solon, G. (1999) 'Intergenerational Mobility in the Labour Market'. in O. Ashenfelter and D. Card (eds.), *Handbook of Labour Economics, 3A*. New York: Elsevier: 1762–1800.

Waldvogel, J. (2002) 'Child Care, Women's Employment, and Child Outcomes'. *Journal of Population Economics*, 15: 527–48.

Warren, J., Hauser, R. and Sheridan, J. (2002) 'Occupational Stratification across the Life Course'. *American Sociological Review*, 67: 432–55.

7
Fighting Inequalities in Health and Income: One Important Road to Welfare and Social Development

Johan Fritzell and Olle Lundberg

Health and economic development

The micro-level relationship between poverty and economic resources in general, on the one hand, and health, on the other, has a long history. A famous example from the past is Friedrich Engels *The Condition of the Working Class in England* (Engels 1969/1845). Today, there is still a clear relationship between economic resources and health, even in the Nordic welfare states (Rahkonen *et al.* 2000; Fritzell, Nermo and Lundberg 2004). In addition, it has been claimed that public health is better in countries and communities characterized by a more egalitarian distribution of income and wealth (Wilkinson 1992, 1996), although this claim has been debated (Kawachi and Kennedy 1999; Lynch *et al.* 2000; Marmot and Wilkinson 2001; Mackenbach 2002).

Parallel with the growing interest in the level and distribution of income and economic resources as important factors behind health and longevity, there has been a growing interest in health as an important precondition for economic development. A healthy population is not only a good in itself; it is also a key factor for economic development and reduction of poverty, which in turn may enhance public health (for an overview, see Subramanian, Belli and Kawachi 2002). For example, Bhargava *et al.* (2001) found a positive effect of adult survival rates on GDP growth, but only among low-income countries. Bloom, Canning and Sevilla (2004) concludes that health has a positive and substantial effect on economic growth. The WHO commission on macroeconomics and health also stressed the importance of investments in health care as an important tool to improve both economic growth and public health (Sachs and the Commission 2001). Just as high degrees of literacy as well as improvements in survival rates and public health were important for economic growth among the Nordic countries at the beginning of the twentieth century, these factors are likely to be important today for economic development and improved welfare elsewhere.

Investments in health (and education, see Webber 2002) are thus likely to pay off in terms of economic development, and economic growth will in turn generate resources for further investments of this kind. It is important to stress, however, that policies aiming at improving population health and knowledge have to be *designed* and *implemented* – they are certainly not realized automatically. Also among poorer countries there are clear differences in public health, because of differences in policies.

Although there are large bodies of literature on health and health inequalities, poverty and income distribution and social and economic development, it is only recently that these traditions of research have been connected. In this chapter, we will draw on recent research on health and economic resources in order to highlight policy alternatives that may enhance the possibilities for social and economic development. The questions around which the chapter will be centred, then, are:

(1) What is the theoretical context that links an interest in income, health and social and economic progress?
(2) Is there a distinct 'Nordic pattern' in terms of income distribution and health inequalities in Nordic countries and, if so, is it related to policies?
(3) What are the links between income and health, on the one hand, and social and economic development, on the other?

Income, health and welfare

Investments in health and a more even distribution of economic resources have been put forward as important preconditions for economic growth (e.g. Aghion, Caroli and Garcia-Peñalosa 1999; Sachs and the Commission 2001). In addition, economic resources and health are not only important features of economic development on a national or international level, but also crucial aspects of people's lives, as well as important resources for a good life in a broader sense. In other words, income and health are central components of people's *welfare*.

In his seminal work on defining and measuring welfare, Sten Johansson (1970) used Richard Titmuss' (1958) work as a starting point, defining welfare in terms of the individual citizen's resources. The definition was made in two steps, where level of living was defined as 'the command over resources in terms of money, possessions, knowledge, psychological and physical energy, social relations, security and so on by means of which the individual can control and consciously direct her conditions of life' (Johansson 1970: 25, authors' translation). Welfare, in turn, is defined as 'living conditions in the areas where citizens seek to influence through collective decisions and through commitments in institutional forms, i.e. through politics'

(Johansson 1970: 138, authors' translation). Welfare is thus defined on an individual level, but it is closely linked to the commitments assumed by the welfare state vis à vis its citizens (Marshall 1950).

By this definition, we can already note a number of important theoretical features. First, this definition of welfare implies a view of humans as *conscious actors*. An individual will, given the resources she commands and the context in which she operates, pursue whatever she regards as a 'good life'. In line with Titmuss, 'resources' should be understood as a broad concept covering both material and intangible aspects.

Second, the definition is indirect in the sense that the good life is not defined but rather left to the individual to decide according to her beliefs and preferences. But welfare resources, such as money, health or a good education, are essential in that they enlarge the *scope of action*. This indirect definition is often discussed with reference to Karl Popper's devastating critique of attempts to create the utopian good society. Popper (1969) claimed that the search for a utopian ideal condition cannot be established without oppression of those who have a different view of what constitutes the 'good society'. Instead, Popper argued, we should aim at 'the elimination of concrete evils'. In line with this argument, Nordic welfare research has focused mainly on the opposite side of welfare – i.e. on welfare problems. Of course, one cannot escape all normative elements in measurements, but it seems reasonable to assume that we can more easily agree what constitutes miseries or inferior living conditions than the opposite.

Thirdly, this definition focuses on 'collective matters that ... arise from the demands and possibilities that all individuals are facing across the lifecycle' (Johansson 1970: 56, authors' translation). This implies that an evaluation of the level and development of welfare should not focus solely on individual resources (e.g. health, income, education), but also on the availability and quality of collective resources. An important part of such resources are welfare state institutions, such as the health care system, the educational system and the social insurance system.

The focus upon resources rather than needs, and upon faring ill as opposed to faring well, has called for objective, or at least descriptive, indicators of living conditions rather than subjective measures of the degree of satisfaction with such conditions. In other words, the tradition has been designed to capture people's actual conditions, not their subjective assessments of them. The latter are likely to be heavily influenced by the level of aspirations, which in turn involve comparisons across both space and time, and these aspirations, in turn, are therefore not uniform across different social categories. Consequently, a focus on satisfaction would run the obvious risk of measuring 'the forbearance of the poor and the discontent of the rich in a both practically and theoretically unfruitful comparison of welfare' (Johansson 1979: 51, author's translation; compare Sen's, 1985a, disapproval of happiness as well-being).

The division of level of living into different components, inspired by work within the United Nations, resulted in the following list of components included in the Swedish Level of Living Surveys:

(1) Health and access to care
(2) Employment and working conditions
(3) Economic resources
(4) Educational resources
(5) Family and social integration
(6) Housing and neighbourhood facilities
(7) Security of life and property
(8) Recreation and culture
(9) Political resources.

Although the list of components was based on rather pragmatic consid-erations, the Nordic welfare approach is nonetheless closely linked to the-oretical or philosophical writings on welfare and well-being, and bears also some similarities to recent discussions to measure social inclusion within the European Union (Atkinson *et al.* 2002). The theoretical foundations of this level-of-living approach have clear parallels with the writings of Amartya Sen on welfare and well-being (see, e.g., Sen 1985a, 1985b). Sen has also high-lighted the Nordic level-of-living studies as an important way of empirically examining diverse functionings (see, e.g., Sen 1992: 39). However, Sen makes a distinction between the *actual conditions* in terms of health, housing, etc. (in Sen's terminology 'achieved functionings') and the *capability to function*, i.e. the means and freedom to reach the conditions desired (called 'capabilities'). In Sen's writings, it is rather the capabilities that constitute resources, or the freedom to achieve functionings. Theoretically speaking, there is much to support Sen's view on freedom. A common illustration is the comparison between two persons who are both starving, one of them because he is poor and cannot afford to eat, the other because he has made a deliberate choice to fast; this freedom aspect is not so easy to capture in empirical research. In practical terms, then, the areas listed above are a mix of living conditions ('functionings') and resources by which functionings can be achieved.

Aggregation and correlation

As already noted, the 'Nordic approach' to welfare research is multi-dimensional. Different areas, or level-of-living components, are investigated, but traditionally there has been no attempt to merge these into one single indicator of welfare. The reason for this is that 'welfare' is seen as multi-dimensional and to consist of what are basically non-comparable dimensions. In other words, there is no common yardstick by which to compare income, health, social relations, political resources and working conditions. Consequently, we note here a break with most welfare economics, that basically strive for an ultimate measure of welfare. A single, generic welfare index could serve as a powerful tool for monitoring purposes, as well as for directing attention to a broader perspective on human development. In fact, the relative success of the Human Development Index (HDI), a composite index based on life expectancy, education and GDP (UNDP 2001), is probably related to its simplicity.

Even if there are clear theoretical problems in lumping together very different types of welfare resources, partial comparisons might still be possible, and surely important from a social policy point of view. To be both poor and sick, for example, is clearly worse than to be in only one or neither of these states. And although the different nature of the dimensions of welfare makes it complicated to add or compare different types of poor conditions it should not lead to a lack of interest in how various conditions correlate with each other. On the contrary, how welfare problems interact and accumulate should definitely be seen as one of the most central topics from such a perspective. One could in fact argue that the comprehensive character of the welfare approach here is one of its main advantages. A deficiency of both welfare policies and standard welfare monitoring is that they have to a large extent been based on a naïve risk perspective that regards all risks or events (illness, unemployment, etc.) as independent from each other. Esping-Andersen (2000: 6–7) puts it nicely: 'Where the risk view tends to see welfare problems as discrete manifestations, the resource view emphasizes how resources (and welfare conditions) bundle together. In fact, it is the welfare correlates that matter.'

The associations of welfare across different dimensions are also key issues for any evaluation of inequality. According to the philosopher Michael Walzer's (1983) theory of distributional justice, inequality in one sphere of life is more acceptable if it does not decide the distribution in another sphere. The comprehensiveness that goes with multi-dimensionality makes it possible to study the interrelations between different areas. Are those with insufficient resources or condition in one respect also the same individuals that are worse off according to another domain of life? We will return to this issue below.

Although welfare is a multi-dimensional concept, we would argue that certain aspects of life are more basic than others. Health in its most basic sense is a matter of life or death; to be alive is on an individual level a prerequisite of any other aspect of welfare. Similarly, a certain level of life expectancy is a basic condition without which it is difficult to imagine human societies at all. Also economic resources are fundamental to provide the means to stay alive and be fed, warm and sheltered. Economic resources are also fundamental since they so easily can be transformed into goods and services. In this sense, health and economic resources are also fundamental preconditions for each other, since poor health will restrict the ability to obtain economic resources and poor economic resources will restrict the ability to avoid poor health.

These links between poor health and poor economic resources are, of course, most striking in a comparison of richer and poorer countries, but can be observed also in mature welfare states such as Sweden (Fritzell and Lundberg 2000). Figure 7.1 gives an overview of the relationship between six dimensions of welfare in Sweden in the 1990s. A bold line indicates a strong correlation. If no line is drawn between two areas, it indicates that the problems are unrelated to each other. There are no systematic 'negative' correlations – i.e. welfare problems tend to accumulate and there is no sign of compensation.

It is evident that many dimensions of welfare are related to each other. Those with severe economic problems also have a much higher risk of having poor health, a weak labour market attachment and weak political resources. Sweden, in other words, seems to be far from Walzer's complex equality since welfare problems actually do 'bundle together'. That aside, Figure 7.1 also provides empirical support for the economy – health relationship on the individual level.

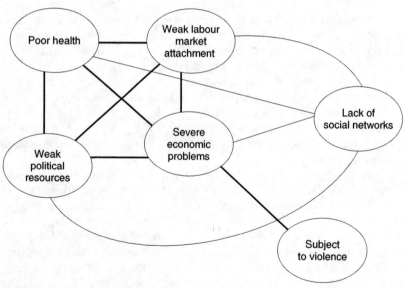

Bold line = Strong association.

Weak line = Significant association, but modest in strength.

Figure 7.1 Association between problems in six different welfare dimensions
Source: Fritzell and Lundberg (2000).

In conclusion, the definition of welfare as an individual and collective resource that citizens can draw upon in order to control and consciously direct the conditions of their lives offers a framework to analyse import aspects of individual living conditions in relation to politics. It thus offers a more nuanced way of monitoring social progress or regress.

Income differentials and welfare policies

Despite the approach to welfare research discussed above, in which welfare is seen as multi-dimensional, it also remains a fact that income and economic resources are a central welfare dimension in welfare capitalist societies. This was supported by the empirical finding concerning the association between different spheres of welfare reported in Figure 7.1. A major aspect of welfare policies in the Nordic countries has thus been to try to equalize the distribution of income.

Historically, it should also be noted that the Nordic countries in general (and perhaps Sweden in particular) have put great emphasis in equalising market income. One way of influencing market income was vis-à-vis employment is reflected in the so-called 'full employment strategy'. Second, trade unions adopted a solidaristic wage policy based on the principle of equal pay for equal work which later was reformulated in practical wage negotiations to imply less unequal pay for unequal work. It should be noted that the solidaristic wage policy was not solely aimed at decreasing social inequalities. LO (the trade union confederation) economists Gösta Rehn and Rudolf Meidner equated this strategy with macroeconomic efficiency and productivity arguments. If companies could not use wage reductions when in economic difficulties the necessary restructuring of the Swedish economy would be fostered driving low-productivity firms and industrial branches out of business. A prerequisite for this strategy would be a centralized wage bargaining system.

As discussed more in detail in other chapters in this volume another cornerstone of the 'Nordic model' concerned various social insurance and income-maintenance programmes to equalize the distribution of income. To what extent is it really the case that the Nordic countries, comparatively speaking, have lower income inequalities than other countries? Is poverty a less frequent phenomenon? To answer such questions, we now present poverty and inequality indices based on the most authoritative source concerning cross-national research on income inequality and poverty; the Luxembourg Income Study (LIS).

Table 7.1 shows the distribution of income in fifteen European countries, in or around 1995, as measured by the Gini coefficient. The higher the Gini coefficient, the more unequal is the distribution of income. We also report the poverty rates as measured by the number of persons living in households

Table 7.1 Income inequality (Gini coefficients) and relative poverty rates (head count below 50 per cent of median income), selected European countries, mid-1990s, sorted by Gini

Country (survey year)	Income inequality, Gini	Relative poverty rates (%)
Finland (1995)	0.217	4.2
Sweden (1995)	0.221	6.6
Norway (1995)	0.238	6.9
Belgium (1997)	0.250	8.0
Netherlands (1994)	0.253	8.1
Germany (1994)	0.261	7.5
Denmark (1995)	0.263	9.3
Austria (1995)	0.277	10.6
France (1994)	0.288	8.0
Spain (1990)	0.303	10.1
Switzerland (1992)	0.307	9.3
Ireland (1995)	0.336	12.9
Italy (1995)	0.338	14.1
UK (1995)	0.344	13.4

Source: LIS, key figures, http://www.lisproject.org/keyfigure.

with equivalent disposable income below 50 per cent of the median income, which are thus total relative poverty rates.

Without going into detail on the figures presented here it is evident that the countries do tend to 'cluster'. The 'Nordic' countries stand out as having low inequality and low relative poverty rates, although Denmark displays a slightly different pattern. The UK, Ireland and the countries from Southern Europe, on the other hand, have the highest inequality and poverty rates, whereas European Continental nations fall in between. Despite the fact that we here have included only West and South European countries, areas that from a global perspective are among 'the low-inequality countries', the cross-national differences are very substantial.

Empirical studies have also highlighted the fact that social policy seems to be a central factor in producing these shifting outcomes. This is linked to the fact that the proportion of total income coming from transfers is generally among the highest in the Nordic countries (Smeeding 2002), while at the same time these income transfers are less concentrated towards low-income groups (Fritzell 2001a). Welfare state redistribution by taxes and transfers has had a particularly strong influence on inequality and poverty reduction in the Nordic countries, when we compare pre- and post-tax and transfer incomes (Ritakallio 2002). Taken together, these results indicate that countries with *less* targeting in their redistribution systems have also been more successful in combating inequality and poverty. Korpi and Palme (1998) label this 'the paradox of redistribution'.

From a comparative perspective, the Nordic countries also seems to be successful in alleviating poverty among specific vulnerable groups. Several studies have indicated that child poverty rates are among the lowest in the Nordic countries (e.g. Bradbury and Jäntti 1999; Vleminckx and Smeeding 2001). The UNICEF study by Bradbury and Jäntti is particularly interesting in that it highlights not only cross-national variations in the redistributional systems of taxes and transfers. The study argues, on the basis of empirical analysis that: 'The higher living standards of the most disadvantaged children in the 'welfare leaders' (particularly the Nordic countries) is due to the higher market incomes in the families' (Bradbury and Jäntti 1999: 71). This finding, of course, relates to relatively high employment rates among both fathers and mothers.

In summary we can clearly say that the Nordic countries, by and large, do have comparatively small income inequalities and low poverty rates. Part of the explanation for this consistent finding is related to the structure of the income-maintenance programmes in these countries, but part also has to do with high employment figures and relatively low wage inequalities. Recent changes in the distribution of income are also much more related to changes in the market than to changes in welfare state programmes. Both Finland (Uusitalo 2002) and Sweden (Fritzell 2001b) have since the mid-1990s witnessed a widening of income differentials that largely seems to be driven by changes in the top of the wage distribution, as well as by increasing capital gains.

Health inequalities and welfare policies

Health problems – illnesses, ailments and premature death – are often seen as a result of bad luck and individual risk factors, either inherited or acquired. This view is reinforced by the facts that medical treatment is individual, and by the health coverage in the media which is focused on behavioural factors such as exercise, nutrition, alcohol and tobacco. Despite this, there are clear and systematic differences in illness and mortality between social classes, educational groups, income strata, men and women, ethnic groups, regions – and, not least, between countries (Mackenbach *et al.* 1997; Macintyre 1997).

Even if there is large individual variation within these groups, differences between groups (i.e. health inequalities) are different in nature than health variation between individuals. For one thing, genetic factors are likely to play a small and insignificant role in the production of systematic differences between social groups, since there is usually no reason to assume health-related differences in genetic set-up between those groups. Similarly, differences in chance or bad luck can be ruled out. Rather, there are systematic differences in living conditions and/or susceptibility to disease that ultimately leads to health inequalities.

Health inequalities, as measured by diverse socioeconomic indicators, have been found for a number of dimensions of ill health all over the developed countries, including the Nordic countries (Fox 1989; Illsley and Svensson 1990; Vågerö and Illsley 1992; Lahelma and Rahkonen 1997). Although equalization has sometimes been predicted (Kadushin 1966) there is no single country where health inequalities have not been found. Health inequalities are thus universal, and concern not only the worst off groups but rather cut across the whole social ladder: the invariance 'the higher the social position, the better the health' holds true in a very consistent way in different countries and for different health as well as socioeconomic indicators.

In the influential British Black Report (Townsend and Davidson 1982), based on data from the 1970s, Norway and Sweden were singled out as countries with significantly smaller mortality inequalities than other countries. Although the empirical underpinning of this statement was not entirely convincing, later attempts to make direct comparisons between Sweden and Great Britain also led to a similar conclusion (Lundberg 1986; Vågerö and Lundberg 1989). More precisely, these studies showed that the size of relative inequalities, particularly for mortality, was larger in Britain than in Sweden, although the hierarchical socioeconomic pattern was fairly similar.

An early comparative study of mortality differentials by education in the 1970s also found smaller relative differences in Nordic countries (Valkonen 1989). The largest relative mortality differences by educational groups were found for France, whereas the smallest differences were found for Denmark, Sweden and Norway. Finland occupied an intermediate position, together with Britain.

However, later and more comprehensive comparative efforts to analyse health inequalities were unable to reproduce these findings. Rather, the general conclusion from a series of papers from The EU Working Group on Inequalities in Health was that inequalities in illness and mortality are as large, or even larger, in the Nordic countries as compared to other European nations (Mackenbach *et al.* 1997; Cavelaars *et al.* 1998a, 1998b; Kunst *et al.* 1998). This was not only at odds with earlier results, but also challenged the view that the egalitarian welfare policies associated with Nordic countries would reduce also inequalities in health.[1]

Health inequalities, as indicated by morbidity and mortality differences between social classes, educational groups or income strata, may be viewed as a very extreme form of inequality. Not only are people's positions in the social structure of importance for their daily living conditions, but these positions also systematically affect their morbidity and mortality risks, resulting in disproportionate levels of illness and premature death among those least well off. In this way, the social structure of society literally affects people's life-chances. Health inequalities also represent an important challenge for welfare policies. The question is, however, what kind of policy implications such inequalities have. In order to address that issue, we need to disentangle inequalities, as measured by relative or absolute differences between social groups, from the underlying levels of ill health or mortality. In Table 7.2, ten European countries are ranked according to three different principles: (1) the relative differences in mortality between workers and others, (2) the absolute differences between these groups and (3) the absolute level of mortality among workers.

Health inequalities are most often reported in terms of *relative* differences, here represented by the rate ratios presented in panel A of Table 7.2. The rate ratios are simply the probability of dying between the ages forty-five and sixty-five among manual classes divided by the corresponding probability among non-manual classes. There are clear differences in mortality risk between manual and non-manual classes in all countries included. The relative differences are of a similar magnitude, except for France and to some degree Finland, where the relative difference is larger. There are no big differences between the other Nordic countries, but we can note that health inequalities measured in this way are no smaller in Sweden as compared to most other countries. But does it follow from this result that welfare policies in Sweden have failed?

Another way to describe inequalities is to look at *differences* rather than ratios. When countries are ranked according to the differences in mortality risk between manual and non-manual classes, the rank order significantly changes. Norway stays in the lead, but is now joined by Sweden. Denmark, with identical relative inequality in mortality as Norway, has a larger absolute

Table 7.2 European countries, ranked according to the relative mortality risk of workers as compared to others (panel A), the absolute difference in mortality risk between workers and others (panel B) and the mortality level among workers (panel C), men aged 45–65 years, 1998

A		B		C	
Country	RR	Country	Diff.	Country	Rate
Denmark	1.33	Norway	5.2	Sweden	19.7
Norway	1.33	Sweden	5.6	Norway	20.9
Italy	1.33	Spain	5.9	Spain	21.1
Portugal	1.37	Italy	6.1	Portugal	22.5
Spain	1.39	Portugal	6.1	England/Wales	24.0
Ireland	1.39	Denmark	6.3	Italy	24.6
Sweden	1.40	England/Wales	7.5	Denmark	25.4
England/Wales	1.45	Ireland	8.1	France	27.6
Finland	1.52	Finland	9.9	Finland	28.8
France	1.70	France	11.4	Ireland	29.1

Source: Kunst *et al.* (1998).

difference between manual and non-manual men and therefore drops in rank. Ireland is another example where the importance of inequalities appears quite different in panel B as compared to panel A. Although the relative differences are the same in Ireland and Sweden (1.39 vs 1.40) the difference in cumulative mortality risk is 8.1 per cent in Ireland as compared to 5.6 per cent in Sweden.

The key to these differences in results when using relative or absolute differences is that the *absolute* mortality levels are quite different (see also Vågerö and Erikson 1997). In the Swedish case, a very low mortality level among non-manual classes in the denominator produces a fairly high rate ratio. And although the absolute differences may be more suited as targets for health policy interventions, they are also dependent on the mortality level of the non-manual, more privileged classes. As a tool for policy evaluation, therefore, neither relative nor absolute differences are optimal. Two questions emerge from this observation: (1) Is there a more policy relevant measure of mortality that still includes an aspect of inequality? (2) What is the reason for the lower mortality levels in Sweden and Norway, and why are they not found in Finland?

A simple answer to question (1) might be to focus directly on the levels of mortality (or ill health) among the unhealthier segments of society – i.e. the manual classes. These data are presented in panel C of Table 7.2, where we find that 19.7 per cent of manual workers in Sweden died between forty-five and sixty-five years, whereas 29.1 per cent of Irish manual workers died between these ages. Life as a manual worker is obviously much more life-threatening on Ireland than in Sweden, despite the fact that the relative differences are about the same.

Inequality in itself is a relative concept, and cannot be defined or measured as the level of health in one group. Inequalities, relative or absolute, might trigger political interest and motivate policy measures. This is not to say, however, that the policies themselves should be directed only to more vulnerable groups, or that the policies implemented should be evaluated against differences in health. If countries are compared in order to established what kind of welfare policies are best in terms of health for all, it might be better simply to focus on the level of health among those who are worst off. The rationale behind this is that inequalities should only be reduced by improving the health among the unhealthier groups.

A focus on the level of ill health or mortality among manual groups, for example, can also be motivated with reference to John Rawls' (1971) 'veil of ignorance'. Placed behind this veil, ignorant about where in society they would find themselves, people would choose principles for distribution of resources that would produce results for those least well off that they would also be willing to live under. If in a similar way we should be forced to choose a country to live in, without knowing whether we would be manual or non-manual, it is hardly likely that we would use the relative differences between classes as a basis for our choice. Given the fact that inequalities appear in all countries, it would be more rational to choose the society where the manual groups have the lowest mortality risks.

As for question (2) we would argue that it is unwize to conclude that all efforts undertaken to equalize living conditions in Sweden have been in vain because the relative mortality risk between social classes remains. Rather, it seems quite likely that a focus on general social policies may have contributed to lower absolute levels of mortality in Scandinavia. The basic idea behind the general social policies is that welfare state institutions (schools, health care, social insurances, etc.) should have such high quality and availability that all citizens want and can use them. A support for the welfare systems is thereby also created among the middle classes, which in turn increases their willingness to pay the taxes needed to run ambitious welfare systems. The quality and extent of services and programmes will thereby also be better and more generous for the working classes and the poor. With targeted and selective policies, the share of the public spending directed to those groups may be larger, but the quality and availability of systems are likely to be less good, and hence the room for improvements in living conditions and survival chances smaller.

But why do we, in that case, see such large inequalities both relatively and absolutely in Finland? In contrast to cross-sectional income data, it is likely that present health is a product of both conditions today and in the past. The same argument holds for the magnitude of health inequalities. This reasoning is particularly relevant in the case of Finland. As seen in Table 7.2, Finland has both large absolute and relative inequalities, but Finland was until recently also a much poorer, and agrarian, society. Finland's welfare state also matured much later than those of the other Nordic countries (Kangas 1991). We would argue that Finland's relatively larger inequalities in health are, by and large, a reflection of historical conditions. A Nordic comparison by Silventoinen and Lahelma (2002) gives support for this inter-pretation, in that they found particularly large health inequalities in older age groups, but not in younger ones.

Income, health, inequality and development

As discussed above, income redistribution programmes are important for a more even distribution of economic resources. We also argued that gen-eral welfare policies may improve survival chances among all groups in society, and thereby also benefit the working classes. But are there any spe-cific connections between equality in income and equality in health and mortality?

There are in fact several links between income and health, on both an individual and a societal level. On the individual level, poverty or low eco-nomic resources has always been connected to ill health and premature mortality. For example, in his famous work from 1845 *On the Condition of the Working Class in England*, Friedrich Engels wrote that the workers were 'so ill-provided with most necessary means of subsistence, cannot be healthy and can reach no advanced age' (Engels 1969/1845: 127). More specifically, Engels pointed to the damaging effects of crowded, poorly ventilated and unclean dwellings, indigestible and unfit food, unsuitable clothing and lack of proper medical care (Engels 1969/1845: 127–34). A half-century earlier Thomas Malthus noted that 'it has been very generally remarked by those who have attended to bills of mortality, that of the number of children who die annually, much too great a proportion belongs to those, who may be supposed unable to give their offspring proper food and attention; exposed as they are occasionally to severe distress, and confined, perhaps, to unwholesome habitations and hard labour' (Malthus 1926/1798).

Some decades earlier the Swedish medical doctor Abraham Bäck had concluded that 'The poverty-stricken are ravaged by pestilence while few of the wealthier fall ill' (Bäck 1765: 6), and he also pinpointed the reasons behind this: 'When I consider the causes behind diseases and excessive mortality among the peasantry, and the worse-off in towns, the first and foremost are poverty, misery, lack of bread, anxiety and despair' (Bäck 1765: 7). It may be noted from these quotations that even early observers of the links between income and health not only stressed the obvious consequences of absolute poverty such as hunger and lack of shelter, but also pointed to the importance of psycho-social mechanisms such as 'severe distress' and 'anxiety and despair'.

Large shares of the world's population live their lives in poverty and poor health today. In most highly industrialized nations, and certainly in the Nordic countries, absolute poverty of that sort is very rare. There is nonetheless a clear relationship between income and health on an individual level in a country such as Sweden (Figure 7.2).

Figure 7.2 shows how the probability of poor self-rated health varies with income. The full sample curve reflects the relationship between household disposable income and poor health, as estimated from a regression analysis including age, income, quadratic income and cubic income.[2] The other curves represent the same analysis carried out separately on three parts of the sample, namely the lowest third, the middle third and the highest third. To aid interpretation we also show where the 10th and 90th percentile value is in the distribution. This means that 80 per cent of the sample lies within the income range given by the vertical lines in Figure 7.2.

As seen from the curves presented in Figure 7.2, these data indicate that there is a clear curvilinear relation between income and health in Sweden. Our results are substantially the same if we stratify our sample by gender. At the same time, these data indicate that the shape of the association may be more complex than the assumption of diminishing marginal health returns

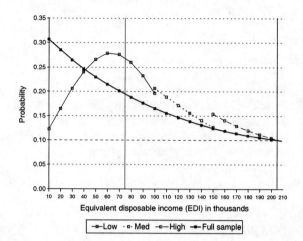

Figure 7.2 Estimated probabilities for poor health, by equivalent disposable income, men and women aged, 25–65, Sweden, 1996–7

Source: Fritzell, Nermo and Lundberg (2004).

of income would postulate. According to the stratified analysis, the slope is not in fact steepest at the very bottom of the distribution. Rather, those at the very bottom of the income distribution appear to have much better health than the full sample model suggests. This reversal of the income and health relationship among those with very low income was also found in earlier research (Ecob and Davey Smith 1999). At the top of the distribution the stratified analysis indicates that the relation between income and health may be sustained even into the top 10 per cent of the income distribution. These observations aside, both these analyses show that the slope is steeper in the middle and lower part of the income distribution.

The main message from Figure 7.2, then, is that there is a strong non-linear relationship between household disposable income and individual health in an advanced welfare state such as Sweden. This, in turn, has several implications. First, simple explanations based on absolute poverty are not sufficient to explain the income – health relationship on an individual level. As seen from the quotations above, such explanations may have been insufficient even 250 years ago at a time when the vast majority of the population in the Nordic countries were still living in poverty. The exact mechanisms involved in producing this relationship today are still to be elucidated, but strong candidates include various stress-related processes linked to relative comparisons of some kind or to the absolute difficulties people with smaller economic resources face in their day-to-day life and in their opportunity to control life circumstances (Lynch *et al.* 2000; Marmot 2002).

Second, assuming that either or both of these types of explanations is important, redistribution of income is likely also to reduce health differences.

As long as at least part of the relationship is generated by causal processes a reduction of incomes in the upper part of the income distribution will have little if any consequences for the health of these people, whereas an increase in income in the lower part of the distribution have a positive effect on health (Rodgers 1979). The public health impact of income distribution from the richer to the poorer parts of the population will therefore be positive, if there is a causal link. In other words, a curvilinear relationship between income and health may provide public health policies powerful with new tools in well-established systems for income redistribution.

In the discussion on the association between income and health on a national level, there has also been a distinction between *absolute* and *relative* effects. When plotting countries wealth in terms of GDP *per capita* against health in terms of life expectancy at birth, a curvilinear relationship is again the result (Figure 7.3). Several observations can be made from Figure 7.3. First, there appears to be an upper limit to life expectancy at birth at around eighty years. However, analyses have showed that this upper limit has increased over time, perhaps due to technological change in general, improvements in medical technologies as well as the lagged effects of improved conditions earlier in life (World Bank 1993; Wilkinson 1996).

Second, only limited public health gains are associated with *per capita* GDP over $20.000 (PPP) or so, whereas small improvements under $5,000 are associated with substantially increased life expectancy. In other words,

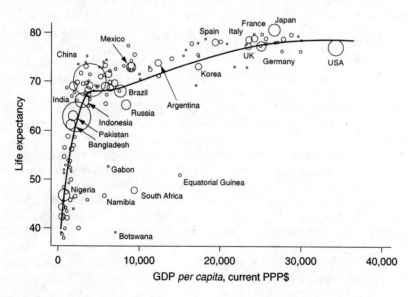

Figure 7.3 Relationship between country wealth and life expectancy, 2000
Source: Deaton (2003).

there is diminishing life expectancy return on increased *per capita* GDP in a way that parallels the individual findings presented in Figure 7.2. This finding has triggered an extensive literature since the mid-1990s. Among richer countries, it has been argued, it is not the economic level as such but rather the *distribution of income and wealth* that is of importance for the health status of the population (for a recent overview, see Kawachi and Kennedy 2002). More specifically, income inequality as such, over and above any individual links between low income and poor health, has been suggested to be a causal factor (Wilkinson 1992, 1996). Although influential, these ideas have not been uncontested. In more recent reviews, the conclusion has been that there is little evidence of a direct effect of income inequality on health, but that the individual-level relationships are reason enough to redistribute incomes in favour of the poorest (Deaton 2003; Lynch *et al.* 2004).

Third, however, the data presented in Figure 7.3 also suggest that there is a wide scope for political action since there is substantial variation in life expectancy at birth at the same level of economic development. Among the poorest countries, life expectancy varies between forty and sixty-five years, although levels of GDP *per capita* distribution are almost identical. Looking at countries with a life expectancy of seventy years or more, on the other hand, there are several examples of countries with far better life expectancy than others at the same level of GDP *per capita*, and indeed as high life a expectancy as much wealthier countries. This may be related to differences in the distribution of economic resources, but also to other policy measures such as the organization of basic living conditions including water supply and health care. The bottom line, we would argue, is that there are different policy options at every level of economic development, and that there is no simple deterministic relationship between economic growth and public health development, even if it obviously is easier to achieve a high level of life expectancy with a fairly good level of economic development.

When it comes to policy, it can be noted that the Nordic countries are characterized not only by relatively small income inequalities but also by ambitious welfare state programmes. These programmes, including child care, schooling, health care and old-age care, to give only a few examples, constitute *extra-individual resources* that enlarge the possibilities for individuals and families to lead the lives they prefer. It is reasonable to believe, we would argue, that income redistribution systems, in combination with welfare services of good quality and availability, helps people to cope with everyday life, and thereby also contributes to better public health. The Nordic countries, apart from Denmark, are also all at the top of the life expectancy league, not least with regard to infant mortality. Statistics reveal that at the beginning of the twenty-first century only seven countries in the world had figures below 4 per 1,000 live births. Four of them were Finland, Iceland, Norway and Sweden. However, that does not preclude the existence of relatively large inequalities between different social strata.

Conclusions

The basic aim of this chapter has been to present how income inequality, population health status and health inequalities are interrelated to one another, as well as to social development and welfare. The framework of the study has been the 'Nordic', or 'Scandinavian', approach to welfare research. Our principal findings and statements are that:

- *Welfare is a multi-dimensional concept.* Welfare measurement and monitoring should (1) study the prevalence of inferior conditions rather than faring well; (2) use descriptive rather than subjective indicators; (3) study how welfare areas are inter-related. Health and income are two key components of level of living.
- Comparative analyses have shown that Nordic countries have *small income differentials and low poverty rates* compared with other rich nations. These outcomes are related to a relatively high and universal social insurance system, but also to high employment rates.
- *Relative health inequalities* are not consistently lower in the Nordic countries in comparison with other European countries. However, this is partly, in the Swedish case, dependent on a very good health status among the upper social strata of the population. In the Finnish case, research evidence suggests that these relatively unfavourable statistics are mostly due to historical conditions and consequently seen only among the elderly. When it comes to infant and child mortality rates, all the Nordic countries perform extremely well.
- Both micro-data and macro-data strongly suggest that the *association between income and health is curvilinear.* In other words, we find diminishing marginal health returns of income for both individuals and for nations. This implies that reducing income inequalities will lead to improvements of population health status.

While our first empirical conclusion, low-income inequality and low prevalence of poverty, is a well known and robust one, we feel obliged to say something more about the other links. Health cannot be redistributed in the same manner as income. Structural forces leading to class differentials in health are not easily counteracted, and to understand these fully is of great interest from a purely scientific view-point. It may be that from a public policy point of view, it is more of an interest to focus on the health status of vulnerable groups as such when making a comparative evaluation. Seen in that respect, the Nordic countries also perform comparatively well here. This in return is likely to foster economic and social growth and development.

Finally it should be noted that we have deliberately refrained from giving more specific reasons, for how population health improvements come about. We have instead returned to the basic welfare approach and argued that what really matters is to improve living conditions and lessen the inequalities of conditions. In other words, we suggest that it is the Nordic social policy model at large that is of greatest importance in understanding the health status of Nordic populations.

Notes

1 A paper by Dahl *et al.* (forthcoming) discusses at length a number of possible counterbalancing forces which could hypothetically be relevant in explaining this outcome. Some of them will also be touched upon here.
2 The curves presented are calculated in the following way: as a baseline, the log odds of poor self-rated health was set to the mean of the other included variable (i.e. age) in the respective regressions. The combined estimates of the linear and any higher-order significant polynomial terms of income were then calculated and transformed into the basic income variable. Finally, the estimates were exponentiated to express the odds of self-rated poor health along the income axis.

Bibliography

Aghion, P., Caroli, E. and Garcia-Peñalosa, C. (1999) 'Inequality and Economic Growth: The Perspective of the New Growth Theories'. *Journal of Economic Literature*, 37: 1615–60.
Atkinson, T., Cantillon, B., Marlier, E. and Nolan, B. (2002) *Social Indicators: The EU and Social Inclusion*. Oxford: Oxford University Press.
Bhargava, A., Jamison, D.T., Lau, L.J. and Murray, C. J. L. (2001) 'Modelling the Effects on Economic Growth'. *Journal of Health Economics*, 20: 423–40.
Bloom, D., Canning, D. and Sevilla, J. (2004) 'The Effect of Health on Economic Growth: A Production Function Approach'. *World Development*, 32: 1–13.
Bradbury, B. and Jäntti, M. (1999) 'Child Poverty across Industrialized Nations'. Innocenti Occasional Papers, Economic, and Social Policy Series, 71 Florence: UNICEF.
Bäck, A. (1765) *Tal om farsoter som mäst härja bland rikets allmoge*. Stockholm: Lars. Salvius. (Speech on Epidemics that Lay Waste among the Country People of the Realm.)
Cavelaars, A., Kunst, A., Geurts, J., Crialesi, R., Grötvedt, L., Helmert, U., Lahelma, E., Lundberg, O., Mielck, A., Matheson, J. Mizrahi, A., Mizrahi, A., Rasmussen, N.K., Redigor, E., Spuler, T. and Mackenbach, J. (1998a) 'Differences in Self Reported Morbidity by Educational Level: A Comparison of 11 Western European Countries'. *Journal of Epidemiology and Community Health*, 52: 219–27.
Cavelaars, A., Kunst, A., Geurts, J., Helmert, U., Lundberg, O., Mielck, A., Matheson, J., Mizrahi, A., Rasmussen, N.K., Spuler, T. and Mackenbach, J.' (1998b) Morbidity Differences by Occupational Class among Men in Seven European Countries: An Application of the Erikson–Goldthorpe Social Class Scheme'. *International Journal of Epidemiology*, 27: 222–230.
Dahl, E., Fritzell, J., Lahelma, E., Martikainen, P., Kunst, A. and Mackenbach, J. (forthcoming) 'Welfare State Regimes and Health Inequalities'. In J. Siegrist and M. Marmot (eds.), *Socioeconomic Position and Health: New Explanations and their Policy Implications*. Oxford: Oxford University Press.

Deaton, A. (2003) 'Health, Inequality, and Economic Development'. *Journal of Economic Literature*, 41: 113–58.

Ecob, R. and Davey Smith, G. (1999) 'Income and Health: What is the Nature of the Relationship?'. *Social Science and Medicine*, 48: 693–705.

Engels, F. (1969/1845) *The Conditions of the Working Class in England*. London: Panther.

Esping-Andersen, G. (2000) 'Social Indicators and Welfare Monitoring'. Social Policy and Development Programme Paper, 2. Geneva: UNRISD.

Fox, J. (ed.) (1989) *Health Inequalities in European Countries*. Gower: Aldershot.

Fritzell, J. (2001a) 'Still Different? Income Distribution in the Nordic Countries in a European Comparison'. In M. Kautto, J. Fritzell, B. Hvinden, J. Kvist and H. Uusitalo, H. (eds.), *Nordic Welfare States in the European Context*. London: Routledge.

Fritzell, J. (2001b) 'Inkomstfördelningens trender under 1990-talet' (Income Distribution Trends during the 1990s. In J. Fritzell and J. Palme (eds), *Välfärdens finansiering och fördelning*, SOU 2001 (57). Stockholm: Fritzes. (The Financing and Distribution of welfare).

Fritzell, J. and Lundberg, O. (2000) *Välfärd, ofärd och ojämlikhet* (Welfare, Disadvantage and Inequality), SOU 2000 (41). Stockholm: Fritzes.

Fritzell, J., Nermo, M. and Lundberg, O. (2004) 'The Impact of Income: Assessing the Relationship between Income and Health in Sweden'. *Scandinavian Journal of Public Health*, 32: 6–16.

Illsley, R. and Svensson, P.-G. (eds), (1990) 'Health Inequities in Europe'. *Social Science and Medicine*, Special Issue, 27 (3): 223–430.

Johansson, S. (1970) *Om levnadsnivåundersökningen* (On the Level of Living Survey). Stockholm: Allmänna förlaget.

Johansson, S. (1979) *Mot en teori för social rapportering* (Towards a Theory of Social Reporting). Stockholm: Swedish Institute for Social Research.

Kadushin, C. (1966) 'Social Class and the Experience of Ill Health'. In R. Bendix and S.M. Lipset (eds), *Class, Status, and Power*. New York: Free Press.

Kangas, O. (1991) *The Politics of Social Rights. Studies on the Dimensions of Sickness Insurance in OECD Countries*. Stockholm: Swedish Institute for Social Research.

Kawachi, I. and Kennedy, B.P. (1999) 'Income Inequality and Health: Pathways and Mechanisms'. *Health Service Research*, 34: 215–27.

Kawachi, I. and Kennedy, B.P. (2000) *The Health of Nations: Why Inequality is Harmful for Your Health*. New York: The New Press.

Korpi, W. and Palme, J. (1998) 'The Paradox of Redistribution and the Strategy of Equality: Welfare State Institutions, Inequality and Poverty in the Western Countries'. *American Sociological Review*, 63: 661–87.

Kunst, A., Groenhof, F., Mackenbach, J. and the EU Working Group on Socioeconomic Inequalities in Health (1998) 'Mortality by Occupational Class among Men 30–64 years in 11 European countries'. *Social Science and Medicine*, 46: 1459–76.

Lahelma, E. and Rahkonen, O. (eds) (1997) 'Health Inequalities in Modern Societies and Beyond'. *Social Science and Medicine*, Special Issue, 44(6): 721–910.

Lundberg, O. (1986) 'Class and Health: Comparing Britain and Sweden'. *Social Science and Medicine*, 26: 511–17.

Lynch, J.W., Davey Smith, G., Kaplan, G.A. and House, J.S. (2000) 'Income Inequality and Mortality: Importance to Health of Individual Income, Psychosocial Environment, or Material Conditions'. *British Medical Journal*, 320: 1200–4.

Lynch, J., Davey Smith, G., Harper, S., Hillemaier, M., Ross, N., Kaplan, G.A. and Wolfson, M. (2004) 'Is Income Inequality a Determinant of Population Health? Part 1: A Systematic Review'. *The Millbank Quarterly*, 82: 5–99.

Macintyre, S. (1997) 'The Black Report and Beyond: What are the Issues?'. *Social Science and Medicine*, 44: 723–45.
Mackenbach, J.P. (2002) 'Income Inequality and Population Health'. *British Medical Journal*, 324: 1–2.
Mackenbach, J., Kunst, A., Cavelaars, A., Groenhof, F. Geurts, J. and the EU Working Group on Socio economic Inequalities in Health, (1997) 'Socio-Economic Inequalities in Morbidity and Mortality in Western Europe'. *Lancet*, 349: 1655–9.
Malthus, T.R. (1926/1798) *First Essay on Population*. London: Macmillan.
Marmot, M. (2002) 'The Influence of Income on Health: Views of an Epidemiologist'. *Health Affairs*, 21: 31–46.
Marmot, M. and Wilkinson, R.G. (2001) 'Psychosocial and Material Pathways in the Relation between Income and Health: A Response to Lynch *et al*'. *British Medical Journal*, 322: 1233–6.
Marshall, T.H. (1950) *Citizenship and Social Class and other Essays*. Cambridge: Cambridge University Press.
Popper, K. (1969) *Conjectures and Refutations: The Growth of Scientific Knowledge*. London: Routledge & Kegan Paul.
Rodgers, G.B. (1979) 'Income and Inequality as Determinants of Mortality: An International Cross-Section Analysis'. *Population Studies*, 33: 343–51.
Rahkonen, O., Arber, S., Lahelma, E., Martikainen P. and Silventoinen, K. (2000) 'Understanding Income Inequalities in Health among Men and Women in Britain and Finland'. *International Journal of Health Services*, 30: 27–47.
Rawls, J. (1971) *A Theory of Justice*. Cambridge, Mass.: Harvard University Press.
Ritakallio, V-M. (2002) 'Trends of Poverty and Income Inequality in Cross-National Comparison'. *European Journal of Social Security*, 4: 151–77.
Sachs, J.D. and the Commission on Macroeconomics and Health, (2001) *Macroeconomics and Health: Investing in Health for Economic Development*. Geneva: WHO.
Sen, A. (1985a) 'Well-Being, Agency and Freedom, The Dewey Lectures 1984'. *Journal of Philosophy*, 82: 169–221.
Sen, A. (1985b) *Commodities and Capabilities*. Amsterdam: North Holland.
Sen, A. (1992) *Inequality Reexamined*. Cambridge, Mass.: Harvard University Press.
Silventoinen, K. and Lahelma, E. (2002) 'Health Inequalities by Education and Age in Four Nordic Countries, 1986 and 1994'. *Journal of Epidemiology and Community Health*, 56: 253–8.
Smeeding, T.M. (2002) 'Globalization, Inequality and the Rich Countries of the G-20: Evidence from the Luxembourg Income Study'. Center for Policy Research Syracuse University/LIS Working Paper Series, 320.
Subramanian, S.V., Belli, P. and Kawachi, I. (2002) 'The Macroeconomic Determinants of Health', *Annual Review of Public Health*, 23: 287–302.
Titmuss, R.M. (1958) *Essays on the Welfare State*. London: Allen & Unwin.
Townsend, P. and Davidson, N. (1982) *Inequalities in Health: The Black Report*. Harmondsworth: Penguin.
UNDP (2001) *Human Development Report: Making New Technologies Work for Human Development*. New York: Oxford University Press.
Uusitalo, H. (2002) *Finland: Changes in Income Distribution*. Helsinki: Central Pension Institute.
Vågerö, D. and Erikson, R. (1997) 'Socio-Economic Inequalities in Morbidity and Mortality in Western Europe'. *Lancet*, 350: 516.
Vågerö, D. and Illsley, R. (eds.) (1992) Inequality, Health and Policy in East and West Europe', *International Journal of Health Sciences*, Special Issue, 3(3/4).

Vågerö, D. and Lundberg, O. (1989) 'Health Inequalities in Britain and Sweden'. *Lancet*, 334: 35–6.

Valkonen, T. (1989) 'Adult Mortality and Level of Education: A Comparison of Six Countries'. In A.J. Fox (ed.), *Health Inequalities in European Countries*. Gower: Aldershot.

Vleminckx, K. and Smeeding, T.M. (2001) *Child Well-Being, Child Poverty, and Child Policy in Modern Nations: What Do We Know?* Bristol: Policy Press.

Walzer, M. (1983) *Spheres of Justice: A Defence of Pluralism and Equality*. Oxford: Blackwell.

Webber, D.J. (2002) 'Policies to Stimulate Growth: Should we Invest in Health or Education?', *Applied Economics*, 34: 1633–43.

Wilkinson, R.G. (1992) 'Income Distribution and Life Expectancy'. *British Medical Journal*, 304: 165–8.

Wilkinson, R.G. (1996) *Unhealthy Societies: The Afflictions of Inequality*. London: Routledge.

World Bank, (1993) *World Development Report*. New York: Oxford University Press.

8

Does the Welfare State Harm Economic Growth? Sweden as a Strategic Test Case*

Walter Korpi

Growth consequences of welfare states

On a world-wide scale, economic growth rates declined markedly after the mid-1970s. In many Western countries, politicians and economists argued that the main causes for this slowdown could be traced back to distorting effects of their welfare states. Such diagnoses were often used to support significant limitations and cuts in social provisions. Welfare states are of major relevance for distribution and redistribution of economic resources among citizens in Western countries. For social scientists, it is therefore of importance to assess to what extent there is an empirical base for the hypothesized negative growth consequences of welfare states. This is important, perhaps especially for those who tend to promote welfare state policies. If major negative consequences remain unrecognized, or nothing is done to abate them, the legitimacy of the welfare state, at least in the long run, is undercut.

Empirical studies of the growth consequences of welfare states have typically been based on comparisons among countries. A relatively new type of strategy is to focus on a country where the assumed negative effects of welfare states on economic growth are most likely to be found. In this context Sweden, widely seen as *the* prototype of a well-developed welfare state, provides such a strategic research site. In this chapter, I will therefore examine the strength of the empirical evidence in recent years purporting to show that because of its welfare state Sweden's economic growth rate has been lagging behind that of other comparable countries. The question here is thus not the general one as to whether welfare states harm economic growth. Instead, I examine the quality of empirical evidence alleged to show that since about 1970 the welfare state in Sweden has in fact made its economic growth rate seriously lag behind that of other comparable countries. Because of Sweden's character as a strategic research site this examination is of relevance for more general debate on the growth consequences of welfare states.

The chapter is organized in the following way. The next section takes up the discussion of the role of welfare states in distributive conflicts, and I justify the use of Sweden as a strategic case for testing predictions about the negative growth consequences of welfare states. I then move to a consideration of overall patterns of GDP *per capita* growth in eighteen OECD countries (1950–97), and discuss the major reliability problems in the measurement of economic growth rates. The basic flaw in efforts to prove empirically the causal effects of Sweden's welfare state on economic growth is the comparison of percentage growth rates among countries without consideration of differences in *initial levels of GDP per capita;* these problems of relative and absolute growth in causal analysis are discussed next. The following two sections analyse the different guises in which the mixing of relative and absolute growth rates have appeared in these efforts, and include an analysis of growth rates when this flaw is controlled for. The background to the Swedish depression of 1991–3 is analysed prior to the concluding discussion.

Welfare states and distributive conflict

In discussions on the potential consequences of welfare states, it is necessary to remember that, because of their role for distribution and redistribution, welfare states are positioned in the centre of distributive conflict among socioeconomically based interest groups. This position reflects the fact that welfare states are the outcome of *tensions* between markets and politics. Markets and politics are two alternative, and complementary, settings for distribution and redistribution; however, they differ in important ways. A basic difference between markets and politics concerns the types of assets or power resources which actors can bring into distributive conflict within these settings, assets which empower actors in defending their interests and in asserting claims.

In market settings, actors are empowered by various types of economic assets, which provide the central resources which actors can use to make claims and to safeguard their interests.[1] Since economic assets can be separated from the individual, they can be more or less concentrated on single individuals or groups of actors. As is well known, economic assets are typically unequally distributed among individuals and households, a distribution markedly correlated with socioeconomic position. Markets thus provide settings for exchange, competition, and conflict among actors which are unequal in terms of relevant capacities. Unlike sports such a golf, markets do not compensate for such handicaps in the final distribution of awards.

Democratic politics provides settings for distribution and redistribution which clearly differ from those in markets. Here, the central power resource, universal and equal suffrage, is by definition uncorrelated with socioeconomic position. Furthermore all democracies have outlawed the sale or purchase of votes. Within the political context democracy thus to a major extent levels the field for competition between different socioeconomic interest groups. To varying degrees inequalities in economic resources continue to influence outcomes of political decision making; yet political democracy is an institutional structure which has decreased the relevance of economic inequality in modern societies to an unparalleled extent. While an individual's single vote in itself, is of course, not a strong asset, its efficacy can be enhanced by collective action. We can therefore expect that individuals, who are relatively disadvantaged in terms of economic resources for market use, are likely to engage in collective action – for example, via political parties and trade unions – to modify conditions for and outcomes of market distribution. The relative role of politics and markets in distributive processes is therefore likely to be a contested one. To differing extents, welfare states modify relations between markets and politics.

The intellectual support for the superiority of market distribution is provided by neo-classical economic theory. Here it is assumed that, apart from some imperfections, the self-regulatory competitive market will via the price system induce economic actors to exert themselves and to adapt to changing conditions, something which will result in an optimal and efficient allocation of resources and rewards.[2] In terms of policy recommendations this theory clearly has *laissez-faire* implications. Political attempts to modify conditions for and outcomes of market distribution are assumed to weaken and pervert market mechanisms, thereby decreasing labour supply, savings and investments, and generating tax wedges as well as deadweight burdens. As a result, the growth potential of the economy is undermined. The theoretical defence for the welfare state is not as well developed and has a much shorter history.

In discussions on the effects of welfare states on economic growth, it is fruitful to remember that diagnoses of impending or real severe negative effects of welfare states have a long ancestry. Over centuries fears of misuse and adverse economic effects were elicited by government attempts to transfer money from the 'haves' to the 'have-nots'. By what in 1834 was the New Poor Law, the British government used the punitive poor house to stem what it saw as grave misuses of overly lax earlier practices. In 1907, the father figure of neo-classical economics, Alfred Marshall, formulated the redistributive dilemma for this theoretical perspective – to what extent was it justified to use political measures to achieve a more equal distribution of wealth when such measures were likely to diminish aggregate wealth (Marshall 1907)?

During the twentieth century, internationally prominent economists from time to time pronounced fears that their home countries were passing or about to pass the point where tax burdens would have grave negative consequences for economic growth rates. Thus in Sweden in the early 1920s, when total government expenditures as a percentage of GDP could be counted in single digits, Heckscher (1921) warned that the country was about to pass an economically dangerous threshold. In the late 1930s, his followers Cassel and Bagge maintained that, at 15 per cent of GDP, the upper limit of taxation had been reached. A decade later, a British economist, Clark (1945) was, however, prepared to raise this deadline to 25 per cent of GDP. In the

USA in 1980, with government expenditures at about one-third of GDP, Schitovsky (1980) stated that while the negative consequences of government size had earlier been limited, they were now threatening the future of the capitalist system. In the 1980s, while total government outlays as percentage of GDP among the then OECD countries ranged from about 30 per cent to about 60 per cent, prominent economists voiced similar warnings of the serious negative growth consequences of large government size.

The historical record thus indicates that when the continuous increase of government size has passed thresholds once defined as 'dangerous', economists' warnings of impending serious growth obstacles have repeatedly been postponed to increasingly higher levels of government expenditures. Theoretically based expectations of negative growth consequences appear to have been important. Yet we must avoid the conclusion that the potential negative consequences of welfare state growth are negligible; my interpretation is that there probably is something in these warnings and that they must be taken seriously. The main task is to attempt empirically to verify theoretically derived hypotheses on serious negative effects to examine circumstances which affect the relative role of these effects and to study the balance between the negative and positive consequences of welfare states. We must, however, remember that when social scientists attempt to adjudicate in such situations of conflict of interests, their objectivity is put to a severe test. In this context it is therefore imperative to base conclusions on good empirical analyses.

Sweden: a strategic test case

As noted above, it is reasonable to argue that to the extent that welfare state expansion leads to theoretically expected serious negative growth consequences, such effects are more likely to be found in Sweden than elsewhere. In 1980, the size of total government outlays as percentage of Sweden's GDP had just passed the 60 per cent threshold and was highest among the then OECD countries, about 20 percentage points above the OECD average. It is therefore not surprising that at this time prominent Swedish economists not only warned about future negative growth consequences; they also argued that during recent decades these problems had already become empirically clearly visible and had made Sweden's GDP growth lag behind that of other comparable countries. The 'Swedosclerosis' diagnosis and 'lagging-behind' thesis were coined to refer to the causes of the malaise which now was seen as affecting Sweden's economy. After the late 1980s, this diagnosis was widely accepted in Sweden and was used in arguments for major reforms of taxes and welfare programmes by social democratic as well as by conservative-centrist governments. The major part of the arguments supporting the 'Swedosclerosis' and 'lagging-behind' diagnoses were presented in the Swedish public debate via newspapers and publications

from business-related think-tanks. I will here focus upon the scholarly publications where the same arguments were made, and scrutinize the quality
of the empirical evidence presented in support of these arguments.

The leading and most prominent spokesman for the 'lagging-behind'
thesis has been Professor Assar Lindbeck.[3] In a thought-provoking evaluation
of 'The Swedish Experiment', Lindbeck writes that 'Sweden had become a
relatively rich country *before* the emergence of a special Swedish model. It
is also worth noting that the *early* build-up of welfare-state arrangements
in the 1950s and 1960s, and the related rise in the share of public-sector
spending from 30 to 45 per cent of the GNP, turned out to be quite compatible with a relatively fast productivity growth during that period' (Lindbeck
1997: 1283, italics in the original). Lindbeck maintains that since about
1970, the expansion of the welfare state and the emergence of a 'Swedish
model' have caused Sweden's relative growth performance to be markedly
poor. The same line of argument has been advanced by all other proponents
of the Swedish 'lagging-behind' thesis. What relevance and weight can we
find in the empirical evidence which has been claimed in support of these
conclusions?

Growth patterns and data problems

The empirical data used as evidence for the 'lagging-behind' thesis consist
primarily of comparisons of GDP growth rates in Sweden with the average for the twenty-four countries which up until the late 1980s constituted
the OECD membership.[4] For causal analysis of the ways in which political
factors and welfare states affect growth it is, however, more fruitful to focus
on comparisons among the eighteen OECD countries which had an unin-
terrupted political democracy during the period after the Second World War
and at least 1 million inhabitants.[5] These countries are Australia, Austria,
Belgium, Canada, Denmark, Finland, France, Germany, Ireland, Italy, Japan,
The Netherlands, New Zealand, Norway, Sweden, Switzerland, the UK and
the USA. In comparisons of GDP levels and growth rates we will rely on
measures based on a common currency (US dollars) with exchange rates for
specified years, as well as so-called 'purchasing power parities' (PPPs), with
exchange rates based on prices in national currencies of a common basket
of goods and services.

An overall picture of the growth patterns we will analyse here is given in
Figure 8.1 which shows the development of GDP *per capita* in our eighteen
countries (using PPPs) from 1950 to 1997. This figure indicates that after
the early 1970s, in most countries, GDP levels tended to rise at lower rates
than was the case before this point, a reflection of the world-wide growth
slowdown discussed above. We find Switzerland at the top, a country with
a GDP level to some extent exaggerated by the fact that while immigrant

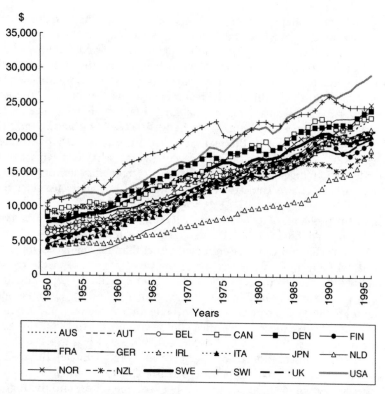

Figure 8.1 GDP *per capita*, selected OECD countries, 1950–96, PPPs
Source: Penn World Tables: Version 6.1.

'guest workers' constitute a sizable part of its labour force and contribute to production of GDP, significant proportions of them are not included in the population figures constituting the denominator. The USA is also at the top, with a growth spurt in the 1990s.[6] At the bottom in 1950 we find Japan, which at that time was beginning its long climb to one of the highest levels among these countries. At a low level we also found Ireland, which after joining the European Community in 1973 experienced a rapid rise, particularly after 1985. Norway started somewhere in the middle in 1950 but had climbed to the top in the 1980s after exploiting its North Sea oil. New Zealand, on the other hand, which started at a relatively high level in 1950, showed a stagnation after about 1985.

Somewhere in the middle of Figure 8.1, in a snake-like muddle, we find Sweden up to 1989. In 1991–3, however, Sweden's growth rates clearly decrease, although showing some resurgence thereafter. Because of this apparent break in Sweden's growth trajectory, I will begin by discussing its growth performance up to 1989, a year by which the 'Swedosclerosis' diagnosis and the 'lagging-behind' thesis were already widely accepted.

Figure 8.1 indicates that in the middle region where Sweden is located, differences among countries are relatively small; only very reliable growth indicators can enable us to distinguish between the growth performance among the several countries in this middle region. Unfortunately, our growth measures suffer from a sizable lack of reliability, a fact rarely recognized.[7] The complicated problems in estimating changes in GDP and in assessing the level of inflation – that is, the real rather than the nominal growth rate – necessitates continuous revision of earlier figures, a process which often considerably changes them. These problems of reliability are of particular importance when we compare growth rates in the middle region where Sweden is located.

Since the problems of reliability of GDP growth figures are rarely observed, even less often publicly discussed and increasingly unlikely to be noted when data become electronically disseminated rather than manually assembled, it is worthwhile to illustrate the scope of the problems, made evident when we follow the growth of real GDP *per capita* for specific years published in successive editions of OECD's *Historical Statistics*. Let us, for example, look at figures for Sweden's percentage growth rate for a single year, 1970, figures appearing in twelve successive annual editions from 1971 to 1982. This gives us the following series 3.7, 4.0, **3.2**, 3.6, 3,9, 3.9, 3.9, 4.1, 4.1, 4.1, **6.2**, 5.5. From the first observation of 3.7 per cent in 1971, estimates thus fall to a low of 3.2 per cent in 1973 but increase to 6.2 per cent in 1981, that is a 3.0 percentage point range of variation between the lowest and the highest estimate for the year 1970. Looking at all eighteen countries and a similar series of estimates for five specific years (1980–4) in the following ten annual editions of *Historical Statistics*, we find an average range of variation close to 1 percentage point (Korpi 1992: 46). Remembering that average estimated growth rates during these years were of the order of 3 per cent, the range of variation generated by revisions is thus about one-third of published growth rates.

Moving from estimates in terms of a common currency to PPPs introduces additional reliability problems. The problems can be illustrated by looking at changes in the rankings of countries for the year 1989 generated when estimates were revised in 1990 (Table 8.1). Comparing the early and the revised estimates for 1989, we find, for example, that Norway drops from rank 4 to rank 14 and Britain from 12 to 15 while Germany rises from 8 to 4 and Austria from 16 to 10.[8] In the debate on Sweden's economic growth, these rankings have played a major role. It has, however, generally been overlooked that such rankings often hide very small differences between countries, differences which in themselves are very unreliable. These problems of reliability must always be kept in mind when discussing Sweden's relative economic performance.[9]

Table 8.1 Rank order, selected OECD countries according to GDP *per capita* for 1989, before and after revision, PPPs

Rank	Before revision	After revision
1	USA	USA
2	CAN	SWI
3	SWI	CAN
4	NOR	GER
5	JAP	FRA
6	SWE	SWE
7	FIN	JAP
8	GER	DEN
9	FRA	FIN
10	AUS	AUT
11	DEN	AUS
12	UK	BEL
13	ITA	ITA
14	NET	NOR
15	BEL	UK
16	AUT	NET
17	NZL	NZL
18	IRL	IRL

Sources: OECD, *National Accounts*, 1, part 7, Table 8.2, 1991 and 1992.

The flaw in causal interpretations

Causal interpretations of data used to support the 'Swedosclerosis' diagnosis and the 'lagging-behind' thesis are marred by a central flaw, which appears in different guises in interpretations of empirical evidence. This flaw is the consistent failure to take into account *absolute levels of GDP per capita* when comparing relative – that is, percentage – growth rates. In the literature on comparative economic growth rates, it has long been recognized that countries with relatively low initial GDP levels tend to have higher percentage growth rates than countries with higher initial levels (e.g. Abramowitz 1990). This fact has somewhat misleadingly been referred to as the 'catch-up effect'.[10] Among the original OECD countries, we find considerable differences in initial GDP *per capita* levels, which can explain about 40 per cent of the total variation in percentage growth rates over 1973–92 (Dowrick 1996). Since the 'lagging-behind' thesis claims a causal effect from Sweden's welfare state to its growth rate, any analysis must consider the major competing causal factors known to be related to percentage growth rates, that is the initial GDP *per capita* level. Proponents of the 'lagging-behind' hypothesis have throughout avoided consideration of the partial dependence of percentage growth rates on initial GDP *per capita* levels; contrary to available evidence, some have even denied its existence (Henrekson 1996). They have thereby failed to consider problems generated when we attempt to make causal interpretations of percentage differences in growth rates among countries differing in initial levels, and in interpretations of changes in absolute growth and relative growth.

This central flaw in causal interpretations mars most of the claims that empirical data support the 'Swedosclerosis' interpretation and the 'lagging-behind' thesis. For many years the main empirical piece of evidence used as support for this thesis was a figure showing the development of Sweden's real GDP compared to the OECD average with 1970 indexed to 100 (Figure 8.2a).[11] Such a figure clearly demonstrates that while average GDP in the OECD area increased by 85 per cent between 1970 and 1989, Sweden's GDP grew by only 46 per cent.

Can we demand stronger evidence for Sweden's 'lagging-behind' caused by its welfare state? Yes, we can. A simple perusal of the OECD table where data on Sweden are found indicates that in the same period a handful of other countries also show a GDP percentage growth rate clearly below that of the OECD average. From 1970 and up to 1989, percentage growth rates were thus 50 in Denmark, 55 in Germany, 59 in the Netherlands, 57 in the UK and 42 in Switzerland (Figure 8.2b). While it is true that in relative terms Sweden's growth rate has been clearly below the OECD average, causal interpretations in terms of negative effects from Sweden's welfare state are invalidated by the fact that several other rich countries shared the same fate. What these countries have in common is not a welfare state on the 'Swedish model' but rather the fact that in 1970 they all had initial levels of GDP *per capita* considerably above the OECD average.

Proponents of the 'lagging-behind' thesis have thus compared percentage growth figures among countries without considering differences in their initial GDP levels. To illustrate the persuasive power of relative growth comparisons in such a situation, we can look at absolute and relative growth of GDP *per capita* in Sweden and in Turkey, the country with the clearly lowest GDP *per capita* among OECD countries in 1970. In terms of changes in absolute levels of GDP *per capita* 1970–89, Turkey had an increase close to $4,000, Sweden about four times as much, $32,000 (Figure 8.3a). When this difference is expressed in terms of percentage growth from the 1970 level, however, the scene is completely changed. As if pulled up by a balloon, Turkey now clearly rises above Sweden with an increase of 63 per cent percent compared to the 46 per cent for Sweden (Figure 8.3b). The spokesmen for Sweden's 'lagging-behind' have consistently preferred the latter type of illustration in attempts to prove their point about the causal effect of Sweden's welfare state. However, if they had also included the relative growth rates of

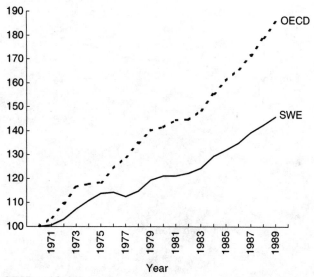

(a) OECD and Sweden

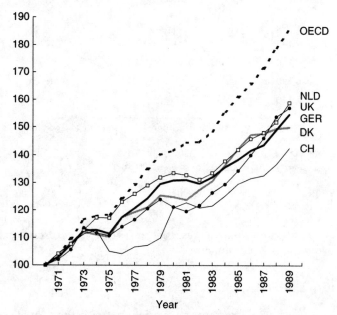

(b) OECD and Denmark, Germany, the Netherlands, Switzerlands and the UK

Figure 8.2 Relative real GDP growth 1970–89 (1970 = 100)
Source: OECD (1991).

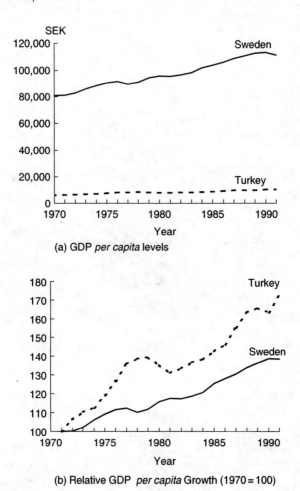

Figure 8.3   Real GDP *per capita* development, Sweden and Turkey, 1970–89
Source: OECD (1991).

other rich countries in their figures, the causal carrying capacity of such a balloon would have been punctured.

Illustrations, no testing

In view of the easy access to comparative growth data in the annual volumes of OECD's *Historical Statistics*, it is surprising that the spokesmen for the 'lagging-behind' thesis do not appear to have looked at the standard Table 3.2 in these volumes. This table shows annual percentage growth rates of real GDP *per capita* for member countries and is reproduced here (Table 8.2 **bold**

Table 8.2 Real GDP *per capita*, selected countries, 1960–89, annual percentage growth

	Average			
	1960–8	*1968–73*	*1973–9*	*1979–89*
USA	3.1	2.0	*1.4*	*1.8*
Japan	9.1	7.1	2.5	3.5
Germany	3.1	4.0	2.5	*1.7*
France	4.2	4.5	2.3	*1.6*
UK	2.4	3.0	*1.5*	2.1
Italy	5.0	3.9	3.2	2.3
Canada	3.6	4.1	2.9	2.1
Austria	3.6	5.4	3.0	2.0
Belgium	3.9	5.3	2.1	*1.9*
Denmark	3.8	3.3	*1.6*	*1.8*
Finland	3.3	6.5	1.9	3.2
Greece	6.7	7.8	2.6	1.1
Iceland	2.8	5.9	4.6	1.5
Ireland	3.8	3.5	3.3	2.5
Luxemburg	2.1	4.9	0.7	2.9
Netherlands	3.5	3.7	1.9	*1.0*
Norway	3.6	3.3	4.4	2.5
Portugal	5.7	8.9	1.3	2.1
Spain	6.4	5.7	1.1	2.1
Sweden	*3.6*	*3.1*	*1.5*	*1.8*
Switzerland	2.7	3.4	*−0.1*	*1.7*
Turkey	3.2	3.4	2.9	1.9
Australia	3.0	3.5	*1.5*	*1.7*
New Zealand	1.4	3.4	−0.2	1.1
Total EEC	3.8	4.2	2.1	*1.9*
Total OECD-Europe	3.7	4.0	2.0	*1.7*
Total OECD	**3.9**	**3.5**	**1.9**	**2.1**

Source: OECD (1991), Table 3.2.

and *italic* added). A quick look at the average growth rates in this table indicates that, in line with their claims, in the period 1979–89 Sweden's percentage growth rate was 1.8, thus lower than the OECD average of 2.1. But looking at the same column in this table, similar growth rates below the OECD average are found not only in Sweden but also in the USA (1.8), Germany (1.7), France (1.6), Belgium (1.9), Denmark (1.8), the Netherlands (1.0), Switzerland (1.7) and Australia (1.7) – that is, countries with GDP *per capita* levels above the OECD average in 1973. Moving to averages for the 1973–79 column, we again find Sweden's growth rate below the OECD average but that this fate is again shared by several other countries: the USA, the UK, Denmark, Switzerland and Australia. The neglect of differences in initial levels obviously invalidates a causal interpretation in terms of the effects of Sweden's welfare state.

Table 8.2 also indicates something of great relevance for the 'lagging-behind' thesis. As noted above, Professor Lindbeck claimed in 1997 that the early build-up of the Swedish welfare state in the 1950s and 1960 had turned out to be compatible with a relatively fast economic growth during that period, and that it was only from about 1970 that institutions and policies in Sweden differed to the extent that they had generated a serious 'lagging-behind'. In a couple of key sentences Lindbeck summarized his whole argument: 'I have emphasized the *growth performance from about 1970* (rather than, for instance, from 1950). The reason is, of course, that *it is only from about this time that institutions and policies in Sweden have differed substantially from those in other OECD countries'* (Lindbeck 1997: 1284, italics added).

A look at the figures for differences in period averages between the OECD and Sweden indicates that Lindbeck's assertion is supported to the extent that Sweden's lag in relation to the OECD average in percentage points was −0.3 for 1979–89 and −0.4 in 1973–9 (Table 8.3). But data show that this lag did not begin after 1970, as a causal interpretation requires. It was already −0.4 in 1968–73, and −0.3 in 1960–8. And, in fact, in 1950–60 this lag was already −0.3.[12] A quick look at easily available sources on comparative growth rates would thus have indicated that already published data had disproved Lindbeck's causal claim years before it was stated. Lindbeck's interpretation of the differences between the Sweden's growth rate to the OECD average after about 1970 is thus untenable. The practically stable and relatively small difference during the four decades 1950–89 indicates instead that it is likely to reflect the year that since 1950 Sweden's GDP *per capita* level was above the OECD average.

The above discussion indicates that prominent scholars appear to have been so convinced about the truth of the 'lagging-behind' thesis that they have not seen the need to test it empirically. Instead they have published

Table 8.3 Average growth of real GDP *per capita*, Sweden and OECD, different periods, 1950–89

	Period				
	1950–60	*1960–8*	*1968–73*	*1973–9*	*1979–89*
OECD	2.9	3.9	3.5	1.9	2.1
Sweden	2.6	3.6	3.1	1.5	1.8
Difference	**−0.3**	**−0.3**	**−0.4**	**−0.4**	**−0.3**

Sources: 1950–60: *Penn World Tables*, Version 5.6; 1960–89: OECD (1991), Table 3.2.

Table 8.4 GDP *per capita*, selected countries, 1870–1988, average annual percentage change

Country	1870–95	1896–1914	1920–39	1948–73	1974–81	1982–8
Sweden	1.69	**2.37**	3.17	3.26	1.00	**2.31**
USA	**1.95**	1.81	0.84	2.23	1.42	3.22
West Germany	1.36	0.77	**3.96**	**5.44**	2.26	2.42
UK	0.82	0.78	1.38	2.49	**0.93**	3.06

Source: Bergman *et al.* (1990: 15).

figures to illustrate what they believed were effects of the thesis. There are a number of cases where this has happened. Suffice it here to take one more example. In a 1990 yearbook from the influential Centre for Business and Policy Studies (SNS), a group of professors in economics published a table which they claimed to support the 'lagging-behind' thesis (Table 8.4). Table 8.4 shows the average annual growth rates of GDP *per capita* in Sweden, the USA, West Germany and the UK during six time periods, 1870–1982. With a heading 'Sweden First in the Lead and Then in the Rear' they summarize the table in the following way: 'Sweden in highest in the growth league in all time periods up to the beginning of the 1970s. Thereafter Sweden falls into the rear' (Bergman *et al.* 1990: 15).

But looking at Table 8.4, it should have been noted that during the four time periods up to 1973, Sweden was second in three and in the lead in only one. Similarly after 1973, Sweden was third in one and in the rear only in one. When I pointed this out, I was thanked for drawing attention to a typographical error. 'The typographical error is that we stated that during all four time periods between 1870 and 1973 Sweden was highest in a group of countries. Our own table clearly indicates that it should have been high (first or second)' (Bergman *et al.* 1991). But among four competitors, the one who comes second or third obviously is in the middle. Therefore the table heading must also have suffered from a typographical error; it should have read 'Sweden First in the Middle and Then in the Middle'.

Ranks and relative distances

As additional support for the 'Swedosclerosis' diagnosis and the 'lagging-behind' thesis, proponents have showed changes in Sweden's rank among OECD countries in terms of levels of GDP *per capita* expressed as PPPs (Lindbeck *et al.* 1994: 10; Lindbeck 1997: 1284–5). Although such rankings are relevant, it must be kept in mind that they often reflect small differences between adjacent countries and, as shown above, are based on figures characterized by significant unreliability. The choice of years for comparisons is also of relevance, especially when it comes to the 1991–3 fall in Sweden's growth rate. Here comparisons have often been made showing changes in Sweden's ranks including the years 1991–3, thereby using this one-time fall in Sweden's rank as support for the 'Swedosclerosis' diagnosis.

If real, the 'Swedosclerosis' syndrome could be expected to result in a gradual decline over a longer time period, rather than in a dramatic one-time decline. In attempt to make causal interpretations of changes in ranks it is therefore necessary to look at the pattern of year-by-year changes during a longer time period. Annual rankings in terms of PPP adjusted GDP *per capita*[13] show that among the eighteen countries discussed here, Sweden's rank from 1950 to 1992 developed in the following way:

66556 65654 54333 33343 34554 44454 55466 65565 579

Here we see a relatively stable picture, with roughly the same ranks in the 1980s as in the 1950s, but perhaps with some improvement in the late 1960s. The years 1991 and 1992 do, however, indicate decline. On the whole, however, during the 1950–90 period changes in Sweden's rankings are not dramatic.

As support for causal interpretations, proponents of the 'lagging-behind' hypothesis have also presented over-time changes in the difference between Sweden's GDP *per capita* (PPP adjusted) and the OECD average, expressed as a percentage of the OECD average. Thus Lindbeck (1997: 1285) demonstrates that while Sweden's level was 115 per cent of the OECD average in 1970, it had declined to 106 per cent in 1990, a decline of 9 percentage points. The same type of logic has also frequently been used in figures showing how Sweden, starting from a relatively high level in 1970, gradually 'fell down' to the OECD average and even below it (Figure 8.4a). The image of Sweden 'falling down' to the OECD average drawn horizontally in Figure 8.4 receives its persuasive power from the implication that the OECD average presents a stable baseline to which Sweden descends.

Again, however, we here see misinterpretations in terms of percentage changes based on differing absolute levels. Instead of being stable, the OECD average GDP *per capita* (in current PPP) quadrupled from 1970 to 1990. Therefore, even if the richer countries maintained the same absolute difference to the OECD average, as a percentage of the growing OECD average this difference would decline. To maintain the same percentage difference to the OECD average, these countries would have needed to have had exponential growth rates, something which in practice is impossible. Lindbeck does not note that his own table shows that in terms of percentage differences from the OECD average, also several other originally rich countries have a similar decline as Sweden. The percentage point decline for Switzerland is 21, for the USA 11, and for Australia and Netherlands 4, for example. The figures showing the Swedish 'fall' in relation to the OECD average can therefore be complemented with figures showing similar declines for these countries

(a) Percentage of the OECD average in Sweden

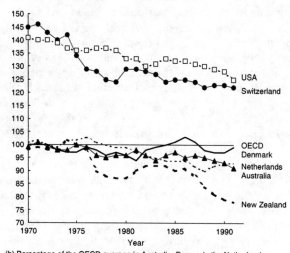

(b) Percentage of the OECD average in Australia, Denmark, the Netherlands,
New Zealand, Switzerland and the USA

Figure 8.4 GDP *per capita*, selected countries, 1970–91, PPP
Source: OECD (1991).

(Figure 8.4b). Again, the problems in causal analysis emerging from comparisons of percentage changes reflecting differing and changing absolute measures have been neglected. A relative decline of this type is not unique to Sweden, but is shared by several other countries with initially high GDP levels but with greatly different welfare states and social policies. Contrary to the claims made, such a decline can thus not be used to support causal interpretations of Swedish policy effects.

Initial levels controlled

The role of initial GDP *per capita* levels for percentage growth rates among our eighteen countries can be analysed by comparing average growth rates during specified business cycles while controlling for initial levels. As discussed above, statistical revisions of national accounts generate sizable changes in estimates of growth rate, changes large enough to shift the peaks of business cycles between adjacent years. In view of the relatively small growth differences between most OECD countries and the lack of full synchronization of business cycles between them, the choice of years for starting and ending periods may have non-negligible effects in comparisons of period averages.

As is well known, although the timing of peaks and troughs in the development of business cycles shows some variation among countries, in its publications the OECD has consistently used 1968, 1973, 1979 and 1989 as breaking-points for major international business cycles. In contrast, the spokesmen for the Swedish 'lagging-behind' thesis have throughout used 1970 as a starting point for average growth rates, without giving any motivation for this choice. Such a starting point makes 1971, a year during which Sweden had about zero growth, the first observation in period averages of percentage growth. In view of the small differences between relevant countries, including a year with a zero growth rate in a period average is likely to give a somewhat lower average for Sweden. In the context of relatively small differences between countries, this choice is problematic.

Because of the considerable unreliability in GDP figures and differences among countries in the timing of business cycles, it would not appear fruitful in comparative analyses to search for any single year as the 'right one' for the beginning or the ending of period averages. Instead, we can focus on intervals of reasonable alternative years and look at the average of these different period estimates. As alternative starting points, we can, for example, take the six years 1968–73, a period which in many countries covers a full business cycle, and as alternative end points the six years 1984–9, which in most countries are characterized by the 'long boom' of the 1980s. This latter interval also includes the years when the Swedish 'lagging-behind' thesis was established. For our eighteen countries and each of the thirty-six alternative time periods we can regress percentage growth rates on initial GDP *per capita* levels. To evaluate to what extent the growth rate of a country during a time period is reasonable, we can use the regression line to estimate its expected growth rates, given its initial level of GDP *per capita*.[14] Thus for each time period and each country we can look at the difference between actual and expected growth rates, and use the average of these thirty-six residuals to attempt to evaluate to what extent growth rates are reasonable. For Sweden, some of the alternative thirty-six time periods differences between actual and expected growth rates are positive, for others they are negative. The largest negative values are consistently found for time periods beginning in 1970, the favourite starting year of the 'lagging-behind' spokesmen.

The overall results indicate that with an average difference of only −0.1 per cent between observed and expected growth rates during these periods, Sweden is found in a large middle category which also includes Austria, Belgium, Canada, Denmark, France, Germany, Ireland, Italy and Switzerland (Table 8.5).[15]

In a review of the arguments in the debate on the 'lagging-behind' thesis and after examining growth rates among the OECD countries since 1950 with control for initial GDP *per capita* levels, Steve Dowrick, professor of economics at Australian National University, came to the following conclusion: 'On balance, it seems reasonable to conclude that *at least up until 1990* there is nothing in the Swedish growth performance which suggests substantial underperformance' (Dowrick 1996: 1777, italics in the original). The analysis

Table 8.5 Average differences between observed and (given initial levels) expected growth of GDP *per capita*, 36 alternative periods, 18 OECD member countries, 1969–73 to 1984–9, per cent

Country	Average difference (Residual)
Norway	1.4
Japan	0.9
Finland	0.8
Italy	0.4
Austria	0.3
Canada	0.3
Germany (West)	0.0
Denmark	0.0
Ireland	0.0
Belgium	−0.1
Sweden	−0.1
France	−0.2
Switzerland	−0.3
Australia	−0.5
USA	−0.5
UK	−0.5
Netherlands	−0.6
New Zealand	−1.2

Sources: OECD, *National Accounts* (1996).

here supports Dowrick's conclusion. Norway, Japan and Finland have had higher growth rates than expected, while New Zealand at least has had lower than expected growth rates.[16]

Sweden's 1991–3 Depression

The above discussion indicates that the empirical evidence mustered by proponents for the 'lagging-behind' thesis has clearly not been up to the mark when we look at Sweden's economic growth over 1950–89. As shown in Figure 8.1, it is, however, obvious that Sweden experienced a major fall in the period 1991–3, when its GDP *per capita* declined during three successive years. In his analysis of the Swedish growth debate, Dowrick (1996: 1778) states that 'there is a stiff challenge for the proponents of the 'lagging behind' thesis. It is incumbent on them to explain why Swedish GDP performance was consistently reasonable over forty years and only shows a marked decline after 1990'.

Dowrick's challenge has, however, not been accepted. Scholars such as Andersen *et al.* (1997: 64) include the decline over 1991–3 as part of their support for the 'Swedosclerosis' interpretation. Although acknowledging the role of macroeconomic factors likely to have contributed to the fall in Sweden's economic growth in these years, Lindbeck (1997: 1312) also assumes that structural weaknesses generated by the 'Swedish model' have played a major role in the decline. For such an interpretation to hold, it would, however, appear necessary to show that these structural weaknesses had already manifested themselves during the preceding decades, something which has not been done. In this situation, alternative interpretations of the post-1990 decline must be considered.

In the years around 1990, some important changes were made in Sweden's economic institutions and economic policy (for a discussion, see Calmfors 1993). Following the trend in many other countries in the late 1980s, Swedish banks were deregulated at the end of 1985, when the tax system permitted direct deduction of interest paid from taxable income. The following three years saw a major boom in bank lending to firms and individuals, not infrequently with shaky collateral, and the household savings ratio dropped drastically (Figure 8.5). Bank deregulation was followed by a tax reform, effective in 1991, which abolished the possibility of deducting interest from taxable income. As a result, borrowers started to pay back their loans, generating a dramatic rise in the household savings ratio in the years 1990–4. Thus from a level of −4.9 per cent in 1988 and −4.8 per cent in 1989, the household savings ratio increased to reach almost 8 per cent in 1992, an increase of about 12 percentage points over a four-year period. In the context of the onset of the international recession in 1990, the result was a major draining of domestic demand, increasing unemployment. Another

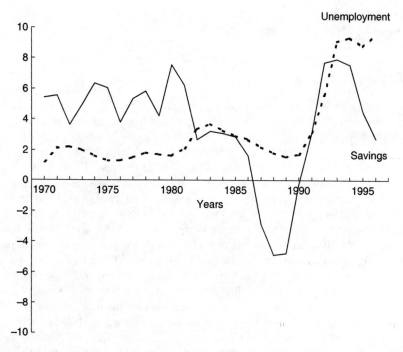

Figure 8.5 Household savings ratio and unemployment, in-Sweden, 1970–96
Sources: Unemployment rate: OECD (1991); Household savings: Lennart Berg, Uppsala University.

result was a major crises in the banking systems, where many large banks had to be salvaged by taxpayers' money.

Another major policy change was made in 1991, when the traditional economic policy focus on maintaining full employment was changed to give primacy to the promotion of low inflation. Interest rates were increased to protect the exchange rate which now had become tied to the European currency unit (ECU). In the context of these circumstance, and the onset of an international recession, mass unemployment made a rapid return in Sweden after 1990. In the earlier post-war period unemployment had normally been very low (in 1970–90 with an average of 2.1 per cent) and an unemployment rate of 4 per cent was regarded as unacceptably high. Now the unemployment level rose above 9 per cent and remained at this level for some years. The Swedish fall in growth rates over 1991–3 thus came in the context of major policy changes and major policy mistakes. These changes provide the proximate causes of this decline. Those who want to use this one-time drop as a part of the evidence for the 'Swedosclerosis' diagnosis have to respond to Dowrick's question above: why did the effects of this sclerosis wait for forty years before becoming visible? The answer to this question is yet to be made.

Discussion

The neo-classical prediction that taxes and other political measures associated with welfare states will generate distortions in the functioning of markets brings us to the centre of distributive conflicts, reflected in differences in view of the relative roles to be accorded to markets and democratic politics. In such a situation of conflicts of interest, if social scientists are to retain impartiality it is important that they base judgements on empirically observed facts. Only some of the Swedish economists have been highly engaged in the promotion of the 'Swedosclerosis' diagnosis and the 'lagging-behind' thesis. As indicated here, their empirical work reveals more efforts to find figures illustrating theoretically assumed outcomes than testing hypotheses concerning outcomes. The Swedish community of economists have long made important contributions to the policy debate and have received international recognition for their intellectual achievements. To paraphrase a well-known statement by Winston Churchill, we must unfortunately say that, as far as empirical evidence is concerned, this was not their finest hour.

The discussion here points to often overlooked problems of reliability in the empirical data used in analyses of comparative growth rates. Although great effort is put into the preparation of national accounts upon which growth data are based, we must remember that because of the great difficulties of this task our measurements remind more of readings through an hourglass than of electronic instruments. This circumstance generates problems, especially in the middle areas where Sweden and a number of other countries are 'clustered'. Because of the 'clustering' of countries, small and relatively unimportant differences among countries affect rankings. Recognizing this problem of reliability, the OECD statistics directorate in a report discussing the use of PPP measures of GDP levels, explicitly warns against their use in detailed country rankings (OECD 2003), a practice which has unfortunately been pervasive in the Swedish debate. Those responsible for producing the these data recommend that they should be used only for broad groupings of countries. In such a grouping, Sweden comes in the same category as Australia, Belgium, Canada, Finland, France, Germany, Ireland, Italy, Japan, the Netherlands and the UK, a conclusion well in line with the arguments made in this chapter.

From a neo-classical theoretical perspective, strong predictions have been derived to the effect that with increasing taxation and welfare state expansion, labour supply as well as growth rates will suffer. A number of empirical studies on the sensitivity of labour supply to taxation has shown only rather limited negative effects, although somewhat more for women than for men (see, for example, Atkinson and Mogensen 1993). In the area of labour supply, social scientists have access to relatively reliable and valid statistical data. In analyses of comparative growth rates, data are much more shaky, but here it has also proved difficult to establish evidence for major negative growth effects, including Sweden, where such negative effects would appear to be most likely to emerge.

The fact that theoretically predicted negative effects of taxes and welfare states are very difficult to verify in areas where they are most likely to turn up and in which we also have empirically useful data should generate discussion on the theoretical foundations of these hypotheses. Instead, however, some economists have turned their attention to the examination of negative effects in terms of decreasing welfare, theoretically defined in terms of deadweight burdens or excess burdens of taxation. Unfortunately these theoretical concepts defy empirical measurement. Here it is instead necessary to examine the definition of the tax wedge assumed to generate excess burdens and lower economic growth. The tax wedge is defined as the difference between what an individual receives after taxes and what employers pay out in terms of wages and wage-related taxes. This definition assumes that taxes collected from employees and employers disappear into a black hole without giving any positive returns to tax payers. In most welfare states, however, most citizens are likely to see that at least parts of their taxes are returned to them in the form of social insurance, health care, schooling, infrastructure, etc. This slip in the key assumption of the theory can explain why it has been so difficult to find empirical evidence for negative growth effects of the Swedish welfare state.

In view of the conflicts of interest in this area, it is necessary to have empirical verification of the bases upon which policy advice is founded. From a policy-related perspective what is needed here are studies where hypotheses on negative effects of taxes and welfare programmes can be empirically analysed. Such studies should focus on the micro as well as on the macro-level. For relevant policy advice, it is also necessary to analyse consequences of welfare states that can be seen as positive, and to attempt to consider and counterbalance positive and negative aspects.

* This chapter draws on my earlier publications, primarily Korpi (1985, 1992, 1996, 2000, 2001).

Notes

1 'Power resources' can be defined as attributes of actors enabling them to reward or to punish other actors.
2 The concept of 'efficiency' used here is Pareto efficiency, describing a situation where no changes can be made without being perceived by at least one actor as having negative consequences, a situation where changes thus require unanimity among actors.

3   Professor Assar Lindbeck was a member of the Nobel Prize Committee in economics from its foundation in 1969 and its chairman 1980–95.

4   As is well known, in the years after 1990, OECD membership was expanded by the inclusion of several new countries.

5   This reflects the 'most comparable cases' strategy proposed by Lijphardt (1975), widely used in causally oriented comparative social science research.

6   For discussions of US growth rates in the 1990s, see Krueger and Solow (2001).

7   As is well known, there is also a debate on the validity of GDP as an indicator of the quality of living, but this discussion cannot be taken up here.

8   Among the twenty-four OECD countries at that time, the average change in GDP *per capita* expressed as a percentage of the OECD average was 5.2 percentage points, with a maximum of 13 percentage points. Among the top seventeen countries, the correlation between these two rankings for the same year was only 0.70.

9   The labour productivity figures also used in the growth debate are even more unreliable. This reflects the fact that information on number of hours worked often comes from sources different from those used for GDP estimates, thereby introducing the possibility that errors in the numerator and the denominator go in different directions. One of the most reliable sources for labour productivity changes are published for twelve countries in the *Monthly Labour Review*. Figures on annual increases in labour productivity for the five years 1985–9 published in consecutive issues during the period 1986–95 show an average range of variation per year and per country of 2.4 percentage points.

10 While countries with relatively low GDP *per capita* levels tend to have higher percentage growth rates than those starting at higher levels, this does not necessarily mean that the relatively poor countries are 'catching up' with the richer ones in the sense that the standard deviation between GDP *per capita* levels is tending to decrease (Korpi 1992: 48–54).

11 Data from OECD, *National Accounts*, 1, 1991, Table 19: 130.

12 Based on *Penn World Tables*, Version 5.6 (Summers and Heston 1991).

13 Rankings based on *Penn World Tables*, Version 5.6 (Summers and Heston 1991).

14 For each of the thirty-six alternative time periods, we thus estimate a simple regression equation: $Y_i = a + bX_i + e$, where Y_i is the average annual percentage GDP *per capita* growth of country i during the period, X_i is the GDP *per capita* level of country i for the initial year of the period, b is a vector of associated parameters and e an error term. The regression line generated by this equation gives the expected or 'reasonable' percentage growth rate for each country during the period.

15 The period-specific figures indicate that, as expected, because of the near-zero growth rate in 1971, taking 1970 as the beginning-of-a-period average leads to the greatest average difference (−0.3 percentage points) between observed and expected growth rates. However, differences are smaller when we look at other reasonable starting points and, as noted above, there is no reason to regard 1970 as 'the right' year for the beginning-of-period definitions.

16 Among these countries, Japan was long a well-known high-growth country while Norway has benefited from North Sea oil and Finland from the special trade relationship with the Soviet Union in the recessions since 1973. Since the formation of the European Economic Community (EEC), New Zealand has faced difficulties in its once-important exports of primary products to Europe.

Bibliography

Abramowitz, M. (1990) 'The Catch-Up Factor in Economic Growth'. *Economic Inquiry*, 28: 1–18.

Andersen, T.M., Gylfason, T., Honkapohja, S., Isachsen, A.J. and Williamsen, J. (1997) *I otakt med omvärlden: Svensk ekonomi i ett internationellt perspektiv* (Out of Step with Other Countries: The Swedish Economy in an International Perspective). Stockholm: SNS.

Atkinson, T. and Mogensen, G.V. (eds.) (1993) *Welfare and Work Incentives*. Oxford: Oxford University Press.

Bergman, L., Björklund, A., Jakobsson, U., Lundberg, L. and Söderström, H.T. (1990) *I Samtidens Bakvatten?* Stockholm: SNS.

Bergman, L., Jakobsson, U., Persson M. and Söderström, H.T. (1991) 'Eftersläpning eller Faktafel'. *Ekonomisk Debatt*, 19(3): 272–3.

Calmfors, L. (1993) 'Lessons from the Macroeconomic Experience of Sweden'. *European Journal of Political Economy*, 9(1): 25–72.

Clark, C. (1945) 'Public Finance and Changes in the Value of Money'. *Economic Journal*, 55: 371–89.

Dowrick, S. (1996) 'Swedish Economic Performance and Swedish Economic Debate: A View from Outside'. *Economic Journal*, 106(439): 1772–9.

Heckscher, E.F. (1921) *Gammal och ny ekonomisk liberalism*. (Old and New Economic Liberalism) Stockholm: Norstedt.

Henrekson, M. (1996) 'Sweden's Relative Economic Performance : Lagging behind or Staying on Top?' *Economic Journal*, 106(439): 1749–59.

Korpi, W. (1985) 'Economic Growth and the Welfare State: Leaky Bucket or Irrigation System?' *European Sociological Review*, 1(2): 97–118.

Korpi, W. (1992) *Halkar Sverige efter? Sveriges ekonomiska tillväxt 1820–1990 i jämförande belysning*. (Is Sweden Lagging Behind? The Economic History of Sweden 1820–1990 in Comparative Perspective.) Stockholm: Carlssons.

Korpi, W. (1996) 'Eurosclerosis and the Sclerosis of Objectivity: On the Role of Values among Economic Policy Experts'. *Economic Journal*, 106(439): 1727–46.

Korpi, W. (2000) 'Welfare States, Economic Growth, and Scholarly Objectivity'. *Challenge*, 43(2): 49–66.

Korpi, W. (2001) 'The Economic Consequences of Sweden's Welfare State: Does the Causal Analysis Hold?'. *Challenge*, 44(6): 104–12.

Krueger, A.B. and Solow, R. (eds.) (2001) *The Roaring Nineties: Can Full Employment Be Sustained?* New York: Russell Sage.

Lijphardt, A. (1975) 'The Comparable-Cases Strategy in Comparatived Research' *Comparative Political Studies*, 8(2): 158–77.

Lindbeck, A. (1997) 'The Swedish Experiment'. *Journal of Economic Literature*, 35: 1273–319.

Lindbeck, A., Molander, P., Persson, T., Peterson, O., Sandmo, A., Swedenborg, B. and Thygesen, N. (1994) *Turning Sweden Around*. Cambridge, Mass.: MIT Press.

Marshall, A. (1907) *The Principles of Economics*. London: Macmillan.

OECD (1991) *Historical Statistics*. Paris: OECD.

OECD (2003) *Main Economic Indicators*, 5: 240.

Schitovsky, T. (1980) 'Can Capitalism Survive? An Old Question in a New Setting'. *American Economic Review*, 70(1): 1–9.

Summers, R. and Heston, A. (1991) *The Penn World Tables* (Mark-5): An Expanded Set of International Comparisons, 1950–1988, *Quarterly Journal of Economics*, 106(2): 327–68.

9
Growth and Employment in the 'Nordic Welfare States' in the 1990s: a Tale of Crisis and Revival

Jaakko Kiander

Introduction

The group of 'Nordic countries' consists of five Northern European states: Denmark, Finland, Iceland, Norway and Sweden. All of them are usually thought to be so-called 'welfare states' – i.e. egalitarian societies with extensive public sectors and income redistribution. They are also rich economies with high living standards and excellent quality of life. The best-known and the largest of the Nordic countries is Sweden, and it is not uncommon that discussions on welfare state simply refer to so-called 'Swedish model'. Although the Nordic countries and their welfare models are not identical there are so many similarities between them and so many differences between them and the other European countries that it is legitimate to speak about a 'Nordic model'. This chapter reviews the macroeconomic performance and the current state of the Nordic welfare states, and focuses especially on the experiences of Denmark, Finland and Sweden in the 1990s in adjusting their public sectors to fiscal consolidation.[1]

In the post-war years – from the 1950 to the 1970s – the Nordic economies enjoyed rapid growth and full employment. However, starting from the 1980s, they, together with other Western countries, suffered from various economic imbalances – inflation, recession, unemployment, currency and banking crises and fiscal deficits – which led many observers to doubt the economic viability and fiscal sustainability of their welfare states. It is nowadays easy to find expressions of an 'orthodox' view which emphasizes the dismal economic consequences of redistributive welfare ('tax and spend') policies.[2] The analytical background to such a view is provided by mainstream economic theory on the one hand, and by the seemingly permanent economic problems of most EU countries since the 1970s, on the other.

On average, the EU economies have suffered from slow growth, continuously high unemployment and low employment and, (as a result) public finance problems, since the mid-1970s. The logic of simple microeconomic models of economic behaviour helps to explain such phenomena by high marginal taxes and income subsidies to the non-employed, which discourage labour supply. The explicit institutional reasons for that kind of economic malaise (sometimes called 'Euro-sclerosis') are hence excessive taxes, regulation, trade unions, large public sectors and too generous social insurance systems. Elements of such arguments occur regularly in the reports of the OECD, policy recommendations of the European Central Bank (ECB) and the European Commission, and in commentaries in the financial press.

The badly performing Western European economies are usually contrasted with the success of anglophone economies: not only the USA, but also the UK, Canada and Australia, and more recently Ireland as well. New Zealand was also used as an encouraging example, until it became evident that its market-friendly reforms failed to deliver rapid growth. Such large-scale analysis does not, however, do justice to many smaller countries. The general picture of European economic gloom over-states the problems because of the problems of large countries. At the same time, many smaller European countries have done better, even the most advanced welfare states, the Nordics. This is of course against 'the OECD theory'. According to the 'orthodox' view, the Nordic economies look like fat birds with heavy burdens; they should not be able to fly, but still they somehow manage to do so.

In this chapter, the macroeconomic crises and structural changes of the 1990s are viewed partly as an adjustment to rapidly advancing integration and globalization processes – especially to financial deregulation – and partly as a result of macroeconomic policy failures. These changes were an essential part of the process of adapting the Nordic economic policies to a European single market and the objectives of European monetary policy. Even then, the Nordic model remains clearly distinctive and in many respects successful. The Nordics have been able to maintain their position among the richest economies in the world and also to avoid the under-employment typical to larger European economies, notwithstanding the alarming rise of unemployment in the beginning of the 1990s. The Nordic societies are still highly egalitarian, and they have maintained high income and employment levels in spite of high taxes and large public sectors.

Although the 'Nordic welfare model' has survived many difficulties, there lie further challenges in the future. The most important are possible tax competition which might threaten the financial basis of current welfare systems, especially in the countries with highest tax rates (Denmark and Sweden), and expected demographic change, which will add an excessive burden to the public finances by 2025. However, all the Nordic countries have currently healthy fiscal surpluses, which gives them a better position than most other Western European countries from which adapt to these future challenges.

The 'Nordic welfare state'

The Nordic countries are often seen as representatives of a special societal model which is usually called a 'welfare state'. Although such a generalization is naturally a simplification it is not unjustified. There are lots of common features in the welfare state models of the Nordic countries and in their historical backgrounds which make them different from other European countries.

The Nordic welfare states and economies have also been successful in achieving good results in terms of general welfare and equity.

Origins

In search for the origins of the modern Nordic welfare models one cannot neglect the decisive impact of long-time political dominance of social democratic parties and their political ideas as one of the most important factors explaining the birth of the extended egalitarian welfare state model in the Nordic countries.[3] That influence began seriously in the 1920s and 1930s, when the social democratic parties formed-governments for the first time. Since then, the social democratic parties have for most of the time been the major governing parties in all Nordic countries.[4] Together with strong trade union movement that has meant a significant position of power for many decades, and this position of power or even political hegemony has enabled the gradual evolution of an increasingly complex systems of taxes and social programmes which today form the essential part of the 'Nordic welfare model'. The creation of a 'welfare state' has been a gradual process. It began before the Second World War, and was in its most intensive phase in the 1960s and 1970s. It started from universal provision of elementary education and basic health care, and proceeded to national pensions and child benefits.

Characteristics

Although the Nordic countries are far from identical, the 'Nordic welfare states' have some important common features. This is why the 'Nordic model' is usually acknowledged as a separate social model. For instance, Esping-Andersen (1990) distinguishes between three different types of the welfare state. The *liberal or marginal* welfare state is based on the social protection provided by private market and family. In such a model social benefits are means-tested and low. In the second model, social provisions are distributed on the basis of *merit and work performance*. According to Esping-Andersen, the Scandinavian model is the third one, based on the *universality principle*. That model promotes redistribution and social equity.

There is a certain 'holistic' or 'universalist' thinking behind the welfare state system in the Nordic model; the society (or public sector) is supposed to take care of citizens from 'cradle to grave' and protect them from the economic and social risks. This is done by providing affordable care, education and decent homes for almost everybody. At the same time, the welfare system redistributes income between households by using taxes and transfers, and thus decreases inequality. The universality of the welfare system is important in the Nordic countries. Everyone is entitled to the same services and to same benefit systems; eligibility does not depend on income and wealth as much as on age or need.

Public sector and social protection

A simple way to measure the size of the welfare state is to compare public expenditure, and especially social expenditure and public consumption, which broadly measures the production of public services. On average, the share of public expenditure as a percent of GDP is clearly higher in the Nordic countries than in other comparable countries. There is no question that the Nordic countries have large public sectors, by any measure.

The public expenditures of the Nordic countries are largely used to finance the production of public welfare services and large-scale income transfers. Social expenditures in the Nordic countries include public provision of day care and other social services,[5] free education (from elementary school to university level), health care and active labour market policy measures. Incomes are redistributed through taxes and transfers. In all the Nordic countries, there are transfers and subsidies to almost everybody: public old-age and disability pensions, child benefits, housing benefits, student benefits, unemployment benefits and maternity (or parental) benefits. The idea of the system is to provide assistance when it is needed (the young and old, for instance), and thus minimize poverty risks (cf. Kangas and Palme 2000). The Nordic systems redistribute income within life-cycles, from middle-aged to young and old.

The level of total public expenditure is higher in the Nordic countries than elsewhere, although some other European countries come close to Nordic levels. The difference becomes clearer when expenditures are adjusted for interest payments on public debt. It is noteworthy that not only welfare expenditures but also all other expenditures are higher in the Nordic countries than the EU average, not to mention the USA (see Table 9.1). The Nordics spend clearly more on publicly provided merit goods – i.e. education, health and social services. This, of course, results from the principle of universal provision. The level of income transfers to households (the largest item of which consists of pensions) is in the Nordic countries not so different from other European countries.

The level of public expenditure and social protection is very high in Denmark and Sweden. Finland is closer to the EU average (see Tables 9.1 and 9.2). There are a few other European countries which also have very high public expenditures, such as France, Belgium and Austria. However, if the level of social expenditure and public consumption is taken into account, one can still argue that on average the group of Nordic countries spends more than any other country on welfare state. The number of public sector employees is very high, more than 30 per cent of total employment in Sweden and Denmark, and about 25 per cent in Finland. These figures

Table 9.1 Decomposition of total public expenditure, 1999, per cent of GDP

Country	Gross expenditure	Primary expenditure [a]	Welfare expenditure [b]	Other expenditure
Denmark	52.5	50.3	34.8	15.5
Finland	47.1	45.5	31.2	14.3
Sweden	55.0	52.3	35.8	16.5
EU15	44.9	41.3	29.8	11.5
USA	29.9	27.1	18.5	8.6

Notes:
[a] Primary expenditure = Gross expenditure minus net interest payments.
[b] Welfare expenditure = Total of merit goods and income transfers to households.

Sources: OECD Social Expenditure Database and *Education at a Glance* (OECD 2001).

Table 9.2 Total public welfare expenditure divided into services and transfers, 1999, percent of GDP

Country	Merit goods [a]	Income transfers [b]
Denmark	18.8	16.0
Finland	13.9	17.3
Sweden	18.6	17.2
EU15	12.8	17.0
USA	10.9	7.6

Notes:
[a] Merit goods = Education, health and social services.
[b] Income transfers = Pensions and social insurance benefits.

Sources: OECD Social Expenditure Database and *Education at a Glance* (OECD 2001).

are clearly higher than in the other EU countries. The Nordic trio spends more money on families, disability and unemployment than the other EU countries, while public pension and health care expenditures are lower in the Nordic countries (Table 9.3). The Nordic countries spend much more on unemployment benefits and active labour market policies (ALP) than the other EU countries.

These differences reflect the strong emphasis which the Nordic model puts on the universal social rights which arise from citizenship. High spending on disability and unemployment helps to prevent poverty and social exclusion within these groups. Similarly, generous support to families and housing subsidizes child bearing and helps to smooth the life-cycle income of families. As a result, child poverty is very low in the Nordic countries.

It is noteworthy that public pension and health expenditures are lower in Denmark and Finland than in the other EU countries, and not much higher

Table 9.3 Distribution of social protection expenditure, 1999, percent of GDP

Country	Education	Health	Social services	Pensions	Disability and family benefits	Unemployment benefits and ALP[a]
Denmark	6.8	6.8	5.2	6.8	4.2	5.0
Finland	5.7	5.3	2.9	8.0	5.4	3.9
Sweden	6.6	6.6	5.4	8.2	5.1	3.9
EU15	4.9	6.4	1.5	11.2	3.5	2.3
USA	4.8	5.8	0.3	6.0	1.1	0.5

Note: ALP = Active labour market policy programmes.

Sources: OECD Social Expenditure Database and *Education at a Glance* (OECD 2001).

than in the USA. The low costs of health care can be explained by the fact that public sector is the main provider and producer of health services in the Nordic countries. It is typical that public health care systems tend to be less costly than those based on public insurance and private provision.

Important aspects of the inclusive nature of the Nordic systems are national pensions systems, family policy programmes as well as unemployment benefits and ALP. In Denmark, pensions are provided by state and financed by income taxes, in Sweden and Finland there are occupational pension insurance schemes[6] funded by compulsory payroll taxes. For those who have not managed to achieve sufficient occupational pension, there is a national minimum award. In 1996, the share of pensioners receiving only the basic pension was 45 per cent in Denmark, 13 per cent in Finland and 18 per cent in Sweden. The average after-tax compensation level of the public pension systems for an average industrial worker with a full qualifying period was about 70 per cent in all the countries (NOSOSCO 1998). Families with children are in the all three Nordic EU countries supported by child benefits, generous parental leave and publicly provided and heavily subsidized day care services.

There is a strong egalitarian ethos in the ideology and practice of the 'Nordic welfare state'. Equality is produced by extensive and universal public service provision and by high and progressive taxation. In addition to this, the wage bargaining system is also dominated by large and mostly social democratic trade union confederations which have aimed at wage compression. A central part of the model has for a long time been the regulation of labour markets through collective agreements between the organizations representing employees and employers.

Earnings-related unemployment insurance is organized in the Nordic countries in an exceptional way. Unemployment insurance is voluntary and is provided by trade unions. Because of the high unionization rate – about 70–90 per cent of workers are union members in Nordic countries – almost all workers are insured. If one is not insured or is not entitled to the unemployment insurance benefit (because of an insufficient prior working period), she is entitled to a means-tested basic unemployment allowance. In practice, the effective after-tax replacement ratios of the unemployment benefits are relatively high in the Nordic countries, especially in Denmark and Sweden, and particularly for low-income families with children.

In addition to generous benefits, the Nordic countries also support the unemployed by providing extensive ALP programmes, which offer training and subsidized work for those who fail to find work in the open labour market. That explains why ALP spending is so high in the Nordic countries in spite of their relatively low unemployment rates – except in Finland, where unemployment exceeded the EU average in 1992–2003.

Well-being and equality

The 'Nordic welfare states' have traditionally been good at improving the well-being of their citizens and the equality between them. The populations of Iceland, Norway and Sweden are healthy and enjoy very high life expectancy. The Nordic social policies are by their nature egalitarian and universal in order to create inclusive systems. They aim to promote equality not only in regard of income distribution but also between the genders.[7] Some of the benefits are universal and independent of family income (such as basic pensions, child and student benefits) while some decrease with income (such as housing benefits) and some are earnings-related (such as unemployment insurance and occupational pensions). Denmark and Sweden are most generous in the provision of public services and income transfers, while Finland is more modest and less ambitious.

As a result of successful welfare policies, measures of well-being and equality usually give high ratings to the Nordics. The best-known measure is the Human Development Index (HDI) which measures a combination of real incomes, life expectancy and the average level of education. It gives highest rankings to Norway, Iceland and Sweden (see Figure 9.1). Denmark and Finland do not perform as well, because of lower life expectancy.

The Nordic welfare states have produced egalitarian societies with relatively equal income distributions and low poverty rates. If measured by Gini coefficients, the inequality of factor incomes in the Nordic countries is almost as high as in other comparable countries. However, after including the income transfers received by the households and the taxes paid by them, the resulting distribution of disposable family income is relatively evenly distributed.

In spite of the increased inequality in the 1990s, the Nordic countries still have the lowest income inequality within the OECD. The Nordic level of income equality is matched only by Belgium and the Netherlands. As a result of extensive income support systems and redistribution, income poverty is also rare. Child poverty in the Nordic countries is lower than elsewhere

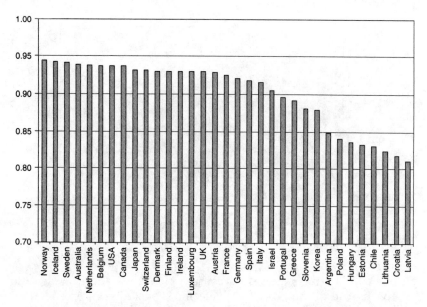

Figure 9.1 The HDI, 2003
Source: UNDP data.

(Jäntti and Danziger 1994 and 2001; see also Smeeding 2000). Even the rise of unemployment in the 1990s did not increase poverty rates.

A study by Eurostat presents the share of population in EU countries, which is 'at risk of poverty'; 'poverty' is here defined as an income level less than 60 per cent of the median income. It can be seen from Figure 9.2 that the Nordic EU countries (together with Germany) have the lowest poverty rates.

The low overall poverty rates and especially the very low child poverty rates of the Nordic countries are due to deliberate social policies which help to maintain disposable incomes of families notwithstanding their labour market position. The egalitarian outcome is helped by subsidized social services such as day care provided by the public sector. The effect of these policies is most visible when one compares the poverty rates of families with single mothers. In most countries, but not in the Nordic countries,[8] the poverty risk of such families is very high.

Taxation

As a result of high expenditure levels, taxes also need to be high. It is not surprising that taxes in the Nordic countries are on average higher than elsewhere. The gross tax rates in Sweden, Denmark and Finland are higher than in any other industrial country, basically due to relatively high and

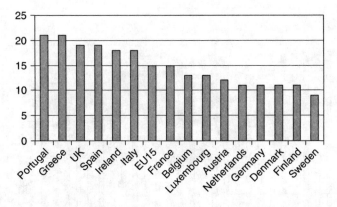

Figure 9.2   Poverty rates, EU countries, 1990s
Source: Eurostat data.

progressive labour income taxes and consumption taxes – and in Sweden also to property and wealth taxes. Corporate and capital income taxes, in turn, have since the mid-1990s been flat and low in the Nordic countries. That can be seen as evidence of *tax competition*; in order to attract mobile capital and firms many small countries have been forced to cut taxes on profits and capital income. In the Nordic countries, however, the introduction of low and flat rates of corporate and capital income taxes in the 1990s did not cause a fall in tax revenue.

Private consumption is taxed heavily in Denmark and Finland. Income taxes are exceptionally high in Denmark, partly due to the very low level of social security contributions (in Denmark, social security is financed by using general tax revenue). Employers' social security contribution rates are in Finland close to the EU average, and higher in Sweden. Average income tax rates and marginal tax rates are highest in Denmark (Table 9.4).

Table 9.4   Indicators of tax burden, 1999, percent of GDP

Country	Total tax revenue	Taxes on income and profits	Taxes on goods and services	Social security contributions	Taxes on property
Denmark	50.4	29.6	16.3	2.1	1.8
Finland	46.2	19.0	14.3	11.8	1.1
Sweden	52.2	21.7	11.2	13.2	1.9
EU15	41.6	14.7	12.4	11.4	2.0
USA	28.9	14.2	4.7	6.9	3.1

Source: OECD revenue statistics.

The level and structure of taxation in the Nordic countries suggests that it is possible to maintain relatively high tax rates on labour incomes and private consumption without doing much harm to the economy. However, as small open economies, the Nordic countries have been forced to respond to international tax competition in corporate and capital taxation, where tax bases can move quickly over borders. Lower corporate tax rates have not yet reduced the tax revenues very far, however.

Growth and employment: crisis and revival

The Nordic recessions and their background

In the 'golden years' from the 1950s to the 1980s, economic policy put emphasis on full employment in all Nordic countries. Full employment was achieved by employing Keynesian ideas of economic policy: active demand management, continuous public sector growth and incomes policy organized through centralized wage bargaining. The Bretton Woods system facilitated this policy model: through regulation of domestic credit markets and international capital movements governments were able to control interest rates and investment activity.

Eventually the policy of rapid growth and full employment caused inflationary pressures. This, of course, was not rare among Western countries in the 1950s and 1960s. However, the Nordic countries (except Denmark) continued this policy longer than most other countries (which allowed unemployment to rise after 1973) and adopted anti-inflationary policies at the beginning of the 1980s.

Until the mid-1980s the Nordic countries were known as a group of small and rich countries with advanced welfare systems and corporatist labour markets. Four of them belonged to the European Free Trade Association (EFTA), a free-trade association of mostly small non-EEC European countries, and they seemed to be immune to the rise of unemployment and related social problems experienced elsewhere in the Western Europe (or EEC countries) at this time. It is noteworthy that in both the 1980s and 1990s the Nordic countries were able to grow faster than the total European Union and to keep unemployment lower. In the 1980s, the Nordic unemployment rates were among the lowest in the OECD while the rate of inflation was slightly higher.[9] In the 1970s and 1980s unemployment rates rose almost continuously in EEC member countries while unemployment in the Nordic EFTA countries fluctuated between 2 and 6 per cent without any serious upward trend. The Nordic countries seemed to escape the perils of recession and mass unemployment plaguing most other European countries; the only exception Denmark, which – unlike the other Nordics – was a member of the EEC at that time and which in the 1980s started to suffer from low growth and permanent high unemployment like other EEC countries (Finland and

Sweden joined the EU in 1995 – Norway's membership was once again rejected in a referendum).

During a six-year period covering the end of the 1980s and the beginning of the 1990s all the Nordic countries finally faced a severe economic crisis. In Finland and Sweden the recession was severe enough to be called a crisis or even a depression.[10] If measured by relative output or job losses, these recessions were worse than those experienced in other OECD countries at the same time (see Table 9.5). While Norway, Denmark and Iceland avoided outright depression, they still suffered from low growth and a rise in unemployment.

The Nordic crises were closely related to changing economic policy regimes in Western Europe (financial market deregulation and a strong commitment to fixed exchange rate) and policy makers' determination to fight against inflation. It is difficult to explain even *ex post* how such deep recessions were possible and what was their ultimate cause. However, it is tempting to argue that the basic factor was a *monetary shock*: a sharp rise of interest rates in 1989–90 bankrupted many debt-ridden firms and forced households to cut their spending, which caused a deflationary spiral and a recession. The recessions of Sweden and Finland were deep and dramatic: they were countries where the build-up of private sector debt was biggest after the financial market deregulation in the 1980s and where the rise of interest rates was sharpest in 1990. Denmark experienced a milder recession, more like other European countries and the USA. [11]

An important explanation for the Nordic recessions were macroeconomic policy failures. The monetary and exchange rate policies were are that time not used to stabilize the economy (contrary to what had happened in earlier crises in the 1970s and 1980s). Things were made worse by stubborn (but in that time fashionable) policy of fixed exchange rates which prevented the necessary currency depreciation and which forced the central banks to maintain high interest rates.[12] The rules-based exchange rate policy doctrine was adopted widely by politicians and central bankers. The idea was to fight inflation by creating 'an anchor' for the value of the domestic currency.

Table 9.5 The recession of the early 1990s

	Annual average rate of GDP growth, 1990–3	Cumulative change in unemployment rate 1990–3
Denmark	0.7	2.5
Finland	−2.7	13.3
Sweden	−0.9	6.5
EU15	1.4	2.8
USA	1.8	1.9

Source: OECD data.

However, the consequences of the deflationary policy were not properly understood at the time, and the resulting recessions were to large extent surprises to both decision makers and economists.

It is likely that both the boom and bust phases could have been largely stabilized by a floating exchange rate. However, all European countries (and the Nordics were no exception[13]) tried to maintain their exchange rates fixed (*vis-à-vis* the strongest currency, the German Mark), which made the European crises worse in 1991–2. In the 'boom' phase, the fixed exchange rate helped to increase currency inflow and supply of credit, whilse in the 'bust' phase, the speculation against the fixed parity caused currency outflow and extremely high rates of interest (see Svensson 1994). The period of high real interest rates caused a collapse in asset prices and domestic demand and wave of bankruptcies and banking crises in Norway, Sweden and Finland. As a consequence, the real economy suffered and unemployment rose, too. This deflationary process ended only when the Nordic countries (together with many other European countries, most notably the UK) were forced to abandon the fixed exchange rate regime in the autumn of 1992.[14] The resulting currency depreciation improved their competitiveness (which helped to increase exports) and enabled the central banks to cut interest rates quickly. The Nordic and other European economies started to recover in 1993.

The Swedish crisis intensified the critique against the 'Nordic welfare state model'. The recession and the subsequent output and employment losses helped to make the case that the crisis and slow growth were not results of a mere macroeconomic coordination failure but instead a deeper systemic malfunction ultimately caused by the structures of welfare states. It was argued that the welfare state was generally bad for growth because it created bad incentives. According to such view, overly generous benefits, labour market rigidities and high taxes would finally discourage investment, job creation and labour supply. Many critics used the dismal growth record of the 1990s as evidence supporting this critical view in both Sweden and Finland. Since the all Nordic countries recovered from the crises, they cannot any longer be used as ultimate evidence of the failure of the 'Nordic model'. It is now more widely admitted that the recessions were related to financial factors and policy failures.

Employment and unemployment

The 'Nordic welfare states' are egalitarian societies with high taxes, organized labour and large public sectors. As such, they have been criticized for being sluggish and structurally weak. Redistributive tax and welfare systems are usually by economists seen as bad for work incentives, and hence bad also for job creation. Moreover, high unionization rates and labour market regulation are also usually thought to be obstacles to employment because they tend to raise minimum wages and compress the wage structure, which should be bad for employment.[15] In all the Nordic countries the employment rate is currently higher than the EU average; the employment rate of Iceland, Denmark and Norway even exceeds that of the USA. The Nordic unemployment rates are lower than the EU average (except in Finland), and long-term unemployment rates are low. But even the Nordics have not been able to avoid problems in the past. The Nordic labour markets faced serious shocks in the 1980s and 1990s, changes reflected in unemployment rates (see Figure 9.3). However, in spite of these negative shocks, Nordic unemployment rates have generally been lower than the EU average. In the 1980s, Finland and Sweden enjoyed very low unemployment (almost full employment), while Denmark suffered from high unemployment in the first half of the decade. In the 1990s, it was the turn of Sweden and Finland to go through a severe macroeconomic crisis and an unemployment shock; in the case of Finland, the shock led to an exceptionally sharp rise in unemployment in 1991–94. The rise was not permanent, and the period of economic recovery was accompanied by a relatively rapid fall in unemployment in 1995–2001.

In the mid-1990s, many observers were ready to conclude that rising unemployment in Sweden and Finland was evidence of the malfunction of the 'Nordic welfare state.' However, the rise turned out be only a temporary shock and unemployment was much less persistent than in that of the large EU countries. Figure 9.4 shows the devastating effect of the economic crisis

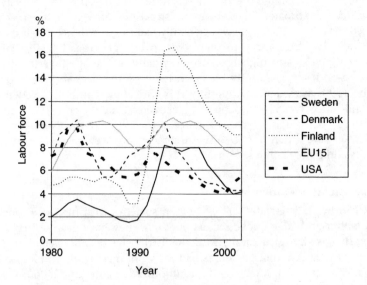

Figure 9.3 Unemployment rates, 1980–2002
Source: OECD, *Economic Outlook*.

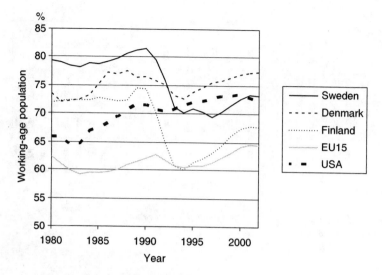

Figure 9.4 Employment rates, 1980–2002
Source: OECD, *Economic Outlook*.

of 1990–3 on Finnish and Swedish employment rates. It also shows that the sudden rise of unemployment was not a result of a long-term deterioration of employment but a consequence of a drastic destruction of jobs within a period of three years. After the crisis, employment in each country recovered quickly, supporting the view that the Nordic labour markets were relatively flexible, after all.

By the end of the 1990s it was clear that the most extensive welfare states in the world – Denmark and Sweden – were still able to maintain high living standards, high employment levels and low unemployment. The labour force participation rates of the Nordic populations at the beginning of the twenty-first were century as high as in the USA and much higher than the EU average; the same applies to employment rates, which in the Nordic countries tended to stay clearly above the OECD and EU averages. Because of the exceptional severity of the economic crisis of the 1990s and resulting high unemployment, Finland was an exception to this rule in the 1990s. However, even Finland had an employment rate above the OECD and EU averages in the year 2000 (see Figure 9.5).

The employment and unemployment figures of Sweden and Denmark were in 2000 very close to the corresponding US figures (see Table 9.6). Four of the five Nordic countries were in 2000 very close to a full employment situation, which was in striking contrast to the more gloomy EU average of an 8 per cent unemployment rate and much lower employment rate.

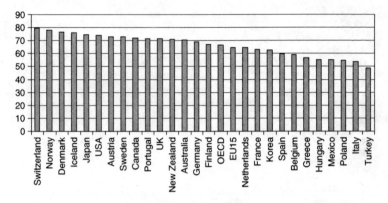

Figure 9.5 Employment rates OECD countries, 2000
Source: OECD, *Economic Outlook*.

Table 9.6 Labour market participation and inactivity indicators, 2000

	Participation[a]	Employment[b]	Inactivity[c]	Unemployment[d]
Denmark	80.1	76.6	23.4	4.4
Finland	74.5	67.1	33.1	9.8
Sweden	76.4	72.9	27.1	4.6
EU15	70.3	64.8	35.2	7.8
USA	77.4	74.3	25.7	4.0

Notes:
[a] Participation: Share of working-age population in labour force.
[b] Employment: Share of working-age population actually employed.
[c] Inactivity: Share of working-age population not employed.
[d] Unemployment: Commonly used unemployment rate.

Source: OECD, *Economic Outlook*.

The 'secret' of the high Nordic employment rates is most likely the 'Nordic welfare state' itself. The high taxes of welfare states may be harmful to private sector employment but the high level of public sector employment more than compensates (Freeman 1995; Rosen 1996). The 'Nordic welfare state' is a system which creates incentives and possibilities to increase labour supply, and particularly the labour supply of women. Taxation based on individual incomes, together with many incomes-related benefits (most importantly pensions, but also maternity and sickness benefits), favour a family model where both parents work. Publicly provided and heavily subsidised day care for children makes that an easy option even for mothers of small children and those with low incomes. The large-scale public provision of social services offers wide employment opportunities, especially to women. As a result, the Nordic countries have labour markets where men typically work in the business sector and women in public sector jobs.

The public sector is a very important provider of job opportunities in the Nordic countries, especially in Denmark and Sweden, where almost 23 per cent of the working-age population (or about 30 per cent of the labour force) is employed by the public sector. In Finland, the figure is lower (17 per cent), which still is much higher than the EU average of less than 11 per cent. As a result of a very large public sector, private sector employment is even lower than in Sweden and Finland in the other EU countries (see Table 9.7). In Denmark, the number of business sector jobs is almost the same as in other EU member countries.

The figures in Table 9.7 suggest that – at least when compared to the other EU countries – the large public sectors of the Nordic countries do not greatly crowd out the private sector employment. The number of business sector employees as a share of population is roughly the same in both groups. The impact of the large public sector is that it has created new jobs in public services and shifted a part of unpaid household work (mostly done by women) to the market.

Economic growth

The good employment record of the Nordic countries would suggest that the real income *per capita* in these countries should also be relatively high, as indeed is the case. The nominal (in dollar terms) incomes of the Nordics are very high. Figure 9.6 ranks countries by their income levels: Norway is ranked 3, Denmark, Iceland and Sweden hold ranks 6–8 and Finland is ranked 13. However, that ranking gives artificially good positions to the Nordics because of their high relative price levels. Figure 9.7 shows the real income levels *per capita* using PPPs which take into account the differences in price levels between the countries. Such a correction causes Finland and Sweden to drop to rank 18 and 19, respectively. Sweden even gets a lower ranking than Finland, Norway, Iceland and Denmark more or less maintain their original rankings.

Table 9.7 Public v. private sector employment, percent of working-age population, 2000

Country	Public sector	Business sector
Denmark	22.9	53.5
Finland	16.9	51.0
Sweden	22.9	49.8
EU15	10.7	53.3

Source: OECD data.

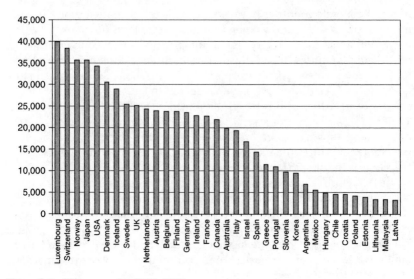

Figure 9.6 GNI *per capita*, 2001, USD
Source: World Bank data.

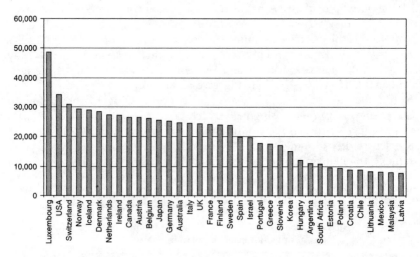

Figure 9.7 Real GNI *per capita*, 2001, USD in PPP
Source: World Bank data.

For Sweden, such a low ranking has been viewed by some analysts as embarrassing given that in 1970 Sweden still belonged to the group of top 5 countries. The fact that Sweden has been surpassed by almost fifteen countries in thirty years has given rise to lots of criticism of the Swedish welfare state ('the Swedish model'). However, at the same time three other countries with 'Nordic welfare state' systems (i.e. Denmark, Norway and Finland) have been able to maintain or improve their relative positions in the ranking. It is therefore (and for reasons put forward by Korpi in Chapter 8) not clear what to conclude. In Denmark and Sweden, the size of the public sector and overall tax burden are almost the same although Denmark seems to have been more successful in economic terms. One explanation may be that the income and price level statistics are not very accurate. Another may be that the structure of taxation and the regulatory framework are better in Denmark.[16]

The evolution of the level of GDP of three Nordics is compared in Figure 9.8 to the EU average and to the USA. In 1980, Denmark and Sweden were above, and Finland slightly below, the EU average GDP *per capita*. After that, the most striking development has been the rapid growth of American GDP.

In spite of the macroeconomic turbulence in the 1980s and 1990s, the long-term growth record of the Nordic countries has not been bad. In spite of very slow growth in 1985–95, Denmark was able to maintain its advanced position *vis-à-vis* the EU average. One has at least to conclude that the Danish welfare state has not been an obstacle to a good macroeconomic performance. Finland and Sweden suffered a serious shortfall of growth in 1990–3, but despite the worst fears the crisis turned out to be temporary. In spite of the large temporary output losses, Finland in the longer run has

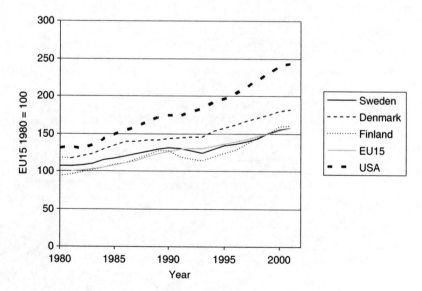

Figure 9.8 Evolution of relative GDP levels, 1980–2000
Source: OECD, *Economic Outlook*.

even been able to catch up other countries and finally surpass the EU average and Sweden. In the light of such a performance the Finnish economy can be viewed as dynamic.

The macroeconomic performance of Sweden was more mediocre in the 1990s. In the 1980s the Swedish economy performed as well as the other industrial countries in terms of output; in terms of employment and unemployment the labour market clearly performed better than others. However, even after ten years the Swedish economy has not been able to recover fully in terms of lost output from the crisis of the early 1990s. This gives rise to two questions: What's wrong in Sweden? It is safe to conclude that it is too early to make a final judgement on Swedish economic performance. In absolute terms, GDP *per capita* in all the Nordic countries is above the EU average; it follows that their advanced welfare states cannot be so bad for economic performance.

The relative growth records of three Nordic countries are depicted in Figure 9.9. Once again, the US economy delivers the most solid and stable growth path over the two decades. The European Union is clearly lagging behind, which means that the relative output difference between the USA and the EU has been widening.

It is interesting to note that Finland and Denmark have on average been able to grow faster than the other EU countries. It is only Sweden which has been lagging slightly behind. Comparisons based on GDP figures are

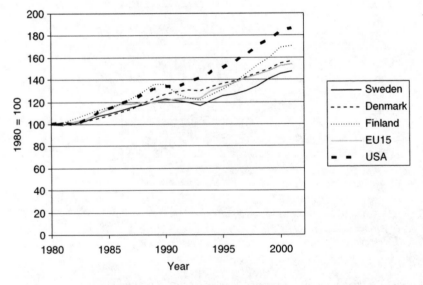

Figure 9.9 Relative GDP growth, 1980–2000
Source: OECD, *Economic Outlook.*

misleading because they do not take into account differences in population growth and in annual working hours. The stronger US growth can be partly explained by faster growth of working-age population in America and by longer average working hours (because of shorter US vacations). A better measure of economic efficiency and economic potential is thus productivity. Figure 9.10 presents the time paths of labour productivity; here one can observe clear convergence among the countries. All European countries have been able to catch up to the US productivity level.

The productivity differences between the countries are small. In the case of Finland, there has been a catch-up process going on *vis-à-vis* all others. Sweden has been lagging behind others and losing relative position mainly in the 1980s, but less so in the 1990s. Danish productivity also improved in the 1990s.

There was a clear productivity catch-up in Finland and Sweden in the 1990s. The economic crisis triggered a process of structural change and rationalization which resulted in the rapid growth of high-tech industries and productivity. The rize of wireless communication technology (the leading firms being the Finnish Nokia and the Swedish Ericsson) demonstrated that change.[17] The rapid growth and strong performance in new technologies improved the image of the Nordic countries as dynamic, innovative and

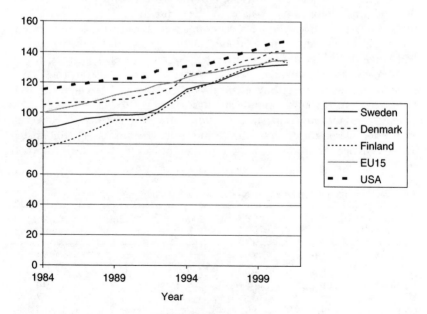

Figure 9.10 Evolution of relative labour productivity levels, 1984–99
Source: OECD data.

modern economies. It has even been argued that the 'Nordic welfare state' may actually be good for such knowledge-intensive growth because it supports research and education and facilitates individual risk taking.[18]

The welfare state and fiscal consolidation in the 1990s

The Nordic recessions caused a lot of strain on the public finances.[19] Initially, the Nordic public sectors were in healthy surplus; in 1990 Finland and Sweden had record fiscal surpluses and the Danish public sector was close to balance. However, the recessions, unemployment and high interest rates changed the situation quickly and fiscal balances deteriorated significantly; on average, the change was more than 10 per cent of GDP in Sweden and Finland. Although the change was big and rapid, it was proportionate to the employment losses so there is no reason to argue that the large deficits had been deliberately caused by expansionary fiscal policy.

The resulting large deficits caused much worry about the economic sustainability of the welfare state. It was clear that the financing of the public expenditure could not permanently rest on large fiscal deficits (Table 9.8). The Nordic governments reacted gradually to the wide imbalances by restricting the growth of public expenditure and cutting the levels of some benefits.

As a response to fiscal deficits, the growth of public demand was restrained in Finland and Sweden in the 1990s and the growth contribution of public demand was almost non-existent in the subsequent recovery. This is a marked difference from the other economic recoveries of the twentieth century when the rise of public spending furthered economic growth. Sweden and Finland differed also from the other Nordic and EU countries, where the growth of public demand was allowed to continue also in the 1990s. It seems to be the case that, especially in Finland and Sweden, the welfare state went through a significant squeeze in the 1990s although there were no outright reductions in social expenditures (Figure 9.11).[20] However, even after these adjustments, the Nordic welfare state model still existed as the most generous and extensive welfare model in most respects when

Table 9.8   General government fiscal balance, 1990–2000

Country	1990	1993	2000	Change 1990–3	Change 1993–2000
Denmark	−1.0	−2.9	2.7	−1.9	+5.6
Finland	5.3	−7.3	6.9	−12.6	+14.2
Sweden	4.0	−11.9	3.4	−15.9	+15.3
EU15	−4.0	−6.3	0.7	−2.3	+7.0
USA	−4.3	−5.0	2.2	−0.7	+7.2

Source: OECD, *Economic Outlook*.

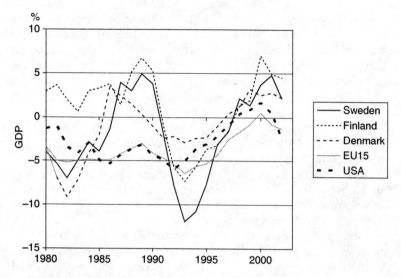

Figure 9.11 General government financial balances, 1980–2000
Source: OECD, *Economic Outlook*.

compared to other European countries – especially in Denmark and Sweden (see Kautto *et al.* 2001).

During the crisis, it was widely thought that the large budget deficits would be incurable without abolishing the welfare state. The economic revival in 1995–2000 changed that picture faster than one would have dared to expect. Public finances moved back to surplus; public expenditures decreased as a share of GDP by more than 10 percentage points and debt ratios even more (see Table 9.9).

Table 9.9 Public finance indicators, 1993–2000, percent of GDP

	Public debt		Public expenditure		Annual growth of public consumption, 1992–9
	1993	2000	1993	2000	
Denmark	83.8	50.4	58.1	51.3	2.4
Finland	56.0	43.5	59.1	44.8	0.7
Sweden	73.7	56.2	67.5	53.9	0.3
EU15	70.0	70.3	50.6	44.3	1.3
USA	75.8	58.8	34.1	29.4	

Source: OECD, *Economic Outlook*.

How was it possible to reduce the GDP share of public expenditures in Finland and Sweden by 15 percentage points within seven years, without destroying the welfare state? The primary answer is rapid economic recovery (which helped to increase tax bases) together with decreasing unemployment benefit expenditure and interest payments. In 1993, non-cyclical public expenditures (i.e. primary expenditures without unemployment-related expenditures) were 45 per cent of GDP in Finland and 52 per cent in Sweden. In 2000, the figures were 38 and 47 per cent, respectively. However, at the same time Finnish GDP grew more than 30 per cent and Swedish GDP more than 20 per cent. As a result, lower shares of larger output were used to finance non-cyclical public expenditure. In real terms, these expenditures grew about 10 per cent in 1993–2000, notwithstanding the austerity measures and fiscal consolidation. So the period of fiscal consolidation in the 1990s did not mean reduced public spending; it meant only that the growth of discretionary public spending was slower than before.

An important factor in the rapid recovery of the Nordic economies is that their labour markets seem to have functioned reasonably well even during and after the economic crises of the early 1990s, and in spite of collective bargaining and generous unemployment benefits. The good standing of the Nordic economies at the beginning of the twenty-first century enables one to use them as counterexamples to the mainstream view professed by economic journalists and the OECD and IMF reports.

Future challenges to the 'Nordic model'

Welfare states have received severe criticism since the 1980s, for many reasons. There is a broad literature which has concentrated on the lack of proper economic incentives in welfare states,[21] a criticism closely related to the functioning of the labour market but also to savings and investment behaviour. It is feared that high taxes and high benefits gradually destroy people's motivation to work hard and take risks, and thus weaken the economic basis of the welfare state.

Integration and globalization can also be seen as threats to the welfare state for the same reason. The current Western European, and especially the Nordic, models of the welfare state are to a large extent based on public expenditure financed by high tax rates. These may not be sustainable in long run if the mobility of capital, labour and services starts to erode tax bases. Another worry for the Nordic countries is that in long run the logic of economic integration may force them to cut taxes closer to the average levels of the rest of European Union. With the enlargement of the European Union, the benefits of the welfare states may also attract a wave of immigrants from poorer countries. These worries raise the question of what long-term effects deepening economic and political integration will have on the 'Nordic welfare model'.[22]

There are also other potential threats. European integration diminishes the autonomy of national economic policies through monetary union and coordination of fiscal policy although at the same time it creates more stability. In the longer run, expected demographic change will reduce the labour supply and increase the burden of pension finance and rising health care costs.[23] These changes will affect all European countries, but the Nordic countries may have less scope to adjust because they already have very high levels of public spending.

Although the Nordic labour markets are capable of delivering high employment and low unemployment rates, it is worth asking what will happen to these regulated and unionized labour market institutions when integration proceeds. There are two reasons to argue that the present institutions may survive. First, most of the other EU countries have similar institutional labour market structures. That is why there will not be much pressure from the European Union to reform or liberalize the labour market. The second reason is that the costs of employment protection and social benefits will probably in future be borne by labour, not by employers. If employees prefer to keep the current level of social protection in a competitive environment with mobile capital, it will be possible, provided that the gross labour cost of the employer stays at a competitive level.

A potentially severe threat to the future of the 'Nordic welfare model' is created by international tax competition. As was argued above, it is likely that the costs of social protection will be borne mainly by labour in the form of high labour taxes. Until now this has been possible without risking the tax base, since labour is rather immobile. However, it is not impossible that in the future increasing mobility induced by general economic liberalization – call it globalization – may have deeper impacts on traditional welfare state systems by intensifying competition for skilled labour and factor mobility. There is already evidence that economic integration has forced most countries to cut their taxes on corporate profits and capital income. The Nordic countries are no exceptions to this rule; they have also reduced their corporate tax rates, but taxes on labour and private consumption have stayed at a high level and even increased in the 1990s.[24]

In the Nordic countries, the tax burden lies mainly on the shoulders of employees and consumers; overall tax rates; average income tax rates and effective consumption tax rates are much higher in the Nordic than in the other EU countries, although the tax wedge is almost the same. Nordic income taxation is highly progressive and marginal tax rates are very high. This holds above all for Sweden, Denmark and Finland.[25] At the moment the tax incidence is on relatively stable and non-elusive tax bases. As a result of high consumption and labour taxes, private consumption *per capita* is not as high in the Nordic countries as one might suggest on the basis of high GDP *per capita* figures.

As European integration proceeds, it will become easier to purchase goods in other countries and to move to work to other countries within the Single Market. This will increase the pressure to harmonize consumption taxes and also after-tax earnings. Although there is evidence from the USA, for example, that some differentials may be sustained between neighbouring jurisdictions (Krueger 2001) such Tiebout-type regional tax competition is likely to put pressure on the Nordic countries to reduce their currently high income tax and consumption tax rates. This applies especially to Denmark and Sweden, but also to Finland. In Norway, the pressure may be felt in a difficulty in maintaining a higher price level of private consumption than elsewhere (due to both agricultural protectionism and high consumption taxes). In Finland and Norway, there is some room to compensate these changes by higher taxes on property. In Sweden and Denmark, all taxes are already so high that tax competition will almost certainly reduce aggregate tax revenue – the only question is by how much. That, of course, is likely to cause difficulties to the financing of current welfare models which rely heavily on public expenditure.

Some relief, however, can be found in the current fiscal surpluses of the Nordic governments which are higher than those of other European countries. Sweden and Denmark, for instance, would be able to cut taxes by 2 or 3 per cent of GDP without a risk of fiscal deficit; Finland and Norway have even more leeway in that direction. Such changes may be sufficient to bring the Nordic tax rates close enough to the tax rates of other EU/EEA countries so that they are sustainable.

Conclusions

After the deep recessions of the early 1990s, all the Nordic countries have experienced a strong recovery. On average, the post-recession Nordic growth rates of output, employment and productivity are almost the same as in the USA in the same period, and much better than the EU average. Within the Nordic group, output growth has been fastest in Finland and Iceland, and employment growth has been about 2 per cent per annum in Finland, Iceland and Norway. The highest productivity growth has been achieved in Finland and Denmark.

The good economic record of the latter half of the 1990s may indicate, that the Nordic economies are still well functioning, notwithstanding the earlier crises. The 'Nordic welfare model' survived the test of the 1990s, when it faced a real crisis when public deficits and unemployment rose to record levels (especially in Sweden and Finland, but to a lesser extent also in Denmark, Norway and Iceland) in the mid-1990s as a result of recession. However, instead of becoming locked in to an 'unemployment trap', the Nordic countries recovered quickly in the latter half of the 1990s; within five years all the Nordic countries had been successful in reducing open unemployment significantly and in turning public finances from deficit to surplus and maintaining their welfare states. The adjustment was made by raising taxes and restricting the growth of public expenditures, but not by changing the basic structure of the national welfare models. The Nordic countries can thus still be regarded as advanced welfare states with high public employment, universal benefit systems, extensive publicly provided welfare services, high taxes, low poverty and corporatist labour market structures.

The Swedish crisis intensified the critique against the 'Nordic welfare state model'. The recession and the subsequent output and employment losses helped to make the case that the crisis and slow growth were not the results of simple failure in macroeconomic coordination but instead a deeper systemic failure ultimately caused by the structures of the welfare state. It was argued by many critics that the welfare state was generally bad for growth because it created bad incentives. According to such view, overly generous benefits, labour market rigidities and high taxes would finally discourage investment, job creation and labour supply. By many critics the dismal growth record of the 1990s was used as evidence supporting this critical view, in both Sweden and Finland. However, since the all Nordic countries recovered from their macroeconomic crises, their allegedly 'bad economic performance' or 'public finance problems' can no longes be used as ultimate evidence of the failure of the 'Nordic model'. It is now more widely admitted that the recessions were related to financial factors and policy failures rather than to institutional weaknesses of the welfare state.

One could even argue that in the Nordic countries labour markets functioned well (and better than in larger EU countries) in the 1990s in spite of high unionization, collective bargaining and generous unemployment benefits. Furthermore, in spite of advanced social welfare systems and high taxes the employment rate in the Nordic countries is higher than the EU average, and the employment rates of Iceland, Denmark and Norway even exceed those of the USA. The Nordic unemployment rates are lower than the EU average (except in the case of Finland), and long-term unemployment rates are low. In the light of these facts, the performance of the Nordic countries could be used as counter-examples to the mainstream view, which is eager to relate welfare states to economic stagnation.

In future, the extensive Nordic welfare systems, although they seem to be functioning well at present, are likely to face further challenges caused by integration, globalization and demographic change. Further integration of European economies may increase pressure for tax competition, which may threaten the financial basis of the welfare state. The Nordic countries have already responded to tax competition by lowering corporate tax rates and taxes on capital income. These changes have been compensated by raising other taxes, and as a result, labour incomes and private consumption are now heavily taxed. It is not clear how sustainable such a regime of high taxes will be in the future if mobility of goods and employees increases. If further pressure to lower taxation emerges in the future, the financing of increasing public pension and health care expenditures of an ageing population may be difficult – possibly more difficult for the Nordic countries than other European countries, because the initial level of taxation is so high and there is not much scope to increase labour supply. Some leeway for the Nordic governments may be provided by their exceptionally good fiscal positions, however.

Notes

1   The chapter focuses mainly on Denmark, Sweden and Norway. Iceland is omitted because it does not have a large public sector, and Norway is omitted because of oil revenues, which help to finance generous public spending.
2   It is easy to find examples of such opinions by reading *The Economist*, or the country reports of the IMF and the OECD, for example.
3   For a survey of the history of 'Nordic welfare states', see (for Sweden) Lundberg and Åmark (2001), (for Denmark) Christiansen and Petersen (2001) and (for Finland) Kettunen (2001).
4   In Sweden and Norway, the social democratic parties have been strong enough to rule alone. In Finland, Denmark and Iceland they have had to rule in coalition governments with other parties. See, for example, Esping-Andersen (1985) and Hicks (1999).
5   'Social services' include mostly services to children, the elderly and disabled persons.
6   In Sweden, the pension system is run by public pension funds, in Finland by private but government-regulated pension insurance companies. In both countries, the systems are partly funded.
7   Tanzi and Schuknecht (2000) argue that increasing the size of public expenditure above 30 per cent does not yield any economic gains. Such a view seems to neglect the equity-improving impact of welfare states of which the Nordic countries offer ample evidence. It can also be said that there is no compelling empirical evidence that large public sectors as such are harmful to growth.
8   Kangas and Palme (2000) show that differences in social policy explain the low family-related poverty rates in the Nordic countries. The same pattern is reflected by the results of Haataja (1999), according to which poverty in the Nordic countries is not connected with unemployment. Forssén (1998) has analysed Nordic family policies and their distributional impacts.
9   It is most likely that the differences in unemployment developments between countries reflect corresponding differences in macroeconomic policies; cf. Blanchard and Summers (1986) and Ball (1999), who emphasize the role of macroeconomic shocks.
10   In the cases of Finland and Sweden the recession of the 1990s was deeper than the Great Depression of the 1930s, if measured by output losses.
11   For literature on the Nordic crises, see Bordes, Currie and Söderström (1993), Jonung, Stymne and Söderström (1996), Kiander and Vartia (1996) and Honkapohja and Koskela (1999).
12   Under fixed exchange rates, high interest rates are needed to defend the exchange rate if investors think it is overvalued, which was the case in most European countries in 1990–2.

13 They could have been an exception since at that time Denmark was the only Nordic country belonging to the ERM, the Exchange Rate Mechanism of the European Monetary System (EMS).

14 Abandonment was forced because market pressure against fixed parities grew too much. The abandonment of the restrictive monetary policy was not deliberate, and was opposed by the European governments and central banks.

15 Some researchers have presented evidence that taxes are not harmful in economies which are characterized by well-coordinated collective bargaining systems; see Summers, Gruber and Vergara (1993) and Kiander, Kilponen and Vilmunen (2001) for more recent evidence. The Nordic countries and Austria are usually used as examples of countries with such systems.

16 It has been argued by Lundvall (2002) that one reason for the economic success of Denmark is the strong population of small and medium-sized firms (SMEs). They are more flexible than the Swedish corporate sector, which is dominated by large multinational enterprises (MNEs).

17 For reviews of the growth of the Finnish wireless technology sector and Nokia corporation, see Paija and Rouvinen (2003) and Rouvinen and Ylä-Anttila (2003).

18 See Castells and Himanen (2002).

19 There have also been studies suggesting that the so-called 'non-Keynesian effects' of fiscal policy might have contributed to the recessions in Sweden and Finland, or that the crises would have partly been caused by excessive deficits (see Giavazzi and Pagano 1995 and Corsetti and Roubini 1996). However, by looking at the timing of the output losses and rising deficits it is very hard to accept such a conclusion – unless one believes that consumers were able to predict the recession well in advance.

20 In fact, a lots of streamlining and organizational change took place in the 1990s, and the number of public sector employees was reduced in both countries (see Palme *et al.* 2003). Towards to the end of the 1990s the welfare state seemed to recover from these measures.

21 See, for example, Lindbeck (1997) and chapter 8 in this volume. It is also a commonplace that international organizations such as the OECD and the IMF repeatedly present policy recommendations which demand further structural changes and reforms (lower benefits and taxes, privatization and deregulation). Such claims are essentially a criticism of the Nordic and other welfare states.

22 There is a broad literature which views the deregulated and globalized capitalism, on the one hand, and European integration, on the other, as major threats to traditional welfare models, and especially to the Nordic ones. See, for example, Stephens, Huber and Ray (1999) and Leibfried and Pierson (2000).

23 The economic and fiscal impacts of the expected demographic change have been analysed by Kiander and Östring (2003), who compare all Nordic countries. More specific analyses on the Finnish and Swedish cases are provided, respectively, by Batljan (2003) and Parjanne and Siren (2003).

24 A report on tax competition commissioned by the Nordic Council of Ministers takes a relatively relaxed view on the potential future threats; see Lassen and Sörensen (2003).

25 It has been shown that in models where trade unions are engaged in wage-setting, progressive taxation may be good for employment; see Koskela and Vilmunen (1996) and Holmlund and Kolm (1995). There is also empirical evidence that even relatively high tax rates do not have significant effects on labour supply (for a survey, see Slemrod, 1998).

Bibliography

Ball, L. (1999) 'Aggregate Demand and Unemployment'. *Brookings Papers on Economic Activity*, 2.

Batljan, I. (2003) 'Macroeconomic Scenarios of the Future and Costs of Health and Social care for the Elderly in Sweden, 2000–30'. In *Sustainable Social and Health Development in the Nordic Countries*. Copenhagen: Nordic Social-Statistical Committee, Seminar Report.

Blanchard, O. J. and Summers, L. (1986) 'Hysteresis and the European Unemployment Problem'. *NBER Macroeconomics Annual*.

Bordes, C., Currie, D. and Söderström, H.T. (1993) *Three Assessments of the Finnish Economic Crisis and Economic policy*. Helsinki: Bank of Finland.

Castells, M. and Himanen, P. (2002) *The Information Society and the Welfare State – The Finnish Model*. New York: Oxford University Press.

Christiansen, N.F. and Petersen, K. (2001) The Dynamics of Social Solidarity: The Danish Welfare State 1900–2000. In K. Petersen and N.F. Christiansen (eds.), *The Nordic Welfare States 1900–2000*. *Scandinavian Journal of History*, 26(3).

Corsetti, G. and Roubini, N. (1996) 'Budget Deficits, Public Sector Solvency and Political Biases of Fiscal Policy: A Case Study of Finland'. *Finnish Economic Papers*, 9(1).

Esping-Andersen, G. (1985) *Politics against Markets: The Social Democratic Road to Power*. Princeton: Princeton University Press.

Esping-Andersen, G. (1990) *The Three Worlds of Welfare Capitalism*. Cambridge: Polity Press.

Forssén, K. (1998) *Children, Families and the Welfare State: Studies on the Outcomes of the Finnish Family Policy*. STAKES Research Reports No 92. Helsinki: National Research and Development Centre for Welfare and Health.

Freeman, R. (1995) 'The Large Welfare State as a System'. *American Economic Review, Papers and Proceedings*, 85.

Giavazzi, F. and Pagano, M. (1995) 'Non-Keynesian Effects of Sharp Fiscal Policy Changes: International Evidence and the Swedish Experience'. *Swedish Economic Policy Review*, 2.

Haataja, A. (1999) 'Unemployment, Employment and Poverty'. *European Societies*, 1(2).

Hicks, A. (1999) *Social Democracy and Welfare Capitalism: A Century of Income Security Policies*. Ithaca, NY: Cornell University Press.

Holmlund, B. and Kolm, A. (1995) 'Progressive Taxation, Wage Setting and Unemployment – Theory and Swedish Evidence'. *Swedish Economic Policy Review*, 2.

Honkapohja, S. and Koskela, E. (1999) 'Finland's Depression: A Tale of Bad Luck and Bad Policies'. *Economic Policy*, 29.

Jäntti, M. and Danziger, S. (1994) 'Child Poverty in Sweden and the United States: The Effect of Social Transfers and Parental Labour Force Participation'. *Industrial and Labour Relations Review*, 48(1).

Jäntti, M. and Danziger, S. (2001) 'Income Poverty in Advanced Countries'. In A.B. Atkinson and F. Bourguignon (eds.), *Handbook on Income Distribution*. Amsterdam: North-Holland.

Jonung, L., Stymne, J. and Söderström, H.T. (1996) 'Depression in the North: Boom and Bust in Sweden and Finland, 1985–1993'. *Finnish Economic Papers*, 9(1).

Kangas, O. and Palme, J. (2000) 'Does Social Policy Matter? Poverty Cycles in OECD countries'. *International Journal of Health Services*, 30(2).

Kautto, M., Fritzell, J., Hvinden, B., Kvist, J. and Uusitalo, H. (eds.) (2001). *Nordic Welfare States in the European Context*. London: Routledge.

Kettunen, P. (2001) 'The Nordic Welfare State in Finland'. In K. Petersen and N.F. Christiansen (eds.), *The Nordic Welfare States 1900–2000. Scandinavian Journal of History*, 26(3).

Kiander, J., Kilponen, J. and Vilmunen, J. (2001) *Taxes, Growth and Unemployment in the OECD Countries – Does Collective Bargaining Matter?* Government Institute for Economic Research, VATT Discussion Paper 23.

Kiander, J. and Östring, T. (2003) 'Den offentliga sektorns effektivitet och hållbarhet i (The Efficiency and Sustainability of the Public sector among the Nordic Countries) Norden'. *Nord*, 12. Det framtida nordiska välfärdssamhället: utmaningar och möjligheter. (The Future Nordic Welfare Society: Challenges and Possibilities.) Copenhagen: Nordic Council of Ministers.

Kiander, J. and Vartia, P. (1996) 'The Great Depression of the 1990s in Finland'. *Finnish Economic Papers*, 9(1): 72–88.

Koskela, E. and Vilmunen, J. (1996) 'Tax Progression is Good for Employment in Popular Models of Trade Union Behaviour'. *Labour Economics*, 3.

Krueger, A.B. (2001) 'From Bismarck to Maastricht: The March to European Union and the Labour Compact'. *Labour Economics*, 7, 2.

Lassen, D.D. and Sörensen, P.B. (2003) 'Financing the Nordic Welfare States: The Challenge of Globalization to Taxation in the Nordic Countries'. *Nord* 12 Det framtida nordiska välfärdssamhället: utmaningar och möjligheter. Copenhagen: Nordic Council of Ministers. (The Future Nordic Welfare Society: Challenges and Possibilities.)

Leibfried, S. and Pierson, P. (2000) 'Social Policy: Left to Courts and Markets?'. In H. Wallace and W. Wallace (eds) *Policy-Making in the European Union*. Oxford: Oxford University Press.

Lindbeck, A. (1997) 'The Swedish Experiment'. *Journal of Economic Literature*, 35(3).

Lundberg, U. and Åmark, K. (2001) 'Social Rights and Social Security: The Swedish Welfare State 1900–2000'. In K. Petersen and N.F. Christiansen (eds.), *The Nordic Welfare States 1900–2000. Scandinavian Journal of History*, 26 (3).

Lundvall, B.-Å. (2002) *Innovation, Growth and Social Cohesion*. Aldershot: Edward Elgar.

NOSOSCO (1998) Nordic Social Statistical Committee: Social Protection in the Nordic Countries. Copenhagen: NOSOSCO.

Paija, L. and Rouvinen, P. (2003) 'The ICT Cluster in Finland – Can we Explain It?'. In G. Schienstock (ed.), *Catching Up and Forging Ahead: The Finnish Success Story*. Aldershot: Edward Elgar.

Palme, J., Bergmark, Å., Bäckman, O., Estrada, F., Fritzell, J., Lundberg, O., Sjöberg, O., Sommerstad, L. and Szebehely, M. (2003) 'A Welfare Balance Sheet for the 1990s: The Final Report of the Swedish Welfare Commission'. *Scandinavian Journal of Public Health*, Supplement 60.

Parjanne, M.-L. and Siren, P. (2003) 'Scenarios for the Long-Term Financial Sustainability of the Finnish Social Protection System'. In *Sustainable Social and Health Development in the Nordic Countries*. Copenhagen: Nordic Social-Statistical Committee, Seminar Report.

Rosen, S. (1996) 'Public Employment and the Welfare State in Sweden'. *Journal of Economic Literature*, 34 (2).

Rouvinen, P. and Ylä-Anttila, P. (2003) 'Case Study: Little Finland's Transformation to a Wireless Giant'. In S. Dutta, B. Lanvin and F. Paua (eds.), *The Global Information Technology Report 2003–2004*. New York: Oxford University Press.

Slemrod, J. (1998) 'How Costly is a Large, Redistributive Public Sector?'. *Swedish Economic Policy Review*, 5 (1).

Smeeding, T. (2000). 'Changing Income Inequality in OECD Countries: Updated Results from the Luxembourg Income Study (LIS).' In R. Hauser and I. Becker (eds.), *The Personal Distribution of Income in an International Perspective*. Berlin: Springer-Verlag.

Stephens, J.D., Huber, E. and Ray, L. (1999) 'The Welfare State in Hard Times'. in H. Kitschelt *et al.* (eds.), *Continuity and Change in Contemporary Capitalism*. Cambridge: Cambridge University Press.

Summers, L., Gruber, J. and Vergara, R. (1993) 'Taxation and the Structure of Labour Markets'. *Quarterly Journal of Economics*, 108.

Svensson, L.E. (1994) 'Fixed Exchange Rates: What Have we Learned?'. *European Economic Review*, 38 (3–4).

Tanzi, V. and Schuknecht, L. (2000) *Public Spending in the Twentieth Century: A Global Perspective*. Cambridge: Cambridge University Press.

10
Financing 'Big-Tax' Welfare States: Sweden During Crisis and Recovery

Ola Sjöberg

Introduction

In the years to come, the Swedish welfare state will face a number of important challenges to the financing of its system of social protection, perhaps the most important of these being changing demographic structures. The proportion of people between sixteen and sixty-four years of age will decrease, which will reduce the relative size of the labour force and thus also reduce the number of potential tax payers. At the same time, the proportion of people above pension age will increase. This group has a high demand for social services, such as health care, and they consume a large part of the resources devoted to social insurance. Consequently, Sweden will have to cope with a situation where a larger portion of the population will have to be supported by a shrinking one. But the support burden issue is not just a question of demography; it also relates to how many of those in their active years choose to work. In this respect, incentives to work are of utmost importance to the financial viability of the Swedish welfare state. Many also predict that the globalization and internationalization of the world economy will put important constraints on the financing of social protection, in terms of both what overall level of taxation is feasible to sustain and the rate at which different tax bases can be taxed.

Sweden is not alone in facing these challenges. In the decades to come, all industrialized countries are facing the same basic demographic problems, and the liberalization of capital and the increased mobility of labour can be expected to affect all countries more or less equally. However, Sweden can in a number of important respects be considered as something of a crucial 'test case' regarding the financial viability of large welfare states. Social expenditures and the total tax burden in Sweden are among the highest in the world. The severity of the economic recession that hit Sweden in the early 1990s was, with the exception of Finland, unparalleled among the OECD member states. The severity of this recession can be detected in the significant fall in GDP, in the dramatic rise in unemployment and the historically unique fall in employment. Between 1990 and 1993 employment fell by over half a million people, the open unemployment rate increased from below 2 to over 8 per cent and GDP displayed negative growth in three consecutive years. Since the Swedish welfare state is heavily dependent upon taxes on work and labour for its financing, the rise in unemployment and decrease in employment put severe strain on both the income and expenditure side of public finances, at both the central and the local government level. Since 1993, most economic indicators in Sweden have shown a positive development; however, the rate of recovery differs between different levels of government as well as depending on what economic indicators one focuses on. Whereas GDP has shown a relatively stable growth since 1993, employment at the end of the 1990s was well below the level prevailing at the beginning of the twenty-first century. And whereas the budget balance of the central government has shown a surplus since 1997, many local governments were still battling with severe imbalances in their budgets.

Thus, if we want to study the financing and financial viability of large welfare states, especially at the time of a rapidly changing economic environment, Sweden seems to be an ideal choice. The purpose of this chapter is to describe and analyse the financing of Swedish welfare in a historical and comparative perspective. The first part of the chapter will be devoted to a description and analysis of how the major social security programmes have been financed in Sweden, as well as in other countries in the OECD area. The next section will focus upon the financing of local government activities in the Swedish welfare area as well as outlining the major components of an alternative way of financing social services, the care insurance (*Pflegeversicherung*) that was introduced in Germany in the mid-1990s. Given the importance of taxes on wages and income from work for the financing of almost all areas and levels of the Swedish welfare state, the chapter will conclude with a discussion and analysis of taxation and labour supply.

The financing of social security programmes in Sweden: an historical and comparative perspective

During the period between 1960 and 1993, social security transfers as a percentage of GDP increased from 7 to 16 per cent among the OECD countries (OECD 1995). The increase in social spending in these countries reflects what has been called 'the revolution of rising entitlements' (Bell 1974: 39). The heavy financial pressure on the state budget accompanying this rise in entitlements has not gone unnoticed by the taxpayers (Figure 10.1).[1] The proportion of the wage an average industrial worker pays in the form of income taxes (state and local) and social insurance contributions increased substantially between 1930 and 1995 in the OECD area.[2] In 1930, an industrial worker paid on cross-national average 1.6 per cent of her gross income in state and local income taxes and

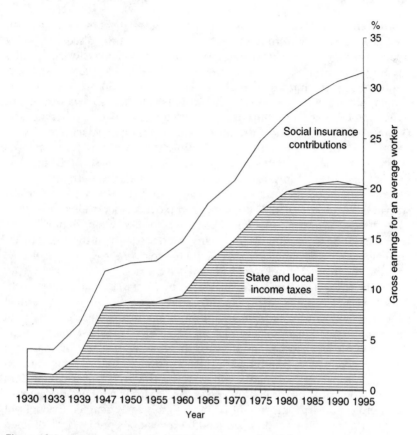

Figure 10.1   Average state and local income taxes and social insurance contributions, as per cent of gross earnings, selected OECD countries [a], 1930–95

Note: [a] Australia, Austria, Belgium, Canada, Denmark, Finland, France, Germany, Ireland, Italy, Japan, The Netherlands, New Zealand, Norway, Sweden, Switzerland, the UK and the USA.

Source: SCIP database.

2.3 per cent in social insurance contributions. In 1995, these figures had risen to 20.2 and 11.3 per cent, respectively.

Behind these average figures, two different stories about the development of taxation in modern democracies can be told (Peters 1991; Steinmo 1993). The first story is about how much modern tax systems have in common. The industrialized countries rely to a great extent on a relatively small number of taxes to generate the vast bulk of government revenues. Besides the growth in income taxes and social insurance contributions, the most noticeable trend in taxation in the post-war period has been the increase in indirect taxes on expenditure, above all consumption taxes. The second story is about how much countries actually differ regarding the relative importance of the different sources of government revenue. If we restrict the discussion to the financing of social security schemes, this cross-national diversity can be illustrated by the distinction between two institutional social policy models and the financing structures they imply: social insurance and non-contributory benefits (Barr 1993). Social insurance benefits is (as a rule) awarded on the basis of previous contributions (usually form the insured, but sometimes also from the employer). Non-contributory benefits are financed wholly by state authorities through general taxes, and can either be in the form of social assistance (targeted) benefits that are awarded on the basis of an income- or a means-test, or 'universal' benefits that are awarded without either a contributions- or a means-test. Historically, conflicts between social actors such as political parties, trade unions and employers' associations have arisen over, first, what institutional form to choose (social insurance/contributory financing or non-contributory financing), and secondly, if the social insurance model was chosen, how to distribute the costs of the reforms instituted between the insured, employers and state authorities.

The social insurance reforms introduced by Bismarck in late nineteenth-century Germany are generally considered to be path-breaking in a number of respects, and in terms of financing these reforms exerted a substantial influence on subsequent social policy reforms. One of the most characteristic features of the Bismarckian reforms were the tripartite structure of financing; a heavy reliance upon employers' and employees' contributions coupled with state subsidies, a structure where the introduction of a compulsory contribution borne by the employer was a major break with prior systems of social protection. This method of financing was widely adapted throughout Europe. However, the proportions paid by the various parties have differed between countries, and the arguments put forward as regards the sources of financing are still largely being advanced today.

The participation of the insured in the financing of social insurance schemes has traditionally been based primarily on the idea that such contributions justify a right to benefit. By making entitlement to benefits conditional upon past performance in employment and/or financial contributions, benefits can be justified as having been earned and the contributor approaches the state as a claimant of an earned right rather than as a supplicant for help. The essence of this argument was captured by the answer by US president F.D. Roosevelt when he was told that the financing of the 1935 Social Security Act in the USA partly by employee contributions was a mistake due to the regressive nature of these contributions: 'I guess you're right on the economics, but those taxes were never a problem of economics. They are politics all the way through. We put those payroll contributions there so as to give the contributors a legal, moral, and political right to collect their pensions and their unemployment benefits' (quoted in Leuchtenberg 1963: 133).

The psychological and moral aspects of contributions from the insured are further illustrated by the debate preceding the Swedish pension reform of 1946. Even though the type of pension introduced by this reform, the People's Pension (*'folkpension'*), was a universal pension received independently of contributions paid, it was nevertheless considered psychologically important that the insured by means of a special tax (consisting of 1 per cent of taxable income) was contributing to her own retirement (Elmér 1960). This demonstrates that how the (visible) costs of social protection are distributed in society can have a political/pedagogical importance. The argument regarding the importance of contributions form the insured was once again brought forward in the discussions preceding the latest Swedish pension reform. An important motive for introducing employees' social contributions in this reform was to make the connection between contributions and benefits more evident and so increase people's willingness to pay taxes (Sjöberg 2001).

Thus, whereas it has been argued that the distinction between contributions from employers and insured is of little importance since employers' contributions in the end will be borne by employees and/or consumers (through lower wages and/or higher consumer prices), history shows that the perception of who is paying for the benefits is of considerable importance for the legitimacy of social security institutions. As Salminen (1993: 150) states: 'in politics the position of "how things look" matters many times more than the position of "how things really are"'.

Even if the 'right to benefit' argument has carried substantial weight throughout history in promoting the financial participation of the insured in social security programmes, other arguments have also been advocated. The financial participation of the insured persons in these programmes has been maintained to promote their financial stability, and consequently also the stability of benefit rates. By relying on social insurance contributions instead of general revenue financing it is, at least in theory, possible to 'earmark' these contributions for specific social insurance purposes. The potential beneficiaries will then be provided with a degree of security that they would not expect if the allocation of funds to the social insurance schemes were dependent upon annual budgetary procedure (Manser 1981; Wilson 1986). Incidentally, this argument has also been claimed to have relevance for the state of democracy. By designing a definite revenue category for each single expenditure, the individual is supposed, through the political process, to be able to participate in public expenditure decisions, as a voter–contributor–beneficiary (Wicksell 1958). In Sweden, a recurrent proposal in the social policy debate in the 1990s was to return to the practice before 1990, when the finances of many individual social security schemes were kept separate from the rest of the state's budget (Sjöberg 2001). Although the economic significance of these arrangements was small, it has been argued that such a solution would make it easier for decision makers and voters to see the financial situation for individual insurance schemes and therefore provide a more unambiguous basis for assessing the need for reforms.

Figure 10.1 gave only an account of the proportion of the gross wage an average worker has paid in social contributions. However, in most industrialized countries in the post-war period social contributions from employers have played a substantial role as a source for financing social security schemes. In Sweden, these contributions increased from 3.4 per cent of the gross wage in 1960 to 33 per cent in the 2000.[3] The most widely used argument in favour of social insurance contributions from employers has been that employers have a responsibility for the economic well-being of workers at times when they are unable to work (Sjöberg 1999). According to this argument, social insurance contributions from the employers should be viewed as a form of 'deferred wage'. This belief in the employers' responsibility perhaps found its clearest expression in the case of work-accident insurance. Since the first reforms in this area, work-accident insurance schemes have in most countries been financed wholly through employers' contributions.

Contributions to social insurance programmes by the employers have often been opposed on the grounds that the employers' contributions will put a too heavy burden on companies, an argument that could be heard even at the time of the Bismarckian reforms. Social insurance contributions from employers have been said to increase production costs, thereby reducing companies' competitiveness with producers in countries where employers do not have to pay such contributions, and ultimately leading to higher unemployment. However, this fear has sometimes been counterbalanced by the need of companies to assure a flow of effective and well-motivated personnel for the company's operation. The need to maintain the quality of labour and reduce labour turnover has in many cases motivated companies to set up company-specific schemes, or to accept employers' contributions to nation-wide compulsory schemes (Sjöberg 1999).

In social insurance schemes, state authorities have usually also contributed with subsidies of varying magnitudes. State subsidies to social insurance were a crucial element in the Bismarckian approach to social insurance reforms as a way of reinforcing a patriarchal structure of society (Rimlinger 1971). Thus, not only social policy legislation but also financial aid from the state has sometimes been considered to promote social and political stability. Furthermore, particularly in the early decades of the twentieth century, it was often argued that since the state in any case had to pay for the protection of the poorest in society, the introduction of social insurance schemes would simply mean that the existing costs of public relief and old-age assistance would be reduced. The contributions paid by the public authorities to social insurance would thus be offset by a decrease in the budget allocated to public assistance. Moreover, the financial resources obtained by contributions from the insured and the employers have sometimes been insufficient to cover the costs of the schemes, especially during periods of economic recession.

In the legislation of many countries, the possibility therefore exists for the state to cover possible deficits in the budgets of social insurance schemes. In addition, it often takes time for social insurance schemes to obtain enough funds, through contributions from employers and the insured, to make possible the payment of legislated benefits. The maturation of social insurance programmes has thus often necessitated high levels of state contributions over a transitional period.

The main argument in favour of non-contributory financing of social security schemes has been that individuals, or social segments, with no or only small prospects of being able to pay a social insurance premium should be protected and guaranteed a decent living standard in the case of sickness, unemployment, or old age. According to this argument, social policy should be organized as to provide a basic security for the whole population. The model of social protection where coverage in the case of a contingency is dependent upon contributions made is closely related to the history of modern labour markets (Alcock 1996). In the post-war economic boom, the image of a full-employment society, where a male breadwinner was committed full-time to employment and providing for his family, was widespread in many countries in Europe. However, labour markets in the European Union have since the 1970s undergone major structural changes. One such change is obviously the re-emergence of mass unemployment, affecting different groups in society to varying degrees. Another change is the replacement of many full-time, largely male, jobs in large-scale manufacturing with jobs in the service sector, often part-time, low-paid and occupied by women. There have also been important changes in family structure, with an increase in the divorce rate and a growth in the number of lone-parent families. These changes in the labour market and family structure have created gaps in the coverage of traditional social insurance schemes where full eligibility for benefits is based on contributions made and thus ultimately on a continuous participation in full-time employment. Particularly vulnerable groups are in this context groups such as long-term and youth unemployed, lone parents (who may not have been able to make sufficient contributions), part-time workers and divorcees (who may lose the full protection of their spouses' contribution records and may have inadequate contribution records of their own). The fact that certain categories will not be contributors to the social insurance system have forced governments to introduce second-tier programmes completely financed from general revenue to complement programmes based on contributory financing. These programmes, as a rule means-tested in character, give protection to those who do not qualify for contributory (social insurance) benefits.

Figures 10.2a and Figure 10.2b show how the average financing shares from the insured, the employers and state authorities for three major social insurance schemes (old-age pensions, sickness and unemployment insurance) have developed in Sweden, as well as on average in the OECD area, between 1930 and 1995.

The most apparent trend in Sweden, as well as on average in the OECD area, since 1930 is the increased importance of social contributions from employers for the financing of social security schemes and the accompanying decrease in importance in the financing share coming above all from state authorities, but also from the insured. Between 1930 and 1995, the employers' share increased from on average around 17 per cent to over 45 per cent in the OECD countries. In Sweden, the employers' share increased even more dramatically, from 0 to 80 per cent between 1930 and 1990. During the same period of time, the financing share from state and local authorities decreased from around 38 to roughly 26 per cent on average in the OECD area and from around 44 per cent to roughly 18 per cent in

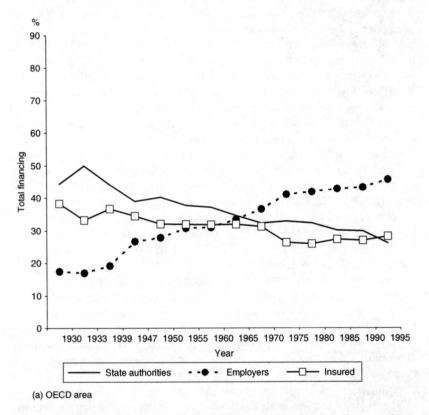

(a) OECD area

Figure 10.2   Financing shares coming from the insured, employers and state authorities in the financing of social security schemes, 1930–95 (a) OECD countries (b) Sweden.
Source: SCIP database.

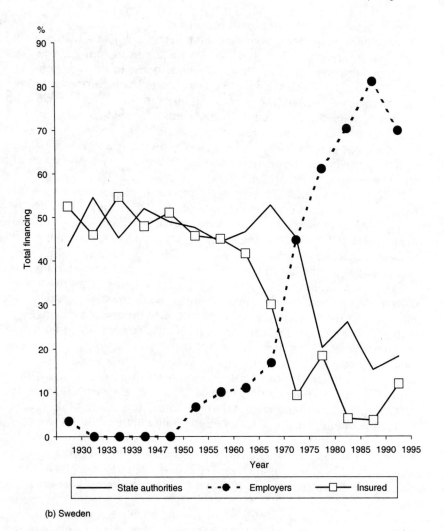

(b) Sweden

Figure 10.2 (continued)

Sweden. Finally, the financing share coming from the insured has shown a long-term decrease (from 38 to around 28 per cent on average in the OECD countries and from 52 to around 12 per cent in Sweden) between 1930 and 1995, a decrease that primarily took place between 1939 and 1950 and between 1970 and 1975. However, since the early 1980s, the financing share coming from the insured has increased on average both in the OECD area and in Sweden.

Even though the Swedish system of social security was put under severe financial pressure in the economic recession in the early 1990s, there are few signs that this recession brought about any radical restructuring in the way in which this system is being financed. The response to the recession and the state's budget deficit during these years was rather to cut expenditures than to increase revenue. The only exception from this general conclusion was the introduction of a funded component in the old-age pension system. This reform, and the introduction of contributions from the insured to the old-age pensions scheme, may be interpreted as a sign of a tighter connection between contributions and benefits in the Swedish system of social protection.

The comparative and historical development of the financing of social security schemes in Sweden, as well as in other OECD countries, can partly be explained by referring to the cross-national variation in institutional models of social policy and the financing structures (i.e. contributory vs non-contributory financing) that is implied by these institutional models. An important distinction in this context is the difference between institutional models aiming at basic security and income security, respectively. The objective of the basic security model is, as the name implies, to provide all (or a majority) of citizens with a basic protection in the case of a contingency such as sickness or old age. This can be accomplished either by social security programmes with universal coverage (i.e. where eligibility is based on citizenship or residence), or through programmes with a weak connection to prior income and/or contributions. Social security programmes which emphasize basic security impliy a high degree of state financing, since many of those intended to be covered by the programme have only a weak connection to the labour market and therefore also only a limited possibility/ability to pay social contributions or to let an employer pay contributions on their behalf. In contrast, in social security programmes that emphasize income security and where benefits are therefore closely related to previous income, the scope for financing through employers' and/or employees' contributions higher.

Since the 1950s, a large number of countries have introduced income-related social security schemes which for their financing have relied heavily upon employers' social contributions (Sjöberg 1999). In Sweden, the introduction of the income-related sickness insurance and old-age pensions schemes in 1953 and 1960, respectively, contributed significantly to the increase in the financing shares from employers in the post-war period. Moreover, the introduction of income-related schemes also tended to decrease the relative importance of targeted and/or universal schemes, which in turn implied a diminished importance of contributions from state and local authorities. A partly opposing trend could be found in those countries which from the implementation of their first legislation in this area followed a 'social insurance' tradition (i.e. contributory financing). These countries, above all on the continent of Europe, frequently introduced in the post-war period programmes of a targeted character, financed through general taxes, in order to give an economic protection to those not covered by the income-related schemes. However, the costs of these schemes were generally lower than for income-related schemes.

Although many industrialized countries reformed the systems of social protection to accommodate both basic and income security, reforms which in turn had important implications for the financing of social security schemes, there has also been a significant degree of institutional inertia when it comes to financing structures.[4] One sign of such inertia is that when countries have changed the institutional form of their social security schemes there has in many instances been a tendency for the old financing structure to exert an influence on the new scheme. The existence of path dependency and institutional inertia demonstrates that the existing financing structure of social security schemes can have important implications for the future financing possibilities of these schemes (Sjöberg 2001).

The financing of local government activities in the welfare area in Sweden

In a comparative perspective, the perhaps most distinguishing mark of the 'Swedish welfare state' is the comprehensive system of publicly financed or heavily subsidized welfare services, such as child care, health care and care for the elderly. Bearing in mind the problem of what activities and sectors to include when estimating the size of the welfare state, an approximation was that local government activities accounted for roughly 50 per cent of total social expenditures in Sweden in the year 2000. Local governments – i.e. municipalities (*primärkommuner*) and county councils (*landsting*) – have traditionally had the primary responsibility for producing and providing a majority of these services.[5] Local governments have also a certain degree of autonomy in deciding how to produce and provide them. The self-government of local governments has a long tradition in Sweden (Bergmark 2001), and an important component of this self-government is the right of local governments to raise their own funds (i.e. the right to tax.).

The care of the elderly and sick has in Sweden traditionally not been considered a matter that should be approached using solutions of a social insurance type, but instead as a part of the state's social responsibility towards its citizens. This means that social services in Sweden have essentially been financed through general taxes. In the post-war period, there has been a gradual transfer of the production of social services from the central to the local government. The most important source for local government for financing the production of these services is tax revenues, which constitute around two-thirds of the total local government revenue.[6] The local government tax is a proportional tax which is imposed upon a tax base consisting of wages and income from most social security schemes (the only major cash benefits which are not taxable, and therefore not included in the tax base of local governments, are social assistance and child allowances). The local government tax varies between different municipalities and county councils, but was on average in 2000 about 20 per cent in municipalities and close to 10 per cent in county councils.

At the end of the 1990s, wages and associated benefits accounted for around 70 per cent of the tax base of local governments, transfer income from old-age pensions for approximately 20 per cent and income from other (taxable) social security schemes for around 8 per cent (Sjöberg 2001). Since the mid-1970s, when income from most social security schemes became taxable in Sweden, the importance of transfer income for the tax base of local governments, and therefore also for their income, increased. Above all, the increase in the number of old-age pensioners and the fact that the group of retirees increased their average income from the old-age pensions system (mainly as a result of the maturation of the income-related pensions, ATP) greatly increased the importance of income from old-age pensions in the tax base of local governments.

The importance of wages for the tax base of local government means that in the long run the development of employment and wages will have a decisive importance for local government finances. Although wage increases mean that the tax base of local government expands, about 75 per cent of the costs of local government consist of wages. High nominal wage increases in the economy as a whole therefore also means higher wages in the local government sector and therefore higher costs to produce most welfare services. From this it follows that it is the development of employment, and above all the total number or working hours, that is decisive for how the tax base and the tax revenues of local governments develops. Figure 10.3 depicts the close relationship that exists between the total number of working hours and the tax base of local government. The main explanation for the sharp increase in the tax base of local government during the 1980s was the growth of both nominal wages and of employment during this decade. In the early 1990s, the economic recession, and above all the decrease in employment (and thus in working hours), meant that the tax base of local government declined. However, at this stage the increased payments of taxable social transfers (above all unemployment benefits) acted as a 'shock absorber' for the local government economy, and the drop in the tax base of local government was therefore less dramatic than the decrease in employment and working hours might have suggested. Since the peak of the economic recession in 1993, GDP has shown a steady rate of growth; however, the GDP growth in the second half of the 1990s was to a large extent accomplished by factors other than increased employment, such as an improvement in the balance of current payments and increased productivity.

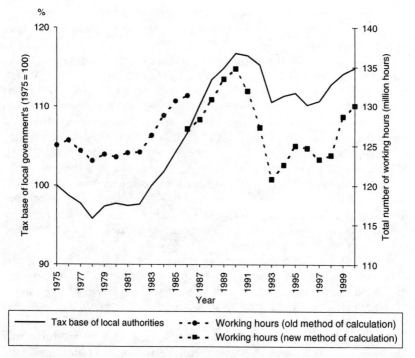

Figure 10.3 Tax base (wages and social security transfers) and total number of working hours, Sweden, 1975–2000
Source: Statistics Sweden (various years).

The decline in employment associated with the recession in the early 1990s and the subsequent slow recovery of employment placed severe strain on the local government economy (Sjöberg 2001). On the income side, the decline in employment during the first half of the 1990s eroded municipal tax revenue. On the expenditure side, costs for social assistance increased sharply at the beginning of the 1990s and did not return to the pre-crisis level for the rest of the decade. Demand for many of the welfare services produced by local governments also increased in the 1990s: there was a 'baby-boom' which meant increasing pressure on the child care system and, a few years later, on schools. The changing demographic structure also meant that the pressure on old-age care intensified. A number of reforms, such as the decision to introduce pre-school activities for children of the unemployed and parents on parental leave also brought further pressure to bear on local government finances. Additionally, there were important changes in the relationship between local and central government that circumscribed local government's scope for action. From a financing perspective, the most important changes in this respect were restrictions on local government tax increases[7] and the requirement on local governments (from 2000) to balance their budgets.

The result for the local government sector as a whole was negative (before extraordinary costs and revenues) until 1997, and in the mid-1990s the financial situation of local governments was serious (Sjöberg 2001). The improved situation in the late 1990s and early 2000s was above all a consequence of increased tax revenues owing to the positive development of employment, especially in 1998 and 1999. This picture of local government's financial situation also conceals important regional variations: in 2001, when the local governmental sector as a whole displayed a positive result, 92 municipalities (32 per cent) and six county councils (out of 20) nevertheless had a negative result (Sjöberg 2001). Severe economic problems thus still linger for many local governments, problems that originate from the fact that the employment rate has not returned to the level that prevailed before the crisis in the early 1990s.

In light of the demographic challenges that lie ahead and the financial difficulties likely to be experienced by many local authorities in Sweden, the question of how to finance social services, and above all the care of the elderly, has received a great deal of attention. The financing of welfare services in the other Nordic countries is rather similar to that in Sweden – i.e. they are mainly financed through general taxes that are paid to either the local or central level of government. To find a more fundamentally different way of financing welfare services, we have to look outside the Nordic countries.

In the mid-1990s, Germany introduced a care insurance, the so-called *Pflegeversicherung* (for an overview of this reform, see Anell, Edebalk and Svensson 1999; Wahner-Roedler, Knuth and Juchems 1999; Kohl 2001). Before the introduction of the *Pflegeversicherung*, the need for long-term care in Germany was seen as a private problem to be solved by private resources, in the form of either paying for the costs of institutionalized care or through social support from the family for care in the home. Only in case of insufficient resources could individuals apply for financial assistance from means-tested programmes.[8] The introduction of the care insurance meant that the costs of medical treatment and personal care were covered by the *Pflegeversicherung* without any means-test, but not other costs (such as food and accommodation). The *Pflegeversicherung* covers the same population as the sickness insurance schemes – i.e. all employees (and their dependent family members) as well as pensioners. In principle, all individuals in need of care can choose between institutionalized care or care in the home (by family members or by professional care givers). However, there are financial incentives that make care in the home by family members more attractive than institutionalized care. The system is a defined contribution system, where the total amount of benefits provided is restricted by the total amount of contributions paid into the system. The system is financed through income-related contributions amounting to 1.7 per cent of gross income (up to a ceiling of approximately 50 per cent of average income), divided equally between employers and employees.[9] Since the contributions are income-related but the services are provided to all, the system implies a degree of vertical redistribution. The system is administered by the existent sickness insurance fund, but the budget of the *Pflegeversicherung* is kept separate from the sickness insurance budget.

The German care insurance reform has attracted a great deal of attention in Sweden, since the introduction of some sort of similar scheme would alleviate some of the financial burden associated with the financing of welfare services. However, the alternatives (and therefore also the content of the reform proposals put forward) are numerous: voluntary or compulsory insurance, publicly or privately managed, a funded or unfunded system. Some combinations – such, as for example, an unfunded private insurance – are in practice unfeasible. On the other hand, a compulsory system can be both funded and unfunded, and be managed either privately or publicly. Different mixes of all these arrangements have been proposed in the Swedish debate, although the majority of proposals seem to advocate an obligatory system (Riksförsäkringsverket 2001).

When describing the German care insurance reform, Kohl (2001) argues that it is a typical example of institutional inertia or path dependency, in which existing institutional arrangements exert a powerful influence on institutional reforms. This path dependence can, for example, be traced in the financial incentives provided for care by family members and the fact that the administration of the *Pflegeversicherung* is managed by the existing sickness insurance funds. Taking into account the different institutional history of the Swedish system of social protection (social insurance and social services), but also the partial break with this history implied by the introduction of fully-funded individual accounts in the latest Swedish pension reform, the design of a possible future system is very difficult to predict.

Incentives to work in the Swedish tax system

As we have seen, the expansion of the Swedish welfare state has historically been heavily dependent upon taxation on labour – in the form of income taxes, employers' social contributions and, in the last few years, employees' social contributions – for its financing. Besides the direct costs that these taxes bring about in the form of lower disposable income for the individual, they can also have indirect costs for both the individual and the economy as a whole. One such indirect cost is the effect of taxes on labour supply. To put it simply, if the individual does not value the economic returns of one more extra hour of work more than the hour of leisure forgone, she will choose not to work this extra hour.[10] And since the economic returns from work are heavily dependent upon how the market income is taxed, income taxes and social contributions (from employers as well employees) can exert an important influence on total labour supply. In this context, there is a complex relationship between the 'benefit side' and the 'financing side' of the welfare state. Welfare state programmes can be, and in many instances, not least in Sweden, have been, deliberately designed in order to encourage participation in paid work. If eligibility and the amounts received from a welfare state scheme are dependent upon participation in paid work, this can work as powerful labour supply incentive.

It can be argued than the welfare state runs the risk of becoming trapped in a 'vicious circle', and that this risk has increased with demographic change and the internationalization of the economy in recent years. In this 'vicious circle', the high taxes required to finance a large welfare state may reduce labour supply and thus the tax base. One way of holding tax revenues constant from a shrinking tax base is to increase tax rates, which might have further negative consequences on labour supply and, ultimately, on tax revenues. It can also be argued that the risk of becoming caught in this 'vicious circle' has increased alongside demographic change, since a smaller number of individuals of working age will have to support an increasing number of retirees. This implies that in order to keep tax revenues at a constant level, taxes on the (relatively) smaller group of individuals of working age must increase. Increased internationalization may lead to a situation where taxes have to be lowered on resources that are mobile, and increased on resources that are immobile. Labour is often considered to be a more immobile resource than capital; increased internationalization may thus imply that the tax pressure on labour has to be increased, with subsequent effects on labour supply and tax revenues.

According to standard economic theory, it is primarily the *marginal tax* that will affect individual's labour supply, where the marginal tax rate is defined as the change in taxes and deductions as a share of the increase in gross income.[11] To what extent are large welfare states associated with high marginal tax rates, and what conclusions can be drawn regarding the effect of such marginal tax rates on labour supply? Table 10.1 displays the marginal tax rates for three different wage levels (67, 100 and 167 per cent of an average production worker's wage) for three different family types (single, single with two children and married with two children), together with net total social expenditure (as percentage of GDP at factor cost), where the latter measure will serve as a 'proxy' for the size of the welfare state.[12] All countries for which data are available are included in the table.

As expected, there is a negative relationship between the 'size' of the welfare state (net social expenditure) and marginal tax rates, which implies that the other aspect of spending resources on social expenditures is collecting these resources through taxation. However, this relationship is neither especially strong nor present for all countries. Although most countries

Table 10.1 Marginal tax rates rate' average for 1997 and 2001, and net social transfers, 1997, different family types and wage levels, ranked according to average marginal tax rate for all family types

Country/wage level[a]	Single person			Single, 2 children	Married, 2 children			Net total social expenditure
	67	100	167	67	100/0	100/33	100/67	
AUS	33.5	33.5	48.5	77.0	48.5	33.5	33.5	21.9
AUT	44.2	42.6	49.6	36.6	42.6	42.6	42.6	24.6
BEL	54.3	55.5	60.3	54.3	51.4	55.7	55.7	28.5
CAN	29.9	41.4	39.7	51.2	46.4	46.4	46.4	21.8
DEN	51.0	51.0	63.4	51.0	45.4	51.0	51.0	27.5
FIN	43.1	48.8	54.4	43.1	48.8	48.8	48.8	25.6
GER	51.1	55.9	53.7	48.4	49.0	51.0	53.4	28.8
IRE	27.3	40.4	47.8	76.1	29.4	29.4	29.4	18.4
ITA	33.1	39.9	43.0	33.1	39.9	39.9	39.9	25.3
JAP	16.9	21.6	29.6	16.9	18.3	18.3	18.3	15.7
NETH	45.9	50.1	51.0	42.7	44.4	50.1	50.1	24.0
NOR	35.8	40.6	49.4	35.8	35.8	40.6	40.6	25.1
NZ	22.5	33.0	36.0	40.5	63.0	33.0	33.0	17.5
SWE	38.1	35.0	53.6	38.1	35.0	35.0	35.0	30.6
UK	32.5	32.5	22.5	51.2	51.2	32.5	32.5	24.6
USA	29.7	29.7	42.5	48.3	50.8	29.7	29.7	23.4

Note: [a] Wage level refer to 67, 100 and 167 per cent of an average production worker's wage.

Sources: Net total social expenditure: Adema (2001); marginal tax rates: OECD (2003a).

with small social expenditures, often referred to as 'liberal welfare states' (Esping-Andersen 1990) such as the USA, New Zealand, Ireland, Australia and Canada, have on average low marginal tax rates, there are countries – such as Norway, Italy and, not least, Sweden – which manage to combine high net social expenditures with relatively low marginal tax rates. If we look at Sweden, with the highest level of net social expenditure, and seen by many as the archetype of a high-tax country, we can note that there are several countries with higher marginal taxes in all income brackets and for both family types. In fact, Sweden's rank is in the lower part of the distribution of countries (ranked between 7 and 14 of the 16 countries) for all income brackets and family types.

However, when analysing the financial viability of large welfare states, the crucial consideration is not the association between social expenditure and taxes, but the degree to which high taxes might have a negative effect on labour supply and thus on the tax base of the welfare state. Figure 10.4 and 10.5 display the cross-national relationship between the average marginal tax rate and two measures of labour supply – the labour force participation rate (Figure 10.4) and the annual average hours worked per person (Figure 10.5), where all data is the average for the years 1997 and 2001.

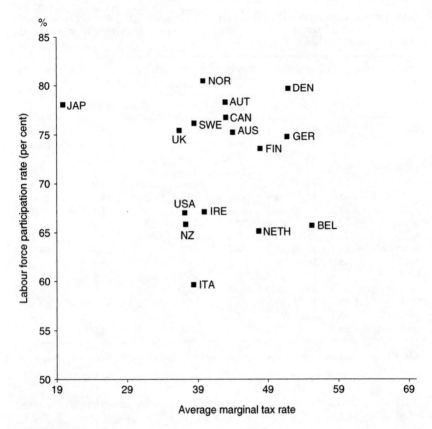

Figure 10.4   Marginal tax rates and labour force participation rate, selected countries, average for 1997 and 2001
Sources: Marginal tax rate: OECD (2003a); Labour force participation rate: OECD (2003b).

There seems to be no cross-national relationship at all between average marginal tax rates and labour force participation rates, whereas there is a weakly significant negative relationship between average marginal tax rates and average hours worked. This might be interpreted as a confirmation of earlier research that has concluded that whereas the marginal tax rate might have an effect on the number of hours worked, it probably has much less impact on the decision to participate or not in the labour force (Agell, England and Södersten 1998). The 'benefit side' and the 'financing side' of the welfare state are closely intertwined in this context, since eligibility for various social benefits in many countries depends on participation in paid work. This eligibility condition can thus work as a powerful incentive for many individuals to participate in the labour market.

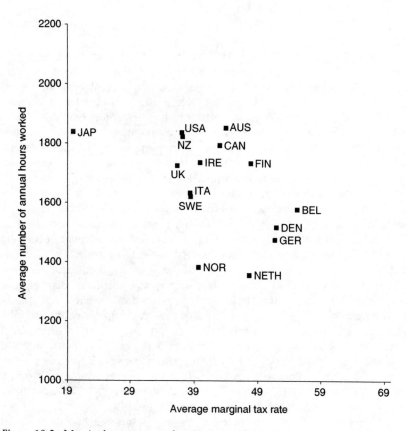

Figure 10.5 Marginal tax rates and average numbers of annual hours worked per person, selected countries, average for 1997 and 2001
Sources: Marginal tax rate: OECD (2003a); Average number of annual hours worked: OECD (2003c).

However, we should be very careful in using aggregated data such as these for drawing the conclusion that there is no relationship between the economic incentives created by the tax system and the labour supply of individuals. For this, we also need detailed micro-level information on both the institutional design of tax systems and the labour supply of individuals. From this viewpoint, the Swedish tax reform in 1990–91, which included significant changes in the tax system and the marginal tax rate, would at first sight be an ideal context to test theories about the association between changes in the tax system and marginal tax rates and the labour supply of individuals. However, the implementation of this reform coincided almost exactly with the economic recession and the decrease in unemployment in the early 1990s, which makes it very difficult to isolate the effects of changes in the tax system from the effects of the general downturn in the business cycle.

A survey of the studies that have nevertheless tried to estimate the effects of the decrease in marginal tax rates in the connection with the tax reform in 1990–1 suggests that the tax reform increased the total labour supply by 1–2 per cent, and that the effects were most significant for individuals working full time (Agell, England and Södersten 1998; Sjöberg and Bäckman 2001). For the group that has been studied most – married couples between twenty-five and fifty-five years of age – a majority of studies indicates that labour supply (measured as working hours) increased as a result of the reform, but that the effects were rather small. For males, the 'average' estimate is that an increase in the net wage by 1 per cent increased their labour supply by 0.1 per cent; the estimates for the increase in the labour supply of females are somewhat higher, but also vary more between different studies. For individuals working part-time and/or with low wages, the effects were considerably lower, and some studies even indicate that the effect for certain sub-groups were negative. Given that the lowering of marginal tax rates was highest for individuals in the upper part of the income distribution, this result is not surprising. There are also studies that contradict, or at least modify, this picture of a positive effect of the tax reform on labour supply. For example, Aronsson and Palme (1994) found that, working with a model where the labour supply of couples was decided jointly, women tended to decrease their labour supply when their spouses increased thesis as a result of the tax reform. This result suggests that for couples where the woman had a partner with a high wage, who in connection with the tax reform experienced a substantial decrease in his marginal tax rate, it could have been rational for the man to increase his labour supply while the woman increased her household production.

Conclusions

Much of this chapter has been devoted to the question of how social security schemes have been financed in terms of the shares coming from the insured, the employers and the state authorities. Two important conclusions can be drawn from this analysis. First, the financing of social security schemes is not only, and perhaps not even primarily, a question of economics. History has repeatedly shown that how the visible costs of social protection are distributed in society will have important, and sometimes decisive, significance for how social policy reform is viewed by the public and for the legitimacy of social policy institutions. Secondly, the way in which social security programmes are financed is to an important extent dependent upon which institutional social policy model is being applied in a country. There are thus important connections between the 'benefit side' and the 'financing side' of the welfare state. However, there is also a certain degree of path dependency in social security financing, in that financing structures tend to persist even though other institutional aspects of social security schemes are changed. This implies that today's financing structures may constitute an important foundation for future reform possibilities.

The financing of the Swedish welfare state is, and will in the foreseeable future continue to be, highly dependent upon taxation on labour for its financing. The population aged eighteen–sixty-five will decrease in Sweden, as in many other industrialized countries, in the years to come. This implies that a decreasing labour force will have to support an increasing number of persons outside the labour force. If the labour force declines, there is also a substantial risk that income from work, and therefore also taxes on wages, will decrease in the economy as a whole. Higher wages will lead to a larger tax base, but wage increases without productivity growth will involve great risks of a 'wage–price spiral' and a deterioration of the competitiveness of the economy. At the same time, it will be very difficult to increase productivity in many of the sectors responsible for the production of welfare services.

This seems to suggest that labour supply – i.e. making as many people work as possible – will be of crucial importance for the financing of the Swedish welfare state. In this chapter, we have concentrated upon the economic incentives for work. But there is also a complex relationship between the 'benefit side' and the 'financing side' of the welfare state. For example, women constitute an important labour reserve; but the supply of female labour is crucially dependent upon the existence of family policies, such as child care services (Ferrarini 2003; see also Chapter 5 in this volume). In Sweden, the production of welfare services is also an area with substantial problems in recruiting qualified personnel, a problem many predict will increase in the nearest future. Many have singled out higher wages as the key factor in making this sector of the labour market more attractive to work in; but higher wages in this sector would mean higher costs for local authorities, which must be financed though taxes on work, which in turn might have a negative effect on the labour supply.

This is only one example of the complex interplay between welfare state financing and the provision of both cash benefits and social services. It is also important not to reduce the financing of the welfare state to a mere technical question about, for example, the effect of economic incentives on labour supply. Ultimately, the size of the welfare state, and the tax burden that is associated with it, is to an important extent an expression of voters' preferences in this area.

Notes

1   Figure 10.1 is based on data from the SCIP database at the Swedish Institute for Social Research, Stockholm University (see Sjöberg 1999 for a presentation of this database).

2 The countries included in the SCIP database are Australia, Austria, Belgium, Canada, Denmark, Finland, France, Germany, Ireland, Italy, Japan, the Netherlands, New Zealand, Norway, Sweden, Switzerland, the UK and the USA. For simplicity, these countries will henceforth be referred to as the 'OECD area'.

3 These figures refer to statutory employers' contributions. In addition, employers pay contributions that are laid down by the parties in the labour market. These contributions amounted to around 5 per cent in 2000.

4 One sign of this institutional inertia (or perhaps of the non-convergence in financing structures) is that the cross-national variation in the different financing shares was no lower in 1995 than it was in 1950. In 1950, the standard deviations for the financing share from employers were 0.20, for the insured 0.19 and 0.28 for state authorities. In 1995, the figures were 0.22, 0.16 and 0.21, respectively.

5 In the remainder of this chapter, municipalities/local authorities (*primärkommuner*) and county councils (*landsting*) – i.e. the primary and secondary tiers of the Swedish local government system – will be treated together under the heading 'local government', unless otherwise stated.

6 The second most important source of revenue is grants from the central government, and the third most important is different kinds of charges and fees.

7 Between 1991 and 1993 local governments were not allowed to raise their taxes, and between 1997 and 1999 the central government punished local governments which increased their taxes by reducing the size of the state subsidy.

8 However, due to the growing number of (elderly) persons in need of care and the increased costs of institutionalized care, an increasing number of individuals became dependent upon these means-tested programmes. Before the introduction of the *Pflegeversicherung*, it was estimated that around two-thirds of the old people in the nursing homes in West Germany, and almost all in the former East Germany, were at least partly dependent upon means-tested programmes to pay for their care (Kohl 2001), which led to a heavy financial burden on the municipalities.

9 As contribution rates can be changed only through political decisions, critics fear that since the number of people in need of care will continue to rise there is considerable risk that the quality of the services provided will deteriorate.

10 According to standard economic theory, the effect of a change in the marginal tax rate on the labour supply of individuals can be divided into a *substitution* effect and an *income* effect. The substitution effect refers to the fact that if the marginal tax is lowered, work will become relatively more profitable, and the cost of leisure (i.e. not working) will increase. The substitution effect thus implies that the labour supply will increase as a result of a decrease in the marginal tax rate. The income effect implies that when the marginal tax is lowered, an individual can afford to consume more. The crucial question is whether leisure is a normal good – i.e. whether the consumption of leisure will increase as a result of an increase in income. If this is the case, a decrease in the marginal tax rate will mean that people will work both more (the substitution effect) and less (the income effect) as a result of an increase in their income. If leisure is not a normal good (i.e. something that people choose not to consume more of as a result of an increase in their income), both the income effect and the substitution effect will work in the same direction as a result of a decrease in the marginal tax, towards an increase in the individual's labour supply. This standard theoretical framework thus makes the total effect of a change in the marginal tax rate on the labour supply an empirical question, and in fact it does not rule out that the total effect of an increase in the marginal tax rate will be an increase in the labour supply.

This theoretical framework can also expanded in a number of ways – for example, by incorporating a time dimension where present-day labour supply decisions are also affected by expected future incomes.

11 An 'extended' marginal tax, which also includes employers' social contributions and the share of an increase in gross income that is paid in value-added taxes when the individual consumes her increase in income, is usually referred to as the 'tax wedge'. The 'marginal effect' usually refers to the total changes in taxes, fees and social transfers as a consequence of an increase in income.

12 To arrive at net social expenditure, gross expenditure has been adjusted for taxes on transfer incomes, taxes on consumption financed by transfer incomes and tax deductions (Adema 2001).

Bibliography

Adema, W. (2001) *Net Social Expenditure*, 2nd edition. Labour market and Social Policy Occasional Papers, 52. Paris: OECD, Directorate for Education, Employment, Labour and Social Affairs.

Agell, J., Englund, P. and Södersten, J. (1998) *Incentives and Redistribution in the Welfare State*. London: Macmillan.

Alcock, P. (1996) 'The Advantage and Disadvantage of the Contribution Base in Targeting Benefits: A Social Analysis of the Insurance Scheme in the United Kingdom'. *International Social Security Review*, 49: 31–49.

Anell, A., Edebalk, P.G. and Svensson, M. 'Resursfördelning och finansiering'. (Resource Allocation and Financing:) In *2000-talets äldreomsorg och äldrevård.* (Old-age Services and Care in the 21st century.) SPRI-rapport, 491. Stockholm: SPRI.

Aronsson, T. and Palme, M. (1994) *A Decade of Tax and Benefit Reforms in Sweden – Effects of Labour Supply, Welfare and Inequality.* Tax reform Evaluation Report 3. Stockholm: Swedish Economic Council.

Barr, N. (1993) *The Economics of the Welfare State.* London: Weidenfeld & Nicolson.

Bell, D. (1974) 'The Public Household'. *The Public Interest*, 37: 29–68.

Bergmark, Å. (2001) 'Den lokala välfärdsstaten? Decentraliseringstendenser under 1990-talet'. (The Local Welfare State? Decentralization trends in the 1990s.) In SOU 2001 (52), *Välfärdstjänster i omvandling*, (Welfare Services in Transition.) Report from the (Welfare Commission) Stockholm: Fritzes.

Elmér, Å. (1960) *Folkpensioneringen i Sverige*. Lund: CWK Gleerup.

Esping-Andersen, G. (1990) *The Three Worlds of Welfare Capitalism.* (People's Pensions in Sweden.) Cambridge: Polity Press.

Ferrarini, T. (2003) *Parental Leave Institutions in Eighteen Post-War Welfare States*. Stockholm: Swedish Institute for Social Research.

Kohl, J. (2001) 'Socialpolitik för gamla i Tyskland'. (Pension Reforms World Wide.) In J. Palme (ed.), *Pensionsreformer World Wide.* (Social Policy for Elderly in Germany.) Stockholm: Pensionsforum.

Leuchtenberg, W.E. (1963) *Franklin D. Roosevelt and the New Deal.* New York: Harper & Row.

Manser, M.E. (1981) 'Historical and Political Issues in Social Security Financing'. In F. Skidmore (ed.), *Social Security Financing.* Cambridge, Mass.: MIT Press.

OECD (1995) *Historical Statistics*. Paris: OECD.

OECD (2003a) *Taxing Wages*. Database edition. Paris: OECD.

OECD (2003b) *Employment Outlook*. Database edition. Paris: OECD.

OECD (2003c) *Labour Statistics*. Database edition. Paris: OECD.

Peters, B.G. (1991) *The Politics of Taxation*. Oxford: Basil Blackwell.

Riksförsäkringsverket (2001) *Socialförsäkringsboken 2001*. (Social Insurance Book 2001.) Stockholm: National Social Insurance Board.

Rimlinger, G. (1971) *Welfare Policy and Industrialization in Europe, America, and Russia*. New York: Wiley.

Salminen, K. (1993) *Pension Schemes in the Making*. Helsinki: Central Pension Security Institute.

Sjöberg, O. (1999) 'Paying for Social Rights'. *Journal of Social Policy*, 28: 275–97.

Sjöberg, O. (2001) 'Välfärdsstatens finansiering under 1990-talet'. (The Financing of the welfare state during the 1990s.) In SOU 2001(57), *Välfärdens finansiering och fördelning*, (The Financing and Distribution of Welfare.) Report from the Welfare Commission Stockholm: Fritzes.

Sjöberg, O. and Bäckman, O. (2001) 'Incitament och arbetsutbud: (Incentives and Labour Supply.)'. In SOU 2001(57), *Välfärdens finansiering och fördelning*, (The Financing and Distribution of Welfare.) Report from the Welfare Commission Stockholm: Fritzes.

Statistics Sweden (Various years) *Statistisk Årsbok för Sverige*. Stockholm: SCB.

Steinmo, S. (1993) *Taxation and Democracy*. London: Yale University Press.

Wahner-Roedler, D.L., Knuth, P. and Juchems, R.H. (1999) 'The German *Pflegeversicherung* (Long-Term Care Insurance)'. *Mayo Clinic Proceedings*, 74: 196–200.

Wicksell, K. (1958) 'A New Principle of Just Taxation'. In R.A. Musgrave and A. Peacock (eds.), *Classics in the Theory of Public Finance*. London: International Economic Association.

Wilson, T. (1986) 'The Finance of the Welfare State'. In F. Forte and A. Peacock (eds.), *The Political Economy of Taxation*. Oxford: Basil Blackwell.

11
The Nordic Model of the Information Society: The Finnish Case

Pekka Himanen

Political choice in the 'information age'

Does the rise of the information age necessarily increase social inequality and exclusion, as seems to be the dominant trend in the world? In many political circles, it is believed that the answer is 'yes.' Many countries have thus chosen the route of competing in the global world by cutting the welfare state.

Yet, if we look at the empirical data on which countries have succeeded as information societies, the picture is much more complicated. For years, the Nordic welfare states have topped the IDC Information Society Index which reflects the adoption of new information technology (IT) in society. If we look at the UN Technology Achievement Index, Finland is the world leader followed by the USA and Sweden (UNDP 2001). The UN Technology Achievement Index is especially relevant because it is based on such key measures of an information society as the creation of technology (the number of patents granted *per capita*, the receipts of royalty and licence fees from abroad *per capita*), the diffusion of recent innovations (the diffusion of the Internet, exports of high- and medium-technology products as a share of all exports) and human skills (mean years of schooling, gross enrolment ratio of tertiary students enrolled in science, mathematics, and engineering).

These above observations already contradict the widespread belief that success in the information age is possible only by following the 'Silicon Valley model' of liberalism: the belief is not based on empirical reality. This has important political consequences: it means that there are real alternatives for countries in becoming technologically and economically dynamic information societies.

However, it is very important to anchor the discussion of these alternatives tightly to empirical facts. Although it makes a lot of sense to talk about 'a Nordic model of the information society', meaning a model that combines a dynamic information economy with the welfare state as its basis, it is more fruitful to analyse one of these cases in depth and thus give a very concrete content to the idea. In this chapter, Finland is chosen because it is currently the most dynamic Nordic information society measured by the UN Technology Achievement Index, a fact that reflects Finland's world leader position in mobile telecommunications (Nokia) and open-source software (the Linux operating system). The strengths of the Finnish IT 'cluster' also include teleoperators, electronic manufacturing services and security software (Paija 2000, 2001).

Other indicators support this choice. According to the World Economic Forum (WEF), the USA and Finland are the two most competitive economies in the world (WEF 2003). The labour productivity of Finnish manufacturing now equals that of the USA, led by the development in the Finnish IT cluster.

From the viewpoint of the less developed countries, the Finnish case also has special interest because until the 1950s Finland was a relatively poor country living mainly from its forests, with over 50 per cent of the population in agriculture and forestry. Figure 11.1 illustrates this developmental perspective.

Simultaneously with technological and economic development, Finland has built a welfare state. Finland not only tops the technological and economic comparisons but also those on social equality and inclusion. Here the distinction from the dominant US model becomes clear. While the USA has moved to the information age with the cutting of the welfare state and

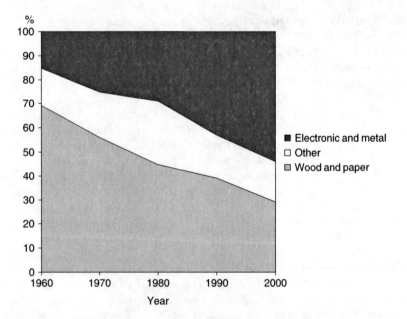

Figure 11.1 Transformation of the Finnish economy, measured by export share, 1960–2000
Source: Etla (The Research Institute of the Finnish Economy).

increases in social inequality and exclusion (as measured by the traditional Gini index and the incarceration rate), Finnish development has created social equality and inclusion. Figure 11.2 illustrates this.

Table 11.1 sums up the current differences of a number of key dimensions of the welfare state.

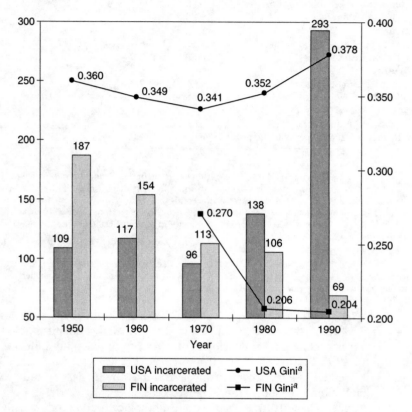

Figure 11.2 Social injustice and exclusion in the shift from industrial society to information society, Finland and the USA, 1950–90

Notes:

The incarceration rate refers to the number of prisoners (yearly average including remand prisoners) per 100,000 in the population

[a] In the Gini index, the value 1 means absolute inequality, in which one person gets everything and all others nothing, and the value 0 means absolute equality, in which everyone gets exactly the same. Figure 11.2 is primarily meant to show the trends of income inequality and incarceration. The figures for the USA are based on household gross income and the figures for Finland are based on *per capita* net income. However, because of the low level of income transfers, the US gross and net income inequality figures are quite close to each other.

Sources: Gini figures are based on Deininger and Squire (1996). Incarceration figures for the USA are based on Cahalan (1986) and US Bureau of Justice Statistics (1992) and for Finland on von Hofer (1997).

Table 11.1 Social comparison, Finland and the USA, mid-1990s

	Finland	USA	Advanced economies
Education			
1 Primary, secondary, and tertiary enrolment (combined ratio)	103.0(4)	95.0	94.0
2 Functional literacy (%)	93.0(2)	82.0	84.0
Health			
3 Life expectancy at birth (years)	77.2	76.5(−5)	78.0
4 Health insurance (%)	100.0	82.0	n.a.
Welfare			
5 Richest 20% to poorest 20% (ratio)	3.6(3)	9.0(−3)	5.8
6 People below the poverty line (%)	3.8(4)	14.1(−4)	10.6
Social capital			
7 Association membership	1.8	1.1	n.a.
8 Incarceration rate (per 100,000 pop.)	62.0(4)	554.0(−1)	126.0

Notes:
The figures in parentheses mark the position within the group of the advanced economies, which include the Western economies (USA, Canada, Australia, New Zealand, Israel, UK, Ireland, Germany, France, Austria, Switzerland, Italy, Spain, Portugal, Greece, Norway, Denmark, Sweden, Finland) and the strongest Asian economies (Japan, Korea, Singapore–Hong Kong and Taiwan are not included because they are not listed independently in all statistics). Only the top five and bottom five positions are marked.
n.a. = Data not available

Sources: 1, 3, 6, 8: UNDP (2001); 2: OECD (2001); 4: *Health Care Financing Review* (1999); 5: World Bank (2000); 7: Putnam (1995) and Siisiäinen (1999). Figures are for association memberships among people with only primary education, mid-1990s.

Table 11.1 shows that the USA is at the bottom of most social statistics among the advanced economies. In fact, in the USA, almost one-fifth of the population is excluded from development: they are functionally illiterate, do not have health protection and live in effective poverty. For many, this leaves only crime as a way of survival: the USA has the highest percentage of the population in prison in the advanced economies.

At the same time, Finland has become a technologically and economically dynamic information society that tops the social inclusion statistics. The Finnish welfare state continues to consist of a free, public and high-quality education system where students receive a student grant at the university level; universal health protection through a free, public, high-quality health care system where benefits do not depend on job or economic status; and universal social protection for unemployment and retirement.

The 'Finnish model' of the information society

The remaining part of this chapter will analyse the specific 'Finnish model' of the information society that has resulted in these techno-economic and social outcomes. The key is the interaction between *business and the state,* between the 'information society' and the welfare state, as I have stated earlier (Castells and Himanen 2002).

Although the Finnish model is market-driven, there has been a conscious government policy to push business towards the information economy. Since innovation is ultimately behind productivity growth in the information economy (Bresnahan, Brynjolfsson and Hitt 2000; Brynjolfsson and Hitt 2000; Castells 2000, 2002), the government's policy has focused on the development of the Finnish innovation system.

A Science and Technology Policy Council (STPC) was formed under the government in 1986 (to continue and expand the work of the earlier Science Policy Council). The Council combines science and technology issues that are usually dealt with separately, and has the highest-level representation from government, industry and the research world: the Council is headed by the Prime Minister and has seven other key ministers as well as the top directors of the Finnish R&D funding agencies, universities and companies as its members. These eighteen members make a very influential council.

The Council's policy is based on the understanding that innovation requires financing, highly skilled people as well as a culture of innovation (Castells 2002; Castells and Himanen 2002, and the government has invested in each of these (for the Council's reports, see STPC 1987, 1990, 1993, 1996a, 1996b, 2000).

Financing

At the beginning of the 1980s, Finland's national R&D investment was about 1 per cent of GDP. The STPC set the goal of doubling this in a decade, and the goal was reached. In the 1990s, on the initiative of the Council, Finland continued to increase its R&D investment even in the recession. By 2000, national investment had exceeded 3 per cent and in 2003 was 3.6 per cent of GDP, which is the highest in the world (with Sweden) and almost double the average in the advanced economies. Figure 11.3 shows this development.

Investment is channelled to universities to make the breakthrough research in basic theory as well as to companies through two agencies: Tekes, the 'technology research and development fund', and Sitra, the 'public capitalist'. Both are autonomous and relatively small agencies, the purpose being to eliminate bureaucracy and dependence on the party politics.

Tekes' funding is meant for new innovative projects that aim at exportable products. The idea is to finance longer-term high-risk innovation that has big promize but that does not sit easily with the 'bottom-line' thinking of business. Tekes strongly encourages cooperation between corporations of different sizes and between corporations and universities in order to distribute new knowledge within the Finnish IT field. In mapping out new areas of R&D funding, Tekes forms cooperative technology programmes whose steering groups include representatives from research, industry and government. This is meant to gather together the ideas of all parties. Tekes is also open

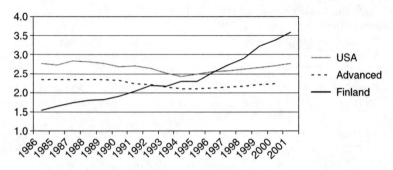

Figure 11.3   National R&D investment, Finland and the USA, 1985–2001, percent of GDP
Source: OECD, *Main Science and Technology Indicators.*

to proposals that are not included in the existing programmes, so that new ideas can also originate from the 'bottom up'. The basic Tekes share in funding is 50 per cent, which encourages an increase in private R&D investment. Currently, Tekes reports to the Ministry of Trade and Industry, although it makes all of its funding decisions independently.

Sitra is called the Finnish 'public capitalist.' As we have seen, R&D funding is available in Finland. However, another form of high-risk investment – venture capital – was still underdeveloped at the beginning of the 1990s. Sitra started consciously to push these markets: as a 'public capitalist', it started to fund the initial and expansion phases of start-up companies. Tekes and Sitra thus provide funding for all the critical stages of private innovation – sharing information with each other in order to be effective in this cooperation. The private venture capital market started to develop, and because private venture capital is available Sitra has started to emphasize pre-seed funding. Formally, Sitra reports to the Finnish Parliament although its decisions are also autonomous.

In spite of this active government policy for increasing innovation funding in Finland, it is important to stress that Finland is still as business-driven as the USA. Private investment in R&D has always been more than half of the total and, in fact, is a slightly larger share than in the 'liberal' USA. Figure 11.4 illustrates this.

People

The ultimate foundation of innovation is people, in which the Finnish government has invested heavily. The basic idea of the 'Finnish model' is that the welfare state (the public education system) should provide equal opportunities for everyone to learn and thus tap the potential of the population. The OECD PISA study (2001) shows that the Finnish pupils top the

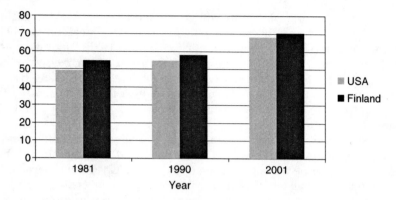

Figure 11.4 Private R&D investment, share of the total, Finland and the USA, 1981–2001, per cent

literacy and math/science tests in the world, with the results not depending on one's social background or the school one goes to. The same basic idea is extended to the university system' – study is free and supported by a student salary. Two-thirds of the school-age population goes to university, and the government's policy has been to emphasize technology knowledge: 27 per cent study science, maths and engineering, almost the double the average in the advanced economies (in the USA, for example, the corresponding figure is 14 per cent) (UNDP 2001).

The public education system provides highly skilled people to innovate in the Finnish IT cluster. It has also helped to create a special culture of innovation – the open-source culture – that has been the basis of some key technological breakthroughs.

Culture

The third key element of any innovation system is the culture of innovation. How thriving a national culture is depends on the innovation cultures of the state, business and people.

In Finland, the state has actively pushed for an open innovation environment by advancing open standards and markets in mobile telecommunications. The Nordic countries cooperated to create the first transnational open (automatic) mobile phone network in the world: the NMT. At the beginning of the 1980s, the small Nordic countries had the biggest mobile phone market in the world, in which they could develop and test their products. Nokia and Ericsson had to compete against the world's leading mobile telecommunications equipment manufacturers, which increased competitive pressure on their innovativeness. At the beginning of the 1990s, the same push for open standards and markets resulted in the European digital GSM standard. Finland was the first to liberalize mobile phone service provision in 1990, and teleoperators had to compete against each other in the innovativeness of their services. The early strategy of open standards and markets gave the Finnish (and the Nordic) mobile telecommunications companies an advantage compared to the protected monopolies in other European countries or the proprietary markets of the American companies, for example. Figure 11.5 illustrates the latter case.

In the Finnish technology business, there has also been a shift towards a culture of innovation. Nokia is a case in point. At the beginning of the 1990s, Nokia was on the edge of bankruptcy; it had expanded to eleven different industries, making everything from televisions to rubber boots (Häikiö 2001) and the conglomerate was managed in the old centralized industrial style. When Jorma Ollila became the CEO of Nokia in 1992, he introduced a new structure and culture. Nokia decided to focus on its most innovative core – mobile telecommunications – and to sell the other businesses. Even in mobile telecommunications, Nokia became more focused on its core expertize and networked with other companies. Nokia is now a network enterprise, working with 300 subcontractors in Finland alone (Ali-Yrkkö *et al.* 2000; Ali-Yrkkö 2001). Internally, Nokia became a decentralized company where units and people form networks based on the changing needs of a given project.

To define the culture for this network enterprise model, Nokia began a process of thinking about what the cultures of innovation had been behind its most important breakthroughs such as the digital exchange and the first mobile phone. The so-called 'Nokia way' was defined by values such

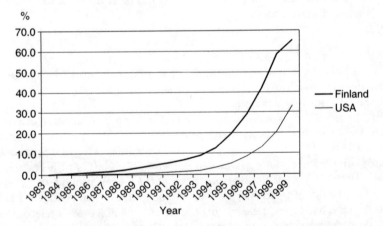

Figure 11.5 Mobile phone market, Finland and the USA, 1983–99, per cent of population as users

as 'respect for the individual' (i.e. a culture of trust where individuals are given space for innovation) and 'achievement' (i.e. a creative culture that continuously exceeds former achievements and rewards people based on their innovative contribution). This new work and management culture has been critical for Nokia to continue operating dynamically in ever-changing markets and to keep its leading position in innovation.

The third element of the innovation culture is that the most important individual actors are found outside the public and private sectors. There is a very strong 'open-source software movement', in which enthusiastic programmers join forces on the Net and give their innovations for anyone to use, test and develop further. Linus Torvalds created the Linux operating system, Jarkko Oikarinen invented the Internet chat room (IRC), Tatu Ylönen developed encrypted Internet communication (SSH), etc., in this way. They were all university students, but their developments were not part of their official studies; instead, they were motivated by the spirit of the open-source movement (Himanen 2001). Eric Raymond, talking about the 'Unix philosophy' which we can read more widely as an expression of the open-source spirit, gives a good summary of this attitude.

> To do the Unix philosophy right, you have to be loyal to excellence. You have to believe that software is a craft worth of all the intelligence and passion you can muster ... Software design and implementation should be a joyous art, and a kind of high-level play. If this attitude seems preposterous or vaguely embarrassing to you, stop and think; ask yourself what you've forgotten. Why do you design software instead of doing something else to make money or pass the time? You must have thought software was worthy of your passions once.
>
> To do the Unix philosophy right, you need to have (or recover) that attitude. You need to *care*. You need to *play*. You need to be willing to *explore*.
>
> (Raymond 2003; emphasis in the original)

It may be argued that the Finnish welfare state has supported this kind of innovation culture. The education system allows students to play with new ideas and explore things, as they do not have an immediate pressure to graduate. It took eight years for Linus Torvalds to get his Masters degree but at the same time he created the Linux operating system!

However, the open-source movement has an impact beyond citizen action and free software. Many prominent open-source people have started their own companies or moved to work in companies so having an impact on the Finnish IT cluster. Figure 11.6 sums up how interactions between the state, business and people form the specific Finnish innovation system.

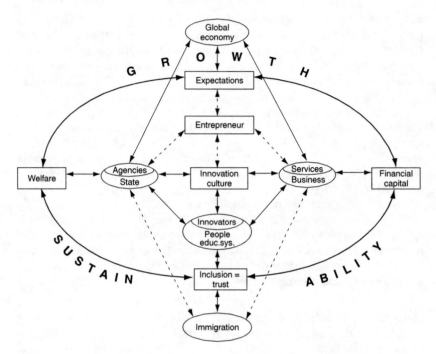

Figure 11.6   The Finnish innovation system

The virtuous cycle

Ultimately, the core of the Finnish model is its combination of a technologically innovative and economically competitive information society with the welfare state that provides both the basis for this growth and makes the growth more inclusive. In other words, the core is an economically and socially positive virtuous cycle between the information society and the welfare state: the welfare state produces highly skilled people to innovate in IT companies, which creates the economic growth that makes it possible to continue the financing of a generous welfare state and further public investment in the nation's innovation capacity. The protection that people feel through the welfare state makes the changes that the information economy requires socially possible, and the fact that the benefits of the growth are enjoyed more equally makes this model socially more sustainable.

This is illustrated by the legitimacy that the Finnish welfare state increasingly continues to enjoy. Figure 11.7 shows that about 85 per cent of the Finnish population support the welfare state even if it means higher taxes (the study asked people if they agreed or disagreed with the statement 'even if good social security and other public services are expensive they are worth it').

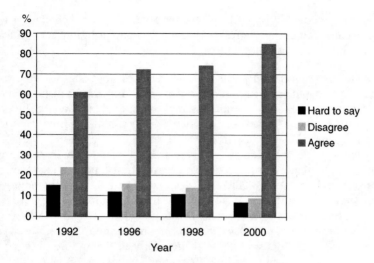

Figure 11.7 Legitimacy of the Finnish welfare state, 1992–2000
Source: EVA (2001).

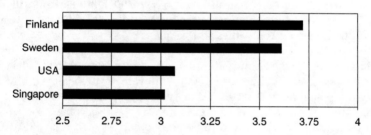

Figure 11.8 Acceptance of flexible work or 'job churning'
Note: Scale 1–5, higher means more accepted
Source: *Global Entrepreneurship Monitor (2001)*.

The same goes for the idea of flexible work, which is more acceptable because of the protection that the Finnish welfare state provides regardless of one's job status (Figure 11.8).

Challenges to the Finnish model

So far, the Finnish model has continued to work well, even with the downturn of the technology field and the world economy. Relative to its competitors, both the Finnish economy and the leading technology companies, such as Nokia, have managed better. Of course, this does not mean that the Finnish model is without its problems. There are several challenges that have become more important over the years. Some of the most significant can be summed up as follows:

1. The level of *start-up entrepreneurialism* is relatively low. Start-up entrepreneurialism would be an important way of expanding the Finnish technological innovativeness to completely new areas, thus broadening the basis for future growth. The history of Silicon Valley has shown how important this is (Himanen and Castells 2004).
2. *Openness to foreign talent* is relatively weak. Finland remains a country with few foreigners: only 2.5 per cent of the Finnish population is foreign or foreign-born. Again, Silicon Valley, where one-third of the engineers are Indians or Chinese and a quarter of the new companies are started by them, has shown how important this is (Saxenian 1999).
3. *Global pressure towards social inequality* is increasing. In the late 1990s, there was some increase in social inequality in Finland, resulting from both unemployment (that in 2003 remained at about 10 per cent of the labour force) and the capital gains for the richest from the global financial markets (Kalela *et al.* 2001). However, this increase was relative as the Finnish Gini index (that measures social inequality) still remained one of the lowest in the world (see also Kautto *et al.* 2001). But Finland will need a courageous policy to create more work and make employment more profitable to both companies and people.
4. The *structures of the welfare state* have not been 'upgraded' to the information age. While the Finnish 'information economy' has reformed its work and management culture and used IT innovatively to increase productivity the public services sector has lagged behind. As the population ages, the pressure on the costs of the welfare state will become stronger and stronger and there will need to be productivity growth to avoid cutting services.

The E-welfare state

These challenges can be called the challenge of the E-welfare state (the 'e' refers to the welfare state in the information age, not only to the use of IT, as the concept also includes organizational and cultural change). It can be seen as a goal similar to the European Union's strategy goals of E-government, E-health and E-learning, although it is a much broader concept that also goes much deeper in system structures.

Because this is a challenge that all welfare states are facing it is useful to conclude this analysis of the Finnish model with some positive ideas on how this shift to an E-welfare state could come about.[1] This is also important for the long-term applicability of the Finnish model in both Finland itself and elsewhere. The common problem is this: with an ageing population, the funding of the welfare state is going to become impossible unless there is a big change. While high economic growth will help, it will not be enough to cover all the costs. There will thus be a choice of change through *reformation* or *deformation* of the welfare state. Deformation would essentially mean giving up the welfare state. The core of reformation – and growth in general in the 'information economy' – is productivity growth through innovation. Figure 11.9 illustrates this challenge.[2]

The situation is very similar in other advanced economies. While the comparison is hardly fair – comparing manufacturing and services is problematic and the measurement of productivity in services is difficult – it does show both the problem and the potential for its solution. The problem is that there has been basically no productivity growth in Finnish public services since the mid-1980s (productivity in telecommunications manufacturing has become ten times higher in the same time period). The positive reading of this is that there is a significant unused potential for productivity growth (although it is true that one cannot expect similar levels of growth as in manufacturing). It is important to underline that here the proposed route for productivity growth in a welfare state is not increasing of the workload of people over a given time – a route that has been much used. As is well known, this is not even possible, as people are already about to break down under their workloads.

Nor has this been what has generated productivity growth in economy, including the telecommunications manufacturing. The key has been productivity growth through *innovation* – technological, product and process. 'Technological' refers here to the use of new IT; 'product' innovation means

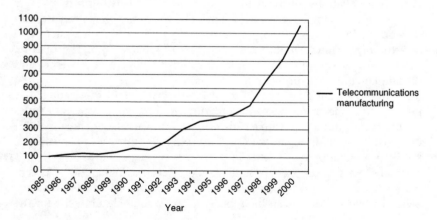

Figure 11.9 Labour productivity growth, Finnish telecommunications manufacturing and public services, 1985–2000 (1985 = 100)

constant development of one's products and 'process' innovation refers to innovative thinking about the actual organization of operations.

In the public sector, the paradox is that the workers are very highly educated and yet there is little innovation. There is no *culture of innovation* – a critical condition – in the public sector and the current work culture militates against it. In the public sector, when an enthusiastic new employee arrives full of ideas, the senior workers look at each other and say: 'Well, wait a week and he'll learn – or we'll teach him!'

A culture of innovation is based on openness, enthusiastic people with new ideas, and encouragment and reward for the creation of new and better ways of doing things. In the public innovation culture, such positive expectations are lacking. The absurd situation infact is that better performance leads to a reduction in the budget and more work for the innovators. In the current situation, it is rational to not innovate!

On the way to the E-welfare state, the first step will be the formation of a *public culture of creativity*, with rewards for innovation When a unit increases its productivity, a significant share of the result must go back to the unit for its future development. The workers must also benefit from increased productivity: innovators should be rewarded and workers must be guaranteed that they can benefit from any time saved by having less heavy workdays: the change has to be motivating for everyone. There has also to be some social contract that gives protection for people's jobs because otherwise workers will not have the trust to carry out the most innovative thinking.

In this kind of an environment, innovative potential can start to be unleashed. Workers can start to think of inventive ways of increasing productivity with the help of IT. All workers can contribute their ideas on product innovations, even small improvements on existing services. The next change is to improve the overall process, where the biggest savings can be won. Such change will eliminate unnecessary work in the system and give the professionals more time to focus on their core job. The Internet can be used as a forum to link innovators in different places together and disseminate their the innovations.

At the same time, it is critical to involve 'outsiders' in innovating. The public sector must be more open to ordering services from private companies so that there can be innovative competition. This can also include the idea of allowing public innovators to start up spin-off companies to spread and sell their innovations to other public services.

Finally, users of the welfare state should be seen as having a big potential for both ideas and feedback. Many users of public health services have ideas about how things can be improved. The system should exist for the customers who also fund the system.

The E-welfare state is about *actualizing the innovative potential* of well-educated workers in the public sector, linking with both the ideas of the private sector and the people. The future of the Finnish/Nordic model of a virtuous cycle between the information society and the welfare state will ultimately depend on each country's ability, and courage, to reform their welfare state into an E-welfare state.

Notes

1 I thank my colleague Antti Hautamäki, with whom I originally developed the idea of the E-welfare state.
2 For the public sector there are not even any measurement of productivity. The standard procedure in the national account is to assume it is zero. That calls for improvement, too!

Bibliography

Ali-Yrkkö, J. (2001) *Nokia's Network: Gaining Competitiveness from Co-Operation.* Etla Series B, 174. Helsinki: Taloustieto.
Ali-Yrkkö, J., Paija, L., Reilly, C. and Ylä-Anttila, P. (2000) *Nokia: A Big Company in a Small Country.* Etla Series B, 162. Helsinki: Taloustieto.
Bresnahan, T., Brynjolfsson, E. and Hitt, L. (2000) *Information Technology, Workplace Organization, and the Demand for Skilled Labour: Firm-Level Evidence* Cambridge, Mass.: MIT – Sloan School Center for E-business, Working Paper.
Brynjolfsson, E. and Hitt, L. (2000) *Computing Productivity: Firm-Level Evidence.* Cambridge, Mass.: MIT – Sloan School Center for E-business, Working Paper.
Cahalan, M.W. (1986) *Historical Corrections Statistics in the United States, 1850–1984.* Washington, DC: Department of Justice.
Castells, M. (2000) *The Information Age: Economy, Society and Culture,* 2nd edn, 3 vols. Oxford: Blackwell.
Castells, M. (2002) *The Internet Galaxy.* Oxford: Oxford University Press.
Castells, M. and Himanen, P. (2002) *The Information Society and the Welfare State: The Finnish Model.* Oxford: Oxford University Press.
Deininger, K. and Squire, L. (1996) *A New Data Set Measuring Income Inequality.* Washington, DC: World Bank, http://www.worldbank.org/research/growth/dddeisqu.htm.
EVA (Finnish Business and Policy Forum) (2001) *Erilaisuuksien Suomi: Raportti suomalaisten asenteista* (The Finland of Differences: A Report on Finnish Attitudes). Helsinki, http://www.eva.fi/julkaisut/ raportit/asenne2001/sisallys.htm.
Häikiö, M. (2001) *Nokia Oyj:n historia* (History of Nokia Corporation), 3 vols. Helsinki: Edita.
Himanen, P. (2001) *The Hacker Ethic and the Spirit of the Information Age.* New York: Random House.
Himanen, P. and Castells, M. (2004) 'Institutional Models of Network Society: Silicon Valley and Finland'. In M. Castells (ed.), *The Network Society: A Cross-Cultural Perspective.* Cheltenham: Edward Elgar.
von Hofer, H. (1997) *Nordic Criminal Statistics 1950–1995.* Stockholm: Stockholm University.
Kalela, J., Kiander, J., Kivikuru, U., Loikkanen, H. and Simpura, J. (eds.) (2001) *Down from the Heavens, Up from the Ashes: The Finnish Economic Crisis of the 1990s in the*

Light of Economic and Social Research. Helsinki: Valtion taloudellinen tutkimuskeskus (Government Institute for Economic Research).

Kautto, M., Fritzell, J., Hvinden, B., Kvist, J. and Uusitalo, H. (2001) *Nordic Welfare States in the European Context*. London: Routledge.

OECD (2001) *Knowledge and Skills for Life: First Results from PISA (Programme for International Student Assessment) 2000*. Paris: OECD.

Paija, L. (2000) *ICT Cluster: The Engine of Knowledge-Driven Growth in Finland*. Etla Discussion Papers, 733. Helsinki: Etla.

Paija, L. (ed.) (2001) *Finnish ICT Cluster in the Global Digital Economy*. Helsinki: Etla.

Putnam, R. (1995) 'Bowling Alone: America's Declining Social Capital'. *Journal of Democracy*, 6(1).

Raymond, E.S. (2003) *The Art of Unix Programming*. (http://www.fggs.org/docs/artes)

Saxenian, A. (1999) *Silicon Valley's New Immigrant Entrepreneurs*. San Francisco: Public Policy Institute of California.

Siisiäinen, M. (1999) 'Voluntary Associations and Social Capital in Finland'. In J.W. van Deth, M. Maraffi, K. Newton and P.F. Whiteley (eds.), *Social Capital and European Democracy*. London: Routledge.

STPC (Science and Technology Policy Council of Finland) (1987) *Review 1987*. Helsinki.

STPC (Science and Technology Policy Council of Finland) (1990) *Review 1990: Guidelines for Science and Technology Policy*. Helsinki.

STPC (Science and Technology Policy Council of Finland) (1993) *Towards an Innovative Society: A Development Strategy for Finland*. Helsinki.

STPC (Science and Technology Policy Council of Finland) (1996a) *Finland: A Knowledge-based Society*. Helsinki: Edita.

STPC (Science and Technology Policy Council of Finland) (1996b) *Tutkimusrahoituksen lisäyksen käyttösuunnitelma 1997–1999*. (A Plan for the Use of the Additional Appropriation for Research 1997–1999). Helsinki.

STPC (Science and Technology Policy Council of Finland) (2000) *Review 2000: The Challenge of Knowledge and Know-how*. Helsinki: Edita.

UNDP (United Nations Development Programme) (2001) *Human Development Report 2001*. Oxford: Oxford University Press.

US Bureau of Justice Statistics (1992) *Sourcebook of Criminal Justice Statistics*. Washington, DC: US Department of Justice.

WEF (World Economic Forum) (2003) *The Global Competitiveness Report 2003*. New York: Oxford University Press.

World Bank (2000) *World Development Report 2000/2001: Attacking Poverty*. Oxford: Oxford University Press.

12
Does the Most Brilliant Future of the 'Nordic Model' Have to be in the Past?

Olli Kangas and Joakim Palme

Emergence and transformation of the 'Nordic model'

We have in this book tried to explore the transformation of the Nordic countries in the twentieth century from a developmental perspective, with the focus on the role of social policy (cf. Mkandawire 2001). We have observed several reasons for why the emergence and transformation of the 'Nordic model' is of interest for the discussion of social policy in developmental perspective. One reason is simply that the Nordic countries have been successful in promoting social policy goals, reducing poverty and inequality while simultaneously increasing employment and social inclusion. We would argue that in the Nordic countries something similar to Schumpeter's notion of a 'constructive destruction' has taken place. Another reason is that each of the Nordic countries is facing dilemmas that are in several respects common to countries in different parts of the world. This second reason is obviously more future oriented: what challenges do the transformation to an 'information society' and more global economies pose for the 'Nordic model'?

In this final chapter we will attempt to be future oriented in three different ways. First, we will describe the pension reforms that have taken place in the Nordic region, relying primarily on Finnish and Swedish cases. These changes have long-term consequences for the sustainability and scope of public intervention in the pension area. Secondly, we will review the state of the universality of the 'Nordic welfare states' with special attention to the places where principles and practices appear to be threatened with erosion. Thirdly, we will try to take a 'holistic' approach to social policy developments, starting from the observation that the old Keynesian legacy has disappeared and that we need to find new macro–micro linkages in both design and evaluation of policies. Here, we try to outline some basic principles that are congruent with a developmental perspective on social policy.

Pension reforms: an example of trust in cuts

Old-age poverty was perceived as a major social policy challenge in late nineteenth century in the Western hemisphere. When the twentieth century came to an end the situation had changed a lot: the older generation had become much more affluent and, according to some, the problem was no longer poverty among the elderly but the overburdened pension system. Yet the advanced industrial nations still exhibit considerable variation when it comes to old-age poverty. As argued elsewhere in this volume, the citizenship/residence-based pension system is interesting from the point of view of the UNRISD project on social policy, since it is encompasses all permanent residents in a country and thus maximizes inclusion. From a development perspective, the fact that the abolition of means-testing provides good incentives for savings and 'long-termism' should be emphasized.

The potential of social insurance for achieving redistribution is often questioned, sometimes rightly so, because the programmes are inadequately designed, but sometimes because the observers fail to recognize that social insurance entails *risk redistribution* as well as *horizontal redistribution*. Vertical redistribution is often part of both. What is also neglected is the importance of social insurance for equalizing the conditions of men and women. Not only do women experience more ill-health, they also live longer. This implies that both sickness insurance and old-age pensions have the potential to redistribute in favour of a group in society that usually are paid less (women), i.e. vertically. With regard to economic efficiency criteria, the following can be noted concerning universal and earnings-related programmes of the Nordic type. The administrative cost-efficiency of universal programmes is, of course, one clear advantage. Another strength of universal systems that are fully earnings-related is that they reduce 'transaction costs' on the labour market. Individuals, firms and unions do not have to spend time negotiating about the provision of basic insurance and services such as health care. Mobility and flexibility in the labour market are promoted because the universal character of the system means that workers do not lose their earned rights when they move from one job to another – the *portability* of social insurance is high. One neglected aspect and advantage of public systems is that it is in principle possible to control the incentive structure.

The financing of social insurance in general, and pensions in particular, is central to the future of the welfare state. The increased needs of ageing societies will put heavier demands on the public purse and the various sources of financing. The critique of the welfare state is based on claims about lack of cost control and eroded incentives to work: as markets for labour capital and products become more mobile, this also makes most tax bases more difficult to control. In the future, it will probably not be enough to deal with programmes at a national level. In reform of pension systems since the 1980s it is apparent that European governments have struggled to achieve goals of both income security and basic security, while trying to control costs in the longer run. It is an advantage to combine earnings-related and residence-based benefits since such a strategy, coupled with an individualization of rights, will promote employment and gender equality.

The pension reform that took place in Sweden is a major exception to the piecemeal 'planning strategy' applied in other spheres of social protection (Lundberg 2003). Pension systems were reformed also in Finland, but in a much more subtle and marginal way (Hinrichs and Kangas 2003). As pension reforms are one of the most crucial ways to combat future cost expansion, a short review of the Nordic reforms is warranted. There have been two options to develop pension schemes. One possibility is to fortify basic security and take national pensions as a basis and build occupational labour market pensions on top of that. That national pension option has been actually applied in Denmark and partially in Norway. In both countries, national pensions in real terms are much higher than in Sweden and Finland (1050, 1201, 747 and 654 Euro/month, respectively, 2000, adjusted to purchasing power, NOSOSCO 2002: 126). Given the functional division of labour in the Danish pension scheme – at bottom are national pensions and occupational pensions are added – above that it seems more likely that Denmark will follow the basic security path, like the Netherlands. In Norway, both the national pension option *à la* Denmark or the employment-related route *à la* Finland/Sweden is open. 'The petroleum funds' that the Norwegians have at their disposal create some room for manoeuvre, just as the public pension funds in Sweden did. To judge from the proposals of the Norwegian Pension Commission presented in January 2004, Norway will introduce elements from both the Finnish and Swedish reforms (NOU 2004: 1).

Reforms in Finland and Sweden followed the other option of developing pension systems but there were also important differences. Both countries followed an employment-related path and what previously was a universal national pension is now tested against other public pension income (i.e. pensions coming from legislated schemes). The key idea was to make work pay: in both countries, employees also are now participating in financing.

In Finland, every year in employment accumulated pension rights in the previous system by 1.5 per cent. After forty years (years were accumulated between twenty-three and sixty-four years of age) the maximum limit of 60 per cent was achieved. The pension giving income was counted on the basis of the four last years in employment and there were no upper ceilings for benefit purposes. In the new system the employee begins to accumulate pension rights at the age of eighteen and up to fifty-two years the annual accumulation rate is 1.5 per cent; in the age bracket fifty-three–sixty-two the accumulation percentage is 1.9 and after that up to the age of sixty-eight it is as much as 4.5 per cent. The pension age is flexible between sixty-three and to sixty-eight years of age. The pension-giving income is now calculated on the basis of life-time earnings, which is detrimental for most salaried employees with an increasing income curve and in fact, this is one reason – in addition to work incentives – why the 'super accumulations' were added in the new scheme.

It was clear by the end of 1980 in Sweden that the old-age pension system (ATP) was under-financed and, given increased demographic pressures that could easily be projected, the problems were going to be aggravated. The price indexing of the system meant that it was unstable in both financial terms and when it cames to social policy goals. The primary focus in the critique of the ATP system was directed towards the benefit formula, where the 30/15 rules (thirty years in employment gave a full pension and the pension amount was calculated on the basis of fifteen best income years) punished those with a long work career and flat earnings profile over the life-cycle, a typical trajectory of low-income persons. Thus the Rawlsian justice principle attached to generations and life-cycles was present.

In 1994, the Swedish Parliament took a decision about 'guidelines' for the pension reform that came into force in 2001, and reshaped the system totally. The reform first replaced the old earnings-related defined benefit system with a defined contribution system where basically 18.5 per cent of earnings became the financial basis of the old-age pension system. 16 per cent went into notional accounts and formed the basis of the *income pension* and 2.5 per cent went into *fully funded* individual accounts. Both kinds of accounts were converted into annuities at the date of retirement, albeit these annuities had different forms. Basic security was ensured by a universal *guarantee pension*, which replaced the old combination of *universal people's pensions* and *special graduated supplements*. The size of this guarantee was graduated in relation to the two contributory public retirement benefits.

When it came to the basis for determining the size of income pension, the reform introduced a number of changes. One fundamental change was that the earnings-related component became the 'first tier'. Another fundamental change was that the benefit formula was to follow the principle of defined contributions. The principle was that all contributions were 'accumulated' and attributed a rate of return, equal to the growth in average annual pensionable income of all insured persons. Even if there was to be no fixed retirement age in the new system, the pension could not be drawn before the age of sixty-one and there was no legal right for employees to continue their employment beyond the age of sixty-seven (employers have the right to fire). The withdrawal was however flexible not only beyond the age of sixty-seven but also in terms of percentage. The size of the pension was to be decided by the accumulated notional wealth and the life expectancy of the cohort (but the pension was to be life-long for each individual).

A strong motive here was to provide a good incentive structure to increase labour supply. An important feature of the reformed system was that it attempted to make all kinds of redistribution that occurred within the system explicit and motivated by social policy considerations. Not only were earnings to give future entitlements to income pension but also a number of other incomes, such as social insurance benefits, as well as credits for having small children, engaging in tertiary education and doing the national service. *Child rearing* was a special motive for giving pension entitlements beside income and earnings. There were to be three different ways of calculating additional entitlements to those generated by parental leave benefits. The most favourable way of calculating these entitlements was applied automatically. Common to all three mechanisms was that the credits applied only until the youngest child was four years old.

The strongest element of redistribution was associated with the provisions for low-income pensioners. As indicated above, the old mechanism of providing basic pensions were the *universal people's pension* and the *special graduated supplement*, now replaced by the *guarantee pension*. The guarantee pension was to be coordinated with the *income pension* (including the fully funded benefit). This meant that only those who lacked an income pension would get a guarantee pension at the maximum rate. Those who had an income pension below the guaranteed level would get a supplement of a guarantee pension. A difference compared to the old system would hence be that those who had earned entitlements to their income pension would get a slightly higher total public pension (sum of guarantee pension and income pension) than those with only a guarantee pension.

The *universalism* of these basic provisions is important when it comes to the classical social policy goal of combating poverty. It also of vital importance in terms of the public and private boundaries of old-age security and the interplay between these two spheres. The reformed public system is insulated from what happens to private provisions since the guarantee pension is coordinated only with income pension (including the funded component) and not with private pensions, whether occupational or individual. This gives strong motives for private savings, since such income will not reduce the public commitments. This diverges from what happens elsewhere in the world in terms of strengthening the means-testing of basic provisions. The fully funded part of the reform changes the boundaries of public and private in the system of old-age security. It opens up the possibility for private fund managers to handle individual contributors within a public framework, where public authorities both collect contributions and pay out the pensions. It also introduces individual risk taking within social insurance, where programmes are usually designed for collective risk sharing.

The Swedish pension reform, as well the more modest Finnish adjustments, can be seen as responses to the pressures and constraints imposed by an ageing society, as well as to the critique of the welfare state concerning eroded incentive structures and poor cost control. Both the Finnish and Swedish schemes offer an interesting 'natural experiment'. In the Finnish case, the departure from the defined benefit formula was not as radical as in Sweden. In a longer run, this may give better pensions than in Sweden but in the same time may lead to financial problems and further cuts. Whereas the application of the defined contribution principle in Sweden puts pensions on a financially stable basis, the fixed contribution rate and price indexing of the guarantee pension means that the system may deliver very low pensions in comparison to the earnings of the working-age population.

In sum, all the smaller welfare reforms introduced in the Nordic countries in the 1980s and 1990s, and especially the 'big' pension reforms show that it is possible to change even a mature public pension system. As Stein Kuhnle (2000) highlights, one central element in Nordic policy making is tendency to find *consensual solutions*. The Swedish pension reform is a good example. It was a result of a political compromise between the political centre-right and the social democrats, reflected in the content of the reform. The left gained support for a large public commitment in an area where there were private alternatives, whereas the centre-right got individual accounts within the public framework. Both sides claimed that the broad support for the reform would contribute to the future stability of the pension system. In fact, the high degree of legitimacy and trust is a Nordic specialty where questions of improving benefits or curtailing entitlements are concerned. This is very much the essence of the 'Nordic welfare state' that tries to combine substantive justice and procedural justice (Rothstein 1998). The former states that welfare policy will provide people with those things they should get, while the latter states that welfare policies are carried out in an impartial way. This also seems to hold in the times of retrenchment.

Reform dilemmas to be solved

The successful adaptation to the economic problems of the 1990s may conceal the fact that there remain challenges and dilemmas for political decision makers. One obvious problem in future concerns financing – the dilemma is to protect and secure the social rights of people while controlling the rise of expenditures. The solution will partly be to find strategies for increasing the number of taxpayers. Another inherent dilemma lives in the reform of the systems of social protection. On the one hand, the aim of these institutions is that they should not, in principle, be changed. They should ideally be robust enough to 'survive' changing economic climates, and thus to contribute to the 'predictability' of conditions for different players, not least on the labour market. The systems should be just and trustworthy. On the other hand, if needs and constraints change to such an extent that the institutions no longer serve their primary purposes well, then this should be a good enough reason for reforming them.

Here we also meet two competing ideas or social policy ideologies: *income equalization* by favouring low-income groups and a more meritocratic *insurance principle* that gives compensation in relation to previous income. These issues have been solved differently in different Nordic countries. It may be argued that Finland, with earnings-related benefits without absolute ceilings, has adopted the latter ideology and Denmark, with generous low-income benefits and low ceilings, has followed the former line, with Norway and Sweden falling somewhere in between. Each strategy has its pros and cons. The Danish system is supposed to be good for the poor, whereas the more earnings-related schemes increase legitimacy among high-income earners. The latter strategy has been hotly discussed in Sweden, struggling with problems of maintaining the 'insurance character' for the large majority of wage earners, since more and more people have earnings above the ceiling for benefits purposes and it is feared that it may have far-reaching effects on popular support for public social insurance it all major groups in the labour market come to rely instead on private, individual or collective insurance alternatives in order to obtain adequate cover. Studies on the paradoxes of redistribution (Korpi and Palme 1998, for example) show that those strategies that are specifically targeted at the poor *de facto* help the poor less than more universal or even earnings-related schemes. However, this is not to say anything about legitimacy: in income maintenance systems, much depends on the interplay or coordination of public and private schemes.

If the publicly financed systems in the welfare services sector are unable to produce care of sufficiently high quality, this may lead to a substantial exit from the public systems by those with higher incomes. In the health care field, faith in the quality of public care is on the wane: health care is struggling with a credibility problem. A growing number of people are taking out private insurance so as to avoid the waiting periods that they clearly feel are too long. To solve this problem, various 'treatment guarantees' have been introduced – the Danish one of 2002 states that if the patient has to wait for treatment more than two months she can be treated in private clinics or seek help abroad (NOSOSCO 2002: 10). Thus opens up new possibilities when the 'free movement' also applies to health care services within the European Union. There is, however, no general increase in the view that private insurance is the solution in the specific case of health care. Voluntary health insurance is no alternative for those who are already in poor health, as insurance companies avoid what are termed 'bad risks' in order to survive as a commercial enterprise. Paradoxically, if private insurance is to serve as a more realistic alternative to national insurance it must be made compulsory, as shown in the earlier historical discussion. The same goes for cost containment.

Home care for the elderly is an area where considerable differences between the Nordic countries have been emerging. Sweden started from the most generous and comprehensive level in the 1980s but has since changed both the character and distribution of home care. Sweden and Finland, and to some extent Norway and Denmark, also seem to be in a situation when universalism in elderly care is being questioned – at least in practice. For the future, the following questions need to be answered:

- What kind of services should be public ones?
- How should they be financed when needs increase in the future?
- What are the limits to user fees if we do not want to create inequities?
- What are the problems and potential of private provision of publicly financed services?

The presence of user charges in virtually all welfare service spheres is nothing new for the Nordic social policy model. The level of user fees, however, and the increase that occurred in the 1990s, could be viewed as a problem for the universality of the model. Economically vulnerable groups forgo health care and old-age care to a greater extent than others. This suggests that the issue of fee levels should be addressed from an accessibility perspective. User fees, especially in cases where the same person is required to pay fees for a number of different types of input, may represent a burden on their economic resources.

For many Scandinavian women, the route to the labour market has been via the public sector employment. The Nordic welfare state has been 'woman-friendly' (Leira 2002). However, there are problems attached to gender segregated labour markets. One problem is the tendency of the public sector to lag behind in terms of both pay and the working environment. As a result, the public sector – and particularly the welfare services sector – risks developing into an employment area characterized by worse working conditions and lower pay than other industries and sectors. This is an important gender issue to be recognized, and bearing in mind the very extensive need for new recruitment that this sector will face over the next ten years, the scenario is a cause of considerable concern. If welfare services are to be properly maintained in future years, this negative trend must be halted. Irrespective of who provides welfare services in the future, the signs are that they will continue to be publicly financed. It will probably thus be decision makers in the publicly financed sector that will be required to meet the extensive challenges that the situation presents. The fact that this sector is politically governed can, on the one hand, prove an advantage, as political decisions concerning pay policy, for instance, can be reached and implemented in a way that is not possible in the privately financed sector. On the other hand, decision makers' room for manoeuvre is curtailed by the fact that they are required to pursue restrictive budgetary policies. As welfare services are such a labour-intensive area, solutions aimed at improving wage and staffing situations may easily result in dramatic increases in costs.

It is important to emphasize that the economic situation of families with children is principally contingent upon the parents' labour market participation. When discussing different support options for families with children, therefore, taking into account any impact these may have on labour market opportunities is of central importance. In that sense, Nordic family policy has a good record. However, the Achilles' heel may be the labour force participation of single parents and (dis-)incentive structures created by various social transfers, each of which has the aim to help the poor but at the end may create such a perverse situation that it is not worthwhile working (see, e.g., SOU 2001: 24; Parpo 2004). There are ways to amalgamate various income-tested systems in order to 'make-work-pay'; however, the problem with such basic-security schemes is that they may increase the initial threshold wage and constitute another obstacle to taking a job. The 'threshold issue' is closely linked to the problems of immigrants in the Nordic hemisphere. As Esping-Andersen's Chapter 6 in this volume hints, it may be that the generous 'Nordic welfare state' may make it difficult for immigrants to get established on the labour market.

The Nordic countries are rightly associated with big public involvement in both cash benefits and care. The debate about the 'proper' public – private mix of welfare is often fought with more or less ethical arguments. On one hand, it is claimed that the state should leave much more room for private alternatives and that a major state involvement in the financing and provision of insurance and services is fundamentally bad. On the other hand, it is claimed that lesser state involvement necessarily means less welfare. It is not always clear what the problem of 'privatization' actually is, and what can be done about it. Privatization can take place along several dimensions. It is not always a question of reducing social rights; private providers can, for example, be used to deliver publicly financed services. Sometimes the private providers are more efficient than the public ones and then it can be seen as a strategy of cost control without intruding on the rights of citizens. There are also examples of public benefits being a very important condition for making private care possible: the care allowance paid to relatives of disabled persons is one way of making it possible for family member to take care of them at home. This is often a much less expensive solution for the public purse if the alternative is institutional care, despite the massive expansion of public care; most care work is still provided by family members. One problem with privatization is that the ideas about what it is and what it can achieve are so vague. An important aspect to consider is that private providers of publicly financed services may enable choice. This, however, is not always the case. Some forms of privatization simply replace public providers in specific geographical areas. It is also evident that the reasons for privatization differ. Some of it is motivated on purely ideological grounds, while some is used to introduce competition.

Another problem of privatization is the potential for poor instruments of quality control. This is not an argument against private providers as such, rather it points to the necessity of keeping a public responsibility for private social services, too. This argument is, of course, especially strong when it comes to publicly financed services. It should be recognized that public alternative may be superior in some areas but that the private solution may nevertheless be better than poor/inadequate/constantly changing public arrangements.

Many people associate privatization with freedom of choice, as regards both the provision of welfare services and insurance schemes of various kinds. While alternative forms of management in the welfare services sphere may enhance freedom of choice, this is not generally applicable. In old-age care, for instance, it is by no means true that private provision always means implementing what is known as the 'customer-choice model'. There are also instances of private provision not being a system that all can in practice choose, and there may also geographical restrictions that limit access in sparsely populated areas. There may be fees or admission procedures, which in practice exclude the economically disadvantaged or people requiring a high level of care input. As far as social insurance is concerned, there is a clearly limited freedom of choice, as in the case of voluntary health care insurance.

As we have observed, the growing presence of user fees could in one respect be viewed as a 'privatization' of financing. It raises a number of important knowledge issues. In general, user fees still mean comparatively little in a total financing perspective. Insofar as people in this area refrain from utilising, say, health care for economic reasons, which is more common among low earners, a regressive redistribution occurs from low earners to others, as low earners still provide a considerable share of financing via the tax bill. Another knowledge issue concerns the extent to which user fees act as a policy instrument for channelling users to different services, such as cheaper primary care instead of expensive emergency care at a hospital. The substantial marginal effects that have arisen in the child care sector as a result of income- and time-related fee scales is a further area in which systematic knowledge, as regards both the structure of systems and the behaviour they engender, could facilitate value-based consideration of how the financing of various benefits and systems should be accomplished.

These developments raise questions with a strong element of value judgement. They concern freedom of choice and social justice, equality and efficiency. A number of questions seem likely to be at the centre of future social policy debate in the Nordic countries:

- What importance do we attach to competition in welfare services?
- How do we value the presence of municipal and other monopolies from a welfare viewpoint, focusing on people's capacity to manage their own lives?
- How do we feel about tax-financed undertakings being used for profit-making purposes?

The end of the Keynesian legacy?

In the wake of the Second World War, numerous important social policy reforms in Scandinavia were carried through and 'the Scandinavian model' social policy gradually took shape of (see Erikson *et al.* 1987; Korpi and Palme 1998). One important aspect of the model was the successful integration of economic and social policies. Social polices mitigated the harshness of the transformation of the agrarian society into an industrial one. Social and housing polices facilitated the migration of agrarian labour force from the countryside to the factories in cities. The lowering of income differences was seen as an important factor of guaranteeing smooth economic growth. During this Keynesian period of economic policy-making, social policy and redistribution through social policy measures was regarded as an important factor for enhancing stable economic growth. Improving the lot of the least advantaged groups in society guaranteed a more stable consumption capacity, which in turn countervailed economic fluctuations. Equality thus not only helped the poor but had a beneficial impact upon economic growth. This was the underpinning rationale in writings by the most important social planners in the Nordic economic community (Myrdal 1960; Kuusi 1966).

In post-war political discourse, equality and growth appeared to fortify each other, and the 'the social' and 'the economic' were regarded as integral and inseparable parts of the same development. In present-day political and economic discourse, the 'economic' is often seen as a valuable producer of social good, whereas the 'social' is regarded as a harmful spender of that good, not having any positive function at all. Equality and redistribution are often regarded as obstacles to economic growth. The comparison of the economic and employment records of the USA and Europe is presented as proof. The economic crisis that Finland and Sweden suffered in the early 1990s often serves the same purpose: the too lavish and excessive welfare states in these countries were deemed to have crowded-out economic activity (for a discussion see, e.g., Korpi 1996). Instead of income equality, there are therefore more cries for income inequality in order to increase incentives to work and thereby to enhance economic growth, so that when economy is booming the worst-off sections in society will also get their share of the rising economic tide. The argument goes that we must now choose between *growth* and *equality*. The old Okunian plea for solving the trade-off between equality and growth (Okun 1975) is still there. The argument of cutting the welfare sector and especially getting the high tax level down is promoted more intensly than ever, further motivated by the globalization of trade, economies and labour markets.

'Globalization' and 'modernization' have become fashionable concepts in analysing the ongoing societal changes in East and West, North and South. Social institutions, including social policy arrangements, based on earlier modes of production are under severe challenge and societies are being pressed to reform existing social programmes and adopt new ones that have a better 'fit' to the global economy. In the vast body of globalization literature, the main focus has been on Western countries. The message has been that in order to be competitive the Western countries – especially those with high welfare expenditures and 'big' welfare states – must cut down their social security to enhance growth and meet the challenges caused by globalization. These challenge are said to be particularly severe for the Scandinavian welfare states known for their equal income distribution, universalism in income maintenance and service delivery, high standards of benefits, high spending levels and, consequently, high cost and heavy taxes that are said to push enterprises out of the country. What is needed is a smaller and cheaper public sector. The big issue here is how to satisfy the demand for 'leaner' but not 'meaner' welfare states, as proposed by Tanzi and Schuknecht (2000).

Despite the expectation that the Scandinavian welfare states will face the most severe challenges in global competition, our study has shown that in international comparison the Nordic countries are not doing that badly when it comes to economic growth and employment. Their performance in terms of economic and creative competitiveness does not lag behind other developed countries. Quite the contrary: the Nordic countries are the leading telecommunication 'clusters' with their intensive mobile telephone and Internet networks. In that sense the history is repeating itself: a hundred years or so ago the mass education created universal literacy among the citizens. Now, the state is trying to expand 'e-literacy' to be in everyone's package of basic capabilities. Florida and Tingali (2004) appraise the Northern European 'creative crescent' that, according to the authors, is challenging the economic power of the USA and 'old Europe'. The top five countries in the Euro-Creativity Index are Sweden, the USA, Finland, the Netherlands and Denmark (see also http://www.demos.co.uk/media/creativeeurope_page373.aspx). The same story is told by world-wide competitiveness indices. By 2004, the leading countries were Finland, the USA, Denmark and Sweden. Norway and Iceland are also among the ten most competitive economies (http://www.imd.ch/wcy/ranking/index.cfm). Against this background, there seems be nothing 'rotten in the states of Scandinavia'. However, there is the challenge of globalization – or perhaps it is more correct to speak about the 'de-industrialization' of the West. Hourly costs in industrial production are about $31 in Germany, $24 in Denmark, Finland and Norway, $21 in Sweden, $17 in the USA and $14 in the UK. In Korea, the costs are about $8, while they are less than ¢30 in China and India (Collier and Dollar 2001). In the era of global production, this situation causes strong pressures for all high-cost countries since there is the threat of the flight of industrial production to less expensive countries.

There are two areas where the globalization of the world economy puts certain limits on what can be done in individual countries. The first is that profitability of enterprises has to be on a competitive level. Otherwise, foreign as well as domestic capital will leave the country. The level of income taxation and the size of social security contributions are not of primary importance, yet employees and their trade unions must recognize the cost of social security: 'there is no such thing as a free lunch.' If the cost of social policy – the social wage – is not taken into consideration in wage negotiations the result may be inflation and eroded competitiveness. This is a lesson which the Scandinavian labour movements have hopefully learned from past decades. Even if profit levels cannot be reduced in single countries, the division between what is paid as 'direct wage' and what is paid as 'social wage' ought to be flexible. In this flexibility discourse centralized, central-level solutions are often argued to be outdated and more local and enterprize variation is demanded to make the 'Nordic employment model' sustainable and competitive in global markets. However, we again meet a dilemma of collective action. The strong and unified labour unions in Scandinavia have participated in decision making via so-called 'social corporatism'. This specific way of decision making has enhanced what we have called 'bridging social capital' unifying large sectors of society, whereas small-group-based solutions fortify 'binding social capital'. The obvious dilemma is how to unify these competing tendencies.

Challenges of globalization and neo-liberal economic doctrines are by no means a problem faced solely by the Western nations. The challenge applies to all countries, not least those that are striving to change their pre-capitalist, non-market-based or socialist institutions to more market oriented ones. The verdict here is very much the same as in the case of European countries: more economic liberalism. Free global markets help poor countries; free trade works like the rising tide that will gradually lift all boats.

However, some words of caution are warranted. There is a strong *chronological bias* in present globalization discourse, displaying the current situation as unique, without any counterpart in history. It is good to keep in mind that when it comes to public policy in general, and social policies in particular, the present situation has a clear similarity with the advent of industrial capitalism and the introduction of social policies in the Western hemisphere. Public policy was then an integral part in attempts to establish social bonds, social identities and even nationhood, as well as in safeguarding stability at times of social unrest. Polanyi (1944) strongly argued that pure market capitalism was not sustainable but needed *social bonds* to work smoothly. The Polanyian argument is still relevant, the more so since issues of social justice and fair distribution of resources have now expanded to be global ones: which people should get what (Deacon with Hulse and Stubbs 1997; Rawls 1999; DeMartino 2000; Turner 2001).

However, when it comes to the relationships between the social and the economic, it is perhaps not all that fruitful to focus on the deficiencies of the neo-classical perspective and to try to seek an antithesis to it. Practices and institutional settings that work perfectly in one situation may become hindrances in another. It is perhaps more fruitful and thought provoking to try to answer to the question: 'What was really wrong with Keynesianism?', than simply pinpointing weaknesses in neo-classical economic doctrine. It might also be useful to examine neo-institutionalism and the challenges it generates for the Keynesian approach, and for the micro-foundations of the neo-classical perspective raised by North (1990) and others (see, e.g., Douglas 1987; Burlamaqui, Castro and Chang 2000), not least as a response to the failures in the transformation of Soviet Union and the Eastern Europe over the 1990s.

There are thus good reasons to elaborate the approach taken in this book: to study the interplay of the 'economic', 'social', 'public' and 'private' in periods of great transformations. The basic policy relevance here is the idea that by analysing how social institutions work we can help states and individuals to adapt to societal transformations. The issue accentuates the importance of old class-based cleavages in society and the question of equality between genders. Recent developments in the Nordic countries, as well as in many other parts of the world, highlight the problems of immigrants in terms of inclusion and participation. If governments fail to respond to needs for social protection and employment, this is likely to reinforce old divisions of welfare and create new ones.

Conclusions

According to the old saying, 'The way to hell is paved with good intentions'. Good intentions and political commitments are not enough to make reforms work successfully. The end-state of the action may be totally the opposite from that intended. The design of the existing programmes thus needs to be critically evaluated, and in this context the Nordic tradition of welfare research can make a contribution. It is based on people's concrete living conditions in a broad perspective, studying not just the economy but also people's health, work and social ties (cf. Palme *et al.* 2003). It is necessary not only to study whether the social policy goals are actually being achieved but also to examine any *unintended consequences* of the programmes.

What we have learnt from developments in the 'Nordic welfare state' is that the expansion and retrenchment of social policy is not just a mechanical reaction to changes in the fabric of society but is also shaped by different values and ideologies, and institutional solutions are likely to impact on those values. The choices of strategy for future welfare policy will be affected by both structural challenges and conditions as well as by existing institutions and political choices. We would thus argue that a strategy is needed for resolving the dilemmas without diluting the socio-political and moral content of the 'welfare state model'. The framework for reform starts from the notion that in order to be successful in meeting new needs with restricted resources, as well as in avoiding trade-offs between equality and efficiency, we must improve (1) incentives, (2) human resources, (3) social services and (4) employment opportunities. In addition, we also need to establish a proper balance between *rights* and *responsibilities* – i.e. re-establish the social citizenship contract. Among the Nordic countries, to maintain, and sometimes restore, the universal character of benefits and services, as well as the earnings-relatedness of social insurance programmes, is a core element of this approach. These issues appear relevant for the reform of social protection in other countries and contexts as well (Palme *et al.* 1998).

The following questions are central when it comes to the incentive structure:

- How can poverty traps be avoided?
- How can marginal effects be reduced?
- How can welfare state programmes be designed so that it pays more to work while protecting entitlements?

To put it differently, the question is how can we design economic rewards so that they induce the desired behaviour? A rule of thumb is to use *universal* benefits and services rather than means-tested ones. As soon as we start means-testing, it will affect the profitability of, particularly, low-income persons – often women – engaging in paid employment. Another strategy is to make social insurance provisions *earnings-related*, making it profitable for people to work and pay social security contributions. The more they earn and pay, the better benefit entitlements will be. Here, different alternative strategies can be identified. A technique that has become popular in the USA and the UK is to have *tax credits* for recipients of means-tested benefits so that benefits will not be fully reduced if recipients start to earn an income. This is very different from the Nordic tradition, where the approach to the problem has been to apply strict activity/work-tests and no one in principle should be able to say 'no' to a job offer. It appears worthwhile to evaluate seriously these different approaches empirically.

Once the *incentive* structure is reformed, the major issue about resources remains. It is not enough to make people willing to work, they must also possess the *resources* to be able to work. This is partly a matter of skills, partly of adequate social services making it possible for adults in families with small children, or frail elderly relatives, to participate on the labour market. The classical strategy is education and training, as well as other forms of active labour market (ALP) policy, such as public relief work and forms of subsidised employment. The aim of these measures should be to improve, or at least maintain, the employability of unemployed persons. The approach of giving heavy subsidies to public services, such as day care facilities is, as argued above, likely to contribute to an overall high employment rate among women.

Even if the labour force is highly skilled, and poverty traps as well as high marginal taxes have been avoided as much as possible, this is of little comfort as long as people do not have the *opportunity* to exercise their skills. If there are no, or too few, jobs to apply for, good skills may not be enough to get employment. Social policies cannot make up for failures in economic policy: this means that a successful strategy has to be based on successful macroeconomic policy making, and the fundamental problem of mass unemployment is that there are too few jobs. But then, on the other hand, successful macroeconomic policies are not likely to be enough, either, if the skills of the unemployed persons do not match what new vacant jobs demand. It is necessary to improve social policy and labour market institutions in several respects: incentives, resources (skills and services), responsibilities and opportunities for selected groups. Reforms of social security systems have thus to be coupled with macroeconomic policy making promoting employment and growth. The conclusion from macroeconomic developments in the 1990s, not least in Sweden and Finland, is that when important macroeconomic decisions have to be made there is every reason to consider carefully the impact they may have on welfare development in the broadest sense.

How successful we are in finding a balance between rights and responsibilities will ultimately depend on the success in providing proper incentives, resources and opportunities for people to enter the labour market. Every strategy will have to deal with the kinds of obstacles – in terms of incentives, resources and opportunities – that face those who seek employment. The position of ethnic minorities, and other groups that are discriminated against on the labour market, is of critical importance here. Citizenship is about the rights and responsibilities of people; social citizenship is about how these principles materialize in the social policy field. While there are strong authoritarian traits in how the discussion about responsibilities has been framed in the Western world in recent years, responsibilities can also be put in a developmental and inclusive perspective (Mkandawire 2001). As argued by Torfing (1999) the ALP strategies in the Nordic countries can be seen in this context. The nature of how rights and responsibilities are balanced must ultimately be decided in the interface between the state and the individual, and whether the state treats the individual as a subordinate or a citizen. The Nordic countries have a long history of the latter. Notwithstanding that social policies often enable people to make choices they would otherwize not have been able to make, individual choice is in some sense circumscribed by state intervention in the form of taxation and social protection. This suggests that state intervention should focus on dealing with social issues that are universally relevant and that it is important to promote individual choice, even in areas that have become subject to state intervention. The Nordic example indicates some of the potential of the approach, but also the problems of maintaining the principles, not least as the economy, and social policy systems, are challenged by macroeconomic failures and various challenges created by demographic transitions, as well as by mismanagement of social policy programmes. This is how we see the lesson from the Nordic experience.

Bibliography

Burlamaqui, L., Castro, A.C. and Chang, H.-J. (eds.) (2000) *Institutions and the Role of the State*. Cheltenham: Edward Elgar.
Collier, P. and Dollar, D. (2001) *Globalization, Growth, and Poverty: Building an Inclusive World Economy*. Oxford: Oxford University Press/World Bank.
Deacon, B. with Hulse, M. and Stubbs, P. (1997) *Global Social Policy: International Organizations and the Future of Welfare*. London: Sage.
DeMartino, G. (2000) *Global Economy, Global Justice: Theoretical Objections and Policy Alternatives to Neoliberalism*. London: Routledge.
Douglas, M. (1987) *How Institutions Think*. London: Routledge.
Erikson, R. Hansen, E.J. Ringen, S. and Uusitalo, H. (eds.) (1987) *The Scandinavian Model*. New York: M. E. Sharpe.
Florida, R. and Tingali, I. (2002) *Europe in the Creative Age*. London: Carnegie Mellon and Demos.
Hinrichs, K. and Kangas, O. (2003) 'When is a Change Big Enough to be a System Shift?'. *Social Policy and Administration*, 37: 573–91.
Korpi, W. (1996) 'Eurosclerosis and the Sclerosis of Objectivity: On the Role of Values among Economic Policy Experts'. *Economic Journal*, 106: 1727–46
Korpi, W. and Palme, J. (1998) 'The Paradox of Redistribution and the Strategy of Equality: Welfare State Institutions, Inequality and Poverty in the Western Countries'. *American Sociological Review*, 63: 661–87.
Kuhnle, S. (2000) 'European Welfare Lessons of the 1990s'. In S. Kuhnle (ed.), *Survival of the European Welfare State*. Routledge/ECPR Studies in European Political Science. New York: Routledge: 234–8.
Kuusi, P. (1966) *Social Policy for the Sixties: A Plan for Finland*. Helsinki: Social Policy Association.
Leira, A. (2002) *Working Parents and the Welfare State: Family Change and Policy Reform in Scandinavia*. Cambridge: Cambridge University Press.
Lundberg, U. (2003) *Juvelen i kronanan: Socialdemokraterna och den allmänna pensionen*. (The Jewel in the Crown: The Social Democrats and Statutory Pensions Stockholm: Hjalmarson & Högberg.)
Mkandawire, T. (2001) *Social Policy in a Development Context*. Geneva: United Nations, Research Institute for Social Development, Social Policy and Development Paper, 7.
Myrdal, G. (1960) *Beyond the Welfare State*. London: University Paperbacks.
North, D.C. (1990) *Institutions, Institutional Change and Economic Performance*. Cambridge: Cambridge University Press.
NOSOSCO (Nordic Social Statistical Committee) (2002) *Social Protection in the Nordic Countries 2000*. Copenhagen: NOSOSCO.
NOU (2004) *Modernizert folketrygd: Baerekreftig pensjon for framtida*. (Modernized People's Insurance: Sustainable Pensions for the Future.) Oslo: Norges Offentlige Utredningar.
Okun, A. M. (1975) *Equality and Efficiency: The Big Tradeoff*. Washington, DC: Brookings Institution.

Palme, J., Koni, A., Pettinger, R., Predosanu, G. and Todorova, V. (1998) 'Welfare State in Crisis: How to Protect the Rights Whilst Controlling the Costs'. Strasbourg: Council of Europe.

Palme, J., Bergmark, Å., Bäckman, O., Estrada, F., Fritzell, J., Lundberg, O., Sjöberg, O., Sommestad, L. and Szebehely, M. (2003) *Welfare in Sweden: The Balance Sheet for the 1990s*. Stockholm: Fritzes.

Parpo, A. (2004) *Kannustavuutta tulonsiirtojärjestelmään: tulonsiirtojärjestelmän muutokset, kannustinloukut ja tulonjako* (More Incentives for the Income Transfer System: Changes in the Income Transfer System, Incentive Traps and Income Distribution). Helsinki: Stakes.

Polanyi, K. (1944) *The Great Transformation: The Political and Economic Origins of Our Time*. Boston: Beacon.

Rawls, J. (1999) *The Law of People*. Cambridge, Mass.: Harvard University Press.

Rothstein, B. (1998) *Just Institutions Matter: The Moral and Political Logic of the Universal Welfare State*. Cambridge: Cambridge University Press.

SOU (2001) *Ur fattigdomsfällan. Slutbetänkande från familjeutredningen*, 2001(24). Stockholm: Fritzes. (Out of the Poverty Trap: Final report from the Family Support Commission.)

Tanzi, V. and Schuknecht, L. (2000) *Public Spending in the twentieth Century: A Global Perspective*. Cambridge: Cambridge University Press.

Torfing, J. (1999) 'Workfare with Welfare: Recent Reforms of the Danish Welfare State'. *Journal of European Social Policy*, 9: 5–28.

Turner, A. (2001) *Just Capital: The Liberal Economy*. London: Macmillan.

http://www.demos.co.uk/media/creativeeurope_page373.aspx;
http://www.imd.ch/wcy/ranking/index.cfm.

Index